T0289791

Uncovered

Uncovered

The Story of Insurance in America

KATHERINE HEMPSTEAD

OXFORD
UNIVERSITY PRESS

OXFORD
UNIVERSITY PRESS

Oxford University Press is a department of the University of Oxford. It furthers
the University's objective of excellence in research, scholarship, and education
by publishing worldwide. Oxford is a registered trade mark of Oxford University
Press in the UK and certain other countries.

Published in the United States of America by Oxford University Press
198 Madison Avenue, New York, NY 10016, United States of America.

Library of Congress Cataloging-in-Publication Data
Names: Hempstead, Katherine, author.
Title: Uncovered : the story of insurance in America / Katherine Hempstead.
Description: New York, NY : Oxford University Press, [2024] |
Includes index.
Identifiers: LCCN 2024015182 | ISBN 9780190094157 (hardback) |
ISBN 9780190094171 (epub)
Subjects: LCSH: Insurance—United States—History.
Classification: LCC HG8531 .H394 2024 | DDC 368/.973—dc23/eng/20240503
LC record available at https://lccn.loc.gov/2024015182

DOI: 10.1093/oso/9780190094157.001.0001

Printed by Integrated Books International, United States of America

Contents

Acknowledgments

Many kind and generous people contributed to this project, and I am glad to have the opportunity to thank them.

Joel Ario helped convince me that there might be an audience for a book about the history of the insurance industry. With deep experience in federal and state policy, which includes serving as insurance commissioner in two states, there is little that Joel doesn't know about insurance regulation and the work of the National Association of Insurance Commissioners (NAIC). He provided major help by reading chapters, providing much-needed context, and sharing his extensive list of contacts.

Walter Licht was extraordinarily generous with his time and wisdom, demonstrating why he is beloved by generations of students at the University of Pennsylvania, where he is the Walter H. Annenberg Professor of History Emeritus. Early on, Walter provided important big-picture feedback on the concept and pointed me to a daunting amount of relevant scholarship. He gave detailed comments on chapters, invited me to give a seminar, and has continued to provide strategic advice. "Be confident!" he once exhorted at the end of a conversation, and I have tried. His support has made that much easier.

Rich Yeselson read sections and provided extremely helpful advice. Roger Grant, who inspired me with his early study of insurance regulation during the Progressive Era, offered valuable comments on the early chapters. Others who helped include Neil Vance, Heather Howard, Tom Baker, Robert Margo, Peter Kinzler, Robert Hunter, and Terry Vaughan. Alex Lemann carefully read the entire manuscript and made thoughtful comments throughout. Seminar participants at the University of Pennsylvania and Rutgers University improved the work with their many helpful questions and suggestions.

I benefited greatly from the expertise and assistance of many archivists and librarians. Mary Beth Davidson, archivist for Travelers, was extremely helpful and patient as the project ranged through different lines of business. She shared a wide assortment of materials and images from the nineteenth and twentieth centuries that contributed immeasurably to the coverage of property and casualty insurance. Duncan Robak of Travelers supplied key materials related to the early development of crop insurance, providing records from the St. Paul Mutual Hail and Cyclone Insurance Company. The vast resources of the Insurance Library in Boston were critical to this project, and research librarian Sarah Hart helped greatly with my many requests for books and images. Librarians at Princeton University, the University of Pennsylvania, Rutgers University, University of California, Berkeley, and Duke University allowed me to access their collections. The A. M. Best Corporation generously provided me with a copy of their excellent company history and permitted me to use a map.

Managing Editor James Cook, Project Editor Emily Benitez, and the rest of the team at Oxford University Press expertly guided this work through the stages of publication, doing much to improve it in the process. My friends and colleagues at the Robert Wood Johnson Foundation provide a wonderfully stimulating work environment where I learn something new every day. Although the scope of this project spans far beyond health, I think they will see something of our mission in the questions I ask in this book and why I ask them.

I am grateful for the support of my family, starting with my mother and father, who always encouraged me, and my children, who give me purpose. I'm sorry that my father is not here to read the final version, but he loved business and stories, so I think he would have liked it.

It is hard to find the words to adequately thank my husband, Andy, who consistently provided me with the perfect doses of wisdom, humor, and encouragement. He found time to read every chapter multiple times and provided thoughtful criticism on matters big and small. His suggestions made this book much better. More than that, he made me laugh and kept me going. Andy is my best critic, my best reader, my best friend. Most of all, I am grateful for the life we share.

Introduction

> The question is cogent and searching, and modern nations must
> find the true answer at their peril, for if the two ideas of free adven-
> ture and economic security admit of no reconciliation, then the fate
> of our civilization is only a matter of time.[1]

The genesis of this book came from a desire to answer some present-day
questions. Working in philanthropy with a focus on health insurance, I became
increasingly aware of the complex dynamic of federal, state, and private insurer
interactions related to the implementation of the Affordable Care Act. Yet the
more I learned, the more I wondered. How have our various insurance markets
evolved to take their current forms? Why is there so much unmet demand for
insurance? How can we understand the unique role of states in insurance regulation? When I learned that the national association of state insurance regulators
had existed since 1871, my curiosity was further piqued.[2] I wondered what had
caused this organization to form and how the regulatory issues it faced had
changed over time. I searched for a book that would tell me this story. Finding
none, I decided to write one myself.

Perched precariously at the intersection of public and private life, insurance
has long drawn the attention of scholars. Theoretical work has illuminated the
criticality of insurance to social organization.[3] Far more than a business, insurance is more broadly a system of risk management and governance that can be
deployed by public or private actors.[4] The choices a society makes about how to
share risk among its members reflect its deepest values about fairness, equality,
and what it means to belong, or to use the words of the British civil servant
Llewellyn Smith, where it has drawn the line between "free adventure and economic security."

Smith was an architect of some of Britain's early social welfare reforms, including unemployment insurance and health insurance. He was not sanguine
about the difficulty of the tradeoff between freedom and security. Noting an increase in both economic instability and demands for social insurance, Smith
asked: "Is this tendency to exalt security as an end a healthy tendency, or should
it fill us with apprehension?" He noted that for some nations, trading freedom
for security might be particularly difficult: "The ideal of security may not at first
sight seem a very heroic aim to put before a country whose economic traditions

Uncovered. Katherine Hempstead, Oxford University Press. © Oxford University Press 2024.
DOI: 10.1093/oso/9780190094157.001.0001

form a veritable romance of adventure, full of the joy of risks encountered and dangers overcome."[5]

That is an apt description of the mindset in the United States, where choices about risk sharing have long tilted toward the individual and private. Historians have shown the important role played by the insurance industry in not just the development of nineteenth-century capitalism, but also the weakening of more communal forms of risk sharing, the erection of the twentieth-century private welfare system of workplace benefits, and the vigorous midcentury defense of that system against the potential expansion of social insurance.[6]

Private insurance retains its great social and economic significance. Without it, much of modern life in the United States would grind to a halt.[7] Most of us need it to protect our health, buy a house, drive a car, open a business, or provide for our dependents. The U.S. insurance industry is mammoth, with nearly $9 trillion in assets under management, employing almost three million people. In 2022, Americans spent more than twelve percent of gross domestic product on insurance premiums.[8]

Yet insurance covers us unevenly. Despite its importance to financial well-being, there is significant unmet demand. In addition to the nearly thirty million who lack health insurance, millions drive without coverage or have inadequate protection for their homes. Those without workplace benefits are more likely to lack not only health insurance but also paid leave, life insurance, and retirement savings accounts. Lack of coverage limits financial protection in the present and constrains wealth generation in the future. These limits have been particularly acute for Black Americans, who have not only have been impacted by historical labor market discrimination and the racist origins of southern resistance to expanding national social insurance programs but also have been the targets of discriminatory underwriting practices. Unmet demand for insurance is an important policy issue with a long history.

Understanding the development of the public and private insurance system in the United States necessitates attention to insurance regulation, for the regulatory structure affects what kind of insurance is made available, on what terms, at what cost, and to whom. State regulation of insurance, which had initially invited my curiosity, turns out to be a critical part of the story. Our state-based system has likely weakened the overall regulatory response and impeded the development of more effective national and public approaches to risk sharing. Seen in this light, a nineteenth-century Supreme Court decision that relegated insurance regulation to the states has lastingly impacted not just the characteristics of insurance regulation, but arguably the structure of much of our social welfare system.

Uncovered is a history of the insurance business and its relationship with government from the late nineteenth through the end of the twentieth century.

During this time, the private insurance industry and the regulatory state grew, but not in tandem. Private industry became increasingly unified and powerful, while regulation developed in a fragmented and piecemeal fashion. The original state-based system was joined over time by various types of federal insurance–related activity, including direct provision of some types of insurance, participation in other markets, and recurring congressional oversight hearings. A Supreme Court decision in 1944 created the opportunity to undo the state-based system, but federal policymakers, under pressure from state regulators and insurers, chose to preserve the status quo.

A major observation is that despite the growing governmental footprint, insurers have been remarkably successful in resolving conflicts between public and private priorities in their favor and have generally been able to leverage the expansion of public sector activity to their advantage. This success reflects neither brilliant strategy nor widespread public satisfaction with insurers' business practices, but rather the unwillingness of state and federal policymakers to seriously disrupt them. A key argument of *Uncovered* is that the role of states in regulation has been critical. State regulation has fragmented and weakened the regulatory response into fifty separate environments where, generally, problems that require public funding can not be solved. This structure has impeded the development of more effective national solutions to risk problems and has allowed private business models to become entrenched.

The regulation of the insurance business in the United States dates from the mid-nineteenth century, when some states began to examine fire and life insurance companies for solvency. From the outset, government largely accepted insurers' claim that their business transcended "mere commerce." A nineteenth-century Supreme Court decision enshrined that point of view and, finding that sales of policies did not constitute commerce, granted regulatory purview to the states. Insurers were thereby able to avoid federal regulation and greatly influence the state regulation that emerged in its stead. There, problems stemming from unmet demand were addressed inadequately, or not at all, though there were some noteworthy reform efforts.

To insurers, their self-proclaimed public role did not imply a desire for partnership with the public sector, and the industry vociferously objected to every perceived state or federal incursion into the business. When in the twentieth century the federal government emerged as a provider of insurance and as a potential regulator of the insurance business, it did so tenuously and incompletely, working around the edges of the private markets it was by then loathe to disrupt. Repeated congressional hearings about the shortcomings and special treatment of the insurance industry resulted in little substantive change.

Insurance is still largely regulated by states, but the federal government has come to play an increasingly important role out of necessity more than desire.

The government is a direct provider of some types of insurance, a major purchaser of others, and a financial backstop in other insurance markets, and government depends on insurers both to participate in private markets and to administer many social insurance programs. Government and insurers have become codependent. While insurers once portrayed their industry as having a public purpose that transcended normal commerce, over time, this persona has eroded and narrowed. Some of the responsibility for unmet demand has been transferred to the government, while much remains unmet. This transition has taken place in several distinct though overlapping phases.

Acceptance

From the outset, insurers portrayed themselves as doing the public's business, describing their role as the socially beneficial act of protecting widows and orphans, thereby reducing public dependency. The idea resonated, and presidents and other prominent citizens went out of their way to heap praise upon the industry. Grover Cleveland even served as the head of a life insurance trade association after leaving office, noting that the management of life insurance involves "a higher duty and more constant devotion than we associate with a mere business enterprise."[9]

Chapter 1 describes the rapid growth of the fire and life insurance business in the decades after the Civil War. Like other business enterprises of the time, such as the railroads, large insurers sought regulation to help tame the unruly aspects of competition. But vexed by the rapidly mushrooming state regulatory apparatus, insurers made an ill-fated attempt to escape state authority. The National Board of Fire Underwriters, the nation's first trade association, created a legal test that challenged a state's right to collect a license fee from an agent of an out-of-state company. The move backfired when the Supreme Court, in *Paul v. Virginia* (1869), ruled that insurance was not commerce and therefore could not be regulated by Congress.

Unable to evade state control, insurers instead sought to control the controllers via the creation of a national organization of state regulators. Chapter 2 shows how insurers organized and heavily influenced the first meeting of the national body of state regulators in 1871. Meanwhile, over the late nineteenth century and early twentieth century, "the companies" regulated themselves, creating a bureaucratic cartel-like structure designed to promote uniform action and disadvantage new entrants. The historiography of the Progressive Era has shown that many businesses feared competition more than regulation. This was surely true of the insurance industry, but unlike railroads and some other industries, insurers were highly successful at organizing themselves into their own "private

government" after federal regulation became an impossibility.[10] Their advantage
stemmed from a natural need in the business to share risk, which curtailed desire
for monopolistic growth and allowed more established firms to collaborate to set
prices and block new entrants.

State Challenge

Insurance may have obtained a special status in the public eye, but it was nevertheless a business, and insurers sought to perform their ostensibly public role on
their own terms and in ways that maximized profitability. This resulted in significant unmet demand, which was met with substandard products such as industrial insurance, a low-value life insurance product sold aggressively to the poor,
or nothing at all. In the early twentieth century, state reform activism on behalf
of consumers was at its zenith, revealing the possibilities as well as the limitations
of what could be accomplished through regulation alone. A cohort of reformist
commissioners tried to increase affordability and protect consumers but met
with relatively little success. An important exception is described in Chapter 3,
which tells the story of how consumer outrage at the business practices of life
insurers was amplified by investigative journalism, resulting in a state investigation with far-reaching consequences. Other state efforts to protect life insurance
consumers and the many ways in which they fell short are discussed in Chapter 4,
which also tells the story of an important though somewhat temporary role of
the federal government as a provider of life insurance during World War I.

The practices of fire insurers were also deplored but even less effectively
countered, as seen in the next two chapters. Chapter 5 describes how scrutiny
of the industry increased after the San Francisco earthquake and fire. However,
largely fruitless antitrust efforts gave way to regulator acceptance of the insurer
position that information sharing was necessary. Powerful regional rating organizations set prices and the cartelized group of large insurers took steps to
erect barriers to entry and also to innovation. The regulated rate-setting practice
that emerged in the early twentieth century is the subject of Chapter 6.

Chapter 7 tells the story of the development of casualty insurance and the
creation of workers' compensation, arguably the crown jewel of state insurance
reform accomplishments. Reformers who hoped workers' compensation would
be the first stage in an expansion of social insurance to include universal health
insurance and old-age pensions would be disappointed as the postwar period
gave way to a period of reactionary "Americanism" that equated expanded government activism with authoritarianism.

While insurers described their own role as "public," they wanted no type of
partnership with the government. At a time when social insurance was expanding

in Europe, insurers vehemently denounced any type of public sector activity in insurance, both criticizing extremely limited attempts at state life and fire insurance and guardedly watching federal wartime activities. Insurers cheered as the federal government's effort to provide soldiers with low-cost life insurance collapsed in the postwar period and embraced the "Americanism" rhetoric of the 1920s, which equated expansions of social insurance with the worst forms of authoritarian societies. Life insurers were already working with large employers in the early phases of the expansion of workplace benefits, the foundation of the privatized welfare system that would emerge in the twentieth century.

Federal Challenge

Until the Depression, the federal government still largely played the role of cheerleader for the insurance industry. In 1929, former president Calvin Coolidge served on the board of New York Life and described the company as a "public service agency." But the federal government entered the story in a significant way during the 1930s, when both the antitrust efforts and the social insurance reforms of the New Deal had implications for the insurance industry. A federal investigation of a St. Louis political boss led to an antitrust suit against a southern fire insurance rating organization with potentially seismic consequences.

As Chapter 8 describes, in *United States v. South-Eastern Underwriters Association (SEUA)* (1944), the Supreme Court reversed the *Paul* ruling, finding that insurance was in fact commerce and could therefore be regulated by Congress. The *SEUA* decision sent a shockwave through the industry. Though they once craved federal regulation, insurers were now terrified of a far more powerful federal government. The decision created an uneasy alliance between companies and state regulators, who were concerned about the potential loss of both power and revenue. In the aftermath of the *SEUA* decision, Congress enabled the persistence of the status quo by passing the McCarran-Ferguson Act in 1945, which essentially preserved the state regulatory structure, conditional on adequate regulation by states.

In addressing the labor market crisis of the Depression, New Deal reformers identified unemployment insurance, old-age annuities, and crop insurance (but not health insurance) as social needs that were inadequately provided by the voluntary safety net created by private insurers. After some initial misgivings, large life insurers concurred, as described in Chapter 9. Narrowing their focus and shrinking their sense of their "publicness," insurers transferred their energy to the rapidly developing group benefits market. During the 1930s, the federal government also began a practice, which would persist for many decades, of holding highly critical yet largely unproductive hearings about the insurance industry. Initial hearings focused on life insurance, particularly low-value "industrial insurance" aggressively sold door to door to the poor. Despite the national attention given to the issue, industrial insurance persisted until it ultimately became unprofitable many decades later.

Retreat

In the mid-twentieth century, insurers wrestled with and often tried to evade the implications of their quasi-public status, which had in many ways become a burden. Life insurers, for example, tried to escape into the world of employee benefits, particularly health insurance. There, as shown in Chapter 10, the size and scope of unmet demand ultimately invited federal attention, as it became increasingly apparent that the private welfare system excluded too many, particularly the elderly. Faced with the threat of government insurance, insurers were forced to acknowledge their public responsibility and joined with hospitals and doctors to try to make the case that the voluntary system could satisfy demand. When this failed, they accepted the inevitability of Medicaid and Medicare, which were built around the structure created by the private employer system and would soon provide additional business opportunities of their own.

In another example, property and casualty insurers initially opposed compulsory auto insurance, knowing that it would create pressure to cover almost everyone, arguing they were being asked to collect a "private tax" on the right to drive. Chapter 11 describes how controversies erupted in many state markets due to high premiums and unavailability, particularly for drivers who were non-White, low income, or elderly. Dissatisfaction with insurers' practices led to multiple rounds of congressional hearings and the growth of a powerful consumer movement, though national reform efforts failed and public controversy about the rating practices of auto insurers persists to this day.

State regulators were largely constrained to a set of tradeoffs between lower rates and less availability, with the threat of market exit always looming if business conditions became too unfavorable. Chapter 12 shows how this dynamic extended to residential and commercial property and liability insurance. The federal government began to serve as a backstop to certain markets. When insurers withdrew from redlined urban neighborhoods, federal riot reinsurance was offered in exchange for participation in an assigned risk plan. After decades of mounting losses from storms, federal flood insurance was created as a collaborative program with industry, but inadequate uptake and insufficient rates minimized the impact on both risk protection and floodplain management. Some states created catastrophe funds and state insurers of last resort in an attempt to compensate for insurer withdrawals, but in a state-based regulatory framework, calls for national disaster insurance were denounced as "beach house bailouts."

Realignment

In both property and casualty and life and health markets, there had long been divisions between larger insurers that generally accepted and even welcomed the growing role of federal government and viewed it ultimately as a complement to their business and smaller insurers, often mutuals, that opposed it for ideological and business reasons. But by the late twentieth century, a new status quo was emerging. It was increasingly clear that insurers could neither completely renounce their public responsibility nor object to government intervention, since most problems involving unmet demand could only be satisfied with public funding. It had also become clear that the public sector would not displace private markets. Collaboration with government was the way forward.

The insurance industry has become dependent on government as a financial backstop and a major customer. Government depends on the insurance industry to participate in markets, including those that are publicly funded. For example, large-scale withdrawal of insurers from residential and commercial property and casualty markets in any state would effectively short circuit the functioning of the economy, and private insurers administer the great majority of publicly funded health insurance.

Addressing early twentieth-century Europe, Smith argued that the ideals of freedom and security could in fact be reconciled, observing that there are "noble and ignoble" versions of both, and suggesting that "the great problem that lies before us in the future is to distinguish rightly between them and to direct our national policy accordingly."[11] This book examines how the tradeoff between freedom and security has been navigated in the United States through the lens of insurance. More than a century later, the "great problem" Smith describes is still with us.

At a high level of abstraction, it could be said that the relationship between the insurance industry and the public sector in the United States has gone through a process somewhat like the famous "stages of grief," only in reverse: initial acceptance of insurers' claims that their business was special and transcended "mere commerce" has been followed by successive cycles of anger, bargaining, and denial, until a new equilibrium between public and private was reached. In this new end state, government and insurers are codependent, the private insurance industry has retained an enormous amount of power and influence, effective national solutions to insurance problems are undersupplied, and significant unmet demand for insurance remains. It is for the reader to judge whether this new equilibrium is sufficiently different from the old.

1

Birth of a Business

Lieutenant Frederick Henry Beecher was planning to make a visit home to see his family that spring in 1868, when he received an order to embark on a new mission. Civil War general Phil Sheridan asked him to assist Major George "Sandy" Forsyth in recruiting and leading a unit of fifty elite civilian scouts to search for Cheyenne and Sioux warriors and engage them in combat. Beecher, shown in an undated photo in Figure 1.1 was stationed at Fort Wallace in Kansas and had previously encountered the Cheyenne during an attack on the fort in the summer of 1867. He was known to be a good shot, and Major Forsyth thought highly of his skills, describing him as "brave and modest, with a love of hunting and a natural taste for plainscraft; he was a splendid specimen of a thoroughbred American, and a most valuable man in any position requiring coolness, courage and tact."[1]

Ongoing conflict between nomadic Native peoples and civilians placed pressure on the under-resourced U.S. Army, leading to the use of civilian scouts. Beecher helped assemble a group known for their tracking skills, and they set off from Fort Hayes, Kansas, heading west for Fort Wallace. They arrived in September and soon learned of an attack on a freight train about thirteen miles east. The next morning, under Forsyth's command, they set out in pursuit of the raiders, following their trail into Yuma County, Colorado. The scouts soon lost the trail, yet their travels did not go unnoticed. As they made camp on the south bank of the Arikaree River, a large party of Cheyenne and Sioux gathered nearby for a massive surprise attack.[2]

A predawn incursion by a small party identified the scouts' location and triggered an onslaught, as hundreds of warriors, armed with rifles, lances, and arrows, descended from the hills. The greatly outnumbered party struggled to establish a defensive position on a sandbar near the Kansas-Colorado border. Casualties from the multiday fighting included the famous chief Roman Nose as well as Beecher, who reportedly dragged himself over to Forsyth before saying: "I have my death wound, general. I am shot in the side and dying." Beecher died along with twenty-one other men, in what came to be known as the Battle of Beecher Island. Those surviving dug sand pits for protection and subsisted for eight days on spoiled horse meat before being rescued by a company of Tenth Cavalry troops.[3]

Uncovered. Katherine Hempstead, Oxford University Press. © Oxford University Press 2024.
DOI: 10.1093/oso/9780190094157.003.0001

Figure 1.1 Lieutenant Frederick Henry Beecher in an undated photograph.

Beecher had been born in 1841 in New Orleans to a storied New England family. He was the grandson of abolitionist Congregationalist minister Lyman Beecher, and the nephew of Harriet Beecher Stowe and her brother, the noted clergyman Henry Ward Beecher. Frederick was the oldest of six children born to Charles Beecher and Sarah Leland Coffin. Charles, also an abolitionist minister and composer of religious music, worked for a time as a church organist in New Orleans. His letters to his sister Harriet provided her with information about slavery that influenced the writing of *Uncle Tom's Cabin*. Frederick attended Andover and was a student at Bowdoin when the Civil War started. With a class-mate, Beecher enlisted on the last day of May before graduation, joining the Sixteenth Maine Volunteers.[4]

He soon saw action and was badly wounded in the thigh at the battle of Fredericksburg. His father brought him home to Massachusetts to recuperate. After recovering, he rejoined his regiment on crutches and fought at Chancellorsville before marching to Gettysburg. In this battle he commanded part of a small, overpowered group of soldiers, who were desperately shredding their flag to keep it from the Confederates. When a shell shattered his right kneecap, he recalled: "I thought I was cut in two and I expected to live but a few minutes but was very happy." His anguished mother got word of his injury and desperately searched the war camps for her son. By finding him, she most likely saved his life. Again, he was removed home, and could not fully recover from his injuries. He was forced to resign from active duty in September of 1864.[5]

The postwar period was not easy for young Beecher. After a lengthy recuper-
ation, he still had pain in his knee and walked with a limp. He served briefly and
unhappily in the Veteran Reserve. In a letter home, he ruminated darkly on his
future: "My fortune has not been good, and I do not know that it will change.
I have much to be thankful for, I know; and yet I sometimes wish I were laid with
the brave men at Gettysburg." Beecher served briefly in the Freedman's Bureau,
before rejoining the army and accepting a commission with the Third Infantry
Regiment. In 1866, he reported for duty at Fort Riley, Kansas, and was detailed
to the Fort Wallace Army Post, on the Colorado line. The posting was difficult
for many reasons. Beecher served as the assistant quartermaster and supervised
much of the early construction of Fort Wallace. The fort was understaffed and
insufficiently equipped to defend against attacks by the Cheyenne, who were
responding to railroad construction and other settler encroachment on their
hunting lands.[6]

As his college newsletter would sadly note, he had longed for a visit home but
accepted a mission that "proved fatal to our dear classmate." Beecher had known
little in life but school and military service. Like his celebrated family, he was
inspired by the ideals of abolitionism, but rather than religion, he was drawn
to the action of military battle. Beecher's obituary paid tribute to his "genuine
courage and unaffected manliness of character" that "will live in the memory of
his friends." Those who served with him praised his skills as a soldier. General
George Custer predicted "had he lived he would have had a brilliant future." His
commander Forsyth, who had chosen him for his fatal mission, described him as
"one of the best and bravest officers in the United States Army."[7]

Given the severity of his war injuries, Beecher's physical condition was poor
for the arduousness of his final mission, which itself seemed ill-conceived. The
Battle of Beecher Island caused far more casualties to the Cheyenne and Sioux
than to the Forsyth scouts. It was not strategically significant to either side and
represented just another deadly episode in the ongoing conflict between the
U.S. Army and Native peoples. Beecher's life and death seem deeply rooted in
the nineteenth-century past. Yet his survivors had an experience that will res-
onate with many today. When his father filed with the New Jersey Mutual Life
Insurance Company to collect on his $2,000 life insurance policy, the claim was
denied on a technicality.

The period immediately after the Civil War was foundational in the development of the insurance business in the United States. Fire and marine insurance were well established, but commercial life insurance was relatively new
and still making its case to a somewhat skeptical public. Casualty insurance had
only just started to develop. Demand for fire and life insurance increased exponentially with the growth of population and economic activity. Although this
took different forms in the two lines of business, firm sizes grew, and national

distribution systems began to develop. The physical contours of the growing industry took shape in New York's financial district, shown in Figure 1.2, as new
firms clustered along Wall Street, Broadway, John Street, and Fulton Street. A vi-
brant trade press emerged to provide information and editorialize on issues of
the day.

Insurers claimed a moral high ground in the world of commerce, arguing
that their industry served the public interest due to its importance in protecting
income and preventing dependency. Yet insurance was very much a business,
and in an environment characterized by rapid growth and minimal regulation,
distinctive market problems emerged. For fire insurance, cyclical insolvencies
driven by underpricing became an ongoing problem, while life insurers
struggled with a number of policyholder issues related to premiums and policy
values. Given the nascent state of regulation, the trade press played an important
role in airing problems, and many issues were resolved on an ad hoc basis. As the
century progressed, established insurers came to believe that competition was a
problem and sought regulation on terms they could control.

Beecher's family was interacting with a life insurance industry that was
growing exponentially, as participants in the rapidly industrializing post–Civil
War economy sought increased financial security and outlets for capital. During
the 1860s, the amount of life insurance in force (or the sum of policy face value)
in New York alone increased from $140 million to $1.8 billion, while assets of
companies similarly grew from $20 million to $229 million. The amount of life
insurance issued in 1868 exceeded the national debt. By 1870, life insurance was
well on its way to being a major American business.[8]

But it hadn't always been this way. The early growth of the industry had been
inhibited by discomfort about the apparent monetization of death, the connection with gambling, and a worry that life insurance would encourage reliance
on something besides hard work and thrift, thereby leading to "relaxation and
decay of those cardinal virtues of society."[9] Similar concerns had emerged in
European countries, where life insurance was also viewed with suspicion, due
to its long association with speculation. In the Middle Ages, wagering on lives
was a popular pastime, especially participants in military combat or the British
peers. This recreational pursuit increasingly came to be seen as unsavory, as
did "graveyard" insurance, a practice that involved speculative buying of
policies on old or ill individuals. By the end of the eighteenth century, a British
antigambling act required that there be an "insurable interest" on the part of the
policyholder.[10]

Another early European form that had both gambling and insurance features
were tontines, an innovation used by Louis XIV of France in the seventeenth century to raise revenue and adopted by private parties thereafter. Tontines were essentially a "life insurance lottery," a collective wager among a pool of subscribers

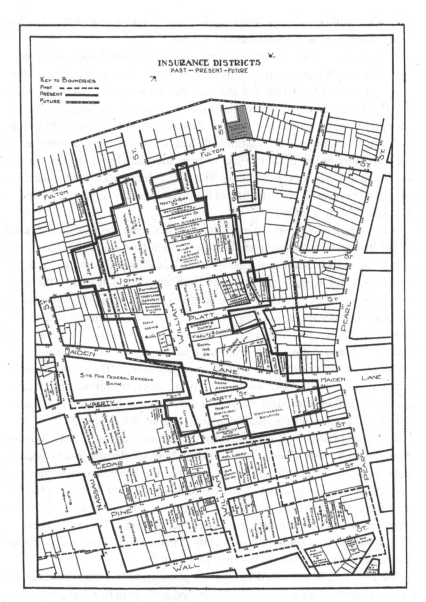

Figure 1.2 Insurance publisher Alfred M. Best drew this map of the New York City insurance district in the early twentieth century. Reproduced by permission of A. M. Best Company.

as to who would survive the longest. There were many variations; in the "last man" tontine the sole survivor was the "winner."[11]

In puritanical early America, life insurance was frowned upon as a type of gambling that threatened the motivation to work. The potential for sudden wealth was considered immoral and potentially corrupting. Saving was preferred as the mechanism for providing for one's heirs and was "as good an insurance policy as any man needs," the *New York Times* admonished in 1853.[12] The early life insurance industry additionally had to counter religious ideas about the sacrosanct nature of human life, in particular the view that life insurance amounted to a form of census taking. The plague that befell the Israelites when King David ordered a census reflected the unacceptability of "illicit attempts to discover the secrets of God."[13]

In the agrarian society of the eighteenth century, there was less practical need for life insurance, as people tended to stay on their land and transmit property to heirs upon their death. Fraternal voluntary societies pooled funds to pay for burial costs. Yet as industrialization and urbanization increased in the nineteenth century, the contours of this agricultural life began to shift. More people worked for wages and didn't have significant property to transmit to heirs. An 1840 New York law permitted married women to take out insurance on the lives of their husbands that would be protected from the demands of creditors.[14]

Despite the fact that there was a religious basis to much of the opposition to life insurance, organized religion was very important in its transformation to a mainstream institution. Protestant clergymen were some of its earliest champions, since they had no property, had low salaries, and needed to provide for widows and children. The earliest life insurance product in the United States was the Presbyterian Ministers Fund, established in 1759 specifically for the widows and orphans of Presbyterian ministers. More conservative denominations as a rule condemned life insurance, and Mennonites prohibit it to this day, but liberal theologians endorsed it as financial prudence and Christian duty. Henry Ward Beecher, uncle of the unfortunate lieutenant, was a major early proponent of life insurance and spoke of it frequently in his sermons. Some life insurance companies even used clergyman as pamphleteers.[15]

Life insurance was justified by its early proponents in religious terms, as a pious and sacred duty to care for one's descendants and in that way achieve immortality. Rather than a renunciation of religion, providing for one's loved ones after death came to be seen as a secular ritual: "He who has done his best to provide for those whom he leaves behind him can look to heaven with far more assurance."[16] A "good death" now included provision for dependents, increasingly important as fewer Americans owned productive land that they could transmit. By permitting some control over the living, life insurance and estate planning in general provided a pathway to immortality. To combat religious critiques,

New York Life issued a circular in 1869. "Wrong Notions Corrected" refuted ten misconceptions about life insurance, including, for example, the argument that "life insurance is not distrusting Providence; for Providence was not designed to preclude self-help."[17] Originally disparaged as immoral speculation, the life insurance industry rebranded itself as a beneficent institution, countering ideological resistance with moral and theological arguments.

After the Civil War, as the economy became more complex, attitudes about risk and death continued to evolve. The funeral undertaking business professionalized and grew, replacing neighbors and relatives who had previously performed this function. The formalization of wills and estate planning also grew in the nineteenth century. These changes normalized the association of money with death, which was important to the acceptability of life insurance. There was soon a tradition of expensive funerals, and dread of "a pauper's burial" stoked demand for life insurance. Life insurance became not only a hedge against uncertainty but also a way to plan for and manage death.[18] As the nineteenth century progressed, life insurance became a powerful corporate institution and grew rapidly. In this pivot toward commercialism, the investment value of life insurance was emphasized over moral and sentimental appeals, although widows and orphans still figured largely in industry rhetoric.[19]

In 1841 there were three mutual life companies, and mutuality was briefly the prevailing form of corporate organization. During the 1840s, nearly twenty more life insurance mutuals would be created. Mutuals, unlike stock companies, had no initial capital requirements, since funds were built from premiums paid by policyholders. This facilitated entry into a rapidly growing industry. This form of organization was dominant at the time for fire insurers too. After disastrous fires and economic instability in the 1830s, mutualization countered investor skittishness and general capital shortages. Life insurance at that time was often a sideline to another line of business. The New York Life Insurance Company, for example, emerged out of the Nautilus Insurance Company, a fire and marine insurer founded in 1841. In 1845 the company amended their charter to add life insurance, before reinsuring the fire and marine risks with other companies and changing its name in 1849. New York Life, along with some other early life insurance companies, also sold insurance on the lives of slaves.[20]

The Mutual Life Insurance Company of New York was founded in 1843 and, along with New York Life, would comprise two of New York's "Big Three." In fact, Mutual Life would be the largest life insurance company in America until the Equitable Life Assurance Society surpassed it in 1886. The emphasis on the noncommercial attribute of mutuality in advertisements echoed preindustrial forms of solidarity and community and helped to offset discomfort about life insurance, as did the potential for sharing dividends. Seeking to pull up the drawbridge, successful mutuals encouraged the enactment of a New York law in 1849 that required a $100,000 security deposit, essentially thwarting the formation of new mutuals.[21]

With the formation of the Equitable Life in 1859, a new period of growth dominated by stock companies began. This trend was accelerated after the Civil War, a period that combined a rising demand for insurance with an abundant supply of capital. More than one hundred new life companies, mostly stock, formed between 1865 and 1870. To give a sense of the rapidity with which the industry grew, the New York Insurance Department reported 56,000 policies in 1860 and 747,000 in 1870, a year when the total adult male population was approximately 9.5 million. The number of companies reporting to New York's department increased from seventeen to seventy-one. The assets of life insurance companies grew twelve thousand percent in the last half of the nineteenth century.[22]

Despite the rapid increase in the number of companies, the so-called Big Three, Mutual Life, Equitable Life, and New York Life, were all established before the Civil War. The Metropolitan Life Insurance Company, founded in 1868, evolved from a Civil War–era accident and health company, National Union Life and Limb, which had unsuccessfully tried to insure soldiers and sailors against disability. The Prudential Insurance Company, founded in 1875, similarly shifted from accident and disability to focus on life. These "Big Five" New York companies would dominate life insurance.[23]

While spurring growth, the Civil War also caused significant disruption to the life insurance business. After Congress prohibited commerce with the South in 1861, it became effectively impossible to collect premiums from Southern policyholders. Companies devised various approaches to the situation. Many permitted policies to be surrendered for a cash value or reinstated at the end of the war. Southern policyholders that joined the Confederate Army were considered to have forfeited their policies. Some policyholders wondered what would happen if they were forced into violent confrontations against their will. One Virginia clergyman inquired: "Suppose an armed force approached the house, or forced themselves upon my premises, and in defending my family and my rights I get killed—will my policy become null and void?"[24]

For Northerners, the standard underwriting prohibition on military service became problematic. Life insurers began to grant a war permit and impose a surcharge known as a war risk premium to policyholders that joined the Union Army, but business practices were not standardized.[25] Companies that were well capitalized took advantage of the opportunity to "do well by doing good," extending generous terms to both North and South to build good will and gain market share. Thus, the president of New York Life opined at the outset of the Civil War that the company would "decline to take advantage of any technicality" to avoid paying claims. Phenomenal wartime growth for the company was attributed to its waiving of its previous prohibition on military service and writing "large numbers of war risk policies at a slightly increased premium." When the ban was lifted after the war, the company sought to resume relations with Southern policyholders, staffing their newly organized "Southern Department" with Confederate Army heroes in senior positions.[26]

The business of fire insurance was also experiencing a period of rapid growth in the post–Civil War era. Marine and fire insurance were the oldest lines of insurance business in the United States, and unlike life insurance, their necessity was never in doubt. Marine insurance played a crucial role in financing whaling ventures.[27] The business was modeled on the British system, where policies were initially underwritten by individual merchants. Much of this business originally took place through informal exchanges based in coffee shops in port districts, most famously Lloyds, which would later become Lloyds of London. Over time, these exchanges evolved into insurance brokerage offices located near ports. By the 1720s, similar offices emerged in port cities in the United States.[28] The Charleston Insurance Company and the South Carolina Insurance Company, both founded in 1776, were the first marine insurance companies in the United States.

In the eighteenth century, lack of capital limited the supply of coverage, which struggled to keep up with the growth of industry. In response, joint stock companies formed, which raised capital through the sale of shares and the distribution of dividends. From the outset, these emerging companies found it relatively easy to get charters from state legislatures. The joint stock structure emerged first in marine insurance, where it was shown to provide greater security than private underwriting. Before the end of the eighteenth century, the first stock insurance company, the Insurance Company of North America, was founded in Philadelphia in 1792. Just as New York Life had emerged from what was originally a marine insurer, the Insurance Company of North America had originally been formed as a life insurance tontine. When unsuccessful in finding a sufficient number of subscribers, the existing members of the Universal Tontine Association voted to transform themselves into a "general insurance company" chartered for marine, fire, and life. They quickly sold sixty thousand shares at $10 each, transforming the nature of marine underwriting in the city, where financial failures of individual underwriters were a problem. After this, the industry grew quickly. By the end of the eighteenth century, there were thirty-three companies underwriting fire and marine losses, and eighty-six charters were formed between 1794 and 1810. By 1810, there were more than seventy joint stock companies in the United States. Philadelphia alone had eleven marine insurers in 1811.[29]

The early U.S. model for fire insurance also hewed closely to the British, where mutual companies had emerged to share risk, particularly after the London fire of 1666. These early mutual companies were primarily not commercial concerns, but rather outgrowths of voluntary firefighting organizations. In 1735, the first mutual insurance company in the United States was formed, the Friendly Society of Mutual Insuring of Homes Against Fire in Charleston, South Carolina. Unfortunately, this firm was significantly undercapitalized and relatively short-lived, going out of business after a fire in 1740. Famously, Benjamin Franklin helped found one of the oldest continually operating mutual insurance companies in the United States in 1752, the Philadelphia Contributionship for the Insuring of Houses from Losses by Fire, also known as the Hand in Hand. Franklin's company focused on insuring loss from fire and made early contributions toward fire prevention.[30]

In the early nineteenth century, demand for marine insurance slowed, as the Embargo Act of 1805–1807 temporarily reduced shipping. In response, joint stock companies originally formed to service the marine industry began to transition into writing fire policies. The demand for fire insurance grew quickly during the nineteenth century, with the development of American manufacturing and the growth of domestic industries like textiles. New companies emerged that specialized in fire from the outset. This line of business increasingly insured the contents of dwellings as the value of personal possessions increased along with real estate prices.[31]

Experiences in the early nineteenth century impressed upon the fire insurance industry the importance of geographical diversification. The business was largely local until the 1830s, a tendency that was reinforced by the common state practice of taxing out-of-state and foreign companies. But such a system created excessive exposure in the event of a large fire. In 1835, a fire in New York City bankrupted twenty-three of the twenty-six companies operating in the city. After this experience, geographic diversification became a priority for the industry. This impetus fostered the growth of the agency system, which became widespread by the 1850s. By 1860, there were thirty-eight out-of-state companies operating in New York. During the ensuing decades, the fire industry evolved into national companies with local agents in various locations.[32]

As fire and life insurance became ever more firmly established in the mid-nineteenth-century social and economic infrastructure, insurers emphasized the special, quasi-public nature of their endeavor. George Savage, president of the New York Board of Fire Underwriters, an early organization of insurers, described his occupation as more of a public service than a business: "I think everybody will confess that the business of fire insurance with which I am connected is a highly important one. It has been my solace, it has been my comfort, during seasons of great despondency and trouble incident to this business, to know that I was engaged in a good work, the work of promoting the welfare of my fellow men."[33]

Life insurers too made frequent references to their role as protectors of widows and orphans. Both fire and life companies were quick to note that insurance prevented financial ruin and public dependency. The benevolent nature of insurance was frequently mentioned by the companies in making the point that their business transcended mere commerce. It was also a good sales pitch, as the societal value of the product strengthened the argument that being insured was a duty.

Despite the frequent statements about social purpose, insurers contended with the pressures that accompanied a rapidly growing business, with accompanying market problems. Fire and life insurers faced different challenges. Fire insurers needed to collaborate with their competitors to spread risk and share loss information, as seen in this list of multiple insurers sharing a large commercial risk shown in Figure 1.3. This led to the early creation of trade associations and cyclical efforts to collectively set rates. Life insurers were able to be more independent and engaged in a different kind of competition. Yet for both lines, rapid growth in demand, combined with very little regulation, facilitated market problems that occasionally threatened the stability of the industry. Most difficulties stemmed from intense competition resulting in price wars and subsequent insolvencies, and an absence of standardized practices related to policy value and the paying of claims.

In the case of fire, the establishment of stable rates was a perennial problem. The evolution of a more geographically diverse industrial structure did not alleviate concerns about solvency. Low capitalization requirements and the widespread adoption of general laws of incorporation facilitated easy entry. The pressure of competition resulted in cyclical underpricing, as firms based premiums on short-term costs with inadequate understanding of risks. The idea of fixing rates arose as early as 1819 with the New York association of fire firms known as the Salamander Society, and periodic attempts to agree on rates during the early nineteenth century collapsed as new entrants undercut prices. After large fires wiped out multiple companies, surviving firms would raise rates, encouraging renewed entry. This was an early version of the underwriting cycle. As fire losses grew along with the size of the economy, so did the negative consequences of these cyclical insolvencies for consumers and the industry.[34]

The issue of a national agreement on rates was raised at the 1866 meeting of the New York Board of Fire Insurance Companies, after an exploding firecracker in Portland had led to a major conflagration on the Fourth of July.[35] This led to the formation of what is considered to be the first national business association, the National Board of Fire Underwriters, an association of seventy-five companies that represented the most serious attempt thus far to cooperate on rates. The need for cooperation was perceived as dire in this admiring early twentieth-century history: "Companies were weakened through rate-cutting

LIST OF INSURANCE AND APPORTIONMENT OF LOSS.

NO. OF POLICY.	COMPANY.	AM'T INS'D.	PAYS.	NO. OF POLICY.	COMPANY.	AM'T INS'D.	PAYS.
21,061	Ætna, Hartford,	$5,000	$3,947 37	509,089	London Assurance, London,	$5,000	$3,947 37
5491	Albany, Albany,	5,000	3,947 37	796,285	London & Lancashire, England,	10,000	7,894 73
9,790	Alliance, Boston,	5,000	3,947 37	168,092	Long Island, Brooklyn,	5,000	3,947 37
100,342	American, New York,	5,000	3,947 37	8,718	Manhattan, New York,	10,000	7,894 73
9,999	American Central, St. Louis,	2,500	1,973 69	27,813	Manufacturers, Boston,	5,000	3,947 37
10,640	American Central, St. Louis,	2,500	1,973 68	51,120	Merchants, Providence,	5,000	3,947 37
58,182	Atlantic F. & M., Providence,	5,000	3,947 37	287,263	Merchants, New York,	2,500	1,973 68
50,396	Boylston Mutual, Boston,	5,000	3,947 37	32,421	Merchants, Newark,	5,000	3,947 37
4,038	Buffalo, Buffalo,	5,000	3,947 37	80,157	Metropole, Paris,	10,000	7,894 73
16,003	Buffalo German, Buffalo,	5,000	3,947 37	5,380	National, New York,	5,000	3,947 37
3,454	Citizens, Missouri,	2,500	1,973 69	56,035	National, Baltimore,	5,000	3,947 37
3,708	Citizens, Missouri,	2,500	1,973 68	28,178	Newark City, Newark,	5,000	3,947 37
98,708	Clinton, New York,	5,000	3,947 37	71,260	New Hampshire, Manchester,	5,000	3,947 37
13,091	Columbia, New York,	5,000	3,947 37	158,820	New York Fire, New York,	5,000	3,947 37
25,445	Commerce, Albany,	2,500	1,973 68	1,037	New York Bowery, New York,	5,000	3,947 37
104,651	Commercial, New York,	5,000	3,947 37	430,106	Niagara, New York,	10,000	7,894 73
111,037	Commercial Union, London,	10,000	7,894 73	331,903	North British, England,	5,000	3,947 37
10,868	Delaware Mutual, Philadelphia,	10,000	7,894 73	2,073	North German, Hamburg,	5,000	3,947 37
49,003	Dorchester Mutual, Dorchester,	5,000	3,947 37	5,524	North-Western National, Milwaukie,	5,000	3,947 37
94,700	Eagle, New York,	5,000	3,947 37	1,001,031	Norwich Union, England,	10,000	7,894 73
87,077	Enterprise, Cincinnati,	2,500	1,973 68	5,195	Pacific, New York,	5,000	3,947 37
40,518	Equitable, Providence,	5,000	3,947 37	127,501	People's Fire, New York,	2,500	1,973 68
3,075	Exchange, New York,	5,000	3,947 37	3,972	People's, Newark,	5,000	3,947 37
8,057	Faneuil Hall, Boston,	5,000	3,947 37	4,499	People's Fire, Trenton,	5,000	3,947 37
69,797	Farragut, New York,	5,000	3,947 37	12,006	Phenix, Hartford,	5,000	3,947 37
139,879	Fire Association, Philadelphia,	10,000	7,894 73	3,715	Phenix, Brooklyn,	10,000	7,894 73
160,207	Firemen's, New York,	5,000	3,947 37	2,008,631	Phenix, London,	10,000	7,894 73
147,409	Firemen's, Newark,	5,000	3,947 37	11,869	Providence Washington, Providence,	5,000	3,947 37
53,167	Firemen's, Baltimore,	5,000	3,947 37	820,119	Queen, England,	5,000	3,947 37
141,487	Firemen's Fund, San Francisco,	5,000	3,947 37	15,199	Relief, New York,	5,000	3,947 37
62,370	First National, Worcester,	5,000	3,947 37	210,720	Rutgers, New York,	5,000	3,947 37
15,681	German, Baltimore,	2,500	1,973 68	172,750	St. Nicholas, New York,	5,000	3,947 37
8,007	German American, New York,	5,000	3,947 37	173,164	Scottish Commercial, Glasgow,	5,000	3,947 37
150,320	Girard, Philadelphia,	5,000	3,947 37	20,648	Security, New Haven,	5,000	3,947 37
2,110	Gloucester, Gloucester,	2,500	1,973 68	22,562	Springfield, Springfield,	10,000	7,894 73
110,737	Greenwich, New York,	5,000	3,947 37	4,385	Standard, New York,	5,000	3,947 37
100,978	Guardian, New York,	5,000	3,947 37	2,298	Standard, New Jersey,	5,000	3,947 37
530,864	Guardian, London,	5,000	3,947 37	114,362	Star, New York,	5,000	3,947 37
4,010	Hamburg-Bremen, Germany,	10,000	7,894 73	965	Toledo Fire & Marine, Toledo,	5,000	3,947 37
5,330	Hamburg-Magdeburg, Germany,	5,000	3,947 37	1,268	Trade, Camden,	5,000	3,947 37
308,201	Hanover, New York,	5,000	3,947 37	75,249	Traders, Chicago,	5,000	3,947 37
15,501	Hartford, Hartford,	5,000	3,947 37	39,890	Traders & Mechanics, Lowell,	2,500	1,973 69
17,033	Home, New York,	5,000	3,947 37	228,051	Tradesmen's, New York,	5,000	3,947 37
7,100	Howard, New York,	5,000	3,947 37	1,061	Transatlantic, Germany,	5,000	3,947 37
103,943	Imperial and Northern, London,	10,000	7,894 73	14,931	Underwriters' Association, New York,	10,000	7,894 73
62,844	Importers & Traders', New York,	2,500	1,973 68	46,911	Union, Philadelphia,	5,000	3,947 37
15,000	Insurance Company of the State of Pennsylvania, Philadelphia,	5,000	3,947 37	14,870	United Firemen's, Philadelphia,	5,000	3,947 37
71,187	La Caisse, Paris,	5,000	3,947 37	4,590	Watertown, Watertown,	2,500	1,973 69
80	La Confiance, Paris,	10,000	7,894 73	10,627	Westchester, New York,	5,000	3,947 37
119	La Confiance, Paris,	5,000	3,947 37	12,845	Western, Toronto,	5,000	3,947 37
3,035	Lamar, New York,	5,000	3,947 37	13,120	Western, Toronto,	5,000	3,947 37
710,098	Lancashire, England,	5,000	3,947 37	249,388	Williamsburg City, Brooklyn,	5,000	3,947 37
63,954	Lenox, New York,	2,500	1,973 68				
2,351,398	Liverpool & London & Globe, England,	5,000	3,947 37		Total,	$570,000	$450,000 00

Figure 1.3 Apportionment schedule shows large number of policies held by a commercial risk suffering a loss in 1880. Insurance Library.

competition and harassed by hostile legislation. Nerves were on edge; everyone was apprehensive, and the zest of combat disappeared in a sudden realization that the entire fire insurance business was in peril." As noted by Mark Howard, president of Merchants' Insurance: "Without an organization of this kind, insurance companies would be in the position of Kilkenny cats. They would devour each other and leave nothing but the tips of their tails."[36]

At their 1867 meeting, the National Board of Fire Underwriters agreed on standard rates and also tried to standardize a claims adjustment practice by additionally pledging to jointly adopt the "Hamburg" form, which limited claims to three-quarters of the value of property. The Hamburg form was designed to combat arson, which insurers believed to be a large and growing cause of fire losses: "Since a large percentage of fire losses was believed to be the work of incendiaries, it was felt desirable to take measures to render the interesting profession of arson less profitable." Although their primary preoccupation was with standardized rates, the National Board of Fire Underwriters was from the outset extremely interested in all forms of fire prevention and decried the extent to which carelessness, inadequate building codes, and arson contributed to fires.[37]

Well before the intense antitrust sentiment that was to come, there was an awareness that the adoption of unified rates would be controversial in some quarters. The resolution in 1867 alluded to the potential pushback: "whereas the efforts of this Board have been met with resistance among merchants, manufacturers and others on the stereotyped ground that it is a monopoly and should therefore be discouraged, on the general plea that all such business combinations are antagonistic to the public."[38] The board staunchly denied any intention to charge excessive rates, but this issue would continue to haunt the fire insurance industry.

The causes of regional variation in risk were considered for the first time in this rate-setting effort, and the board divided the nation into six territories, each staffed with paid representatives. There was an attempt to inject some underlying knowledge about risk into the setting of rates and a recognition that the market alone was not resulting in accurate pricing, since "degrees of hazard varied so bewilderingly with local conditions, the construction of buildings, the nature of occupancy, it was necessary to have some better basis of charge than the rates fixed by competition." This question reportedly "dominated all others and was attacked with energy."[39]

As always, the cooperation of agents was far from assured. Anticipating this, several firms signed the "Chicago Compact," which promised to dismiss any agent that violated the National Board of Fire Underwriters' rates more than twice. For the first several years, cooperation on rates was observed, but by 1869, the agreement had begun to unravel. A cautionary essay in the trade journal the *Insurance Times* warned that in the recent years of prosperity too many have become "indifferent, or lukewarm, and in too many cases have tired of holding up their agents to a faithful and honest performance of their pledges and duty."[40]

These concerns soon became a reality. Committee chairman E. W. Cowell noted in the December meeting: "Candor compels us to say we are not as efficient a board today as we were in our last meeting. . . . [T]he outside public being made aware that our hold on local boards is not as strong as formerly, have redoubled their efforts for cheaper insurance, and many companies are giving discretionary power to their agents to meet this demand." By early 1870, the board had accepted defeat and alerted local rating boards to "modify, suspend, or declare advisory any or all rates fixed by them."[41]

In the sharp-elbowed life insurance industry, firms jockeyed for market share. The industry had abandoned its pious rhetoric, and many firms appealed to the more speculative interests of consumers by marketing policies as investment vehicles. An intense rivalry developed between the two largest New York firms, Equitable Life, led by entrepreneurial upstart Henry Hyde, and the older and stodgier Mutual Life, whose president Frederick Winston embodied a more conservative tradition.

Hyde was widely considered to be a phenomenal talent, especially in the area of marketing. Hired as a teenager to work for the Mutual Life, he left at age seventeen to start Equitable Life, opening an office with a large sign immediately above his former place of business. His force of personality and sales skills were legendary, and his personal involvement in sales was critical to the firm's early growth. One former clerk recounted that "Many prominent men who called to see (Hyde) failed to get away until after they had applied for a policy leaving their checks for the first premium. It was not uncommon to get out a policy in fifteen minutes when Mr. Hyde was behind the application."[42]

Hyde pioneered a national distribution system of home office sales management, where local sales managers hired, trained, and supervised agents. He traveled relentlessly around the country, recruiting agents away from other firms and encouraging general agents to be on the lookout for good talent. At the time, agents were still relatively untrained, relying largely on pamphlets and articles in the trade press to educate themselves. Many agents sold life insurance as a sideline activity, and the practice of direct personal solicitation was just emerging. The growth of the industry required a constantly increasing pool of agents, and commissions also increased throughout the nineteenth century as firms sought to attract agents and increase volume.

Hyde's innovative spirit and insatiable quest for growth led to the introduction of deferred dividend policies, a distant cousin of the tontine, which encouraged policyholders to speculate by waiting for larger dividends in the future. Winston responded with a brutal competition that involved agents, marketing, and the insurance press. Their fierce rivalry, known as the "Thirty Year War," would rage for much of the rest of the nineteenth century. One way that Mutual Life tried to respond to the threat posed by Equitable Life's deferred dividend policies was to offer premium reductions, a practice that became widespread. While not successful for Winston, this practice became common among other firms, some of whom were less well capitalized.[43]

The war between the companies had many fronts and was not limited to Equitable Life and Mutual Life. In terms of sales, it led to wars over dividends, policy liberalization, and agent compensation, including commissions, bonuses, and expenses. As described in one mid-century account, it became a contest over "who could give away the most business, hire the most agents away from a competitor, or cast the worst light upon him to his disadvantage with the public."[44] Part of the incentive came from the strong demands for capital, as the growing industrial and agricultural sectors sought loans. The investment imperatives as well as the growing demand for life insurance led to the valuation of increased production over everything else.

The big companies blanketed the land with agents, following the path of the railroads into newly settled towns where the demand for life insurance was strong. One New York Life agent noted that "the field was so ready for the harvest" that he received $15,000 in advance premiums before delivering a policy. Companies increased coverage in established territories as well. As population grew, real income increased, and transportation networks improved, life insurance became easier to sell and easier to buy. Increasingly, large companies were able to organize and control a national sales force. Additionally, New York's Big Three and several other companies had considerable success in marketing overseas.[45]

The aggressive tactics of the life firms caused reputational damage to the industry, despite the growing popularity of the concept of life insurance. The constant denunciation of competitors by agents in their quest for new business eroded consumer confidence, leading to the feeling that "a life company was not a safe place in which to leave funds." Another major factor was a constant stream of firm failures, starting in approximately 1867. The press did much to disclose misdoings and corruption, which did not improve consumer trust of industry, as even if not suffering a loss, the public "worried lest its turn might be next." Winston did not share Hyde's killer instinct and at one point sought unsuccessfully to cap enrollment in Mutual Life to a hundred thousand policyholders to tamp down the contest. In a prophetic insight, Winston speculated that "In the future, the struggle will be between conservatism and audacity," and ultimately, these fierce battles subsided, and the big firms learned that they generally had more to gain by working cooperatively.[46]

One front of competition concerned policy liberalization. Just as the fire industry was beginning to try to factor in the importance of building materials, municipal water supply, and the quality of fire departments, life insurance in the 1870s struggled with adequately measuring mortality risk. The profession of actuarial science, a branch of mathematics that specializes in the calculation of insurance premiums, was still in its infancy in the United States. The big life firms had actuaries, and preliminary life tables existed.[47] Yet they were crude and did not account for many individually varying conditions, where lack of data was an issue. Many companies attached surcharges to account for hazardous activities, such as serving in the military or travelling to California. During the Civil War, many companies established war risk surcharges of approximately two percent for existing and five percent for new policyholders. Yet these practices were not standardized and were driven by competition more than actuarial science. Firms didn't always provide clear information about their policies to consumers.[48]

Another major issue was surrender or nonforfeiture values in life insurance policies. A surrender value is an estimate of the equity that consumers have in their life insurance policy if they stop paying premiums. Earlier in the nineteenth century, life insurance policies were treated more like commercial contracts, meaning that when a consumer stopped paying, the contract was considered void. But as insurance increasingly came to be thought of as an investment, there was a change in expectations and a growing consensus that policyholder investment in their policy should be protected.

This change in sentiment was in large part due to the efforts of Elizur Wright, the famous actuary and first insurance commissioner of Massachusetts. Wright was born in 1824 on a farm in Connecticut and studied mathematics at Yale. One of his instructors was Lyman Beecher, the grandfather of the unfortunate lieutenant. Like Beecher, Wright was a committed abolitionist. A trip to London in the 1840s exposed him to the speculative secondary market in life insurance policies that existed there. In the outdoor market where poor men sold their policies to buyers who would profit by their imminent death, the horrified Wright could even see a similarity to a slave auction. This strengthened his commitment to creating a standardized approach to policyholder equity through nonforfeiture regulation.[49]

However, consensus was lacking about how that value should be calculated and in what form it should be made available to consumers. In 1858, New York Life introduced a simple approach to surrender values based on the number of premium payments made. In 1861, due to the efforts of Wright, Massachusetts

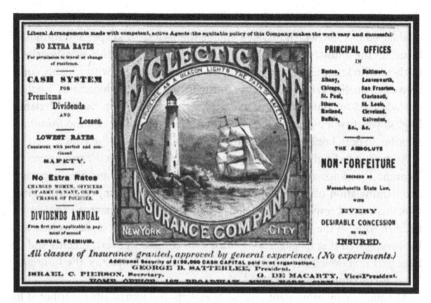

Figure 1.4 Eclectic Life advertisement, *Insurance Times*, 1871.

passed a nonforfeiture law, but its application was limited to Massachusetts companies doing business in the state, with the result that practices varied significantly between companies.[50]

In their advertising, life insurers sought to differentiate themselves by describing their approach to surcharges and surrender values. Eclectic Life's advertisement in 1871, as seen in Figure 1.4, makes a number of important claims. One is that they will not charge extra rates for women, military officers, or travel. Eclectic also claims they will offer policyholders the "Absolute Non-forfeiture decreed by Massachusetts state law," a reference to the standard set in the 1861 Massachusetts law, which was voluntarily adopted by companies in other states. Some companies also began to guarantee specific cash surrender values to policyholders, although the practice was not widespread.

In this highly competitive but still relatively unregulated industry, an aggressive trade press played a major role. Important examples include the *Insurance Monitor*, the *Insurance Record*, and the *Insurance Times*. While these papers made pertinent comments about issues of the day, they also served as paid propagandists for companies that would pay them to carry out their wars against one another or critique state regulators or industry practices.[51] The transactional nature of the relationship between the companies and the trade papers was not a secret; in fact, the editor of the *Insurance Record* was known by the nickname "Dollar-a-Line."[52]

Perhaps the best known of these papers was the *Insurance Times*, a monthly established in 1868, which played a unique role as a score keeper and sounding board for the industry. Its editor and publisher, Stephen English, was described by those who knew him as a crusader, "violent as a warrior," with a highly combative personality. With an "intense egotism that was at times ludicrous," English was addicted to conflict and did not back away from a fight. Born in Ireland, English was first a police officer in London. He then worked for the *Insurance Monitor*, in both London and New York, but soon left to start the *Times*.[53]

According to English, the *Insurance Times* was devoted to the promotion of "genuine insurance and sound and honorable companies" and the "exposure and denunciation of all their unreliable and fraudulent competitors." English took this second responsibility seriously and devoted many pages to castigating bad behavior on the part of insurance companies, agents, and state regulators. However, given that its pages were filled with company advertisements and in large part functioned as paid propaganda for specific companies, the *Insurance Times* was an unreliable narrator.[54]

Although many prominent insurance experts and journalists contributed to the *Insurance Times*, the journal reflected English's intense personality, a relationship that was compared to that between Horace Greeley and the *New York Tribune*.[55] As a rule, the *Insurance Times* carried the flag for what might now be called "big life" and "big fire" in New York, defending the large and established companies and denouncing those considered to be poorly run, undercapitalized, or speculative.

English had several grievances that were repeatedly addressed. One was a fierce opposition to life insurance companies organized on the cooperative or "assessment" principle, meaning that they did not use actuarial methods in determining premiums. Additionally, the *Insurance Times* critiqued other life firms that were thought to be undercapitalized "wildcats" or excessively disputed claims. English also decried inadequate fire prevention efforts, criticized the performance of many fire departments, and argued that arson was an underrecognized problem. A third theme was a generalized disdain for the insurance industry in all states other than New York and Massachusetts, but particularly in the South and West. A final editorial priority was to criticize state insurance regulation. English was an advocate for national supervision or, as a second best, uniform state regulation. Inadequate regulation permitted the bad business practices that the *Insurance Times* decried, while excessive regulation and taxation of out-of-state firms impeded the national growth of the New York companies.

The 1870s saw an increase in cooperative or "assessment" life insurance companies, which were often organized as fraternal organizations or mutual benefit societies. These assessment plans emerged in response to the distaste many consumers felt for the large insurers and to the growing demand for a lower-cost product. The assessment plans presented themselves as a noncommercial alternative to the large "investment" companies. Unfortunately, their disinterest in commercialism included a disregard for actuarial principles, and many of these companies quickly became insolvent.[56] Many of these plans were part of fraternal societies, while others adopted some of the outward appearance of a fraternal society but had a more commercial orientation, including the offering of dividends to attract business.[57] The distinctions between the two were not always clear—"the essentially commercial companies were not always easily distinguishable from the more purely mutual aid 'cooperative' or fraternal associations because the former sought so shrewdly and persistently to identify themselves with the latter."[58] The embrace of communitarian rhetoric by these firms was seen by the *Insurance Times* as a deceptive ploy: "The sentimentality that would make it a benevolent or charitable institution is too sickening to be listened to."[59]

The *Insurance Times* shared the position of the National Board of Fire Underwriters that high rates inevitably flowed from "improvidence and inattention . . . arson and incendiarism." The journal was critical of conditions that contributed to fire hazard, often discussing the quality of local fire departments and other safety issues, and supported the necessity of pricing for the existing level of hazard, echoing insurers' position on the Hamburg principle. The fact that the United States had far greater rates of fire loss than Europe was a source of embarrassment to those in the insurance world. Ascribing the disparity to a defect in the national character, English began an aptly named editorial called "A Fiery Circle" with an admission of guilt: "We are, from some cause or other, the greatest fire-raisers in the world." Better safety, rather than cutthroat competition, was the path to sustained lower rates, and "shallow advocates of cheap fire insurance" would do more good by "helping to lessen the frequency of arson" rather than starting new companies "founded on false premises and certain to fail in the end."[60]

The *Insurance Times* hailed from New York, and sectional battles were a major theme. Evidence of protectionism and incompetence in southern and western states was regularly noted. For example, in a lengthy takedown of the Southern Life Insurance Company of Memphis, the *Insurance Times* declared the company to be "totally unworthy of confidence, and on the highway to bankruptcy."[61] The recency of the Civil War was clear in some of the coverage. While denying any "hostility to this or any company merely because it is in the South," it was nevertheless noted that northern companies had attained their "unparalleled size and vigor" because the "ablest minds in the country have been employed in perfecting their organization." On the other hand: "The Southern people are as yet inexperienced in the management of life insurance interests, and it can hardly be expected that they will escape committing some grave errors." English suggested that southern companies adopt "a better standard of mathematical knowledge to enable them to avoid the blunders" and to aspire to "a little less of the clannishness which sees perfection in everything which appeals to sectional prejudice."[62]

The South was not the only region in the crosshairs. A dissection of the insurance industry in Cincinnati was contemptuous, starting with the observation that residents of the Queen City were unjustifiably proud of themselves and had a proclivity for cliquishness. Their business circles "wind about in beaten paths," ending up "about where they began." After a disparaging discussion of the "forty-five little fire insurance companies here," the *Insurance Times* dispensed one at a time with the city's four life firms, ending with Cincinnati Mutual, "the puniest infant of the four," sparing details on the grounds that it is "idle, if not cruel, to upbraid one so near passing away." The piece closed with some characteristic tough love from English: "Cincinnatians, a parting word! Break up your cliques, set the world before you as the field of your operations, and build up one grand and good company. This you can do."[63]

Quite often the *Insurance Times* took the side of companies against consumer complaints. Typical is a case where they defended the right of the Railway Passengers Assurance Company of Hartford, which was part of the Travelers Insurance Company, to issue policies that covered men for injury or death but women for death only. Accident or "travelers" insurance was at the time a new and relatively small line of business. While conceding that "it is probably very ungallant to make distinctions in business on account of sex," the *Insurance Times* concluded that was unavoidable since "business is regulated only by questions of profit and loss." The publication threw their full support behind Travelers: "Mr. Batterson says that his company cannot afford for twenty-five cents to insure a woman against all sorts of accidents for twenty-four hours, and that the figures in their office sustain his assertion." English reasoned that, "using the language of fire insurance, women are *extra hazardous*," and no "judicious company" should insure extra hazardous property without a special application. It was suggested that the aggrieved consumer might wish to make such an application, so that she could potentially pay more for protection against a "shattered limb or a disordered curl."[64]

Yet consumer protection was also sometimes a theme, and the *Insurance Times* was not reluctant to point to inadequacies of state supervision. In an excoriating piece on the New York Workman's Benefit Company, which was an example of the growing business in industrial insurance, a type of life insurance where small weekly premiums were collected from working-class customers, the *Times* labeled it as one of the "delusive swindles which are springing up all over the country." The customer base was "laboring men," and the "projectors of the scheme take it for granted that this class is less informed than any other on the subject of life insurance and are therefore more easily imposed upon." After describing in detail the flaws in the company's business model, they close with a caustic question aimed at New York's first insurance commissioner, William Barnes: "Why is it that these bogus insurance schemes are allowed to flourish under the eyes of Mr. Barnes, who receives from $6,000 to $10,000 per annum to protect the public from being defrauded by the promoters of these palpable swindles?"[65]

The *Insurance Times* advocated for more transparency about the terms and conditions of life insurance policies. They also argued that when claims were made, properly run companies, while alert always to the prospect of fraud, should pay quickly. Delays involving technicalities of coverage were viewed very dimly. When widows and orphans are in need, a well-run company comes "promptly to their succor, and without quibbling or litigiousness or giving a particle of superfluous trouble or a moment's unnecessary delay, pours into their lap the fruit of the providence of the departed." However, this ideal was not always met, and there was a class of "pseudo insurance companies" that appeared to be in the business for the "wrong reason" and who strategized to "yield to the heirs of the insured as little and themselves as much as possible by every quibble and quirk of law and cunning devise and trap that legal ingenuity can adopt and devise." In the dark days of sorrow, these companies are eager to "blast the hopes" of the unfortunate widows and orphans, robbing them of the "fruits of the lost saving and foresight of their deceased protector." Notwithstanding their observation that it was "sickening to read the details," the *Insurance Times* often recounted examples of this type of malfeasance.[66]

Therefore, it was no surprise that the *Insurance Times* seized on the Beecher story with glee, running a column headlined "A Delusional Insurance Company" in its October 1870 issue. A family friend had conveniently written a letter recounting the facts. Beecher, while enlisted in the army, took out a $2,000 policy with his mother as the beneficiary. New Jersey Mutual contacted him and asked for a five percent war risk surcharge to his premium. Beecher did not make this surcharge payment, writing to the company that he would "take the war risk himself." He also failed to make his third premium payment and shortly thereafter was killed. When his father filed a claim, expecting a reduction in the payout to reflect the missed premium, New Jersey Mutual refused to pay anything, arguing that Beecher had forfeited the entire policy by refusing to pay the war risk surcharge. The fact that the policy could not be found was used by the company to argue that Beecher had canceled it.[67]

The *Insurance Times* first castigated New Jersey Mutual for charging Beecher a war risk premium after the fact, since he was in the army when he bought the policy: "Unless a soldier is insured as such—as a fighting man—his insurance is a delusion and a mockery." Since there was no clause in the policy requiring surcharges from policyholders that were already in the military, "Lieutenant Beecher was right in declining to submit to any such demand." The insinuation was that New Jersey Mutual Life would resort to any type of argument to avoid paying a claim, since the company "lives by its wits and is often at wits end to live." English even used Beecher's military status to wring a little more drama out of the issue: "It is hard that the heirs of a soldier who died fighting in the service of his country should be so shamelessly treated, but we trust that this melancholy example will prevent others from becoming the victims of such a soulless and merciless corporation."[68]

The issues that arose in the Beecher claim showcased the unsettled nature of life insurance at the time, particularly the way in which certain policy features, such as surrender values and surcharges, often were applied in an unstandardized and discretionary manner. The *Insurance Times* welcomed the opportunity to criticize these business practices, but their interest in New Jersey Mutual was more than casual. An analysis of the company's financial statements appeared the next month and unearthed a host of discrepancies. Projecting the ratio of future claims to reserves, the *Times* concluded that bankruptcy was "palpable" and that New Jersey Mutual must think that state officials were "as blind as owls at midday to the insurance jugglery." Financial distress had led to quibbling with policyholders: "The policies of the company are fast maturing into claims which it is divesting itself of the ability to satisfy. It is already resorting to the miserable expedient of disputing them."[69]

The following month New Jersey Mutual responded, noting that, "a certain in-surance journal having seen fit to reflect severely on this company," they wished to defend themselves. In an attempt at damage control, Vice President Charles Lathrop opened the door to some potential softening with regard to Beecher: "If our Board have done any injustice, or acted unadvisedly in this case, I am sure they will readily reconsider it." Regarding their finances, Lathrop seemed to wel-come transparency and called upon the New York insurance superintendent to make "an immediate and thorough examination of our company." The *Insurance Times* expressed grudging approval: "Let the company first do justice to its own deceased policyholders and the public will be prepared to receive a vindication of its general management."[70]

Meanwhile, the story of Frederick Beecher's insurance claim took another turn when the lieutenant's policy was "providentially discovered in an old mil-itary trunk." New Jersey Mutual was informed of its existence by way of corre-spondence from the deceased's brother, who also noted "in the most friendly spirit" that financial hardship on the part of Lieutenant Beecher had resulted in the nonpayment of the third premium. Furthermore, the cause of his death was upon further reflection not strictly speaking a "battle"; rather, the lieutenant's unit had been "overtaken by a roving band of Indians." The *Insurance Times* contributed to the spin, describing Beecher's activities in Kansas as a "peace mission" that resulted in an "unexpected fight."[71]

The discovery of the policy "had the effect of a bombshell in the home office of the company," leading New Jersey Mutual to reconsider its position. After reviewing sworn statements by General Sheridan and Major Forsyth and conducting an in-person interview with Beecher's brother, the company paid about two-thirds of the policy, deducting for the nonpayment of the third year but forgiving the lieutenant's failure to pay the war risk surcharge. The company turned the episode into a publicity opportunity, publishing a letter from Beecher's brother, in which he praised their generous forfeiture policy: "As Lieutenant Beecher had failed to pay the third annual premium, which fell due before his death, had he been insured in any of the 'forfeiting companies,' the policy would have been void. But as he had the good fortune to be insured in your Company, the policy held good, and produced on your 'Lapse Plan' the above-mentioned sum."[72] The Beecher claim was finally paid. Stephen English even made the unusually charitable observation that "Repentance in time is itself almost a virtue."[73]

Despite his passionate defense of Beecher, the real object of English's ire was the insurance officials in New York and Massachusetts for their apparent complacency about the finances of New Jersey Mutual, a company that had "long been tottering on the brink and is now sliding down the steep, catching at twigs to sustain itself." If state regulators do not "arrest its descent and save what is yet left for the insured, they will become passive partners in its iniquity."[74] The deteriorating financial status of New Jersey Mutual led to a set of fraudulent transfers of risk to reinsurance companies that were subsequently indemnified. These activities began as early as 1872. The company finally lost its license in 1877. The New Jersey insurance commissioner's report of that year describes a lengthy list of misdeeds, which "fully sustained and justified the action taken to wind it up and disclosed a degree of corruption and crime in connection with its management that has rarely been paralleled. For years the annual statements of the company have been deliberately falsified . . . and the moneys which they represented appropriated by those in control to their own use."[75]

New Jersey Mutual was able to conceal its fraudulent behavior from the insurance supervisors for quite some time. Even Elizur Wright, hired by the state as a consulting actuary, was initially fooled. But an examiner's report leaves little doubt that there were some irregularities: "There is frequent want of explicitness in important entries; there are dubious entries; from one place in the Journal three consecutive leaves have been cut out."[76] At the time of the commissioner's

1877 report, New Jersey Mutual's president had been indicted and was a fugitive from justice, along with disgraced former Connecticut commissioner Benjamin Noyes, who had been part of the scheme.

While insurers liked to speak of themselves as serving a public interest, the sharp elbows of the late nineteenth-century business often functioned to the disadvantage of policyholders. State regulation was minimal, and while there were thoughtful and principled exceptions like Elizur Wright, most regulators were not professionally or ethically equipped to protect consumers. The travails of Lieutenant Beecher's survivors provide an example of the unsettled state of much of the insurance business and the ad hoc way in which many disputes were resolved.

In this regulatory void, the trade press played an important role in airing grievances and drawing attention to individual stories that illustrated broader patterns. Yet insurance journalism itself was far from objective, and journalists often served as a mouthpiece for the companies that paid them most. Beecher came from a prominent family, and the *Insurance Times* took on his cause as a way to develop a line of attack against New Jersey Mutual, with comments aimed squarely at state insurance officials. Yet five years passed before regulators intervened. During this time many others likely had an experience similar to that of the Beecher family, but perhaps with a less favorable resolution than in the case of the unfortunate lieutenant.

2

A Permanent Body of Barnacles

> As the people of every state are interested in procuring insurance
> which shall be reliable, and ... cost as little as possible, it would seem
> that some measures might be adopted, which would promote the
> general interests of the insurer and the insured.[1]

With these words, on February 3, 1871, New York insurance superintendent
George W. Miller invited all state commissioners, directors, and superintendents
to come to a meeting in New York City, which he termed the "National Insurance
Convention" (NIC). When Miller's invitation letter was published, editor
Stephen English trumpeted the news in the *Insurance Times*: "It is our privilege
to announce a brightening prospect of insurance." There were high hopes for
the convening and the potential to create an "equitable adjustment" of the "conflicting regulations and vexed questions that at present oppress and embarrass
every branch of underwriting."[2] But less than two years from this auspicious beginning, Miller would be ousted from his position as superintendent and English
would find himself in jail.

As the insurance industry grew, interactions with government grew as well.
Fire and life insurers portrayed themselves as having a special quasi-public role,
due to the economic and social benefits of insurance and its potential to reduce
demand on the public sector. Arguing that their business transcended "mere
commerce," more established insurers sought the credibility that came with regulation but tried to shape and control it as much as they could.

As the relatively minimalist role that states initially played in insurance supervision expanded, some insurers engaged in an unsuccessful campaign to shuck
off state control in exchange for a hopefully less active federal government. The
effort resulted in a critical 1869 Supreme Court decision, *Paul v. Virginia*, which
established that insurance regulation should be left to the states. And while
insurers might have been disappointed with the outcome, they would have been
hard-pressed to disagree with the ruling, which read in part that "issuing a policy
of insurance is not a transaction of commerce."[3] The *Paul* decision would prove
to be extremely consequential in shaping the future path of insurance regulation.

Uncovered. Katherine Hempstead, Oxford University Press. © Oxford University Press 2024.
DOI: 10.1093/oso/9780190094157.003.0002

In a second-best effort to create more uniformity, fire and life insurers pushed for the creation of a national body of state insurance regulators. In 1871, twenty-nine states met in New York City to form the NIC. The evolving role of that organization, now called the National Association of Insurance Commissioners, is a critical element in the story of the insurance industry and its relationship with the public sector.

There was little reason to expect much from an organization of state regulators that was heavily influenced by the insurance industry. State officials focused on the interests of their domestic companies. Sectional rivalries and retaliatory taxation were major concerns. Consumer interests were not prioritized, and professionalism among state regulators was uneven. But as the century progressed, policyholder issues emerged in both life and fire insurance that would demand the attention of regulators and would demonstrate not only the potential but also perhaps more importantly the limits of state regulation.

Insurance regulation has a long history in the United States, dating back to a 1799 Massachusetts law. During the early nineteenth century states saw their role as primarily to promote the growth of the industry by approving corporate charters, and barriers to entry were generally very low. As a result, solvency quickly became a problem, and Massachusetts was the first among states to take action. In 1807, the state began to require some simple financial reporting by insurance companies.[4]

A Massachusetts law from 1820 required that no company could write a fire risk that exceeded ten percent of their capital stock. Subsequent laws increased financial reporting requirements for joint stock companies, creating a standardized form with twenty-one questions. Later on, the state created similar requirements for mutual companies. Financial reporting was also required from out-of-state companies. In 1853, Massachusetts appointed two commissioners to compile all state insurance laws, which were published in 1854. The next year, the state established a board of three insurance commissioners, which was reduced to two in 1858. Elizur Wright, seen in Figure 2.1, was appointed as one of these two commissioners.[5]

New York established their first general insurance laws in 1849. Before that time, insurance companies were chartered by special acts of the state legislature. This transition followed similar developments in state banking regulation, where New York played a leading role from an early date. New York transitioned to "free banking" in 1838, permitting banks to be chartered by administrative processes subject to regulatory requirements rather than through acts of the legislature. The law of 1849 required companies to file incorporation papers with the New York secretary of state. It also established a state comptroller with regulatory powers, who was authorized to require companies to submit financial statements. Importantly, the comptroller was also empowered to deny a

Figure 2.1 Elizur Wright, actuary and abolitionist. Undated photograph from the collections of the Massachusetts Historical Society.

company the right to operate in the state if their financial status did not appear to be secure. Solvency criteria would become a fundamental aspect of insurance regulation in all states. In 1859, the legislature established the New York State Insurance Department, the nation's first state department of insurance.[6]

Examinations of fire insurance companies were critical in the development of New York's department, which started officially in 1860. As William F. Barnes, the first commissioner, recalled of these early days: "I appeared in a very modest and unpretending manner, with my little carpet-bag, in Wall Street; the denouement and subsequent history I will not take up your time to repeat." The role of insurance companies in shaping New York's insurance supervision was clear from the outset. Barnes described the department as being established "mainly in consequence of those examinations in the summer of 1855, and almost solely on account of and for the benefit of the fire insurance interests of this state."[7]

While Massachusetts and New York had the most early regulatory activity, other states sought to establish formal supervision over insurance in the mid-1850s. Often insurance was initially under the supervision of the secretary of state before the establishment of an insurance department, which in many states occurred in the 1860s or later. New Hampshire was actually the first state to appoint an insurance commissioner in 1851, when the state passed a statute appointing a board of three commissioners.[8] The state issued regulations in 1870 that required companies to be licensed and permitted the insurance commissioner to revoke a company's license at any time. Yet the dominance of New York and Massachusetts among states was apparent. In his annual report of that year, Commissioner Oliver Pillsbury made clear that his department lacked the resources of Massachusetts and New York, describing himself as "much indebted" to these states for "statistical and general information."[9]

After solvency, the most important objective of state insurance supervision was the protection of home state industry, though the two objectives often worked at cross-purposes. Solvency regulation operated through licensure that was conditional on meeting certain standards, including requiring initial deposits and on-going financial reporting. To promote the growth of domestic companies, states tried to restrict competition by complicating the entry of "foreign" or out-of-state companies through measures such as taxation, the requirement of large deposits, and the placement of restrictions on agents. States that created two tiers of regulation, with looser requirements for domestic companies, protected insurers who were more likely to become insolvent.

Insurance regulation in the nineteenth century focused on companies rather than policyholders, with a few exceptions. In fire insurance, one controversial issue was the "valued policy" provision. In the wake of significant losses from conflagrations, fire insurers had begun to adopt stricter loss settlement practices, attempting to limit recovery strictly to the value of the loss incurred, with results that left many policyholders deeply unsatisfied. In response, a movement arose to require insurers to pay the entire face value of the policy.

Advocacy for the "valued policy" law was associated with agrarian activism in the late nineteenth century, particularly Populism and the Granger movement, which promoted economic cooperativism and self-advocacy among farmers.[10] Rural support for valued policy laws reflected a deep antipathy toward largely eastern fire insurers.[11] With strong backing from farmers, Wisconsin passed the nation's first valued policy law in 1874 despite enormous opposition from insurers, who viewed it as an invitation to arson. The "Wisconsin problem" was a frequent topic of conversation among fire insurers in the late nineteenth century, as similar efforts emerged in other states. Yet one underwriter acknowledged some responsibility for the situation, observing that the movement was "a reaction on the part of the public against the schemes and systems which we have ourselves made."[12]

Another critical issue for regulators was nonforfeiture in life insurance. In the early days of life insurance, it had been generally accepted that policyholders who stopped paying premiums would forfeit the entire value of their policies, but by the mid-nineteenth century this practice was increasingly seen as inequitable. The trade press played an important role in influencing public opinion on this issue, and pressure on industry grew.[13] By the late 1850s, most companies provided some type of surrender value, but company practices were not standardized. Most required at least five years of premium payment, and conditions were generally quite restrictive.

Elizur Wright was an early exponent of the view that nonforfeiture was a policyholder's right. While insurance commissioner of Massachusetts, Wright conducted an analysis that demonstrated that firms profited handsomely from lapsed policies and argued that individual premium payments could be decomposed into insurance and reserve components. He argued that nonforfeiture values should be calculated based on the share of the premium reserves, with certain deductions for adverse selection and administrative costs. Wright's early work helped further the case for nonforfeiture. One industry response was the "Ten Pay" policy introduced by New York Life in 1860, which standardized the calculation of the surrender value based on the share of ten premiums that were paid.[14]

The 1861 Massachusetts nonforfeiture law mandated a standardized calculation of surrender values for all life insurance policies sold in Massachusetts by firms that were chartered in that state. After its passage, Wright and his staff maintained a registry that could inform any policyholder of the surrender value of their policy at any time. The surrender value was based on Wright's calculations of the "net value of the policy," or the net level premium reserve at four percent interest. The surrender value was not cash, but rather took the form of paid-up term insurance for a length of time that varied based on the net value of the policy. An incontestability clause was added in 1864, strengthening consumer protections.[15]

The Massachusetts nonforfeiture law was significant in a number of ways. First and foremost, it made surrender values a right. The law established the concept of individual reserves, which previously was not considered meaningful by actuaries. It was also significant from a policy perspective, since the Massachusetts legislation interfered with private contracts, which was uncommon for the time, but reflected the special quasi-public role of insurance. The Massachusetts law only applied to a small share of the life insurance market—policies sold in Massachusetts by companies chartered in Massachusetts—but it spurred more competitive developments in the industry, as consumer expectations rose.[16]

Due perhaps to his excessive zeal for the rights of the policyholder, which particularly antagonized agents, Wright was essentially driven out of the commissioner's office in 1867, but he retained a very important role in the industry as a consulting actuary and the pre-eminent American expert on life insurance. In 1870, Wright was again approached to help develop a stronger nonforfeiture bill for Massachusetts, which would apply to all firms doing business in the state. After an initial defeat due to strong pressure from New York firms, particularly Mutual Life, a revised bill was passed in 1880.[17]

New York regulators had a different outlook on surrender values, which reflected the influence of insurers, the majority of whom were headquartered in New York City. William Barnes, New York's first commissioner, had expressed a preference for competition rather than regulation to solve the problem of surrender values, and the big New York life firms opposed the Massachusetts regulation. By 1871, New York was beginning to formulate a more industry-friendly regulatory approach, with a three-year blackout period and a different basis for calculating the net premium value that was more favorable to the companies.[18]

Despite these differences, these two earliest commissioners of New York and Massachusetts, Barnes and Wright, were exceptional regulators, particularly in the context of the generally low quality of public service at the time. Both men had high moral standards, which, as one twentieth-century history noted, stood "in sharp contrast to the general business thinking of the day." Wright focused primarily on life insurance, while Barnes had gained much of his experience in the financial supervision of fire insurers. Both were concerned about the quality and compensation of agents. Wright lamented that "no business was more afflicted with quackery, or suffered more from an unworthy and unwholesome advocacy." Barnes too expressed concerns about the nature of the life insurance business and agent compensation, noting prophetically that "when competition is severe, and the compensation of agents depends entirely on the amount of policies secured, without regard to their character, the business of insurance becomes excessively forced, and future years must bear a sad record of early lapses and deaths."[19]

From the outset, state insurance regulation displayed signs of ethical compromise. Elizur Wright was driven out of his position by state legislators, who, "offended at his unsparing integrity . . . pretended to consider the expense excessive, and resolved to get rid of him." Stephen English criticized the decision: "Never was more good done for so small a sum," and doubted the state could retain Wright's successor, "a practical mathematician and scholar," at the current salary of $2,000. Given the role of Massachusetts as a standard-setter, the potential quality erosion was consequential: "One incapable or dishonest Commissioner would sink the Insurance Department of Massachusetts as low, and render it as futile as it now useful, superior and honored in the estimation of the public in America and Europe."[20]

In New York, the vast cash reserves of life insurance companies made them a tempting target for ethically compromised elected officials. In an early version of "pay to play," an insurance committee composed of Tammany-affiliated New York state legislators initiated an "investigation" of life insurance companies that was reported by English to be a thinly disguised shakedown: "It has been currently rumored that the committee's purpose is simply to black-mail the insurance companies and coerce them to pay $40,000 or $50,000 to secure a whitewashing report."[21]

Conflict of interest among supervisors was also commonplace. Benjamin Noyes, while commissioner in Connecticut, served as chief officer of American Mutual Life of New Haven, alleged by English to be a "life corporation founded on the wild cat principle of doing its deeds in the dark." While this company was "ignominiously driven" from other states, "Connecticut alone is content to harbor this feline depredator." Due to the lack of standards in the Connecticut Insurance Department, "sound and strong" companies desirous of a "reliable endorsement from government of their solvency and good management" had to do business in Massachusetts and New York.[22]

Massachusetts and New York had the most rigorous supervision standards, so companies that were licensed in these states could use that fact as a type of national credential. Southern and western states, which had little capital and relatively underdeveloped home industry, sought to tax and otherwise encumber eastern companies, and at first engaged in little supervision, holding home industry to very low standards. The top priority of these state insurance supervisors was to protect their domestic insurance companies, and regulatory practices were driven by sectional rivalries.

Insurers trying to establish national markets opposed the extra taxation and deposit requirements placed on foreign companies. They also critiqued what they considered to be an excessive number and variety of state regulations, which they claimed created inefficiencies and administrative burdens. State legislatures were unpredictable and might pass "valued policy" laws or other legislation unfavorable to insurers as a result of constituent pressure. Yet at the same time, the insurance industry wanted to be regulated. As was the case with railroads, regulation provided protection against the effects of often brutal competition by creating standards that disadvantaged undercapitalized competitors.[23]

In response, some insurers advocated for a federal charter that would provide uniform and hopefully weaker regulation. Life insurers unsuccessfully proposed a national bureau of life insurance in 1868. *The Nation* reflected on the idea favorably, arguing that a central bureau would allow the "same security for all." This was seen as an advantage to consumers in a world where some states did nothing to supervise insurance, while others placed restrictions on out-of-state companies that "in many cases are vexatious only to responsible organizations and advantageous only to the unscrupulous." National regulation also seemed like a better approach to combat the growing size of corporations, a concern

The Nation feared would only get worse as the century progressed: "It is becoming evident, day by day, that there are men and corporations in our country stronger by far than all the authority of any single State, men and corporations that may someday test even the strength of the general government." Life insurance companies in particular "are gradually developing into bodies of the most extraordinary power and importance."[24]

The fire insurance industry had similarly proposed a federal charter in 1866. While the bill stalled in the Senate, the insurers tried a legal strategy. Alexander Stoddard, the head of the New York Underwriters Agency and one of the founders of the National Board of Fire Underwriters, felt strongly that insurance was interstate in nature and should have national supervision. He sought to put this to a test. Colonel Samuel Paul, a Virginia native and a Confederate Army veteran who served as counsel to the New York Underwriters Society, was the plaintiff in a lawsuit that ultimately came before the Supreme Court.

In the case, Paul, a licensed Virginia insurance agent, refused to pay state licensing fees, in order to test Virginia's jurisdiction over insurance. Paul alleged that Virginia's practice of taxing "foreign" or out-of-state companies was unconstitutional. The suit claimed that Virginia's differential taxing practices violated the "privileges and immunities" clause of the Constitution, which pertains to the legal rights of residents of other states, and improperly regulated interstate commerce.

Justices on the Supreme Court accepted neither argument. In their 1869 decision, the court ruled that the privileges and immunities clause applied to people, not corporations. Importantly, they ruled that insurance did not constitute interstate commerce, finding that "issuing a policy is not a transaction of commerce." As a result, it was left to states to tax and regulate the industry.[25] The decision was a disappointment for the National Board of Fire Underwriters, as recounted in an early history: "There was an earnest hope that insurance might be freed from the harassment of the infinite variations of State law, by establishing its national status, but the Supreme Court decided otherwise."[26] The *Paul* decision left the regulation of insurance to the states, with the associated challenges created by the growth of both the insurance industry and state regulatory agencies.

The idea of industry-created uniform regulation for states was proposed even before the *Paul* decision. In the *Insurance Times* it was suggested that the National Board of Fire Underwriters "might frame a complete and uniform system of insurance laws that would, by its simplicity, superiority, and approximate perfection, commend itself to the adoption of every state Government." Nor should the life industry stand on the sidelines. Leaders of this line of business should also construct "a perfect body of laws" to present to state legislatures, since "conflicting, harassing and oppressive State laws form the greatest impediment to their growth and prosperity."[27]

Useful source material for such a project would naturally be the laws of "Massachusetts, New York, and some other states." Accompanying this compendium of laws should be a "commentary showing the defects of extant systems and the advantages of the ones proposed. The quicksands, dangers, and weaknesses to be avoided, and the real object and efficient points of governmental supervision, should be clearly and succinctly described." "Thus instructed," the respective state legislatures and insurance departments would quickly see the wisdom of this preferred new system, in which "the laws of all the States would be made to approximate . . . and the greatest legal benefit attainable by insurance companies would be secured to them." This approach was described as a desirable second best to federal regulation, as it would "come as near possible" to the "unity, simplicity, economy, universal sweep and effect of a National Insurance Bureau established by the general government at Washington." To complete their plan, the *Insurance Times*, clearly speaking on behalf of the large New York fire and life insurers, proposed a national meeting of insurance commissioners at which these new ideas could be disseminated.[28]

The first meeting of the NIC took place in New York City from May 24 through June 2, 1871, with representatives from nineteen states. Miller of New York was appointed president, and Llewellyn Breese of Wisconsin was made vice president. Attorney Henry S. Olcott of New York City was the secretary and wrote notes of the proceedings, along with a long and discursive introductory essay. Absent was Julius Clarke, commissioner of Massachusetts.[29]

Due to the incipiency of state supervision, not all of the delegates were actually insurance commissioners. The Wisconsin delegate Breese, for example, was the secretary of state, as was the delegate from New Jersey. Maryland sent representatives from the Treasury Department, and Indiana and Pennsylvania sent auditors. Minnesota sent the governor's private secretary. California was represented by a Mr. Skeel, who was not even a California state employee and at one point confessed he had never set foot in the state.[30]

New England and the Middle Atlantic region were well represented at this first meeting, as was the Midwest and California. Yet other than Kentucky and Tennessee, southern states did not participate, reflecting perhaps some sectional aloofness but also the very early stage of insurance regulation in that region. This plaintive note from invitee George E. Bovee, secretary of state of Louisiana, provided a perspective from a southern state: "I presume there will be no objection to my occupying a seat on the floor of the convention, unless someone appears with better credentials as a representative from Louisiana. All the bills presented to the legislature of this state at its last session relative to the subject of insurance failed; therefore, we have no laws to repeal and can profit by the combined wisdom and experience of other states at the outset." Unfortunately, Bovee was not able to attend.[31]

Some states hoped the gathering could help resolve conflicts between states. Ohio's insurance supervisor, Jason Godman, communicated his support for the upcoming meeting in his annual report, noting that while state supervision of insurance was critical, it was "attended with some evils" arising from retaliatory legislation. He hoped the meeting would help to counteract the "narrow-minded sectional feeling" that had given rise to "unfriendly legislation" directed at out-of-state companies. He also hoped to mitigate a practice by which a commissioner from "another state" (most likely New York) was authorizing third parties to charge Ohio companies that did business in that state for inspections that seemed unnecessary. "It seems to me that such supervision as this is against the spirit of all just laws, and I enter my protest against it."[32]

The influence of the insurance industry was palpable throughout these first proceedings. To start, insurers funded the convention. The meetings were held at the headquarters of the New York Board of Underwriters. It was even initially suggested that representatives of the industry be permitted to join the deliberations as members of the convention, but Miller declined. However, representatives from insurance companies made formal statements to the convention and also sought to interact more informally with the attendees. For example, the president of the Equitable Life encouraged the delegates to visit and "receive and partake of their hospitality at such times as may be convenient to them, either personally or in a body." There were also various industry-sponsored social and recreational events that took place during the convention.[33]

Olcott's introduction gave some insight into the mindset that motivated the interstate convening, as he sought to provide readers with "a clear idea of the rise and development of the insurance idea, the abuses which have attached to it and impeded its progress—as barnacles decrease the speed of a ship."[34] He praised state regulation, particularly as practiced by New York and Massachusetts, in contributing to the progress of the industry thus far. At present, bad actors and inefficient regulation stood in the way of further growth and societal benefit, and the NIC meeting was to chart a course that would obtain these outcomes in the least restrictive manner possible.

Concerns about life insurance were foremost in the minds of most attendees. George Miller, in his opening remarks, drew a contrast between fire and life insurance. The value of the former "needs no demonstration," while it is with life insurance that "all the doubt exists."[35] Miller's hope was that the convention could help to establish an "intelligent, comprehensive and uniform" system of supervision that would ensure that any company "had the ability to meet its obligations." Frederick Winston of Mutual Life struck a similar tone in his remarks, reflecting his fierce struggle with Henry Hyde of Equitable Life and the general problems of the industry: "The business of life insurance is now on trial before the American public, and its verdict will greatly depend upon the course marked out for it by your convention."[36]

For the New York companies that orchestrated this initial gathering, the major objective was to improve business conditions. Increased state regulation and the lack of uniformity that came with it were inconvenient. Particularly problematic was the proliferation of laws in southern and western states that imposed higher taxes and deposit requirements on foreign companies. In a perfect world, states would adopt uniform regulations that were the same as those in Massachusetts or, better yet, New York.

Miller acknowledged the reality that every state would regulate insurance: "There is no reason why every State should not have its insurance bureau, and why all should not prove great public blessings." But he suggested that too much regulation could be as problematic as too little: "With these rapidly increasing state departments, and the various, and in some cases crude legislation of the different states accumulating, it began to look as if there might be a danger that supervision would be overdone, and the companies supervised to death." He espoused a minimalist philosophy of ensuring through regulation that companies would be able to meet their obligations, rather than "dictate their details or terms."[37]

Former New York commissioner Barnes similarly acknowledged that New York, along with Massachusetts, had come to exercise a somewhat "extra territorial authority," given the historical absence of regulation in other states. He begrudgingly acknowledged that other states had the right to regulate, but it was clear that he wished they did not: "It is, of course, entirely plain, and upon which there can be no controversy, that . . . the state of Rhode Island . . . has precisely the same rights as the state of New York, and the state of Nebraska the same rights as the state of Massachusetts." Barnes exhorted the attendees to seek unity, since it is "exceedingly detrimental" when states pass laws that are in direct conflict with each other. Barnes also noted that the current legal status of insurance regulators was not as sturdy as it should be, since departments were "creatures of statute" that could be wiped out by legislatures.[38]

The heavy influence of business was clear in repeated statements that the interests of insurers and their customers were the same. Regulators described themselves as equally allied with the companies and the public. Commissioner Paine from Maine noted: "We are here, as I understand it, as the friends of the companies and as the friends of the public, and if there is any conflict between the companies and the public, I hope we are the intermediate parties who may be able to settle or compromise that matter and bring them to one. But I don't understand that there is a great want of harmony."[39] Barnes made the same point: "It is entirely certain that the true interests of the people are precisely identical with those of the companies. Their interests are precisely identical, and the very best friends of the companies in the country, and the very best friends of the whole public are the insurance superintendents."[40]

Insurers stuck the same note and, stressing their quasi-public role, repeatedly noted that they welcomed regulation. To demonstrate the reasonableness of the fire insurance industry, a spokesman for the National Board of Fire Underwriters ended his formal remarks by saying that "no underwriter, worthy of the name, will ever be found complaining of the strictures of your enquiries" since they permit the public "to judge the soundness of the companies . . . and protect itself against the designing and unworthy." The New York Board of Fire Underwriters similarly allowed that "whatever is really adapted to promote the public good will be to the advantage of every well-conducted fire insurance company."[41]

Yet the companies used the convention to lobby for their regulatory priorities, one of which was greater uniformity among states. Speaking on behalf of life insurers, President Frederick Winston of Mutual Life advocated for common approaches to the valuation of policies and the calculation of reserves, and the universal acceptance of financial statements and valuations from the state of domicile. He complained that under the current system, companies were besieged with "many questions . . . asked by persons without practical experience, which really develop no important point." George Hope made a similar plea on behalf of fire insurers: "The companies are subjected to great labor, expense and annoyance by the numerous and generally unimportant variations which are found in the blank forms adopted by the different states."[42]

Another objective was stricter financial supervision. Hope argued that the social importance of preventing an insurance insolvency was greater than preventing bank failures but had received less attention: "It is of much greater importance than it is to save the billholders of banks from losing by the failure of banking institutions, and the last was long the object of great care and supervision, while the former was almost neglected." Adopting a fairly cavalier stance toward bank failure, he suggested that "no one, as a rule, is likely to suffer severely, excepting those comparatively well able to sustain the loss." On the other hand, "the failure of an insurance company involves individuals, not, in small losses, but in large ones; the parties who hold its policies having in many cases a large portion, and sometimes all they possess involved in the failure of the company." Invoking the hallmark rhetoric regarding the role of insurance in preventing poverty and public dependency, he continued: "Many such a property holder dispirited and heart-broken by the failure of an insurance company to pay his claim of a few hundred or thousands of dollars, has sunk into beggary and become a tax upon the community."[43]

The closeness between the regulators and insurers present was seen in the joint animus toward financially unstable companies. Spokesmen for the big fire insurance companies complained about companies that practiced "enormous practical untruths" by misrepresenting their financial soundness and suggested that "the interests of the public demand that by some legal regulation companies be required to present to the public not only nothing that is untrue, but also all that is true respecting their condition."[44] The financial examinations of former New York commissioner Barnes were enthusiastically recalled by California's representative Skeel with a graphic metaphor: "We want a man who can put the knife up in to the hilt and turn it round until it has disemboweled the rotten corporations which have so long disgraced our business; that man is William Barnes."[45]

The public benefit of excluding unsound companies was cited by regulators as a major objective, with Georgia's representative noting that "much good has been accomplished and considerable evil repressed, especially by reason of the inability of unsound or bogus companies to come up to the standard laid down by law, by which they have been entirely excluded from the state."[46] Financial regulation also benefited existing companies by complicating new entry.

Insurers lobbied hard against taxation, leaning on their special social role. Speaking for fire insurers, Hope suggested: "A tax upon insurance is a tax upon the providence of the people, and someday states will become so wise as to refuse to perpetrate such a wrong."[47] Frederick Winston of Mutual Life made a similar argument: "It is a burden upon the prudence and forecast and affection of a class of the community generally far from wealthy, and very often poor, who are striving from year to year to lay aside something for the benefit of their families and to keep them from want and from becoming pecuniary burdens upon the state." To the extent to which taxation was necessary, industry representatives suggested that only enough revenue should be raised to fund the work of insurance departments and complained about state legislatures that seemed to think insurance companies "do not confer any great advantages upon the community; that they should be restricted and hampered, and taxed heavily."[48]

Fire insurers complained about the valued policy laws. Hope commented that a "vulgar and unjust prejudice" among some state legislators led them to think that companies habitually tried to skimp on their claims payments: "That ALL of the companies in all parts of the country are already ready to meet such claims with a manly recognition of the truth ... is not asserted, but it is asserted and can be proved ... that no business is conducted with greater fairness and justice than that of fire insurance in this country." Hope also castigated regulators for their naivete about arson: "The convictions for incendiarism about the country prove that the crime of arson is perpetrated with sad frequency ... yet members ... introduce bills ... which are calculated only to foster crime and to prejudice the best interests of honest citizens."[49] The New York Chamber of Commerce also participated and lobbied against valued policy laws.

Differential treatment of out-of-state companies was one of the most divisive issues. Both fire and life insurers criticized the concept of state deposit laws, noting that they tied up their capital in ways that made it impossible to run a national business. Winston's comments about interstate taxation reflected the relative recency of the Civil War: "Onerous taxation is politically bad. It engenders retaliatory legislation and provokes sectional prejudice and bad feeling. When one state struggles to extract through taxation all that is possible from corporations or individuals, chartered or resident in other states, it creates and keeps alive a feeling of jealousy and distrust inconsistent with that fraternal feeling which should be cherished by our people in every part of our common country."[50]

George Savage from the New York Board of Fire Underwriters named the sectional tension between newer and older states: "There is a jealousy, and there is no use in disguising the fact, on the part of some of the states against the eastern companies, from the impression that we are deriving a large profit by this insurance business and drawing money from the other parts of the country to enrich the east, and New-York in particular." He admonished newer states to cease the practice of taxation for their own good: "By and by, when you get to be rich, and have surplus capital, you can form companies as fast as you want; but till then you can insure cheaper upon eastern capital."[51]

There were several concrete accomplishments from this first meeting. Committees were formed to create uniform "blanks" (forms used to require financial reporting from companies) and standards for assets and investments, reserve values, taxation and deposits, dividends, and other miscellaneous questions. Not surprisingly, the regulators tabled the resolutions put forth on the controversial issues of interstate taxation and retaliatory legislation. Participants spoke of creating a list of common legislative priorities to share with their respective states. Barnes, seemingly encouraged, described his evolving support for state supervision: "The true policy on this subject is to have an insurance department in every state in the union."[52]

One of their most important decisions was to continue to meet as a body. In the short run, they scheduled to continue their current meeting in October, planning to gather once again in New York, since delegates found it hard to consider another location "after the generous hospitalities of the insurance companies of this city."[53] On that note, there were numerous references to Miller's hospitality, including this gushing testimonial from Mr. Paine: "pleasures have swarmed upon us to an extent which I never before enjoyed in connection with any public gathering, and I think this will be the testimony of all here, and principal among those who have been the means of our enjoying ourselves to such an extent has been our President."[54] A story in the *New York Herald* alludes to some of these pleasures, describing an excursion on the steamer *Josephine*, "composed of as jolly fellows as ever popped a cork or swallowed chowder." The amenities included the provisions of New York's famous Delmonico, who "with his hampers of the good things of life and innumerable baskets of wine, was on hand, and with his usual grace catered to the cravings of the inward man."[55]

Not everyone appreciated these distractions. Mr. Pillsbury from New Hampshire complained about the pace of the work and the degree of socializing: "I say I came here for work. But perhaps it is unfortunate that I am associated on a committee whose chairman, deservedly popular, has a great many friends and acquaintances in the city, and we find it very difficult to get together for consultation, for the reason that he is constantly interrupted by friends."[56] The accused chairman, Mr. Smith of Kentucky, acknowledged his popularity but ceded no ground: "It is true. I have many friends in this city, but notwithstanding the gentleman's remark, I have not yet had an opportunity of visiting my nearest and best friends who reside near our hotel. I am very sorry that this kind of talk has occurred. It does not advance our object." Miller too scolded Pillsbury for the insinuation of impropriety: "I am rather apprehensive that the honorable gentleman from New Hampshire has created a wrong impression. . . . [F]or my own part, I have no knowledge that the convention has as yet visited, or been present, at any amusement of any kind."[57]

As the meeting wore on, some delegates appeared weary. Mr. Brinkerhoff of Illinois at one point seemed to almost beg for it to end: "We have stayed here eight days. It will be nine days to-morrow evening. We find that we have enough subjects presented to us; and we have heard enough on the different subjects which are before the convention to keep us thinking for some time."[58]

When the NIC resumed its meeting in October of 1871, once again in New York, there were twenty-nine states in attendance. This meeting also lasted ten days, during which time a constitution was adopted and officers were elected. The states also agreed on a uniform set of blanks and agreed that statements of company assets would be accepted from the state in which the company was chartered, or "domiciled."[59]

The birth of the national organization of state regulators was driven by the big New York insurance companies, who sought a second-best solution after they failed to obtain national regulation. States at the time did not have particularly strong incentives to act cooperatively, particularly in the area of taxation. Protectionist desires to benefit home industry outweighed any interest in uniformity, and there was considerable ill will between the states in the immediate postbellum period.

Yet the fact that so many states would elect to gather in New York reflected the growing importance of fire and life insurance in economic modernization.

States did have a pragmatic need to learn from each other. The dominant status of New York and Massachusetts had at first made it easy for other states to invest little in supervision. But as they tried to develop their own insurance industries, they soon came to realize that this placed their home companies at a competitive disadvantage. Early challenges in the establishment of this national organization of state insurance regulators reflected the conflicting impulses toward nationalization and sectional competition and the tension between bureaucracy and corruption that characterized the Gilded Age.[60]

Some mainstream newspaper accounts pointed approvingly to the willingness of commissioners from around the country to set sectional rivalries aside. The *Nashville Union* noted that "men from the extreme South" have met those who "boast an honorable record in the Union Army, in a spirit of perfect mutual respect and good will." The paper had high hopes for the gathering, describing it as "one of the most important business meetings ever held in this or any country" and anticipating benefits such as better regulation, reduced insurance speculation, and "greater protection for the policy holder."[61] The recency of the Great Chicago Fire, which had occurred earlier that month, gave the meeting additional currency, prompting the *Waterloo Courier* to note that the fire has "proved very clearly the intimate relationship of the insurance systems of the States, and it is now evident that regulations intended for the good of one will redound to the advantage of all."[62] Bringing up the consumer angle, the *Weekly Commonwealth* from Topeka praised the creation of an insurance department in Kansas, without which "the insuring public are left no protection against fraud and have no means of distinguishing between an honorable and solvent company and a dishonest and insolvent one."[63]

Not all observers were impressed. The *New York Times* was scathing in its criticism of both George Miller and the initial NIC meeting, accusing the former of criminality and castigating the latter as an extravagant boondoggle. Using a combination of investigative reporting and editorializing, the *New York Times* reported that insurers were intimidated by threats of retaliation from Miller if they did not pay large "inspection fees" for required financial examinations. Miller was accused of instituting "a new system of formal and needless examinations, for which he has charged at the rate of about a hundred dollars an hour to fire companies." Referring to some irregularities in the "summary winding up" of several companies, the paper noted that "the least accusation commonly whispered against Superintendent Miller was of arbitrary, unwise, and queer policy."[64]

The meeting of the NIC incited particular fury: "All it has done and all it can do might have been accomplished at a thousandth part of the outlay, and infinitely less trouble. Nothing else has been or will be done by this mighty and costly combination, which styles itself 'The National Insurance Convention of the United States.'" The choice of Olcott as secretary was criticized, and Olcott was described as having "no more knowledge of insurance than the topography of the further side of the moon."[65]

The *New York Times* dispensed with the convention's attendees, who "ranged over the whole field of underwriting, displaying their ignorance and incapacity at every step, much to the amusement of practical adepts. But their contentment with themselves experienced no abatement and finding a visit to New York and a sojourn at the St. Nicholas hotel at the companies' expense a delightful relief to their ordinary official routine, they determined to perpetuate the pleasant joke and proceeded to organize themselves into a permanent body of barnacles." The article further complained of the convention's cost, which was borne by insurers, and claimed that the payment was far from voluntary, as companies were told they "must pay or be crushed." As for the money, the *New York Times* rhetorically asked whether it would come from "the sacred funds reserved for widows and orphans." The paper urged the policyholders to come to the defense of the companies, since "the managers of the little entertainment prepared in this City a few weeks ago, under the sounding title of the 'National Insurance Convention', have now figured up their bill of expenses and are sending out circulars to the life insurance companies, requesting them to call up to the Captain's office and settle."[66]

The *Insurance Times*, while more measured, also raised some questions about the cost of the meeting, supporting those firms that chose to "decline to pay the assessment until an exact account of particulars," agreeing that there was no reason for any "superfluous disbursements."[67] This observation reflected a growing disillusionment with the meeting. With his usual immodesty, publisher Steven English had claimed to have himself been the originator of the idea to convene a national body of state commissioners and more than once provided an exact citation to the place where this suggestion had first appeared.[68] Yet before the convention even occurred, the *Insurance Times* had turned negative on the meeting. English objected to the fact that Miller had proposed legislation that would grant the insurance supervisor additional powers. Miller's seeming complicity with the activities of the legislative Insurance Committee was also a factor.

From that point, things deteriorated rapidly. Shortly after the first NIC meeting, the New York State Legislative Committee accused Miller of "maladministration" and advocated for his removal. To the *Insurance Gazette*, the most "astonishing feature of this remarkable event," which increased "the surprise and bewilderment of the underwriters," was the fact that these complaints against Mr. Miller were "evoked so soon after the closing up and completion of the proceedings of the great National Convention of Insurance Commissioners, Superintendents, and other state officials." Despite some expressions of support from insurers, the *Gazette* reported, this "failed to appease the rancorous hate of his enemies," who had resolved to "carry the war into Africa."[69]

The *Gazette* wondered whether Miller's "struggle for official existence may serve to render him a wiser man and a more efficient public servant." Yet it was not to be, and Miller's resignation was soon announced.[70] Stephen English at the *Insurance Times* commented sourly on the ouster: "The fact is that Mr. Miller is not a man of figures but a mere politician." Next time, English suggested, the governor should "consult the companies . . . so as to profit to some extent by their knowledge of the fittest person to fill the place."[71]

Apparently, Miller had cultivated a climate of extortion, where companies were asked to pay large sums for a clean financial examination. The superintendent's life insurance report in 1872 was inaccurate, seemingly by design. Thundered English: "It is indeed worse than useless, for it is absolutely pernicious, being replete with gross blunders and injurious and inexcusable errors." The truth may lie somewhere in the middle. Whether it would be more accurately described as extortion versus the taking of a bribe, Miller had apparently received a payment of $2,500 from Mutual Life for a favorable financial report. The original transcript had allegedly been recorded by a stenographer in Mutual Life's employ and kept from the public.[72]

Upon learning this in March of 1872, English, an erstwhile admirer of Mutual Life, became instead a fierce opponent, repeatedly criticizing Miller and the allegedly fraudulent examination. But English was also likely being paid by Henry Hyde of Equitable Life to carry out his war against Mutual Life, so the degree of moral outrage is suspect.[73] English, who "never felt so good as when denouncing something," ignored repeated warnings from Mutual Life's vice president Richard McCurdy to "let up on Miller or be crushed." The retribution came in the form of a six-month stay in New York City's Ludlow jail on a charge of libel brought by Frederick Winston of Mutual Life and accompanied by an insurmountably high bail.[74]

Incarcerated, English continued to publish the *Insurance Times* while protesting the unreasonableness of his imprisonment. A New York State investigation led to his release, which was accompanied by an undisclosed payment from undisclosed sources, likely combined funds from Equitable Life and Mutual Life, which realized that this public affair was damaging to them both. This led to a temporary truce between the two companies as Hyde "called off his dog and we called off ours," in the words of Mutual Life's McCurdy.[75]

The inglorious exit of George Miller and the incarceration of Stephen English fit the pattern of ethical compromise pervasive in Gilded Age insurance regulation. There was little reason in these early days to expect much from an association of state insurance regulators. In 1877, English described the annual meeting of the association he once championed with a decided lack of enthusiasm: "our state supervisors of insurance, who are desirous of impressing the public with the erroneous idea that they really know something about insurance, and meet once a year to display their ignorance on the subject, held their usual annual convention."[76] English had brought Miller down but he paid a steep price, suffering as he did through "false imprisonment, loss of business, loss of property and everything else." By 1877, the *Insurance Times* had folded, and English had changed sides once again. He was working for Mutual Life.[77]

3

The Road to Armstrong

Wolf Silverman stepped out into the sunlight on a July morning in 1896. After two months in "the Tombs," the dank and unsanitary Egyptian Revival–style building in lower Manhattan that housed New York City's infamous Halls of Justice and House of Detention, he was a free man. This outcome had initially seemed far from certain. Charged with grand larceny and attempted fraud, the evidence against him appeared overwhelming. Silverman had allegedly played the "substitution" game by having "a healthy Irish woman" apply for life insurance under his wife's name. After several policies were obtained, Silverman reported his wife's death from consumption. Two companies contested the claims, and Mrs. Silverman was exhumed. The medical examiners would testify that due to significant differences in height, weight, and hair color, the deceased "could not have been the Irish woman whose life was insured."[1]

At trial, the district attorney's office presented further evidence tying Silverman to an organized gang engaged in insurance fraud. To bring the point home in the courtroom, two locks of hair, one blonde and one black, were presented as evidence that the two women were different.[2] Yet after just two hours, the jury voted for acquittal, handing Metropolitan Life another in a string of "severe defeats in the courts."[3] The Empire Life Company fared even worse when Silverman sued them the next year for his outstanding claim. Despite the repeat testimony of the medical examiner (who had personally witnessed the exhumation) that the deceased was not the woman he examined, the jury awarded Silverman the entire amount he sought, $1,642.50.[4]

To say that life insurance companies were unpopular in the late nineteenth century would be an understatement. By that time, a generalized antipathy toward the insurance industry as a whole was well established. This chapter tells the story of how the growing importance of life insurance to Americans in the late nineteenth and early twentieth century increased concerns about access to reliable and affordable coverage. As the late nineteenth century progressed, life insurance was perceived by an increasing number of Americans to be a necessity. In the absence of pensions or a significant labor movement, there were few alternative ways to manage the financial risk associated with early death. But

Uncovered. Katherine Hempstead, Oxford University Press. © Oxford University Press 2024.
DOI: 10.1093/oso/9780190094157.003.0003

as demand soared, dissatisfaction with cost and quality also grew. Consumers' unhappiness centered on business practices of life firms, such as complicated and expensive policies with investment features, disingenuous agent behavior, unclear claims adjustment practices, and the inconsistent disbursement of dividends.

Unmet demand and distrust of the big companies led to the growth in popularity of cheaper alternatives, although they too had shortcomings. There was a new crop of reformist state insurance commissioners who were not sympathetic to the insurance industry. In the early twentieth century, a period known as the Progressive Era, an aroused consumerism was amplified by investigative journalism. In the context of a growing wariness about the power of large corporations and the concentration of wealth, the vast financial assets and investment practices of the large life firms invited further negative attention. The crisis came to a head in 1905, when revelations about financial misbehavior by the big firms resulted in the appointment of the Armstrong Committee by the New York legislature. The result was a broad package of legislation designed to curb industry practices, much of which was adopted by most states. In an attempt to avoid the mounting pressure, insurers made another unsuccessful attempt to trade state for federal supervision.

The Armstrong investigation and its aftermath showed the potential of state insurance supervision, but also its limitations. While there were meaningful reforms to insurer practices, large companies were ultimately able to use the new standards to their advantage by showcasing their compliance. And while these laws did better protect consumers, they did not address the issue of unmet demand, which had resulted in the growth of two substandard products, assessment insurance and industrial insurance. These products were largely unaddressed by the Armstrong investigation and would persist well into the twentieth century before collapsing under their own weight.

As urbanization and industrialization increased, the demand for life insurance grew. The amount of life insurance "in force," essentially the value of all existing policies, grew from $622 million in 1875 to more than $5 billion by 1895, a sum nearly three times larger than the total amount of deposits in savings banks. In that year, the estimated number of policyholders was about two million, nearly three times as many as in 1875.[5] In the transition away from a largely land-based society, fewer Americans could rely on transmitting property to heirs. Even for many with land, especially farmers, life insurance became an increasingly common way to secure mortgage debt. In the absence of pensions, workplace benefits, and well-functioning credit markets, life insurance was the primary way to provide for dependents and obtain credit. After multiple bankruptcies of life insurance companies during the Panic of 1873, when a wave of insolvencies led to a widespread run of bank failures and a subsequent recession, the "Big

Three"—New York Life, Mutual, and Equitable—gained market share. These three firms grew from about a third to more than one-half of insurance in force between 1875 and 1895.[6] Competition between the big firms raged, and in the quest for growth, policies were marketed aggressively, often promoted as investment opportunities.

Emblematic of the problems with the life insurance business in the late nineteenth century was the deferred dividend policy, a product that was marketed as both an investment and insurance. These policies were also known as "semitontines" and contained both a traditional and a speculative element. Tontines were first used in France in the seventeenth century as a way to finance a war for Louis XIV. The namesake, Lorenzo de Tonti, was an Italian banker and governor who was living in France at the time, though many believe he did not originate the tontine but rather appropriated existing ideas.[7]

Sometimes called "life insurance lotteries," tontines rewarded survivors by deferring payments. There are many variations on the concept. The original tontine required the deposit of an initial investment, which was never returned. Surviving participants shared the interest payments, which increased over time. In a "last man" tontine, a sole survivor receives all the proceeds. In deferred dividend policies, the tontine aspect was centered on the dividends. Policyholders would agree to forgo annual dividends for specified periods on the promise of larger dividends later from the "tontine fund." The growth of the tontine fund was in part a function of the deaths or lapses of other policyholders. Deferred dividend policies had no surrender values. If a policyholder died before the end of the dividend period, the beneficiaries would receive the face value of the policy only, and no share of the tontine fund.[8]

Henry Hyde of Equitable Life first brought tontines to market in 1859, followed by New York Life in 1871 and Mutual Life in 1885. Immensely profitable, they soon became the preferred insurance policy for the big firms. Agents were paid more for selling deferred dividend policies, and "annual dividend business," or the selling of whole life policies with level premiums, was actively discouraged. Mutual Life reported that within three years of offering deferred dividend policies, only one-half of one percent of new business was sold with traditional annual dividends.[9]

Deferred dividend policies were controversial. Their actuarial soundness was not really at issue; however, implicit in their design were several attributes that many in nineteenth-century America considered to be unsavory or at least inappropriate as a life insurance mechanism: profiting from the death of others, seeking excessive benefits while living, forfeiting surrender values, and risking the financial protection for dependents.[10] Elizur Wright castigated them as "life insurance cannibalism."[11] Connecticut Mutual refused to sell deferred dividend policies and in their advertisements implored consumers to choose "pure Life" with the "full, absolute and simple protection needed," rather than "gamble with it or try to make a speculation out of it."[12]

Conservative Frederick Winston, president of Mutual Life, initially resisted, then unenthusiastically offered deferred dividend policies in 1870, before withdrawing them in 1872. The company's annual report from that year explained the decision, describing the policies as an "unequal wager" where "the most needy, whom life assurance is especially designed to protect, are pretty sure to prove the losers." The report also noted the feature of the policies that would ultimately spell trouble for the companies: "the large accumulations" in the tontine fund, which offer "a strong temptation to wasteful expenditure."[13] Companies that passed on tontines lost market share, but ultimately their concerns were well placed. Tontines created huge accountability issues, as firms accumulated enormous cash reserves that they didn't report as liabilities. Additionally, potential customers received highly inflated estimates of future payments from the tontine fund.

In the context of an extremely fierce competitive battle with Equitable Life, Mutual Life attempted to meet the competitive threat by lowering premiums instead, which created its own set of controversies. The battle between the two companies escalated to the trade papers. When Stephen English of the *Insurance Times* repeatedly attacked Winston, while being paid to do so by Hyde, Winston charged him with libel and saw to it that an unaffordable bail was imposed. English remained in jail for six months, during which time Mutual Life and Equitable Life jointly participated in a new cooperative organization, the Chamber of Life Insurance, which was developed to oppose "oppressive legislation." Somehow through the auspices of this group, funds were raised for English's bail, and a truce of sorts was called.[14] By then the companies were beginning to realize that the industry as a whole would be stronger if they attacked one another less. Nevertheless, Winston would ultimately feel compelled to offer deferred dividend policies again in 1884 as Mutual Life's market share continued to deteriorate. After his death in 1885, this practice was enthusiastically continued by his successor, Richard McCurdy.[15]

Dissatisfaction with the costs and practices of the mainstream life industry combined with an inability to understand how insurance worked made consumers receptive to lower-cost alternatives, even if their reliability was questionable. New to the life insurance market in the late nineteenth century were "cooperative" or "assessment" plans. These emerged as an alternative to what came to be known as "investment" or "ordinary" insurance sold by what came to be known as the "old line" companies. Some of these assessment plans were sold by fraternal societies, and insurance benefits were combined with the social benefits that came from lodge membership. While the tradition of voluntary mutualism goes back far longer, the three decades after the Civil War were the heyday of fraternal organizations, which offered working men friendship, solidarity, and the prospect of mutual aid. It is impossible to measure precisely, but fraternal membership has been estimated at approximately twenty percent among males at the turn of the century.[16]

The popularity of assessment plans was a rebuke to the investment focus and high agent commissions of the old-line companies. Assessment societies were generally advocates of "pure protection," meaning their plans provided term insurance, with no investment enticements, surrender values, or policy loan options. The term "assessment" referred to the way the plans worked, which was primarily by assessing members when a death occurred. (Some plans also covered sickness and accidents.) There were no actuarial estimates, premiums, or reserves. A selling point of assessment plans was their simplicity. "Pass the hat" and "Pay as you go" were common talking points for salesmen who drew a contrast to the more expensive and more complex policies of the old-line companies. Yet this feature was also a bug. As members aged, the assessments became inadequate, leading to insolvencies and the rapid dissolution of many of these societies.[17]

Former Massachusetts insurance commissioner Elizur Wright's son Walter referenced these difficulties in an article in which he admired the disruptive impact of assessment plans despite considerable failures, noting that while it would be an "arduous task to collect a full list of these failed or abandoned societies," the plans were "not slow to learn" from their early mistakes.[18] Like his father, Wright laid the blame for the popularity of assessment plans at the feet of old-line companies who alienated consumers, particularly high-pressure agents who "played the part of the boor who slew the goose that laid the golden eggs."[19] By 1895, assessment plans had in fact overtaken the old-line companies in terms of the amount of insurance in force,[20] "providing food for the reflection of those agents who resisted a simple, moderate, and effective measure of reform when their business was in the height of public favor."[21]

Assessment plans caused headaches for regulators from the outset. Some were intentionally fraudulent, like the failed "United Order of the Golden Lion," described in a court proceeding as "one of the rankest of the collapsed assessment endowment swindles. The officers got together shortly after the order was started and voted themselves outrageous salaries."[22] But the majority of failures were likely unintentional, with the most common problem being unsustainably low rates. Unlike the old-line companies, which predominantly sold whole life insurance with level premiums, assessment plans operated on a term basis, and assessments were not fixed. As members aged, assessments rose, deterring new members and setting the stage for an inevitable collapse. News of a failed assessment plan would often be communicated via a circular calling for a final payment, like this one received by members upon the collapse of the Mutual

Benefit Association of Illinois in 1895: "True you paid for and bought some life insurance, but have none now—the same thing is liable to happen with any other commodity you purchase, and especially when you pass the hat around to pay for it. So we hope you will comprehend the situation and remit to us at once as delay only means expensive litigation which we are confident you do not desire."[23]

Assessment plans escaped regulation since they were not classified as insurance companies. As the insurance commissioner of Minnesota noted in 1896: "The present laws are very loosely drawn: in fact, it is about as easy and cheap to incorporate an insurance company upon the assessment plan in Minnesota as it is to start a peanut stand on a street corner." His comments reflected a growing sense of accountability among regulators as the purchase of life insurance spread to a less affluent population: "It is not to the credit of the state that it allows the creation of companies and their continuance . . . whereby the father of a family pays a portion of his hard-earned wages for the premium on a policy which, when the dread messenger of death does come, proves to be either worthless or worth less than its face." He implored the legislature to create some "almost radical legislation" to address this issue, noting the state's duty to "protect the people patronizing this class of companies. As a rule, they are those who can least afford to lose their money, and their families are those who suffer most when the insurance upon the life of the husband and father proves worthless."[24]

The Kansas supervisor of insurance in 1899 acknowledged that many fraternal orders were well run, yet some "owe their birth to one or two faulty causes." The first was the "ultra-sentimental craze" that placed an "imaginary brotherhood" over "actual business merits." The other was a more "reprehensible birthmark," schemers who were mainly trying to enrich themselves. He looked forward to a time when the "vagary of one and the knavery of the other" would be recognized, since these traits should "preclude their being entrusted with a country grocery. Why should they be encouraged as custodians of a member's assessments or a widow's benefits?"[25]

The old-line companies and the conventional trade press were extremely critical of the assessment model, which they viewed as a major competitive threat. Assessment organizations responded in kind, dismissing critiques and branding members of the trade press as "hirelings of monopoly." The insurance journals, which were widely read by agents, seized on moments when assessment plans were forced to acknowledge inadequacies in their rates, as did the *Baltimore Underwriter* when the Northwestern Masonic Aid Association announced a transition to the actuarial approach: "It must go hard with the chief representative of this towering assessment association to get down from his high seat, to cast himself at the feet of the tables of mortality, to throw up the sponge, and come out in favor of level premiums."[26] Yet the old-line companies could not ignore the threat posed by the fraternal organizations. At a meeting of the Detroit

Life Underwriters Association in 1908, members heard a presentation about the "lodge plan," which "by the aid of diagrams showed how they worked to the ultimate loss of the members." After sharing anecdotes about bad outcomes, one agent remarked that while "all this was true," the orders were nevertheless popular because "the fraternal spirit appealed so strongly to a large number of people. This had to be combatted in competition."[27]

As the demand for life insurance spread to a broader share of the population, affordability became an issue. Another newly popular product for an even less affluent customer was "industrial insurance," offered by the commercial life industry. Originating in England, industrial insurance operated through weekly in-person collection of small premiums. Policies had a small payout and required no medical exam. Industrial insurance also covered the lives of women and children and was often sold as a way to cover burial expenses. Two of the "Big Five" firms specialized in these products, first Prudential, with Metropolitan Life following in 1879, joined later by John Hancock and others.[28] The business grew extremely quickly. Metropolitan Life sold its first industrial policy in 1879; in 1880 it sold more than two hundred thousand.[29]

Industrial plans had a very high lapse rate, due to the low income and variable circumstances of the policyholders. For example, Metropolitan Life reported a fifty-one percent lapse rate in 1904.[30] Accordingly, industrial insurance was extremely profitable, and companies in the business built huge cash reserves. Like ordinary insurance, industrial insurance was also based on actuarial methods and sold by licensed insurance companies. Both products were also referred to as "legal reserve" insurance, in contrast to assessment or fraternal insurance. For this reason, industrial insurance concerned regulators less than assessment insurance.[31]

Among the old-line companies, fierce competition had led to large agent commissions for new business. This practice had been accelerating throughout the nineteenth century. As early as 1863, New York's first insurance supervisor, William Barnes, had expressed concern that "in the fervid and zealous competition indulged in by the companies, some offices have been tempted to over-step the bounds of prudence and propriety in regard to the amount of commissions and compensation paid to successful agents and canvassers."[32] In this environment, commissions of fifty percent on new business became common, expenses that were loaded into the costs of premiums. Thus, due to the distribution system, increased competition between firms raised the cost of life insurance to policyholders.

Agents reacted to these incentives in predictable ways. The huge differential between commissions on new and existing business was conducive to "rebating," where agents offered discounts to new customers, a practice that was described in the late nineteenth century as "so general that it may almost said to be common."[33] This was often coupled with "twisting," where agents convinced people to switch policies, usually by lying about their competitors. In doing so, consumers often lost what they had invested, since many policies had no surrender value. The essence of twisting was deception. James Alexander, president of Equitable Life, typified the response of company leaders when he criticized twisting in 1904: "Lying about other companies is pernicious and must be stopped."[34] Yet while executives may have publicly decried these practices, the profitability of new business and the impetus for growth created strong incentives for their persistence for the companies as well as the agents.

The agency system had begun to develop in the 1860s, when out-of-state companies needed to appoint someone who was authorized to accept legal summons and complaints. The principal selling agent was a feature of both life and fire insurance, but while fire agents often represented more than one company, in life insurance this was less common. A home office system developed, pioneered by Equitable Life, where general agents would recruit and hire agents and split commissions. Early on, many agents sold life insurance part time as a side job and would often limit their sales to their circle of acquaintances. As the nineteenth century progressed, in-person solicitation to wider circles of prospects became more common.[35]

By the late nineteenth century, the big life firms had national sales organizations with home offices managed by general agents. Individual agents were still relatively unsupervised and poorly trained, but competition for agents was strong, and standards were relatively low. The commission structure provided its own attraction and created an environment that favored volume at the expense of all else. By 1897, for example, Mutual Life was providing commissions as high as eighty percent of the first year's premium for new sales, with steeply reduced commissions for renewals. New York Life created the "NYLIC" association for agents that sold more than $25,000 with different membership categories, some of which provided pensions. Critics of the industry, including New York's first supervisor, Barnes, worried that "these absurd donations to agents" corroded the culture of the industry by effectively transferring power from "responsible officers" into the hands of "a set of irresponsible and reckless agents, combined and confederated for the purposes of selfish gain, without regard for the public good."[36]

Agent behavior heightened generalized distrust of the industry. Barnes suspected that discomfort over commission sizes tempted companies concerned about "deserved condemnation" from policyholders and others "to evade the rendition of fair and honest statements of expenses to this Department."[37] Connecticut's commissioner lamented how "fierce competition between companies is fast descending into an unseemly struggle to pull their agents away from each other and twist policy-holders from one company into another."[38]

Legitimate agents feared the reputational damage that came from "lightening so-licitors" who would resort to any means to sell policies: "He is ruining our busi-ness! If a stranger is seen upon the streets of a town and upon inquiry it is learned that he is a lawyer or a doctor or a banker or a preacher or a professor in some college or a merchant from somewhere, a feeling of respect toward him is estab-lished; but if it be said that he is a life insurance agent, every man instinctively gets away from him—thanks to the lightening solicitor."[39]

Sensing trouble, organizations representing agents joined together to form the National Association of Life Underwriters (NALU) in 1890, the beginning of a long effort toward professionalization. The year before had seen the formation of the Actuarial Society of America.[40] The industry as a whole was suffering from consumer outrage, as noted by a Kansas agent concerned that "some morning I expect to see a mob with clubs outside the office. Reforms must come."[41] Yet it was difficult to change. The powerful New York City branch, home of the Big Five, called for antirebate regulation as early as 1888. John McCall of New York Life, formerly New York's insurance superintendent, drafted a rebate bill in 1895, which stipulated that there be "no distinction or discrimination in favor of individuals between insurants of the same class and equal expectation of life." The New York legislature adopted the measure a year later. The New York su-perintendent further ruled in 1895 that the acceptance of rebates invalidated contracts. The underwriters' organization backed the state and made additional efforts to enforce discipline.[42]

At the NALU meeting in Milwaukee 1891, the members there also endorsed an antirebate bill, on the grounds that "Rebating makes the insurance busi-ness a disreputable and beggarly makeshift, instead of an honorable and prof-itable calling."[43] The National Conference of Insurance Commissioners was supportive, endorsing a resolution calling for "the absolute suppression of the vicious practice of rebating commissions" and encouraging the enactment of stringent antirebate law in all states at their 1891 meeting, where they addition-ally opposed twisting and lapsing.[44] The quest for government regulation to pro-vide relief from excessive competition was not unique to life insurance. Railroad executives too were seeking protection in the form of antirebate legislation, which would result in the federal Elkins Act of 1903.[45]

The push against rebating initially appeared to gain traction. By 1895, twenty-one states had antirebate statutes. But enforcement was difficult. An agent explained how there were "a thousand ways" of giving rebates: "For instance, I sell an insurance policy to a hatter, and collect the full premium. A few days later I buy a silk hat from him and pay $30 for it. Can't I pay what I like for a hat?"[46] Many, like Wright, believed that the problem indeed lay further upstream, with the structure of commissions. Commissioner Wadell of Missouri dismissed antirebate efforts on these grounds: "so long as extravagant commissions are paid to agents in order to secure business . . . rebating will continue."[47]

The life firms attempted to form an antirebate compact, agreeing to discharge any violating agent, with no rehire for one year. Additionally, the NALU offered a reward for anyone found cheating and attempted to create a blacklist of all agents in 1891. Yet the experience of the life insurers was like the unsuccessful attempt of the National Board of Fire Underwriters to establish fixed rates. By 1898, increased competition caused the agreement to crumble. "We are reluctantly compelled to admit that neither legislation nor the compact between the companies has been effective to do anything like the extent hoped for," reported Equitable Life in late 1899.[48]

To combat twisting, the Big Three—New York Life, Equitable, and Mutual—signed an "anti-competitive literature" compact in 1903, restricting advertising literature to content that companies had agreed to be fair and prohibiting "hostile criticism or attack" on any company. Some other companies joined this effort too, including Northwestern Mutual Life, while still others attempted but failed. The industry also turned their attention to tontines, producing a somewhat less speculative "modified tontine plan" in the mid-1880s. Many companies also added various ad hoc enhancements to their policies, such as cash surrender amounts, insuring of females at the same rate as males, and the extension of grace periods. These efforts were influenced in no small part by the growing unpopularity of the industry and the rising threat of more substantive regulation.

The large firms were incentivized to try to self-regulate, to the extent that it would harm their less established competitors and stave off more significant supervision. They were beginning to realize that cutthroat competition was not in their best interest. The quasi-public posture of the insurance industry placed a premium on the appearance of responsible conduct and an openness to scrutiny. The introduction of industrial insurance had magnified the ostensible social mission of life insurance, as the underprivileged joined the familiar widows and orphans as vulnerable beneficiaries. The leaders of the big firms continued to describe themselves as engaged in a noble effort, which, in the words of Mutual's Richard McCurdy, "combined business with philanthropy, business with great and ennobling ideas of humanity." At the same time, the size and profitability of the big firms was growing to mammoth proportions, with the life insurers collecting, as one industry source noted, "more money each year than the Government itself."[49]

Large life insurers may have struggled to regulate themselves, but they had been fairly successful in controlling state regulation up to this point. Industry influence over state legislators and insurance regulators had so far prevented substantive reforms that would have meaningfully benefited consumers.

Given the location of the large life firms, control of New York regulators was critical. Starting with the first insurance supervisor, New York's early insurance regulators were closely allied with political machines, industry interests, or both. There was a general tendency to regulate as little as possible. State "examinations" of the big firms routinely turned up nothing uncomplimentary. They were often exchanged for expensive trips to New York or other kinds of favors. The big companies' influence on what supervision did occur was considerable. For example, life insurers successfully had a clause inserted into the New York nonforfeiture bill in 1879 allowing the protection to be waived as long as the warning was in red, famously leading Equitable to print policies entirely in red ink.[50] New York's attempt to tax insurers was stalled for years and then, when finally freed of legal encumbrances, was repealed in 1880 on the strength of industry lobbying.

In the early days of state insurance regulation, commissioners were minimalists and concerned themselves primarily with solvency. These commissioners often came from the insurance industry and returned there after their stint in public service. Yet even among this first generation, some commissioners sought to do more to protect consumers. Elizur Wright of Massachusetts was clearly a standout in this regard, and others such as Daniel Wester Wilder of Kansas and William Fricke of Wisconsin also sought more consumer-friendly reforms and the general professionalization and modernization of insurer practices. Yet they could hardly be viewed as antibusiness, and most believed that eliminating the unscrupulous elements from the market was mostly what was needed, or as Wilder put it: "most of these nasty letters from policyholders will cease when the best company men with the ideas assume control."[51]

Yet the rise in anticorporate sentiment in the late nineteenth century was accompanied by the influx of a new cohort of insurance commissioners that were far less sympathetic to the insurance industry. In the populist South and West, reformist commissioners were driven by both a desire to protect policyholders and an anti-eastern sentiment that translated into antipathy for the New York firms. Campaigns to tax life insurance companies were high-profile public issues in a number of other states, including Wisconsin, where the Orton Law in 1899 was supported by a bipartisan majority. In states like Kansas and Texas, the tax issue was mingled with a concern about a "money drain" to New York as premiums exceeded claims. The desire to require domestic investment and protect domestic industry grew from these concerns.[52]

The Kansas superintendent of insurance set a tone in 1896 by issuing a warning to insurers that if they excessively contested claims, their license to do business in the state could be revoked. The trade press howled at this new flexing of regulatory muscle: "The picturesque superintendent of Kansas tells, with

much use of words, what he means to do to insurance companies that are liti-
gious.... [H]e is going to bounce them from Kansas." Using a common rhetorical
device of aggrieved business interests, they drew an unfavorable comparison to
Europe: "Meanwhile, it may be well for all of us to consider whether it is conducive to good government to have officials who hold out threats to businessmen,
that if they avail themselves of their undoubted rights in the courts, they will be
deprived of the privilege of doing business. . . . Pay up without hesitation or attempt to compromise or get out! This is the ultimatum of Kansas. And yet we talk
of the tyranny of Prussia."[53]

The next Kansas superintendent of insurance, Webb McNall (1897–1899),
exemplified the crusading reform spirit. A member of the short-lived Kansas
Silver Republican Party, McNall had sought to regulate railroad rates while
serving in the Kansas House. In addition to being a former legislator, farmer, and
lawyer, he had also previously worked as a deputy sheriff and published a newspaper, which "on all subjects will be found on the side of the people." McNall
chafed at the consensus-driven national body of insurance commissioners. At
one point he revoked the licenses of Mutual, New York Life, and Connecticut
Life after a dispute over a policyholder matter, and in 1898 he imposed a two percent surtax on out-of-state companies.[54]

Yet like many reformist commissioners, his candle burned brightly but
briefly, and his term lasted for only two years.[55] Not only did the Kansas
populists lose the elections of 1898, but also McNall himself was charged with
an offense similar to that allegedly committed by George Miller of New York
in 1872, the collection of "exorbitant fees for pretended examinations of the
financial condition and standing of certain insurance companies" and the ap-
propriation of "such fees to his own use and benefit." The eastern insurance
community could not be happier. The *Travelers Record* closed a celebratory account of McNall's swift descent with a final thought: "Those companies which
fought him day in and day out and refused to enrich him have the right to feel
satisfaction, and those who weakly yielded to his every demand have the occasion for philosophic meditation. *Vale*, McNall!"[56]

In defense against mounting reform tendencies, the big firms formalized and
increased the sophistication of their system of political influence, employing a
network of agents and influencers with national reach, who attempted to head
off legislative threats at their inception, often through well-placed financial
contributions. Increasingly the firms found it advantageous to work together,
but the difficulty in combatting state efforts mounted. A harried John McCall
of New York Life reflected: "I daresay it is the feeling of every executive officer . . . that we shall be badgered and harassed to death in every state of the
union by the introduction of bad bills of every kind." McCall, a former state supervisor himself, further complained that lobbying and bribing state officials

was becoming increasingly expensive and estimated that three-quarters of state insurance bills were introduced for the purpose of blackmail.[57]

The firms' financial assets had traditionally been a source of pride, emphasized in their advertisements. For example, an 1896 ad for New York Life in the *Weekly Underwriter* was simply a "notice" announcing that the "books for the year of 1895 have closed, and the record shows over $127,000,000 of business on which the first premium was received by the Company in cash during the year."[58] New York's Big Three in particular reveled in their growth, seeking additional markets overseas; investing in railroads, oil, and other ventures; and encouraging their leaders to become involved in economic and political life at all levels.

Investment opportunities became more interesting than life insurance marketing for some of these leaders, who prized their roles as suppliers of capital and cultivated close relationships with affiliates in the financial sector. Working often through banking intermediaries, life insurance firms made large investments in railroads and other securities. Trustees directed investments to entities where they had financial interests. For example, George P. Baker, trustee for Mutual and chair of the Finance Committee, was a director for dozens of railroads and the president of several banks in which the company invested.[59] George Perkins of New York Life was one of the most notorious of these financial multitaskers, simultaneously serving as New York Life's president and a partner at J.P. Morgan.[60]

Yet the size, profitability, extravagance, and political influence of these firms became a focus of suspicion and anger, as public concern about consolidation and corporate power mounted. Even worse, investment activity was linked to the much-hated monopolistic trusts and "syndicates." The investment issue also exacerbated longstanding sectional tensions and led to support in some southern and western states for policies requiring life insurance companies to invest in states where they did business. This was accompanied by a focus on what was perceived as excessive operating costs of life insurance firms, including high salaries and lavish commissions for agents. Another flashpoint was the political power of industry. When insurers successfully lobbied to have New York's tax bill repealed, the press blasted the outcome.[61]

These financial concerns joined the list of other consumer grievances such as marketing practices, disputes over policies, slowness to play claims, and the rising cost of coverage. The economic troubles of the 1890s led to another round of premium increases.[62] Life insurance was considered essential to many Americans by this time, so these issues created a sense of crisis.

This lament of the mayor of the Ozark community of Ellington, Missouri, captured the frustration felt by many: "Not only do those damn life outfits make it difficult to collect on, but now they go and jack up their charges. I have a big family, I work part time in the saw mills and in town. I must have protection on my life, but I don't know if I can afford it for very long."[63] While willing to support moderate reforms, especially those that encumbered their smaller competitors, the big firms resisted efforts to tax premiums or create any oversight of rates or investment practices. Evoking their quasi-public status and claiming a higher social purpose, the companies argued that they needed freedom. A tone-deaf 1904 editorial from the trade publication *The Spectator* suggested that the public was misinformed:

> Efforts should ... be made to inculcate more just and reasonable ideas as to the beneficent position occupied by insurance in the business and social systems of this country; and to demonstrate, as forcefully as possible, the desirability of allowing insurance interests the greatest freedom of action consistent with a wise though mild supervision. The latter should contemplate the protection of the public from fraudulent concerns but should permit legitimate companies to operate untrammeled by useless restrictions, and no greater fee or taxes should be collected from insurance interests than are necessary to maintain supervisory departments.[64]

Yet widespread dissatisfaction mounted. As early as the 1890s came the first calls for publicly sponsored life insurance, based on much-envied similar systems in European countries and New Zealand. As a further indication of their growing unpopularity, court decisions increasingly went against the big firms in the 1890s and early twentieth century, as seen in the case against Wolf Silverman. This drift reflected antipathy toward industry, social expectations consistent with the quasi-public role of insurance, and a perception that policyholders were at a significant disadvantage. Another category of insurance litigation covered the role of the agent, and company attempts to disavow responsibility usually did not prevail.[65]

Life insurers renewed efforts for federal supervision as concerns about increasingly activist state reform grew. John Dryden, president of Prudential and later a U.S. senator from New Jersey, expressed the widely held view among the big firms that "Every company would naturally prefer just one set of regulations, for that would make it so much easier to shape policy."[66] The profederal trade publication *The View* was established in 1904, with publisher Max Cohen making the case for national regulation.

Life insurers had long sought federal supervision, arguing that anarchy reigned in the states. In 1865, representatives of the life insurance industry petitioned Congress for a national act to make insurance companies federal institutions that could be supervised like banks, resulting in an unsuccessful bill that was considered in the Senate. The *Paul* decision in 1869 firmly established that the federal government could not regulate the industry, as insurance was deemed a contract in indemnity rather than interstate commerce.

The industry-orchestrated organization of state regulators in 1871 had initially appeared to be an adequate substitute, but as states became increasingly activist, enthusiasm for federal regulation returned.[67]

By 1895, McCurdy of Mutual had become a strong exponent of federal supervision, a position influenced in part by his interactions with the federal government in the context of the company's difficulty with overseas expansion. George Perkins of New York Life and John Dryden of Prudential were also outspoken advocates of a Washington bureau, and Equitable came on board by 1900. In 1892, there was an unsuccessful legislative proposal to create the National Bureau of Insurance as part of the Treasury Department. Under that plan, a national commissioner would license firms and only Congress and the state of domicile could regulate or tax. Senator Orville Platt of Connecticut reintroduced a similar bill in 1897 that permitted more state options for taxation. This received more support from federal lawmakers but also died.[68]

Though formal efforts stopped, informal advocacy for federal supervision continued, and when Theodore Roosevelt created the Bureau of Corporations in 1903, the issue was once again revived. The chief executive officers (CEOs) of the big life firms, including Perkins and McCall of New York Life and McCurdy of Mutual, had contributed to Roosevelt's campaign and were strong proponents of federal regulation. An efficiency argument was made against the confusion of state regulation, but insurers also hoped that federal supervision would allow them to escape "consumer triumphs."[69]

Theodore Roosevelt favored the idea of large corporations being supervised by the national government. It was consistent with his concept of "New Nationalism" and his advocacy for greater federal supervision of the railroads. Roosevelt endorsed a plan to make the newly established Bureau of Corporations, within the Department of Labor and Commerce, a national home for the industry. He asked Congress to consider whether the bureau could supervise interstate transactions in insurance. John Dryden, who was both a U.S. senator from New Jersey and the president of Prudential, introduced a bill for a national insurance department that could issue licenses and require a $100,000 guarantee bond from firms. Roosevelt's friend and close advisor George Perkins, CEO of New York Life, strongly encouraged him in this thinking.

Yet despite this prominent support, by 1905 the insurance industry position had become muddled. Some feared federal supervision for competitive reasons. Morgan Bulkeley, who was one of Connecticut's senators and the head of Aetna, worried about the domination of federal regulatory machinery by giant and politically powerful New York firms. Smaller companies in the South and West were concerned that national regulation would tip the deck too strongly in favor of the East. State commissioners opposed the move too, fearing a loss of their powers. Momentum toward stricter federal regulation of railroads, which would ultimately result in the 1905 passage of the Hepburn Act, dimmed the enthusiasm of fire insurers for federal regulation. Beyond the insurance industry, there were broader concerns about excessive federal involvement in business. Some insurance industry critics doubted that federal regulation would be sufficiently strict. Finally, a robust consideration of the constitutional implications of *Paul v. Virginia* cast doubt on the feasibility of a federal bureau. With criticism of life insurers escalating, the companies dreaded a legal battle that would result in a public reaffirmation of state power.[70]

As momentum for reform increased, journalists played a critical role. Unlike the insurance trade press, which largely functioned as paid propagandists for the big insurers as they waged war against one another, the life insurance industry became the target of reporters writing for widely read publications. Investigative journalists, known by some at the time as "muckrakers," were a relatively new and increasingly important feature of the Progressive Era. Their reporting sought to expose corruption and graft among political and economic elites, with a particular focus on concentrations of wealth. Contemporary examples include Ida Tarbell's series on Standard Oil, which appeared in *McClure's Magazine* between 1902 and 1908, along with Ray Stannard Baker's investigations of railroads and Upton Sinclair's *The Jungle*.[71]

A set of exposés about the New York life insurance companies were catalytic. Tomas Lawson's "Frenzied Finance" series, which was published in 1904 in *Everybody's*, focused on the financial dealings of the Big Three. Lawson's credibility was not unimpeached, since he was a reformed stock speculator who had allegedly participated in an attempt to wrest control of Equitable.[72] The trade publication *American Underwriter* predictably dismissed the piece as an opportunity to "raise hell and sell papers," but the public was responsive.[73]

The "Despotism of Combined Millions" quickly followed, focusing on how the life insurance industry invested policyholder premiums in much-hated trusts, or "syndicates," in which company leaders had financial interests. Writer John Ryckman pulled no punches and went right after the Big Three, which "with their billion of assets and with their million of surplus withheld from the policyholders have been the main allies of the creators of great watered stock schemes in sucking blood from the public." The series hewed closely to other contemporary journalistic takedowns of trusts, and while the insurance industry itself wasn't explicitly monopolistic, the largesse of the Big Three and their incestuous financial relationships with the trusts made them part of the same storyline. Ryckman investigated the intersection between financial behaviors and political influence and accused the companies of a long list of misdeeds, including financial self-dealing, undue influence over state legislatures, retention of too much premium revenue, misrepresentation of dividend returns, and many other lapses, conveying to readers his sense of horrified amazement: "The investigation into the affairs and conduct of the life insurance combine leads one into such a tangled jungle of financial intrigue, gross delusion and deception, broken faith and political corruption, that I find my greatest difficulty lies in isolating certain and distinct parts of this whole ugly mess."[74] Ryckman called for sweeping financial reforms, including regulation and greater transparency around investments and expenses. In an early form of data journalism, he sought to illustrate with graphs how dividends had dwindled over time due to industry speculation in trusts. The trade press denounced the stories as irresponsible and the journalists as "dangerous individuals," yet the findings were welcomed by people across the country who read them avidly. Letters from readers urged Ryckman to stay on the trail, like one from a Texas man who implored, "Don't let up, publicity is the thing."[75] Cartoons, such as Figure 3.1, depicted nepotism and greed by life insurance companies.

The popularity of these two series led the *New York World* to start an investigation of their own, which initially focused on Equitable. Their point of departure was a lavish Versailles-style costume ball hosted by the young James

A VERY 'MUTUAL' FAMILY AFFAIR.

Figure 3.1 This political cartoon satire alleged nepotism in the family of Richard McCurdy, president of Mutual Life. Library of Congress.

THE ROAD TO ARMSTRONG 61

Hazen Hyde, son and heir of the deceased founder. In some ways, Hyde Jr., a foppish twenty-something who indulged in a host of elitist affectations such as violet boutonnieres, became a poster child for the industry's excesses and lack of accountability. An internal struggle for control of the company, precipitated by founder Hyde's death in 1899, likely resulted in the leaked and probably false story that the ball was paid for by policyholders' premiums. Uncovering nepotism, corporate extravagance, and other malfeasance, the *World* accused New York's insurance regulators of sharing responsibility for the company's bad financial practices and called for an investigation by the legislature.[76]

An initial response to the series in the *World* was an investigation and report that recommended a major reorganization of Equitable. Yet perceived problems with the industry were far more extensive, and a subsequent editorial by the *World* called for a broader investigation. Shortly thereafter, New York Senator William Armstrong established the "Joint Committee of the Senate and Assembly of the State of New York to Investigate and Examine into the Business and Affairs of Life Insurance Companies Doing Business in the State of New York." Progressive reformer Charles Evans Hughes, who had entered public life fighting urban gas monopolies, was appointed chief counsel. Hughes would go on to become New York's governor in 1906 and would later become a U.S. Supreme Court justice, a candidate for president, and secretary of state.[77]

The Armstrong investigation is notable for its time, and in fact for any time, as a highly public and searching scrutiny of a group of major corporations and is also unique in the extent to which it produced a substantial policy response. What started in reaction to internal dissension within Equitable ended up including all of the Big Five, whose executives responded to questions from Hughes before a packed crowd at city hall. The investigation focused on investment practices, administrative expenses, and political contributions. Though not criminal, the hearings were structured much like courtroom proceedings, with the well-prepared Hughes described as "complex, probing, patient yet relentless." A number of the intended witnesses made themselves scarce, becoming indisposed or suddenly leaving town. News of the hearings filled the front pages of national newspapers. The investigation lasted nearly four months, culminating in a report and a set of recommendations in December of 1905.[78]

The Armstrong investigation substantiated most of the charges made against the big life firms. The reputational damage was profound. As Attorney General William A. Moody noted of Equitable, "This tremendous insurance power was pulled down like a house of straw—not by any prosecutions, but by public opinion." In addition to financial improprieties and excessive administrative expenses, the investigation also exposed the lobbying practices of the insurance industry companies and the extent of their influence on state regulators.[79] In his report, Hughes issued a warning, charging that the Big Three in particular had grown so large and unaccountable that "their management, if permitted to grow unrestrained, will soon become a serious menace to the community."[80] The New York Division of Insurance Supervision did not escape criticism for their passivity. But the problems were not limited to New York, as the companies had extended their political reach to many other states where they did business.

A letter to the editor of the *New York Tribune* expressed the near-universal response to the Armstrong hearings: "The developments of the life insurance investigation now in progress are such as to shock and sicken mankind."[81] The call for reform was strong: "Government should protect people from these sharks and grafters, and should severely punish everyone who attempts to defraud the public."[82] As Lawson put it, the big life firms, once "the greatest, most respected and most venerable institutions in our land," were now seen to stand for "all that is tricky, fraudulent, and oppressive."[83]

In the aftermath of the investigation, the leadership of the Big Five collapsed mentally and physically under the weight of their public condemnation. As one New York Life lobbyist noted, "I am in such a nervous condition and like all the rest of our company, have been under the doctors' care." Equitable's James Alexander went abroad in 1905, "broken down under the weight of his troubles." Young James Hazen Hyde, always a Francophile, went to Paris for "a rest," which lasted thirty-five years.[84] Mutual's Richard McCurdy stepped down in 1905, claiming ill health.[85] He would die in 1916. Prudential's John Dryden stepped down under similar circumstances in 1907 and died in 1911. Metropolitan's Hegeman was indicted for forgery and perjury though ultimately acquitted.[86] New York Life's George Perkins, friend and advisor to Roosevelt and one of the most well known and outspoken of the Big Five CEOs, left the company in 1906. He would die shortly after World War I, depressed and disillusioned.[87] New York Life's John McCall was the last of the Big Five to step down, after resisting repeated calls for his resignation. Finally, in a letter to trustees in early 1906 he made his announcement, citing both declining health and the "erosion of his peace of mind," resulting from the "continuous misunderstanding and misrepresentation of his actions and distortion of facts and misquotations of his utterances."[88] Before dying "of worry" in 1906, he foreshadowed a potential redemption: "I go to a higher court to render my account."[89]

The Armstrong investigation was a strong counterpoint to the notion of regulatory "negativism"—that is, the idea that only solvency and marketing practices should be regulated. The big firms, which for so long had supported regulation that functioned to thwart potential competition from undercapitalized upstarts, now found themselves on the receiving end of regulatory attention. Many of the recommendations from the Armstrong Committee were enacted in 1906 by the New York legislature. Included were laws requiring (1) the divesture of investments in equities; (2) the regulation of lobbying and the prohibition of

campaign contributions; (3) the standardization of the policy form; (4) limitations to agents' activities, such as rebating; (5) democratizing management, by
requiring more policyholder representation in mutuals; and (6) limitations on
the volume and expense of new business. Bills based on these recommendations
were swiftly drafted, passed, and signed by New York's governor. These included
the controversial sections 96 and 97, which targeted the structure of the industry
itself and sought to reduce growth by placing a limit on the amount of new business that depended on firm size.[90]

Many states followed New York's lead in regulating the life insurance industry.
There were forty-two state legislatures in 1907, and thirty considered life insurance regulation, with twenty-nine passing laws. Significant change occurred in
many states, including New Jersey, Massachusetts, Delaware, Maryland, New
Hampshire, North Carolina, West Virginia, Louisiana, Missouri, Texas, Ohio,
Indiana, Illinois, Michigan, Minnesota, Montana, North Dakota, Colorado,
and California. A number of other states held hearings of their own, including
New Jersey, Wisconsin, Iowa, Massachusetts, and Tennessee. The Wisconsin
investigations focused closely on the local firm Northwestern Mutual and were
led by legislator Herman Ekern, who would later become the insurance commissioner.[91] Not every state was on board. An editorial in the *Hartford Courant* by
an unnamed "life insurance man" argued that Connecticut's current laws were
strong enough and that, moreover, "the public should find encouragement to
insure, not be discouraged by sensational stories and laws which may not be
necessary."[92]

Outrage from these sensational stories led many to cancel their policies. When
combined with the growth restrictions of the Armstrong laws, new business for
the Big Three plummeted in the years after the 1905 investigation, as seen in
Table 3.1. This may have been the most painful consequence of all. Just as massive, unfettered growth had characterized the establishment of these companies,
their contraction was the most drastic penalty possible.[93]

The Armstrong investigation and its aftermath showed the potential of state
insurance supervision, but also its limitations. While there were meaningful
reforms to insurer practices, large companies were ultimately able to use the
new standards to their advantage by showcasing their compliance. And while
the Armstrong laws did better protect consumers, they did not address the more
fundamental issue of unmet demand, which had resulted in the growth of two
substandard products, assessment insurance and industrial insurance. These
products were largely unaddressed by state reformers and would persist well into
the twentieth century before collapsing under their own weight.

Yet in their weakened state, the companies could at the time do little to resist the momentum for reform. Their ability to influence state regulators, even
in traditionally friendly New York, was at an all-time low. Attempts to obtain

federal supervision had gone nowhere. Ultimately, the companies would adjust and find ways to benefit from the new regulatory environment by taking credit for meeting the standards, while at the same time developing new products and markets. But in 1905, the Big Five were newly powerless. As George Perkins sourly observed: "The Armstrong recommendations have all become law, and a nice mess they are going to make of the New York life insurance companies."[94]

4

The Life Insurance Moment

Now, what has happened? Let us talk sensibly—what has happened?

Lee Frankel was speaking at the 1910 New Jersey State Conference on Charities and Corrections. He had been asked to discuss Savings Bank Life Insurance, a Massachusetts effort to provide low-cost coverage to workers through a partnership between the state department of insurance and savings banks. Though it wouldn't please his audience, the main point he wanted to make about savings bank life insurance was that it did not work. Despite the efforts of the "best men and women in Massachusetts" and "lectures, propaganda literature, meetings of every kind," there were by Frankel's estimation only 2,500 policyholders, mostly from several large factories whose owners had purchased the insurance on behalf of their employees. By and large, Frankel said, "the industrial classes of whom we speak today have not accepted it."

This was a regrettable but unavoidable fact of life:

> It is almost with despair that it must be said that you cannot get that element of the population to provide for itself unless you have got the missionary and the propagandist going to him and almost by the throat compelling him to do so. And that service must be paid for. That service is always paid for by the poor man. He pays for it in his coal; he pays for it in his rent; he pays for it in every necessity of life. You know that as well as I. Whether he gets it through insurance or any other wise, it is the poor workingman paying the bill in the long run.[1]

From his prior experience as the executive director of the United Hebrew Charities, Frankel understood well the fragile position of industrial workers and the case for some better means of protection. He had traveled to Europe to study social insurance at the behest of the Russell Sage Foundation. Yet in his new role as the assistant director of the industrial department at Metropolitan Life, Frankel also understood the potential threat that public life insurance or old-age

Uncovered. Katherine Hempstead, Oxford University Press. © Oxford University Press 2024.
DOI: 10.1093/oso/9780190094157.003.0004

pensions posed to the highly profitable industrial insurance business. His hiring was a major coup for Metropolitan and reflected the way in which the company sought to pivot in the post-Armstrong years.

Frankel exuded empathy and expressed unequivocal support for the goal of savings bank life insurance: "I contend that any insurance man . . . will welcome . . . any scheme of insurance cheaper than the ones that are now in vogue." He further let it be known that Metropolitan Life had gladly lent a hand, "when these lovely men and women in Massachusetts with good intentions developed it without any actuarial experience of their own." Frankel pointed out that the savings bank idea was nothing new, referencing both "old Elizur Wright back in the seventies" and other countries: "It has been tried in some form or other in every state in Europe." And while he tacitly acknowledged the costliness of industrial insurance to the poor, he maintained that these well-intended alternatives were doomed to failure.

The development of Savings Bank Life Insurance and the recruitment of Frankel to the industrial insurance department of Metropolitan Life reflected changes in the way that the boundary between what was public and what was private about life insurance was being navigated in the early twentieth century. Insurers had historically affirmed the quasi-public nature of their business. Yet the travails that had led to the Armstrong investigation had given cause for reconsideration. The gap between social need and what insurers were willing to supply was increasingly apparent. Now more stringent regulations were combined with scattered attempts to provide life insurance publicly. While some companies publicly sympathized with the intention behind these efforts, most viewed them as a threat.

The early twentieth century was a period of significant emphasis on both the public and private importance of life insurance as the reform impulse reflected in the Armstrong investigation rippled throughout the country. Influenced by examples of social insurance in Europe, some states tried to implement ambitious reforms, including the establishment of state-run insurance. Other states used this moment to act on populist and sectional impulses, enacting protectionist measures that favored local industry and had little benefit for consumers.

The "Big Five" unsuccessfully pursued federal supervision, guarded against threats from new competitors, adjusted their business models to conform with new expectations, and sought new opportunities to serve a broader range of policyholders, most notably with group insurance. Assessment and fraternal insurance began to decline under the weight of actuarial requirements and competition from group insurance. The federal government made an unexpected entry, providing low-cost life insurance to soldiers in World War I, a move that challenged private industry by demonstrating the potential for government involvement in insurance on a large scale. The postwar collapse of Progressive reform sentiment contributed to the passing of the life insurance moment by the 1920s, although individual and group life insurance itself continued to grow exponentially throughout the twentieth century.

The Armstrong investigation raised the threat of aggressive state oversight and increased the desire for federal supervision among large life insurers. The American Bar Association supported federal supervision in 1905. Even the National Convention of Insurance Commissioners (NCIC) collectively concluded that the troubles with Equitable and other life insurance scandals necessitated at least some federal oversight. But support among state regulators was not uniform. Southern and western states felt they had much to lose, and more reform-minded commissioners generally opposed federal supervision on the grounds that it would be too soft on industry. "We want to maintain the meaningful reform which is possible only at the state level. . . . Federal supervision is an anathema to those who desire justice for the policy holder."[2] Others feared the result would be the consolidation of power by the leaders of the New York companies. A column in the *Independent* warned of ceding control to "a comparatively small number of men in the insurance business who would co-operate in controlling the Federal Bureau, just as they have controlled the insurance commissioners and legislatures of certain states."[3]

The tide ultimately turned against federal regulation, which came to be widely seen as something that would be beneficial to industry. The fact that the political contributions unearthed during the Armstrong hearings were to the Republican Party did not escape notice. Senator John Dryden's advocacy for federal control struck many as self-serving. His bill failed to win support, and the White House was deluged with anti-Dryden letters. "If his bills are passed," warned one commenter, "you will find that . . . his power of appropriating the savings of the middle class are greatly increased."[4] A New Jersey editorial acidly reinforced the connection in the public mind between life insurance companies, monopolistic trusts, and political corruption, cynically asking: "Will the Jerseys be unfaithful to this revered statesman, this friend of humanity, this warm unselfish and generous soul? We cannot think it. We will not believe it. No Jerseyman rides in a trolley car, consults his gas meter, pays his electric light bill or his taxes or provides for his funeral without praising and blessing John Fairfield Dryden."[5] In the aftermath of Armstrong, the eastern companies coalesced in a new trade organization, the Association of Life Insurance Presidents, formed in December of 1906 and initially headed by friend of the industry and former president Grover Cleveland. The goal of the organization was to create a more publicly acceptable way to advocate mutually against hostile legislation, now that the Armstrong investigation had exposed the ways in which the companies had sought to control the state legislative process.[6] Earlier that same year, another new trade organization had formed. The American Life Convention was composed of small southern and western companies, newly emboldened by the setbacks to the Big Five and staunchly opposed to federal supervision.[7]

Theodore Roosevelt ultimately came to believe that Congress lacked the constitutional authority to regulate insurance. Yet he generally sought more uniformity and was alarmed by some of the more anti-industry reforms being proposed in southern and western states. Another idea for a greater federal role, proposed by Congressman Butler Ames of Massachusetts, was for Congress to create model insurance laws for the District of Columbia, which could then be copied by other states. These matters were among those discussed at the National Insurance Convention of Governors, Attorneys General, and Insurance Commissioners held in Chicago in February 1906, several weeks before the release of the Armstrong report.[8]

A committee of fifteen was appointed at the national convention, which was largely composed of insurance commissioners, including many who were highly critical of eastern companies. These included Reau Folk of Tennessee, W. D. Vandiver of Missouri, and Zeno M. Host of Wisconsin. This commission advocated for uniform legislation on a limited platform of life insurance issues, including the prohibition of deferred dividend policies, more policyholder power in mutuals, restrictions on investments, and standardized policy forms.[9] Creation of model laws became an important tactic that the NCIC would use to build consensus among states and try to increase national uniformity. Attendees at this convention also expressed support for the Ames bill, which would have placed the District of Columbia Insurance Department in the Department of Commerce to serve as the nucleus of a national system of regulation. While Roosevelt and the industry supported this bill, it never got out of committee, and Congress concluded in the spring of 1906 that it lacked the authority to regulate life insurance. Momentum for federal regulation was then largely exhausted.[10]

New York was the source of the Armstrong investigation and the ensuing reforms, but it remained the home of the financial industry, including the big life companies. While the Armstrong laws were significant, they did not seek to overturn the basic structure of industry. The Armstrong laws can be viewed as a baseline set of reforms that reflected broadly shared goals and were generally adopted in most states. However, the Armstrong investigation presented an opportunity for some states to pursue additional objectives. For example, in the South and West, the broadly shared Progressive reform goal of restraining the life insurance companies was joined with incentives to act on longstanding sectional desires to reduce the power of eastern companies and grow domestic industry. Revelations about political contributions made by the "Big Three" to the Republican Party were received negatively in the largely Democratic southern and western states and increased their desire to limit the power of the New York companies.

Elsewhere, the opportunity created by Armstrong allowed some to think about life insurance reform in the context of the growing interest in social insurance. While affordability was not the only problem for life insurance consumers, it was broadly recognized that many assessment plans were unreliable, and industrial insurance offered low-income policyholders little protection. Progressive reformers were keenly aware of policy innovations from abroad, where old-age pensions, workmen's compensation, and health insurance were under various stages of development in Germany, England, France, and New Zealand. In some states, reformers sought to take advantage of the reform moment in life insurance to attempt to achieve broader social welfare objectives through state-provided life insurance.[11]

In Texas, reform efforts focused on investment practices, marrying Armstrong-related outrage at the companies with sectional interests in keeping capital in state. The result was the Robertson Law, which required that seventy-five percent of life insurance company reserves from Texas policyholders be invested locally and subject to state taxes. This approach had a considerable amount of public support, feeding into a longstanding view, propagated by local politicians, that the life insurance industry had been "taking" from the people of Texas. Yet there was also a counterargument, that a regulation like the Robertson Law would actually hurt Texas policyholders, because premiums would be higher if companies could not get as good a return on capital. Similar investment bills were proposed but did not succeed in some other states, including Kansas and Oklahoma.[12] In the run-up to the adoption of the Robertson Law, advertisements reflected the regional politics of the domestic investment issue, with Equitable taking credit for El Paso's paved streets because had they purchased their bonds, "after the city tried every place" to sell them.[13] Meanwhile, ads for newly formed Texas insurers like the Southwestern encouraged customers to "Keep Texas money in Texas."[14]

The Robertson Law resulted in a mass withdrawal of life insurance companies, which were very concerned that these practices would be adopted by other southern and western states. Missouri and Kansas also considered investment bills in 1907, and the issue continued to be raised over the next several years. State financial interests, particularly banks, sometimes opposed investment bills, as they did not wish to compete with New York life insurance companies in the mortgage market.

Metropolitan complained the act created "such burdensome conditions" that it threatened "the independent solvency of the Texas business."[15] Most exiting companies kept their existing policyholders and serviced them from nearby offices located on the border. Meanwhile, many new life companies emerged in Texas and formed a powerful lobby, successfully thwarting New York firms' repeated efforts to weaken the Robertson Law's provisions.[16] There were periodic arguments that the law slowed the state's economic development by restricting the supply of capital; those opposed wanted to come to terms with the eastern companies so that they could reenter. Attempts to modify or repeal the Robertson Law started in 1912, yet the regulation persisted until 1963.

The issue of political contributions was also particularly salient in southern and western states. In Democratic strongholds such as Missouri, the revelation that life firms were using policyholder money to contribute to Republican campaigns was galling, and the outspoken Missouri superintendent, W. D. Vandiver, suspended New York Life's license in 1905 on the basis of that company's political contributions. He also caused "quite a flurry" by attempting to oust Equitable, Metropolitan, and Prudential because their executives' salaries exceeded the $50,000 limit set by Missouri law.[17]

In the aftermath of the Armstrong laws, the geographic distribution of the life industry shifted west and south. In 1905, there were seventy-nine life firms, of which more than half were from the Northeast and Middle Atlantic, and ninety-four percent were from either the Northeast, Middle Atlantic, or Midwest. The years after the Armstrong laws saw the rapid emergence of new companies, as the growth restrictions combined with the unpopularity of the New York firms created opportunities. Between 1905 and 1910, 151 new life firms were created, and of these, only 9 were from the Northeast and Middle Atlantic. The West had 3 life companies in 1905. By 1910 there were 47.[18]

The East Coast insurance establishment resented the newly aggressive legislation from southern and western states and the new firms that emerged in the changed regulatory climate. For example, when the Nevada commissioner challenged New York Life over a deposit law, the *Indicator* noted that "It is amusing how 'cockey' some of these little states become when they need to remind the public of their existence."[19] There was a similar view toward Missouri's salary limits and the highly restrictive Wisconsin laws. The animosity extended to new firms. The Robertson Law was a clear manifestation of the tension between new and old companies and was criticized in New York for driving from Texas many of the "strongest insurance companies in the world."[20] The Mutual's bulletin scolded: "The many newer companies—not all—that from the very first seek to court local favor by attacking and maligning the older institutions as oppressors of the people, draining the West and South of their money for the purpose of enriching eastern stockholders and Wall Street gamblers. When the representatives of the older companies point out the falsity of such charges . . . they are charged with assailing the latter unjustly and maliciously."[21] The Association of Life Insurance Presidents lobbied against the Texas law, while the American Life Convention did not take a position.[22]

Much of the Armstrong investigation had focused on the Big Three, which were purveyors of what had come to be known as "ordinary insurance," largely a middle-class product. The Armstrong laws were designed to improve the market for that product in ways that would benefit policyholders, but some wanted to do more to broaden the base and increase the prevalence of insurance. The Armstrong investigation also coincided with a global interest in social insurance and growing concerns in many countries about the vulnerability of low-income workers. Life insurance reform ideas in the United States were highly influenced by policy developments abroad. While the insurance industry often referenced Europe negatively, reformers drew positive examples where insurance was used as a tool of public policy. In the aftermath of the Armstrong investigation, several states sought to create public or quasi-public alternatives to commercial life insurance.

In Massachusetts, future Supreme Court justice and antimonopolist Louis Brandeis took advantage of the opportunity presented by the Armstrong investigation to pursue his long-time goal of establishing a "savings bank" life insurance program geared at low-income consumers. The idea of using savings banks as a way to sell low-cost insurance had originally been attempted by Elizur Wright.[23] In fact, Wright received considerable criticism from otherwise admiring insurance industry associates when in 1876 he introduced his concept of a family bank, which combined savings with life insurance. The *Insurance Times* castigated Wright for "wasting his old age." The family bank had never become a reality, and the idea had faded away when Wright died in 1885. Centralized postal savings systems were important features in several European social insurance efforts, and Brandeis was pleased to revive the concept, claiming that his state had "established for the world the scientific practice of life insurance by the work of its great insurance commissioner Elizur Wright."[24]

Massachusetts Savings Bank Life Insurance, which originated in 1907, was essentially a public-private partnership, in which the state contributed some in-kind resources to support the actuarial work and medical examinations, but the policies themselves were actuarially priced.

The target market was wage workers who would otherwise purchase industrial insurance or go without protection. Savings banks in New England at the time largely served low- and middle-income depositors and operated with very low margins, so the partnership seemed to make sense. The almost charitable nature of savings banks was described as a selling point, as they were "managed by gentlemen of long experience in the handling of the savings of our people in small amounts at the lowest possible cost."[25] Savings Bank Life Insurance was supervised by both the insurance and banking departments of Massachusetts, and their investment of premiums conformed to the conservative regulations governing savings banks.

In promoting the plan, Brandeis associate Herman LaRue Brown stated what was by then self-evident to Progressive Era reformers: "The necessity of life insurance in some form to the wage earner has long been accepted by the student of social conditions." He acknowledged the importance of "the turning on of the searchlight" (a reference to Armstrong) as galvanizing the Massachusetts plan, revealing as it did "conditions which astonished even a public which had begun to have some acquaintance with the devious operations of so-called high finance." Most of the Armstrong probe had been focused on "'ordinary' life insurance . . . because that is the sort of insurance with which the more influential of our citizens are most concerned."[26]

But in fact, the Armstrong investigation had also yielded revelations about industrial insurance that "called no less earnestly for remedy." Though not the main focus, industrial insurance had been exposed during the hearings as a low-value financial product for the poor, with an estimated forty percent of premiums going to administrative costs and profits. Due to the costliness of the insurance, along with "oversolicitation" by aggressive agents, lapse rates were extraordinarily high. Because of the costly system of sales and premium collection, "the wage earner buying on the industrial plan pays about twice as much for one dollar's worth of insurance as it costs the professional man." Brown termed this the "innate vice" of the industrial insurance system: "All the members of this great field organization must receive their compensation out of the premiums paid by the policyholders."[27]

To counteract these tendencies, Brown argued that the design of Savings Bank Life Insurance "struck at the very root of the evil and forbade the employment by the banks of paid solicitors or collectors, and here is the great strength and the one possible weakness of the movement." Prohibiting marketing and sales came at the cost of enrollment, as even Brown would acknowledge, as he also acknowledged that the Savings Bank plans were only fifteen percent less expensive than commercial insurance. To compensate for the lack of sales, Brown noted that assistance from employers and labor unions was encouraged, as "solicitation, even direct and personal, has not been frowned upon" so long as it is "voluntary and unpaid." Employers could also purchase insurance on behalf of their employees, creating one of the early models for group insurance. The admittedly modest goal was to "primarily appeal to that class of our citizens who voluntarily use the savings banks."[28] Another challenge was that savings banks were generally unsupportive, believing that "nothing experimental" should be done to risk the security of their deposits. The majority of banks in Massachusetts did not participate in Savings Bank Life Insurance.[29]

A column in the trade paper *The Indicator* suggests that the doubts that Metropolitan Life's Frankel had about the viability of Savings Bank Life Insurance were widely shared: "And now that the plan is fully underway, it is expected that the industrial classes, for whom it is especially designed, will flock to the bank by the thousands to get insurance. In the meantime, industrial agents, who can secure applications only by dint of much hard work and patient plodding, are no doubt looking on with much interest, curious to see to how great an extent people will voluntarily go after what they find so much difficulty in taking to them. The companies are not greatly worried over the prospective loss of business."[30]

While the Savings Bank Life Insurance received some in-kind support from the state of Massachusetts, Wisconsin provides the sole example where life insurance was literally sold by the state. Wisconsin's insurance hearings resulted in legislative proposals, seventy-seven in all, that went far beyond the Armstrong laws and, "climaxing with drastic impracticabilities," sought to regulate many more aspects of life insurance.[31] Bills drafted in Wisconsin attempted to democratize the governance of life insurance companies, ban rebating, prohibit political contributions, limit salaries, and restrict the amount of expenses that could be loaded onto premiums.[32] Included among the successful legislative proposals was a study bill to consider the future implementation of state insurance, which would potentially include life, disability, and old-age benefits. The example of New Zealand's public life insurance was used in making the case.[33] New Zealand sold low-cost insurance through the post office as early as 1869, and by 1877 the government had the largest market share, a position it retained until the 1980s.[34]

Many of the New York firms exited Wisconsin in response to these laws, creating a vacuum that reformers attempted to fill by pressing their case for a public option. The *Insurance Field* accurately teed up the challenge for the upcoming legislative session: "From one side the Socialists will take advantage of the exodus of companies to urge a constitutional amendment permitting state insurance and from another side will come arguments for such modification of the law as will permit the return of companies that have withdrawn."[35] The advocates for state life insurance prevailed, and "The Wisconsin Plan for State Life Insurance" was signed into law in 1911 by Governor McGovern, a Progressive, and was implemented in 1913. Under the plan, each Wisconsin resident between ages twenty and fifty could purchase a policy with a coverage maximum of $3,000.[36]

Compared to Massachusetts Savings Bank Life Insurance, the Wisconsin Life Fund had more of a middle-class target and was designed with the Big Three in mind. Industrial insurance was far less established in Wisconsin, and there was a longer tradition of small mutual insurance companies, both fire and life. Commissioner Ekern alluded to the Big Three's cost structure in justifying state insurance: "Of the total expense of old-line companies, more than one half is commissions and salaries to agents. Under the state life plan, the policyholders are saved this great expense." Like Savings Bank Life Insurance, the Wisconsin Life Fund was designed to have a very small bureaucratic footprint; there would be no advertisement or agents, nor would any new agency be created. The insurance department would manage the plan, and government employees would sell policies to anyone who requested them, for a tiny commission. "Every factory inspector, clerk, and treasurer of every county, town, city and village and every state bank are insurance agents for the state." When the plan first rolled out, newspaper articles listed the names of all the initial policyholders, along with their age, height, and weight.[37]

Despite this low profile, the fund faced headwinds from the outset. A connection with socialism was frequently made. From the *Calgary Herald*, a 1912 article made an accusatory point: "To the complaint that the idea of state insurance is socialistic, the Commissioner answers that insurance is public service and should be under state control. . . . As a matter of fact . . . the law was passed by the aid of the socialist members of the legislature."[38] Yet Ekern was not a Socialist. Using the type of arguments Progressive Era contemporaries made to justify the regulation of transportation and power companies, he suggested that the private market could not deliver a sufficient quantity of affordable insurance, and public provision was the only way to obtain the social benefits of widespread ownership of insurance.

In the same way that Progressive reformers supported mothers' pensions and no-fault workers' compensation, Ekern emphasized the public interest in life insurance as a protection against government's exposure to the consequences of poverty, as a "recognition of the economic necessity of extending the facilities for safe insurance beyond the field of private enterprise, to include practically all residents of the state, that the state may be more fully safeguarded against the burdens of pauperism and its people protected against the evils of improvidence and dependency."[39] This was the same argument made by life insurance companies themselves as a justification for their special quasi-public role.

Ekern's argument that greater public involvement in insurance was a way to protect the government is a recurring theme. It is but one manifestation of a long string of state and federal insurance policy actions that are motivated by a desire to minimize government exposure to risk. Ekern makes clear that not only individual citizens but also the state of Wisconsin would be at risk if the prevalence of insurance was low. Like their contemporaries in Europe, Wisconsin progressives made the case that extending social insurance was not socialist but was instead a way to thwart socialism. In an approving appraisal of a program in New Zealand that provided low-interest credit to farmers, the Wisconsin Board of Public Affairs argued that state aid was "one of the strongest antidotes to socialism," since anything that helped men become more independent will add them to the ranks of the "political parties which represent the interests of the property-owning classes."[40] Brandeis similarly argued that Savings Bank Life Insurance would counteract socialist tendencies.[41]

The big New York firms were largely indifferent to the Wisconsin Fund, since most had withdrawn from the market. Yet complaints came from other quarters. A somewhat unexpected source of opposition was fraternal societies. While one might think their anticommercial ethos would lead them to support a state-sponsored effort, in fact, the reverse was the case. The *Kansas Workman*, a fraternal society publication, editorialized incessantly against the Wisconsin plan in particular and state insurance in general, in part because similar legislation was under consideration in Kansas. Somewhat ironically, considering the source, the *Workman* accused Wisconsin of careless management of their reserves, leading them to earn only two percent. Inadequate premium loadings, they warned, would lead the state to rely on the General Fund. "State insurance is a burden on the people," proclaimed one article, which went on to warn, "premiums have been less than the cost of operations, and people have paid the deficiency."[42]

The *Workman* also had the standard industry perspective on marketing, sounding much like Metropolitan Life's Frankel, and referencing European experience: "The fallacy that people will buy insurance without solicitation has caused the failure of state insurance wherever tried."[43] The Mutual Life Underwriters Association, a trade group of nonfraternal assessment plans, also opposed state insurance, considering it of "paternalistic hue" and "un-American." Yet they were able to remain calmer than the *Workman*, deeming current efforts "not of moment," since insurance "is no longer bought but has to be sold. State effort thereon is not so much to be feared." Compulsory insurance, however, would be another matter altogether, "a real threatened cloud to all existing life insurance organizations of our country." When the popularity of social insurance was ascending, the Mutual Life Underwriters Association was concerned. While the press "teems with European accomplishments in governmental insurance ... we must not be blind to it."[44]

Like Massachusetts Savings Bank Life Insurance, the Wisconsin Life Fund was plagued by low take-up. By 1915, for example, only 328 policies were in force. It was also not helpful that premiums of the Wisconsin Life Fund were not markedly lower than commercial rates and that the maximum amount of coverage was quite low. Yet despite its tepid sales, the Wisconsin Life Fund was a potent symbol, with ardent supporters as well as detractors. A number of states considered emulating the approach, and Kansas came extremely close, with a very similar bill, although it would have employed agents to solicit business. It passed the House but was killed in the Senate by the Insurance Committee.[45]

The Wisconsin Life Fund and other state insurance legislation were products of the uniquely reformist culture of Wisconsin in the early twentieth century. The German university education of nationally famous University of Wisconsin faculty such as John Commons and Richard Ely, the mutualistic values of the many Scandinavian and German residents, and the outsized influence of Robert La

Follette were some of the factors that made Wisconsin a vanguard of Progressive reform. Commissioner Herman Ekern, with his Norwegian heritage and deep Lutheran faith, was emblematic of Wisconsin reform sensibility.[46]

Less publicly renowned but also representative of this time was prominent surgeon and Madison resident George Keenan. Keenan was born in Dane County and attended the University of Wisconsin and Rush Medical College. Despite a brief stint as American counsel-general to Bremen during the Cleveland administration, he was a Republican and became involved in local civic life after returning to his home in Madison.[47] Dr. Keenan was Robert La Follette's friend and physician and occasionally spoke to the media about the senator's health, in 1910 informing them about an episode of illness ("undoubtedly gallstones") that required surgery.[48] With Keenan attending, the "knife work" was performed by the Mayo brothers in their Rochester, Minnesota, medical clinic, in a procedure from which La Follette reportedly emerged feeling "sore, but bully."[49]

Keenan continued to treat many of Madison's most eminent citizens and was appointed to a position as a local public health officer in 1913.[50] Yet his own health was poor, and after a hospitalization and a lengthy illness, Keenan died of pneumonia in 1915, at the early age of fifty-nine, leaving his wife Matilda and their five children. While Madison mourned the untimely loss of their "thoughtful, helpful, and scholarly citizen,"[51] Keenan's death was also notable for another reason, as it represented the first claim on the Wisconsin Life Fund.

By 1915, the political climate, nationally and in Wisconsin, had started to change. Reformer interest in including life insurance as a component of broader social welfare policy had waned. Much energy had instead been diverted into the implementation of workmen's compensation, the subject of a future chapter, which had first appeared in Wisconsin and Ohio in 1911 and was rolling out in other states. The Wisconsin Life Fund was the symbol of a prior administration, and existential threats loomed. Conservative businessman Emanuel L. Philipp, elected governor in 1915, opposed the fund. The negative view of the Wisconsin Life Fund was most likely also colored by controversy surrounding state fire insurance, also a subject of a future chapter.

When Keenan died, the Philipp administration exploited their leverage and held up the payment, while the treasurer Henry Johnson asked the attorney general to certify the "validity" of the state life and fire insurance laws, expressing his "grave doubt" as to their constitutionality. In a somber piece headlined "Wisconsin Experiment Hurt," the *Chicago Tribune* stated the obvious: "The fact that death claims may not be paid promptly will no doubt interfere with the growth of the fund."[52] Yet Attorney General W. C. Owen informed Johnson that the insurance laws were constitutional and, "declining to become a party to any arrangement" for the purpose of "attacking the law in the courts," directed that the claim be paid.[53]

In 1916, Wisconsin commissioner Cleary had the department's actuary examine the Wisconsin Life Fund. Not surprisingly, it was deemed unsound, with the actuary reporting that if the fund were a private company, it "would not be given a license." The *Wichita Beacon* reported: "Commissioner Cleary is said to believe that state insurance is impracticable, and this report verifies his opinion."[54] Given the notorious nature of the Wisconsin Life Fund, the report received widespread coverage, with the *Hartford Courant* reporting in "State Life Fund Fiasco" that the state actuary, L. A. Anderson, "severely criticizes the methods used in the conduct of the fund."[55]

Paradoxically, the publicity surrounding the actuary's report in 1916 increased consumer interest at least a little. However, at the end of 1916, the fund had only 381 policyholders, versus more than 575,000 for the rest of life companies doing business in the state. At around the same time, a new study of the fund identified some weaknesses, including the lack of marketing and the potential for adverse selection resulting from low fees paid to medical examiners. The *Hartford Courant* concluded that the fund "serves little purpose and faces an obscure future."[56]

For Wisconsin, this turned out to be the case, for enrollment was low, the policies were not notably cheaper, and the low maximum coverage amounts essentially consigned the fund to irrelevance. In the same manner in which the fund was held up as a shining example to other states, its failure was influential as well, and interest in state life insurance began to fade after 1915 as Progressive reform efforts in general lost momentum. Meanwhile, the New York companies that had exited Wisconsin slowly returned, now willing to comply with all of the 1907 reforms. Although he represented the first claim, by the time George Keenan died, the movement for state life insurance was essentially dead as well. While proponents of the fund had a bill passed to authorize more active solicitation, Governor Philipps promptly vetoed it.[57]

Massachusetts Savings Bank Life Insurance similarly limped along in semi-obscurity, although compared with Wisconsin Life Fund it was a great success. In 1916, there were four banks participating with ten thousand policyholders, leading the sympathetic but dubious commissioner of Connecticut to suggest that "before the plan can be successfully extended so that the industrial world can share its benefits, there must be either a very much wider support given to it ... or else it must blossom out—into what it is now in bud—something akin to state insurance."[58]

The potential to create a pathway to public old-age pensions was seen by opponents of state insurance as the greatest threat. In 1909, an old-age pension system administered by post offices was initiated in England. This program was taxpayer funded, to the consternation of the insurance press both in England and in the United States, where there were worries that the Massachusetts Savings

Bank Life Insurance might ultimately be used for old-age pensions. The small footprint of Savings Bank Life Insurance was described with relief: "The experiment has only been taken up by two of the 189 savings banks in Massachusetts.... The scheme has not worked out to the satisfaction of the theorists."[59] There were similar concerns about the potential for the Wisconsin Life Fund to develop a system of annuities.

In the pages of the *Kansas Workman*, state involvement in insurance was described as a disaster on par with "Europe's invasion of one of the little American republics." Although potential mismanagement was the purported risk, a deeper mistrust of government was at the root of the *Workman*'s objection, in addition to the obvious competitive threat. Readers were presented with a dark scenario of self-interested politicians, who, "pretending to create reforms, induce dissatisfaction with privately administered business in order that the government might be persuaded to take it over, and in this manner furnish forth fat jobs for themselves and their fellow drones." A dystopian society would be the result: "In the end, all individual effort would be killed, enterprise and thrift would be things of the past, and we should become a mass of officials governing each other like driven cattle."[60]

The Armstrong reforms initially put the life insurance industry back on its heels, particularly the New York firms. Being reviled by the public and deprived of political influence, and having avenues to federal supervision closed off and business opportunities constrained by multiple state regulations, the industry found itself at an inflection point. Most of the New York life firms experienced transitions in leadership and made strategic adjustments. The pivot was away from emphasis on financial largesse and investment activity and toward the cultivation of a reputation for soundness.

The life industry ultimately accepted Armstrong and sought to profit from the credibility that came with compliance. An advertisement by Mutual in 1908 noted the company was "under a new management" and further claimed that their policies met the standards of New York's law—"the most exacting ever established." While they couldn't resist bragging that their "vast resources were greater by many millions than those of any other country in the world," this largesse was now "closely invested" in profitable securities in a way that was "consistent with safety."[61]

Blustery Darwin Kingsley of New York Life, in an advertisement that took the form of a letter to policyholders, insisted: "The Company is sound in every respect."[62] An ad from Equitable leans on the enhanced regulatory climate when it assures potential agents that "the State endorsement of the standard policy convinces the most skeptical applicant that its provisions are absolutely in his interest."[63] In the aftermath of Armstrong, the outlook for agents changed considerably, given the reduction in commission structure and other regulations, and a long process of professionalization began. The National Association of Life Underwriters promoted education for prospective agents, and courses on insurance as well as the science of salesmanship became widespread.[64]

The reforms came to be widely viewed as necessary. A telling exchange took place in 1908 when Charles Evans Hughes, now New York's governor, made a surprise visit at a gathering of Metropolitan's industrial department. President Hegeman introduced him, joking that "As you all remember, I had the honor of co-operating with Governor Hughes in a very important public movement. . . . At times, I remember, I perspired profusely." Hughes defended the investigation: "And so it was that certain restrictions were imposed." These restrictions had thus far prevented "a recurrence of those evils which the business cannot stand." Alluding to the fact that the Armstrong laws did not reform industrial insurance, he implored his audience of industrial agents to do the best they could for their customers, arguing that no part of the "life business" was more important than that which "relates to the insurance of the poor ... in which patriotism, in which a real genuine interest in one's fellow man should predominate so entirely in the determination of outlays."[65]

This is not to say that all aspects of the reforms were accepted. Certain parts of the Armstrong laws, particularly section 96, which restricted the volume of new business, continued to rankle industry. New York Life's Darwin Kingsley, protégé of George Perkins, was one of the most outspoken opponents, arguing that the state had it backward: "The real aim of legislation should be to encourage a larger production."[66] In discussing the travails of New York insurance supervisor Otto Kelsey, who was forced out for perceived laxness toward industry, *The Indicator* noted that "The agitation for reform placed him in a most trying position."[67] Similarly, the trade press cheered when Metropolitan's Hegeman was exonerated, describing him as a fall guy: "Something had to be done to satisfy the newspaper clamor following the Armstrong investigation."[68] The industry press sought to make the point that the real object of state regulatory focus should be directed elsewhere, at the "horde of wildcats and insolvent mutuals which infest the country," rather than the "good companies."[69] By 1909 and 1910, some of the regulations had loosened, and the caps on volume were eased.[70]

The last serious industry attempt for federal supervision occurred in 1913. Darwin Kingsley advocated using the courts to force a challenge of the *Paul* decision. If that failed, the next step would be an attempt to amend the Constitution. A test case was chosen regarding a Montana premium tax, but in *New York Life v. Deer Lodge County*, the Supreme Court's decision affirmatively supported state authority.[71] There was no support for a constitutional amendment, either from federal lawmakers or from policyholders. The state system was entrenched.

While accommodating themselves to the new regulatory climate, life insurers sought new avenues for growth, which led to a keen interest in activities in Europe.[72] The growing interest abroad and among reformers at home in social insurance led the big firms to focus more, at least rhetorically, on making life insurance available to those of modest income. At Equitable's fifty-year jubilee in 1909, President Paul Morton announced a "greater sphere of usefulness" as a goal for the future, "in which I hope to see the Equitable do its full share. That sphere is to give protection to the people who cannot afford to carry a big line of life insurance. I refer to the artisan, to the man behind the plow, to those engaged in the humbler walks of life."[73]

One way to broaden the base was to create new products marketed to employers. The first group life policy was offered by Equitable to the Pantasote Leather Company in 1911. Equitable established a group insurance department in 1912, and Montgomery Ward was another important early client. Along with Equitable, Metropolitan led in building the market for group insurance. At the National Civic Federation (NCF), the powerful executive association frequented by Perkins, Kingsley, and other advocates of federal regulation, the conversation increasingly turned to employers' responsibilities for workers' insurance, an important concept in the emerging ethos of welfare capitalism. Worker's compensation was also first introduced in that year and rolled out slowly across states for the next several decades. It was at a NCF meeting in 1909 that Lee Frankel made a presentation about his study of government insurance in Europe. Haley Fiske of Metropolitan Life was in attendance, and shortly thereafter Frankel came to lead Metropolitan's industrial department.[74]

Life insurers also developed a more explicit interest in the health of policyholders and began to develop "life conservation" agendas. This emerged first in the context of the tuberculosis epidemic. Several of the New York firms made efforts to improve treatment. Metropolitan Life, for example, opened up the Bureau of Cooperation to collaborate with others on tuberculosis prevention and unsuccessfully sought permission from New York's supervisor to erect a hospital for policyholders. Ultimately, they were able to create a facility for their own employees. Even some of the fraternal societies constructed "tent cities" for affected members.[75]

Metropolitan Life, more than any other firm, embraced health-related activities. Particularly through its industrial department and ultimately a welfare division led by Frankel, the company began to realize the opportunities for improving the health of members using the tools of public health and social welfare. In the post-Armstrong world, Metropolitan Life occupied a unique place among the Big Five. The volume restrictions did not apply to them, because at the time of the Armstrong laws their sales of ordinary life policies were below the quota. While the Armstrong Committee had discussed problems with industrial insurance, they did not propose new regulations for this line of business.

Some complained that Metropolitan was the "pet" of the Armstrong Committee, even though their chief executive officer was indicted. Escaping relatively unscathed, Metropolitan had an opportunity to grow at the expense of its rivals, which it did, greatly expanding its ordinary life business. Internally, there was a sense of having dodged a bullet, as a company history from 1914 notes: "To sum up, the Metropolitan was given a free hand and the old tontine companies were restricted."[76] Yet the company tempered their pursuit of this opportunity with a recognition that it must behave differently, realizing that, as the New York insurance supervisor noted in his 1914 report, "organized wealth under private management must, if it is going to be allowed to exist at all, assume certain public responsibilities which were not dreamed of under the old philosophies."[77] The hiring of Frankel and the expansion of the life conservation efforts reflected that new awareness.

Metropolitan's objective with regard to the industrial division was to exude corporate responsibility and pre-empt state insurance or other public activities. Under Frankel, industrial insurance developed a highly visible public health and social welfare orientation, with an emphasis on education and disease prevention.[78] The company collaborated with New York City's health department in a "clean-up" campaign in 1913, then encouraged leaders in eleven other cities to undertake similar efforts. They collaborated with settlement houses to arrange for home visits from nurses, provided health education, distributed fly swatters, and created programming for children. The "Health and Happiness League" for boys and girls required members to pledge to commit to sanitary behaviors such as not spitting and trying to kill as many houseflies as possible.[79]

The visiting nurse service began in New York in 1909 and spread to a number of cities by 1913. In that year, Metropolitan Life reported over one million visits, at a cost of $570,000. Visits were limited to cases where there was a "strong possibility of recovery," and the nurse was encouraged to provide general information about sanitation and health behaviors. While the company did not study the impact of the service on mortality and net costs, they were confident in the value of the program, reporting, "Had it not been for the care of the nurse, many patients would not have been restored to health."[80]

Metropolitan Life also engaged in advocacy for public policies and activities that they thought would benefit the health of their policyholders. For example, in St. Louis, they distributed a hundred thousand copies of a pamphlet emphasizing tenants' rights under a new housing law. In 1913, Metropolitan contacted city health officers, offering to help distribute materials to their policyholders for any campaign designed to improve health conditions. They further did not hesitate to encourage their policyholders to vote for policies that the company believed were in their interest, such as authorizing bonds for a municipal tuberculosis sanitarium in Chicago. The company even became involved in a limited way in the construction of housing for wage workers and offered buyers a unique financial instrument that combined the mortgage with a life insurance policy based on the home.[81]

Additionally, Frankel encouraged statisticians and actuaries to conduct analyses of their voluminous policyholder data and publish annual reports on the mortality experience of the "industrial classes," recognizing that their data assets exceeded those collected by vital registration areas in some respects. A publication in 1919 analyzed policyholder data from 1911 and 1916, which represented fifty million life years and 635,000 deaths from a population that was over twelve percent Black, permitting analysis of racial differences in mortality by cause.[82] Arguing with some justification that the study should be seen as a supplement to the census and other government documents, Metropolitan made a new argument for the quasi-public role of the insurance industry: "It is appropriate that the insurance companies should contribute to the advance of medical science and to the public health movement."[83]

For assessment insurance (which largely consisted of fraternal plans but also included other associations that used the assessment method but were not fraternal orders), the peak came in the late nineteenth century, but the decline of this category took a surprisingly long time. In 1895, the amount of insurance in force in assessment plans exceeded that in ordinary insurance, and while this would not occur again, the assessment category basically maintained its size in absolute terms throughout the first several decades of the twentieth century. Yet other forms of insurance grew far more quickly. While the amount of ordinary and industrial insurance in force each nearly tripled between 1910 and 1920, assessment insurance stayed fairly constant at approximately $10 billion.

In 1922, an important milestone was achieved when the amount of industrial insurance in force exceeded the assessment and fraternal category; group insurance in force would surpass assessment and fraternal insurance by 1930. The ascendance of assessment insurance to popularity reflected reputational problems with the old-line companies as well as affordability concerns. As some of the former issues improved due to better regulation and the latter situation improved due to the emergence of other options such as group insurance, the competitive edge of assessment insurance eroded. And while these plans represented an alternative to, if not a refutation of, the commercial model, many ultimately had to adopt the very actuarial methods they critiqued to survive.[84] While this occurred, the story does not end with a convergence into the old-line model. Many fraternal associations maintained the assessment system well into the 1920s. And even those associations and orders that mutualized and adopted legal reserve status maintained a distinct outlook and a deep antipathy toward both regulators and the rest of the industry.

The Mutual Life Underwriters Association, a trade group of assessment plans, considered themselves advocates of "pure protection," rejecting investments, endowments, surrender values, and policy loans and even disapproving somewhat of the "lodge activities" favored by their ostensible brethren, the fraternal associations. This group faulted the Armstrong laws for making it difficult for new assessment plans to form and blamed regulators for not coming to the aid of struggling plans, failing to help "tens of thousands of families who today are unprotected because the insurance they depended on has been destroyed." It was grudgingly acknowledged that the disregard from regulators was at least partially understandable, since "a large number of life associations have been formed and are now trying to continue on inadequate rates." But they nevertheless proudly defended the concept of pure protection ("It takes a noble fellow to sell straight protection"), finding it superior to the expensive investment products sold by the old-line companies, the "tremendous octopus" of industrial insurance, and their somewhat naïve "fraternal brethren" who were slow to recognize that "social features, which used to be a magnet, are now wholly ignored by four fifths of the membership."[85]

'Pure protection' was term insurance, and the association plans represented by the Mutual Life Underwriters Association could see that the old-line companies were increasingly gravitating to this product. One of the ways in which this was happening was through the growing sales of group insurance, which the association correctly viewed as a mortal threat. The 1913 meeting opened with a resolution that the issuance of life insurance without a medical examination "is a menace to the future interests of all life insurance organizations, unfair in principle and dangerous in practice." Group insurance was also deeply threatening to insurance agents, due to the use of salaried brokers, and was initially viewed dimly by state regulators.[86]

There was a discernible streak of paranoia or at least a very strong sense of grievance in the proceedings of the Mutual Life Underwriters Association. They did not view the old-line companies as simply seeking new markets but rather saw their behavior as motivated primarily by a desire to eliminate the association plans. The organization's president, reacting to the encroachment of group insurance, denounced it as "simply a sandbagging confidence game, and we all know the reasons for it. It is a direct drive especially at assessment insurance in all forms. It is one more old-line scheme to wipe us off the slate. Don't think for a moment it is a philanthropic movement on the part of our old-line friends. They are not afflicted that way."[87]

While many assessment plans had become insolvent in the late nineteenth and early twentieth centuries, others had either raised rates or adopted the legal reserve system and become insurance companies. Some, like the Woodmen of the World, which was one of the largest, insisted that "ample and adequate assessment rates are charged," negating the need to become an insurance company. A fair amount of underwriting was involved, requiring a medical exam and a background check by a panel of members. Applicants in hazardous occupations were banned, and the amount of insurance was limited, usually to $1,000. Many plans wouldn't pay claims for indemnities resulting from "intemperance, immoral conduct, or vicious habits."[88] Unlike the "pure protection" advocates, the Woodmen offered annuities and disability payments but not policy loans or surrender value. In 1909 they were comfortable about their financial position, stating that they had profited from the experiences of similar organizations, and that the plan was "completely safeguarded against the disasters so fatal to many of its unfortunate forerunners."[89]

Assessment plans were a constant problem for regulators. While many failed in the late nineteenth century, those that survived did so by raising rates in some fashion. While the most sophisticated of the associations joined together to form the National Fraternal Congress and adopted a set of mortality tables in the manner of commercial actuaries, others continued with the assessment strategy, raising their rates to what they hoped would be sufficient levels. But for many, they were not adequate.[90] As one mid-century assessment noted, by the time problems are identified they are hard to solve: "The hat-passing custom looks absurdly simple; and the dangers that lurk within the device when men undertake it innocently as a long-term contractual proposition came to light only when injuries have been sustained by many participants, and remedies are hard to apply."[91] The unwinding of an assessment plan was a classic version of the "death spiral" scenario, as an aging membership necessitated rate increases, which drove out younger members, necessitating a further need to raise rates, until no members remained.

By 1920, many states had banned assessment plans altogether or limited permissions to plans that were already in business and restricted fraternal plans to those that used the National Fraternal Congress mortality table to set rates. Additionally, many states required that assessment plans indicate their "assessment" status in red ink on the front of the policy.

A legislative ultimatum of sorts had been devised by the National Conference of Insurance Commissioners in the "Mobile bill," a model code named for the location of the conference in which it was developed in 1910. The bill raised the stakes for assessment plans and required a solvency test as a condition of licensure by 1920. In 1915, West Virginia's commissioner Darst spoke optimistically about the process: "The cleansing fires are now at work. . . . Some have already emerged beautifully purified, others unfortunately have been consumed."[92]

By 1918, a variant of the bill had passed in close to forty states. As 1920 approached, regulators feared (correctly) that many fraternal plans were not ready. As one commissioner warned: "Many will, I fear, find themselves as the foolish virgins, without oil and unprepared."[93] And the size of this segment was not inconsequential. In 1920, there were still approximately eleven million members and $10 billion of insurance in force in fraternal and other assessment plans.[94] The National Fraternal Congress, in 1920, acknowledged the pressures created by the new financial requirements and the dwindling interest in ritualistic lodge activities: "The moving picture now receives that interest." Both trends eroded the competitive advantage of fraternal plans, membership in which declined sharply after 1930.[95]

Fraternal plans were an important source of insurance for Blacks, who formed societies in the South and in northern cities. DuBois, in *The Philadelphia Negro* (1899), described high rates of fraternal membership among working males in Philadelphia.[96] These societies experienced the same difficulties as other fraternal plans, and in a quest for more security, a number of Black-owned insurance companies came into existence to sell insurance on an actuarial basis. One of the best known was the North Carolina Mutual Life Insurance Company, which was formed in 1898 by men with prior experience in fraternal plans. Several other similar companies formed in other parts of the country.[97]

A major motivation for Blacks in forming their own insurance organizations was the discrimination they faced in the commercial market. While during Reconstruction commercial industrial companies sold insurance to Blacks and Whites on an equal basis, many began to explicitly discriminate after studies revealed that Black mortality rates were higher. Prudential, which published a number of such studies, explicitly adopted this policy in 1896, and most other companies followed suit.[98] While many states adopted "antidiscrimination" regulations, this referred not to racial discrimination but to the practice of price discrimination to attract new business—that is, rebating. New Jersey was one exception; that state's antidiscrimination statute included the statement "Discrimination against colored persons also prohibited."[99]

By 1916, there was a new life insurance policy issue that crowded out talk of state insurance and the future of assessment plans. With the entry of the United States into World War I, the question of pricing war risk arose once again. During the Civil War, intense competition between firms led them to develop different ad hoc approaches to war risk. A version of this same approach was followed during the Spanish-American War, although the number of policyholders affected was considerably lower. Due to the lengthy peacetime period, many life insurance policies contained no war clause, causing chaos as thousands of young men enlisted in the army. This created an uninsurability problem that challenged the private market.

By now the life insurance industry had become more collaborative, suggesting that a consensus position would need to be found. Companies sought available mortality data from Europe, and the NCIC created a committee to produce a model war risk policy. While there was a general agreement about the structure of such a policy, firms did not reach consensus about how such risk should be priced. Some companies, like Equitable, added a policy rider to exclude war casualties. The Wisconsin Life Fund announced that they would not increase their rates.[100]

Yet even if the companies and state regulators had been able to agree on how to price war risk, the greater market problem concerned how to properly assign it. Soldiers in the Union Army and the Spanish-American War essentially paid for their additional cost of their life insurance, if they had policies. In World War I, this responsibility fell to the federal government. The federal War Risk Insurance Act was originally created in 1914 to protect commercial vessels during wartime, but over time multiple amendments added additional protections. In October 1917, the act was amended to add three important benefits to soldiers: (1) a family allotment to help compensate dependent family members for the absence of a breadwinner, (2) a disability provision that would provide compensation in the event of death or disability and (3) voluntary government life insurance.[101]

The War Risk Insurance Act was designed with a great sensitivity to the prevailing view about Civil War pensions, which were widely believed to have been excessively expanded in 1890 as a political giveaway. These feelings were one of the reasons that old-age pensions had become a third rail in discussions about social insurance.[102] An explanatory address to enlisted men took pains to distinguish the new insurance provisions from pensions, which were "regarded by many as a gratuity."[103]

The War Risk Insurance Act was designed to avoid the future need for war pensions through its three-pronged strategy of family allotments, access to life insurance, and compensation in the event of death or disability. Unlike commercial workmen's compensation, the amount of the disability compensation was based on a "new principle," family need—essentially the number and characteristics of dependents—rather than the wages or prior wages of the affected servicemen, a precursor to some of the design elements in Social Security. The disability provisions also included the coverage of medical treatment and rehabilitation services that would ultimately form the basis of the Veterans Administration. The goal of this comprehensive strategy was to make "supplementary pension legislation for those involved in this war wholly unnecessary."[104]

The life insurance provision of the War Risk Insurance Act was a recognition that the existence of a death and disability benefit did not address the issue of the potential future uninsurability of enlisted men. It was explained to the men that this element of the act was voluntary and should not in any way be considered a handout: "It is not giving you the insurance because it did not take the insurance away from you. It is giving you the insurability because the war did take your insurability away from you. But if you do not want to avail yourself of your now new insurability that is your privilege."[105]

In structuring the benefit, the government considered but rejected the idea of attaching some type of rider to cover war risk to policies in the existing commercial market. In explaining that choice to the men, it was noted that the private companies were ready to be "very fair" had such a plan been adopted. But that approach necessitated the endorsement of a variety of commercial and fraternal policies in an industry that the federal government did not regulate, and while "most of the companies are good and many excellent, the United States is not ready to say that it will back up any company."[106]

The government had another reason to offer the insurance themselves. They wanted to do more than merely cover the current war risk; they deliberately priced the coverage well below "peace rates." They were able to keep their costs low since they had the benefit of recent medical examinations on the soldiers, they did not use sales agents, and as "it seemed only right and proper that the cost of administering it should not be charged up to the men"; administrative costs were counted as general war expenses and not loaded onto premiums. The terms were generous as well, with a maximum coverage amount of $10,000, considerably above the current average policy size, which was approximately $2,000 in ordinary life at the time. And while soldiers were encouraged to take out the lowest-cost term policies while serving, they would be able to convert to a number of other policy forms after the war ended and retain the insurance for life. The hope was to create an offer that was too good to refuse: "This opportunity is so wonderfully attractive that a man must be a fool or crazy and not fit to be in the service if he does not avail himself of it to the utmost of his financial ability."[107]

This was a far more muscular version of the type of "public option" represented by the Wisconsin Life Fund, and although it was offered only to a specific subset of the population, it was similarly motivated by a desire to reduce government exposure to risk. In this case, the risk was a future demand for a service pension. By incentivizing self-protection, the hope was that men would not feel "compelled, as our Civil War veterans felt compelled," to ask for help. "Surely we will all rejoice if, through this insurance opportunity, the heroes of this war will be spared the necessity of asking for service pensions."[108]

War risk insurance was priced twenty-five to thirty percent below commercial rates and contained extremely generous terms regarding conversion to other forms of life insurance in the future. While voluntary, the government had an advertising budget and a semicaptive audience with above-average interest in their possibility of death. As a result, take-up was extremely high. By 1918, ninety-five percent of those eligible had purchased $23 billion worth of insurance, with the average person applying for eighty-five percent of the maximum amount of coverage. By 1920, the Bureau of War Risk Insurance reported over four million policyholders, a sizable slice of the market since about sixteen million ordinary life policyholders were reported by the commercial life insurance industry that year. Given the higher policy values, war risk insurance in force in 1919 exceeded $40 billion, briefly surpassing the ordinary life category.

The life and disability provisions of the War Risk Insurance Act were considered a significant accomplishment by many progressive reformers. The government studied European models and consulted with academics and experts in private industry, including Metropolitan Life's Frankel and former Wisconsin insurance commissioner Herman Ekern, now in private practice. Columbia sociologist Samuel McCune Lindsay described the legislation as a "democratic expression of a new sense of social solidarity and a unity of national purpose."[109]

Yet, as is often the case with ambitious social programs, implementation proved daunting. After the war, the Bureau of War Risk Insurance was faced with significant logistical challenges. During wartime they were able to deduct premium payments from the pay of servicemen and servicewomen, but with rapid de-escalation, collections became extremely difficult. There was a high degree of lapse as soldiers returned to civil society. Many were short on funds, while others may have no longer seen the value of insurance once the elevated risk of the war had passed. However, the government was very eager to retain their military policyholders and offered generous reinstatement terms and additional benefits to sweeten the pot. A number of subsequent amendments liberalized the insurance benefits. Additionally, a "civil relief" amendment was passed in 1919, in which for a short while the government paid commercial premiums on behalf of policyholders who were serving in the military.[110]

There were similar implementation challenges regarding the disability compensation. A major problem was the poor quality of address information. The bureau had temporarily moved into the National History Building of the Smithsonian during the war, as shown in Figure 4.1. With the aid of greatly expanded staff and modern office technology such as the addressograph machine, they attempted to contact soldiers and answer a voluminous amount of correspondence, approximately ten thousand letters a day. In 1920, an advisory panel chaired by Charles Evans Hughes recommended the creation of regional offices and an advertising budget to facilitate communication and retention of insurance. The American Legion and the American Red Cross also assisted with Bureau of War Risk Insurance activities.[111]

Figure 4.1 Clerks at the Bureau of War Risk Insurance. Reproduced by permission of the Smithsonian Institution Archives, #MAH-23905.

Life insurers accepted the federal government's incursion into the life business as an unfortunate necessity, comparable to other war sacrifices like buying liberty bonds and helping the Red Cross. George E. Ide, chief executive officer of the Home Life Company, head of the industry committee appointed by Secretary of Treasury McAdoo, argued that the "menace" of government insurance was greatly exaggerated as long as the government "realizes the necessity" of operating the program on the "basis of credit and debit similar to that which is compulsory in the management of private corporations," that is, with all of the administrative expenses incurred.[112]

That is not what happened, and the potential effect on sales was not lost on anyone. A keynote at the 1918 NCIC meeting exuded sympathy for agents: "When we see the Federal Government going into the life insurance business, our hearts go out to the men who have made a study of protection," but it chalked it up as a justifiable patriotic service and a tribute to the indefatigable spirit of insurance men, who have been the "first to begin and the last to quit" in their support of the war.[113] Insurers were vigilant for signs of activities they considered to be overreaching, particularly evidence that the government was disparaging commercial companies or encouraging enlisted men to drop their existing policies. There was widespread suspicion that there were forces within the government

that sought to exploit the circumstances to permanently expand federal involvement.[114] When George E. Ide publicly criticized the federal effort, an angry letter
from Secretary McAdoo seemed to imply that the federal insurance powers
might be expanded. This sent a chill through the profession. At the 1918 meeting
of the National Association of Insurance Agents, the importance of fighting socialist tendencies was a theme.[115]

By this point, the reformist element in state insurance regulation had all but
evaporated, and the ideological space between commissioners and insurers was
generally very small, making it possible for the Kansas commissioner in 1918 to
sound much like an insurance executive when he referenced global events while
expressing uneasiness about the potential for excessive government intrusion
into business: "Already all sorts of topsy turvy ideas are choking the progress of
certain unfortunate countries, and they will have their echo here and must be
resisted."[116]

As it turns out, the insurance industry need not have worried. The postwar
collapse in war mountinsurance was nothing short of spectacular. By 1920, approximately three-quarters of policyholders had dropped their coverage. The
causes were many, but one factor was surely logistics. The government was not
able to put a system in place to collect premiums. At a congressional hearing in
1920, a representative of the American Legion discussed the possibility of using
postal workers to aid in collection, remarking, "I find that in these large insurance companies they make it a point to keep in touch with the insured."[117] But by
then it was far too late.

There was also evidence that suggested that at least some soldiers
misunderstood the coverage. It was apparently widely thought to protect "life
and limb," and returning soldiers with partial disabilities were surprised and disappointed to find they were not covered. Wounded soldiers encouraged the passage of additional legislation to expand their coverage, with many writing letters
to their congressmen from Walter Reed Hospital describing their plight: "Now
that I am crippled with the loss of a leg I find that my insurance is worthless
to me."[118] The third cause was probably lack of demand. Accounts by soldiers
suggested the government made an extremely hard sell, sometimes closing the
doors of rooms so soldiers could not leave until they signed. Many felt at least
somewhat coerced to buy insurance. With the imminent threat of death past,
motivation to pay premiums on large life insurance policies lagged among this
largely young cohort. Ultimately the Veterans Bureau was created in 1921, which
consolidated the Bureau of War Risk Insurance with other veterans' services.[119]

After the war, anxiety about state-run insurance mounted. The conservative
Los Angeles Times denounced a recent "craze to put the state in the insurance
business," citing multiple examples of state fire, hail, and auto insurance around
the country. Touching on the Wisconsin Life Fund as the sole example of state

life insurance, it was noted that "although the Wisconsin Life Insurance Fund has been in existence for more than twelve years, only 430 persons have availed themselves of the alleged advantages of the plan."[120] In Wisconsin, the state fund narrowly escaped repeal, and legislation that would have permitted more direct marketing of policies was predictably vetoed by Governor Philipp.[121] In language that reflected growing contemporary concerns about radicalism, state insurance was described as a way to "drive the Socialist and Communist wedge into American industry."[122]

By the 1920s, individual life insurance's public moment was over. Life insurance was no longer important to reformers as a potential part of a system of social insurance, due to both the postwar collapse of Progressive reform sentiment in the United States and the early development of several alternative sources of risk management—workmen's compensation and group life insurance. The use of life insurance as an anchor of regional economic development in southern and western states had similarly lost salience as a public issue, although the Robertson Law in Texas would persist until the 1960s. Two small and extremely incremental state experiments with the public or quasi-public administration of life insurance had been irrelevant in terms of enrollment but reflected and contributed to an ongoing discussion, which would continue to unfold, about the proper role of government in insurance. The large and abrupt wartime entry of the federal government, while considered by most to be necessary and justified, stoked anxiety among insurers and state regulators, and while it did not leave a large permanent mark, it demonstrated that the federal government was able to use insurance at scale as a tool of public policy.

The war risk program was probably good for the commercial industry, as it publicized the importance of coverage and normalized the idea of a larger policy amount. In the largely prosperous twenties, the amount of ordinary life insurance in force increased from $33 to nearly $80 billion. The amount of industrial insurance in force increased as well, from about $7 billion in 1920 to more than $18 billion in 1930. Given that the average size of industrial policies was much smaller, approximately $150 compared to roughly $2,000 for ordinary insurance, there were many more industrial policyholders, fifty million in 1920, as compared with sixteen million with ordinary insurance.

Yet fraternal and industrial insurance—the two products that arose in response to the late nineteenth-century crisis in the life insurance market—would essentially disappear as the twentieth century progressed. The fraternal segment stayed very constant at approximately ten billion in force before starting a swift and final descent in the 1930s. One important statistical milestone was in 1922, when the amount of industrial insurance in force surpassed the fraternal and assessment class. In 1930, there was another important inflection point, when the amount of group insurance in force also exceeded the assessment category.

Table 4.1 Life insurance in force in the United States, 1900–1960, millions ($)

	1900	1910	1920	1930	1940	1950	1960
Ordinary	6,124	11,783	32,018	78,576	79,346	149,071	340,268
Group			1,570	9,801	14,938	47,793	175,434
Industrial	1,449	3,125	6,948	17,963	20,866	33,415	39,563
Total	7,573	14,908	40,540	106,413	115,530	234,168	586,448

Institute of Life Insurance, Life Insurance Fact Book, 1961.

By 1950, the amount of group insurance in force exceeded the industrial category and signaled the decline of that line of business. By 1960, themountt of group insurance in force was nearly half the amount of ordinary individual life insurance, as seen in Table 4.1.

Fraternal organizations ultimately disappeared as a specific category of life insurance, yet several successful individual fraternal organizations exist today, such as the Modern Woodmen of America, a "member-owned fraternal financial services organization," which in 2021 had nearly 750,000 members and more than $42 billion of life insurance in force.[123] Former Wisconsin insurance commissioner Herman Ekern in 1920 cofounded a religious version of a fraternal, the Lutheran Brotherhood, which evolved into Thrivent Financial, today a Fortune 500 corporation.

While the reform movement was over, it left some important traces. Largely because of the anti-industry sentiment that powered the Armstrong investigation and other Progressive Era state reform efforts, life insurers were unsuccessful in their pursuit of federal supervision in the early twentieth century. The state system that remained would prove to be fragmented and inconsistent, but the NCIC became more professional and effective during the early twentieth century and developed a process of model legislation. While most states implemented at least some reforms that addressed the most problematic aspects of traditional life insurance, and to a lesser extent assessment insurance, significant variation remained. As a result of economic, cultural, and regulatory differences, the amount of life insurance in force per capita varied significantly by state, with approximately a five-to-one ratio between the highest and lowest state in 1920, as seen in Figure 4.2. Levels were lowest in the southern states, where poverty, racial discrimination, and a regulatory culture more focused on aiding local industry than policyholder protection contributed to significantly lower rates of life insurance coverage.[124]

Reformist tendencies among state insurance commissioners were relatively short-lived and largely gone by the beginning of World War I. By the 1920s, most

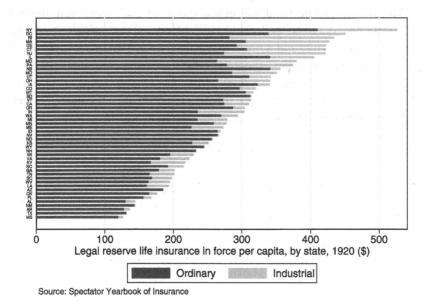

Figure 4.2 Legal reserve life insurance in force per capita, by state, 1920 ($).
Spectator Yearbook of Insurance.

state regulators were friendly with the life insurance industry, especially their
domestic companies; generally distrustful of assessment plans and fraternal
societies; and uninterested in industrial insurance. To varying degrees, the
Big Five successfully reinvented themselves after the Armstrong investigation,
maintaining both their profitability and industry domination, while finding new
markets and ways to stay relevant in discussions of public issues related to health
and social welfare. None did this more effectively than Metropolitan Life.

The growth of group insurance, along with workmen's compensation,
deputized the employer as an important part of the safety net and added to the
fragmented nature of the insurance system, in which the ability to protect one-
self from risk depended on not only income but also state of residence and place
of employment. The inadequacies of industrial insurance as a response to the
affordability problem were well understood, and while it was not a problem that
could be solved with regulation alone, the fact that industrial insurance continued to exist maintained the status quo. The private sector had no incentive to
change, and the few examples of state insurance were not able to increase coverage. A meaningful response would not be forthcoming until the Depression
and the Social Security Act of 1935, and despite that industrial insurance would
persist until it finally became unprofitable in the 1970s.

The Wisconsin Life Fund still exists, and as of 2021 there were upward of twenty-two thousand policyholders.[125] Massachusetts Savings Bank Life Insurance exists as well and is now a national mutual life insurance company.[126] Despite the controversy these programs once caused, the motivation to destroy them never rose to the necessary level, perhaps because their enrollment was so insignificant. Once seen as a radical state incursion into private commerce, their quiet persistence reflects the waning public interest in individual life insurance.

5

Collusion and Its Discontents

Early in the morning of April 18, 1906, Charles Stetson Wheeler Jr. was awakened by a violent earthquake. He was away at school in Belmont, California, about twenty miles south of San Francisco. When his headmaster mentioned that brick structures do not fare well in quakes, he and several classmates set out for their homes in San Francisco, not knowing what they would find. "We must have gone about eight miles when the van of the thousands leaving the city met us. They were principally hobos and riffraff, packing their blankets on their backs. We stopped and anxiously inquired the plight of the city. Some said that the city was burned to the ground, some that the whole town was submerged by a tidal wave, but all agreed in this particular: that it was time to leave the city, for soon there would be nothing left of it."[1]

The San Francisco earthquake lasted less than one minute but in that brief time ignited scores of fires as chimneys fell and gas lines were severed. The fires combined and spread. "We could see mothers wheeling their babies in buggies, limping, dusty, and tired. Men lashed and swore at horses straining at loads of household furnishings. All were in desperate haste. This increased our speed in the opposite direction. We began to see the dense black cloud of smoke hanging above the skyline ahead of us. We almost ran."[2]

A series of setbacks compounded the disaster. The earthquake had broken the main pipes that supplied the city's water. The highly regarded fire chief Dennis Sullivan was fatally injured at the outset when a crumbling chimney struck his head.[3] The absence of his leadership led to the inappropriate deployment of dynamite "by those who were unfamiliar with its use"—in a way that greatly furthered the fire's spread.[4]

Conversations with those leaving San Francisco increased Wheeler's panic: "As we passed over each mile we heard more distressing tales from those leaving. Men called us fools to be going toward the doomed town. Thousands were traveling away; we were the only ones going toward San Francisco."[5]

Jack London, on the scene for Colliers, described how even the wind pattern fed the flames: "Strong winds were blowing upon the doomed city. The heated air rising made an enormous suck. Thus did the fire itself build its own colossal chimney through the atmosphere."[6]

Uncovered. Katherine Hempstead, Oxford University Press. © Oxford University Press 2024.
DOI: 10.1093/oso/9780190094157.003.0005

Finally, Wheeler was able to glimpse San Francisco:

"At last we came to the old Sutro Forest. We toiled up to the summit of the ridge and looked down for the first time upon the city we were raised in. In my mind it was a sight that shall always be vivid. The lower part of the city was a hell-like furnace. Even from that distance we could hear the roar of the flames and the crash of falling beams. We were paralyzed for a moment with the wonder of it. Then we began to run, run hard, down the slope toward the city."[7]

Wheeler Jr's panic intensified as he got closer to home:

> Fear grew stronger and stronger in my heart as I saw that all the chimneys of the houses were littering the streets through which we passed. They were of brick and so was my father's house. As I came within four blocks of the house I looked anxiously over the roofs of other houses for its high chimneys that hitherto had been visible from that point. I could not see them! Then I was sure that it was all over, that my father, mother, and sisters were lost forever.[8]

The fire would prove to be far more damaging than the earthquake. "The earthquake shook down in San Francisco hundreds of thousands of dollars worth of walls and chimneys," wrote London, "but the conflagration that followed burned up hundreds of millions of dollars worth of property."[9] One symbolic victim of the quake was the ornate city hall, built by corrupt political boss Chris Buckley at great expense in the 1890s. This quickly toppled, allowing the chamber of commerce to achieve an aesthetic and political putdown by observing that the earthquake damage "stands as a monument almost entirely to cheap, dishonest and insincerely ostentatious construction," while in "well-built brick buildings it was almost nothing."[10]

The well-built Wheeler house survived: "Then as I reached the curb before the door I never expected to enter again I looked up. The house, though shorn of its chimneys, stood staunch and strong—they were safe. For a second I stood still. Then, like a poor fool, I began to laugh and shout. That was the most joyous home-coming of my life."[11]

Even before the quake, the fire risk in San Francisco was considered high. Just months earlier, the National Board of Fire Underwriters had issued a warning, deeming the congested downtown "unmanageable from a firefighting standpoint" and concluding that the city was overdue: "San Francisco had violated all underwriting traditions and precedents by not burning up; that it has not done so is largely due to the vigilance of the fire department, which cannot be relied upon indefinitely to stave off the inevitable.[12]

The earthquake caused at least fifty separate fires, and the burning lasted for three days, consuming about 3,000 acres, 520 blocks, and 25,000 buildings, about half of which were residences. On April 21, the burning stopped due to a combination of firefighting efforts and natural exhaustion of fuel.[13] Churches, libraries, and banks were burned, as were the three major newspaper buildings and the Pacific Stock Exchange, among many others. More than 3,000 people died. Another 200,000, half the city's population, were homeless and largely without possessions. In the immediate aftermath, survivors slept in tents and in parks and for some time had to do their cooking in the street to avoid starting new fires. President Roosevelt signed the California Relief Resolution on April 19, sending $1 million to the sufferers in San Francisco.

By April 22, $2.5 million had been appropriated. Roosevelt encouraged Americans to contribute to another fund managed by the American Red Cross, and donations came in from across the country. Congress would appropriate more funds for food, water, blankets, tents, and medical supplies, and would also ultimately provide funds to rebuild damaged federal buildings.

The campus of the University of California, Berkeley became a temporary shelter. Others camped at Golden Gate Park. There was an urgent need for food, clothing, and medicine. Warned the *Los Angeles Times*: "Unless supplies are rushed in and arrangements made for their distribution, trouble is feared within a few days. Even men of wealth cannot obtain food with all their money."[14]

The San Francisco earthquake and fire was one of the worst natural disasters in the United States, and the worst metropolitan fire in history.[15] It is a catastrophe on a scale that transcends any specific historical period. Yet it is also an important milestone in the development of the fire insurance industry—a trajectory that had thus far been characterized by persistent conflicts about rates punctuated by conflagrations and insolvencies. While fire insurance was less frequently included in broader Progressive Era conversations about social insurance, there were significant distributional issues in pricing, availability, and claims adjustment, making it a potent public issue. At a time where there was little else in the way of a safety net, fire insurance was a critical lifeline, particularly in the wake of a catastrophe. The scale and complexity of San Francisco challenged fire insurers to an unprecedented degree, while desperate policyholders clamored for relief and an increasingly skeptical national audience evaluated their response.

The total damage was estimated at approximately $350 million, approximately $250 million of which was insured. There were 234 foreign and domestic fire insurers with business in San Francisco, in addition to many foreign reinsurers. Widespread destruction of policyholder and company records compounded the difficulties in claims adjustments. Representatives of firms from all over the country flocked into town to assess the damage, as shown in Figure 5.1, while their home offices waited for the news.

An early hope among insurers that damage from the earthquake would reduce the fire losses was quickly dashed by those on the scene. The "fall of building" clause, common to fire insurance policies at the time, would void coverage if part

Figure 5.1 Adjusters of the San Francisco conflagration in front of the ruins of city hall, July 1906. The 1906 San Francisco Earthquake and Fire Exhibit. Reproduced by permission of the Bancroft Library, University of California, Berkeley.

of the insured property fell due to a cause other than fire.[16] A letter to New York from Insurance Company of North America representative Sheldon Catlin delivered the bad news succinctly: "I find the earthquake damage is comparatively slight in San Francisco, the great loss being occasioned by fire. We can count on very little salvage."[17]

Beginning on April 21, companies met daily to forge a common approach to adjustment, since many risks were covered by multiple firms. A "committee of fifteen" was appointed to jointly adjust claims where six or more firms were involved. Many companies initially sought to discount claims significantly to adjust for earthquake damage. A small number of companies, mostly foreign, had clauses excluding damage from earthquakes, but they were not explicit about whether indirect damage from earthquakes was covered.[18] European reinsurers believed that fires caused by an earthquake should not be covered and urged their direct insurance partners not to settle claims. The arrival of the foreign companies at the scene took some time. In the meantime, the few domestic companies with earthquake exemptions came under fire as policyholders pursued litigation.[19] The president of Williamsburgh City Fire, which had an earthquake clause, responded to heavy pressure from policyholders and city and state officials by saying that "his heart beat strongly for San Francisco, but he was running an insurance company and not a charitable institution and his company would not pay,"[20] and that paying these claims would be an "act of philanthropy" that the company could not, "in fairness to their stockholders, undertake."[21] Ultimately, the state insurance commissioner received a legal opinion from the attorney general that found Williamsburgh to be liable.

The twenty most involved companies met on May 31 and reached the "New York Agreement," which formalized a more liberal approach to coverage. An informal and ostensibly private vote was taken on whether there should be a "horizontal cut" at seventy-five percent or whether the face value of the policy should be paid if the earthquake damage was deemed immaterial. The results of this vote were leaked, and the media excoriated those favoring the cut, quickly dubbed as the "six-bitters" or the "shavers." The pressure led several firms, including the Insurance Company of North America, to quickly shift their allegiance to the camp of the "dollar for dollar" companies.[22]

Policyholder organizations swiftly formed and planned litigation and other actions. Motivated by the necessity of insurance settlements for rebuilding and future investment prospects, state and local officials aided their cause and downplayed the significance of the earthquake. The Board of Realtors referred to the event simply as the "San Francisco fire." The insurance commissioner, E. Myron Wolf, opined that the earthquake damage was immaterial and took an active role on the side of policyholders, as did the mayor and governor.[23] Insurers chafed at the pressure. "Your people are making a great mistake in minimizing the earthquake damage," complained the St. Paul Fire and Marine Insurance Company in a letter to Governor Pardee. "I can understand why this is being done, but it immediately puts the Insurance Companies on the defensive. The whole thing is too serious a matter to justify any unfair methods on either side."[24]

The San Francisco Policy Holders Protective League was formed in June, with the sole goal of obtaining payment in full. A small fee was collected for the purposes of waging a publicity campaign against the "six-bitters." The league pledged to publish the list of "such companies as may be prompt and diligent in adjusting and paying their actual losses in the San Francisco fire, and also such companies as may fail to do so."[25] This strategy was described approvingly by the *San Francisco Call* as a "conservative form of blacklisting." A "roll of honor" listing the dollar-for-dollar companies was ultimately posted in the Ferry Building.[26] California representative Julius Kahn suggested in a speech before the House of Representatives that the list of "six-bitters" be read into the Congressional Record.[27]

The press played a key role in publicizing the dispute. The *Call's* headline thundered the news of the league's formation: "Powerful body is to demand fair treatment," noting that "dishonest companies have an enemy to be feared." The newspapers covered every detail of the controversy, lingering on the "foreign corporations with such impossible sounding names" with their earthquake clauses and mysterious role as reinsurers. Who knew that the friendly local agent selling fire insurance answered to an unknown general agent, who answered to one or more insurance companies, who were themselves subject to reinsurers? And that was not all. There were falsified photographs used by disreputable adjusters and questionable use of a "fallen chimneys" clause by companies seeking to evade paying claims. There was the disgusted agent of a German company, who quit and joined forces with the policyholders. San Francisco's German consul Bopp took a star turn as he tried to pressure his countrymen to pay their claims in San Francisco. There were even allegations of bribery leveled at Commissioner Wolfe. While the fire insurance industry could not be portrayed as dominated by monopolistic "trusts" in the same manner as the railroads, banking, and life insurance, there was more than enough unflattering material to engage the press.

The *Call* ratcheted up the pressure on the six-bitters, covering accounts of various California municipalities and other entities that were dropping their policies with companies that had not paid their San Francisco losses in full. Commissioner Wolfe supplied powerful copy in the form of plaintive letters from nervous policyholders across the country, such as this one from Ohio:

> I am a widow and have my own home. That is about all I have in the world and my little garden supplies me with most of my food. I carry an insurance policy in the _____ Company. I understand that this company has forced widows in San Francisco to take less than half the money due to them. I would go to the poorhouse if my place should burn and my insurance company makes me take half of what was due me. Please let me know the truth of the reports about the _____ Company so I can transfer my policy to a good company.[28]

Well before intense public pressure greatly raised the costs of being a "six-bitter," the benefits of paying claims were recognized by many firms. As early as April 20, the British Atlas Insurance Company was ruminating on how instrumental the Chicago fire had been to the reputation and profitability of companies like Hartford and Aetna, and envisioning a windfall for those who paid claims in full: "We should act with promptness to take the full advantage of the next few weeks, when there will be a re-adjustment of business from bankrupt and weak companies to those of demonstrated strength." From a market share perspective, the catastrophe was seen as a bonanza: "This conflagration will check adverse legislation, it will advance rates, it will reduce competition, it will stimulate demands for insurance." The main challenge was beating the competition: "Meanwhile, our colleagues who are alert and energetic will be striving for the best of the things which we want." Not surprisingly, the Atlas joined the ranks of the "dollar for dollar" companies.[29]

Ultimately, approximately one hundred thousand claims were adjusted, and insurers paid out roughly $180 million—approximately eighty percent of insured losses.[30] Firm performance was mixed. A handful of German and Austrian companies paid nothing and left the U.S. market. A group of large and established companies paid the entire value of their claims, and others fell somewhere in between. About one dozen U.S. companies went bankrupt.

The trade publisher Alfred M. Best Company spent six months at the scene and issued a special report that evaluated the behavior of each company. Since conflagration was a risk for many policyholders, the performance of firms in these extraordinary circumstances was an important benchmark. For this reason, "coupled with the normal American distaste for repudiation of obligations," the audience was national. Best singled out for particular rebuke those firms that "met their creditors with an arbitrary and technical spirit," despite being able to pay their losses. Relying on research that they were (original emphasis) "PREPARED TO SUBSTANTIATE TO THE FULLEST EXTENT," Best warned that those who evaded their responsibility would find that their actions "will not be forgotten by that great insuring public from which their support is drawn."[31] The role that A. M. Best played as an advocate for consumers and as a source of objective information about the financial position and business practices of insurers was a major innovation, particularly at a time when much insurance journalism was unreliable. Both the Baltimore fire of 1903 and the San Francisco earthquake and fire were major opportunities for the young company to demonstrate the value of its reporting to consumers and also to credit markets.[32]

At the 1907 National Convention of Insurance Commissioners (NCIC) meeting, San Francisco was described as a "staggering blow, which swept away the entire underwriting profits of nearly half a century." Yet the assessment was largely positive, as the fire insurance industry had fared better than in prior conflagrations: "Nevertheless, adjustments were made with remarkable promptness and, in the main, with fairness and liberality. While some may be weaker financially than before, they are far stronger in that priceless asset, the merited confidence of the people."[33]

But in reality, that confidence was in short supply. In a caustic editorial, the *Call* observed that two months into the recovery, San Francisco had learned the early lessons of fire insurance and was now "opening the first book of the advanced courses." These hard lessons revealed that "fire insurance isn't the simple business proposition that San Francisco thought it." The rest of the nation would do well to learn from the experience, one that has "brought the whole institution of fire insurance into question."[34] In a November report summarizing the settlement, the chamber of commerce sounded a similar theme, noting that while public pressure caused some companies to pay more than they had originally intended, thousands of mostly poor residents settled their claims quickly for much less than they deserved. While some companies tried to be helpful, others "apparently tried to make as much trouble as possible," helping to feed "a wave of popular indignation." Their report referenced the Armstrong investigation in its wary conclusion: "The lesson that the insured will take most to heart is that insurance will not take care of itself, nor will his broker take care of it for him without some watching. The insurance interests of a business house are immensely important and should be looked after by a trained person. The conflagration has shown, as has the recent life insurance investigation, the need of popular education in insurance."[35]

Fire insurers also came away from San Francisco feeling worse for the experience. Many felt that they had been pressured to overpay. While consumers wanted more coverage to better protect them, underwriters instead wished to standardize earthquake exclusions, feeling that the industry "should not be called upon again to meet such enormous drains on their reserves, where a conflagration arises from a source or hazard not contemplated by them nor the insured, at the time the policy was issued."[36] Even the "dollar for dollar" companies found little cause for celebration. A glum dispatch from the Atlas in August expressed disappointment that the competitive situation turned out to be "not at all parallel" to that which occurred after Boston and Chicago, where market share was gained at the expense of companies that failed. Too many companies had remained solvent, and what's more, since those great conflagrations of the past, "mutual companies have grown strong and vigorous" and competed strongly in many markets. Worst of all, hoped-for rate advances were meeting with "serious opposition in many quarters," a situation that was also explained with a resentful allusion to Armstrong: "The ignorance, selfishness, and narrowmindedness which develop in almost every locality are something astonishing. It is pretty clear that no discrimination is made in the public mind between the fire companies and the life companies."[37]

In the global property and casualty insurance industry, the San Francisco earthquake is known as the world's first "super catastrophe," a term that refers to an event that causes massive damage and a cascade of subsequent losses. Hurricane Katrina is a more recent example of a super catastrophe. The San Francisco earthquake and fire had international impacts on insurance. The enormous transfer of capital to the city to settle claims was one of the events that contributed to the financial Panic of 1907.[38] As direct insurers began to pay their claims, European reinsurers saw that their interpretation of the damages would not prevail. Under the rules of reinsurance, they honored their treaties with direct insurers, but some, such as Swiss Re, took terrible losses and had to withdraw from the U.S. market temporarily. Later, an earthquake commission would standardize the treatment of earthquakes in insurance contracts in multiple languages. Reinsurers would also begin to take a more active role in their contracting with direct insurers. For direct insurers, San Francisco showed the complexity of a modern catastrophe, where "beyond actuarial techniques, issues of causality, legislation, reserves, treaties, politics, organization, past income, current losses, future profits, threats from competitors, and limited cooperation also had to be taken into account."[39]

The federal government has come to play a major role in catastrophes—both ex ante, in prevention and in insurance markets, and ex post, in direct relief and rebuilding. Yet in San Francisco, the federal role was relatively modest. The military was involved in fighting the fire and occupied the city for some time thereafter. Additionally, the federal government provided limited humanitarian aid and rebuilt federal buildings. The House of Representatives Claims Committee heard appeals from San Franciscans seeking reimbursement for property destroyed by federal authorities. Saloon owners in particular sought compensation for alcohol destroyed by the military to prevent fires and mob violence. While state and local policymakers applied pressure to insurance companies and provided temporary relief to those who were displaced, the vast majority of the loss was borne privately, particularly by the poor, many of whom lacked insurance and lost all of their possessions.[40]

San Francisco stands on its own as one of a small handful of historic global catastrophes. Yet it also is a useful milestone in understanding the evolution of the fire insurance industry. There had been a considerable amount of progress since the last epic conflagration, the Great Chicago Fire of 1871. This was seen in the higher degree of solvency, the use of reinsurance, a coordinated approach to claims adjustment, and the longer-term outlook taken by many firms. Yet standards for industry behavior had risen even more. Progressive Era skepticism about corporate behavior made for a watchful national audience, informed by journalists, investigative financial reporting, and organized groups of policyholders. The San Francisco experience elevated the reputation of a subset of firms, but it diminished regard for the industry as a whole. This came at a time when the cost of fire insurance was already a major public issue, and problems with the life insurance industry were on full display.

The San Francisco earthquake and fire occurred at a time when the regulatory climate around fire insurance was in transition. To understand that transition, it is useful to look back to what had previously been the biggest fire in the United States, the Great Chicago Fire, which took place on October 9 and 10 of 1871. This blaze, which may or may not have been started by a kick from a cow, incinerated nearly three and a half square miles (two thousand acres) of the city, burning nearly twenty thousand buildings, and leaving approximately a hundred thousand residents homeless. Approximately half of the property burned was covered by insurance, with insured losses estimated between $90 and $100 million.[41]

About one year later, the Great Boston Fire of 1872 destroyed forty acres in the city's downtown. With losses exceeding $50 million, the rate of insured losses was higher, seventy-five percent, due to the highly commercial concentration of the fire.[42] Out of two hundred companies doing business in Chicago at the time of the fire, sixty-eight were bankrupted by the blaze, and policyholders recovered only forty percent of their covered losses. After the Boston fire, policyholders fared somewhat better and about seventy percent of claims were paid, but thirty-two firms went out of business. Out of four thousand companies, only one thousand survived.[43]

As the nation urbanized, fire became an increasingly important problem for public safety and economic growth. By the time of the Chicago fire, there had already been over four hundred large fires, which had collectively destroyed almost $200 million worth of property in other major cities. As the built environment changed in the nineteenth century, with more dense construction and the increasing use of incendiary materials, fire hazards changed as well. Fire danger was a major threat to urban life, particularly conflagrations that could blaze for days, destroying large residential or commercial areas.

Both firefighting and fire insurance were longstanding activities and had evolved somewhat jointly in many areas from bucket brigades and mutual aid societies. Firemarks, logos of insurers placed on the outside of a building, were a literal symbol of the relationship, indicating for firefighters that the building was insured. Insurers would often reward firefighters for being the first to reach a dwelling. In the early and mid-nineteenth century, fire insurance companies also provided general support for the activities of volunteer firefighters, by purchasing their equipment and paying for the decoration of their engines. In New York, Aetna paid to have Thomas Scully paint the engine-sides of a firefighting company.[44]

As the century wore on, the relationship began to erode as fire insurers were increasingly likely to have a national focus and fire departments began to professionalize in larger cities. Fire insurers expressed interest in fire prevention and often decried "fire waste" in trade publications, yet they lacked a systematic approach. Despite being a long-established business, fire insurance at this time was not technically sophisticated. Risks were evaluated in a fairly informal manner, and the risk and potential cost of conflagrations were particularly hard to estimate. A major business strategy at the time was diversification.[45]

In this climate, fire insurance underwriting would be very profitable for a number of years if there were few fires, but periodic conflagrations exposed the structural problems with the industry.[46] Due to an inadequate scientific basis for underwriting, premiums were largely set by underwriters' instincts and more importantly by market competition. Agents had considerable latitude in pricing and were incentivized to seek new business. There were minimal barriers to entry, and fierce competition between firms resulted in rate wars, which drove premiums below safe levels. When conflagrations occurred, insolvencies often followed in their wake. In the aftermath, survivors raised their premiums, encouraging the entry of other firms, and the continuation of the cycle.

In the late nineteenth century, the fire and life insurance industries differed in some important ways. Fire insurance firms were smaller and geographically more diversified and lacked the need for enormous capital assets, since the time horizon of policies was much shorter. While there were a number of well-established firms, such as Aetna and Hartford, there was no equivalent of the grandeur or market share of New York's "Big Three." Firms worked together, sharing parts of large risks, and trade associations became important early. Unlike life insurance at the time, competition in fire insurance was seen as ruinous. The National Board of Fire Underwriters, formed in New York in 1866 in the wake of a fire in Portland, Maine, became a national voice of the industry and an early advocate of collaborative rate setting.

Compared with life insurance, the demand for fire insurance was better established. While life insurance was still a relatively novel product in the post–Civil War era, the necessity of fire insurance was well understood, and the importance of selling was less important. But despite the fact that fire insurance had more historical longevity than did life insurance, the underwriting had a less scientific basis. While life insurers had access to fairly reliable mortality tables, there was no equivalent source of truth in fire insurance, especially given the rapid changes in the built environment resulting from industrialization.[47]

In both life and fire insurance, business problems in the late nineteenth century involved the role of agents. To achieve geographic diversification, many fire insurers early on adopted a national strategy, which resulted in the development of a system that empowered agents. Unlike in life insurance, fire insurance agencies, like the one shown in Figure 5.2, usually represented multiple companies. Since they had no stake in underwriting, agents were not motivated to avoid bad risk. Fire underwriters in financial trouble resorted to legal technicalities to avoid paying claims. As in the case of life insurance, growth in demand increased agent leverage and commissions, and therefore premiums.

Figure 5.2   Fire insurance agents in San Antonio, Texas, 1890s. Permission granted by Travelers Archives.

Since the mid-1860s the industry had made a concerted effort to deal with the issue of rate wars and cyclical insolvencies. As early as 1819, New York's Salamander Society had promoted cooperative ratemaking, but the effort failed to gain traction. The National Board of Fire Underwriters was established by approximately one hundred firms with the objective of creating an industry pricing strategy. The board essentially sought to replace competition with cooperation between firms, creating more standard practices and wresting control of pricing from the agents.[48] The board advocated the development of uniform rates. Their initial approach was to create two hundred rating boards, supervised by district organizations. By 1869, there was a rating bureau, which divided the nation into six departments, each with paid employees.

At the same time, the board advocated for policies that would prevent fire, such as safer construction, enforcement of building codes, prevention of arson, and better firefighting capabilities. It began a very early effort to associate rating with characteristics of cities such as municipal water supply and the presence of a fire department. Threatened by the prospect of increased state regulation, the board advocated unsuccessfully for federal regulation, creating the legal test that led to the *Paul* decision.[49]

The first attempt to standardize rates was extremely short-lived. Large companies with higher costs dominated the National Board of Fire Underwriters' process, and small firms and mutuals acted on their temptation to undercut rates, cooperating with the board "when it pleased them."[50] The system was perceived as being top-down and was disliked by agents. Meanwhile, demand for fire insurance was growing rapidly in an urbanizing nation. Between 1866 and 1876, the value of insured property nearly doubled from $3.4 to $6.2 billion, and premiums rose from $29 to $65 million.[51] The effort at price control collapsed after a general rate war in 1869.

The wave of insolvencies that accompanied the Chicago and Boston fires gave new urgency to the board's mission. Surviving firms joined the board and cooperated with their rate-setting agenda. By 1874, ninety percent of premiums and ninety-five percent of insurance capital were represented by the board. The recent memory of conflagrations gave them great advantage. The board enforced the uniform rates with enthusiasm, employing staff to sanction violating agents, meanwhile pursuing various agendas related to fire protection and municipal codes. Yet once again, the equilibrium was disrupted. Consumer displeasure with rates that were too high was one factor. The agreement was challenged by the Panic of 1873 and was falling apart by 1875. A main factor was that the board rates were generally thought to be too high. A mostly admiring fifty-year retrospective acknowledged as much: "It was arbitrary in its actions, and it used its power for the increase of profits by reducing commissions and raising rates. The rates became excessive, as was afterward admitted. While the term had not yet become current, the National Board of Fire Underwriters was in fact the first great American trust."[52] Acknowledging defeat, the board in 1876 suspended its efforts to fine agents who violated rate agreements. The aptly made "Committee of Retrenchment" agreed in 1876 to stop national rate setting and devolve the responsibility to local boards. Meanwhile, the national body continued to focus on statistics, fire prevention, combatting arson, and legislation.

In the late 1870s, the board was nearly dormant, with greatly reduced staff and influence. Yet, the concept of rate standardization was by no means abandoned. Part of the board's failure stemmed from the fact that their national system of rate setting had become outdated, and underwriters had become more sophisticated about incorporating local information into rates. The board's "flat rates" emphasized the internal conditions of buildings and did not account for important variation in environmental factors such as the supply of water or the professionalism of the municipal firefighting forces. Local and regional underwriters' associations had begun to develop their own rates, which included more of these features. The use of detailed maps and systematic rating schedules was growing as the empirical basis of fire underwriting improved.[53]

The next attempt at collusion emerged in the 1880s and this time was dominated by state and local boards. Given the failure of the prior effort, a more decentralized approach was taken, using local boards that were composed of agents. Some insurers began to institute early forms of what would come to be called schedule rating, where characteristics of both individual risks and municipalities were considered in the establishment of rates. Local rate setting became established by the 1880s in major cities, and municipal boards rated surrounding communities. Agents worked collaboratively since companies would split risks. There was a great emphasis on diversification and no incentive to compete on price. Rapid economic development in the 1880s increased insurance take-up and the valuation of property. Between 1880 and 1889, insurance coverage rose by an average rate of 4.6 percent a year, increasing 50 percent overall. By 1890, more than half of all property burned in fires was insured. By the 1910s, this figure exceeded 70 percent.[54]

By the late nineteenth century, rate-setting boards were entrenched in many cities. Nevertheless, instability in many markets continued, since barriers to entry were low, and new companies would come in and offer agents higher commissions to undercut board rates.[55] Despite the growing power of the boards, local rate wars persisted into the twentieth century. An 1896 account of a "compact war" in Lexington, Kentucky, provided a sense of its dysfunctional nature. One agent reported he had "instructions to write at any rate. The object in doing so is simply this: all along, ever since the compact war, the agents have been cutting rates, first from one dollar to ninety cents, then to eighty cents, etc., until it became a nuisance. Every effort to have an established rate sustained proved futile. We will, by our action, either make them stand by one rate or kill the business entirely. We will write it for nothing, if necessary."[56] During this period, policyholders were by and large unhappy. Rate wars led to insolvencies and failure to pay claims. Cartels, on the other hand, enforced rates that often seemed too high and differentiated between customers in ways that seemed arbitrary. Many policyholders complained about what they perceived to be discriminatory pricing. This took many forms; large businesses were favored over smaller ones, urban locations over rural, and eastern states over western.

Yet companies generally avoided discussing these issues and tended to emphasize arson, carelessness, and the poor practices of fire departments. A major theme was "fire waste," which was attributed to not only arson but also poor building practices, inadequate firefighting capacity, and general carelessness. An 1895 account in a trade paper of a Maryland fire referred to the "list of wooden Eastern Shore towns with no means of fire extinguishment," noting that since "insurance companies decline risks of this class, the property owners are obliged to be their own insurers, and to suffer accordingly in the event of loss."[57] State and municipal efforts to improve fire prevention and firefighting capacity were unevenly evolved. In a speech before a fire underwriters' association, the nation's only fire marshal (from Massachusetts) confessed to feeling lonesome, "not personally or individually, but as a state fire marshal, I am officially lonesome."[58]

Debates over "valued policy" legislation revealed the poor state of the relationship between fire insurers and their customers. These laws, which were passed by many states beginning in the late nineteenth century, required insurers to pay the entire face value of insured property in the case of a total loss. This represented a response to a practice among insurers to pay only a portion of the policy's face value at a time of the loss, arguing that the property's actual value was less than the face value. Poor policyholders in particular often settled for a fraction of what they were owed, due to their pressing needs for funds and their inability to afford litigation. The widespread downward adjustment of claims after the Great Chicago Fire increased support for valued policy laws.

The popularity of these laws was highest among poor farmers and other low-income consumers. Fire insurers and some of their larger customers argued that valued policy clauses encouraged arson and raised premiums. In their view, they led to "overinsurance" and were thus conducive to moral hazard, which was a major industry concern. When combined with a dishonest agent, the valued policy law created a pathway to fraud, as "a man may insure his house worth only $1500 for $3000, and recover the whole amount."[59] The author of a sympathetic fifty-year anniversary history of the National Board of Fire Underwriters glumly assessed the impact of valued policy laws: "Thus the honest were compelled to pay for the crooked few; things usually work that way."[60]

The first valued policy legislation was passed in Wisconsin in 1874, with the strong support of the agrarian Granger movement. Several years later, Ohio, Missouri, and Texas enacted similar bills, sometimes labeled "Wisconsin laws." Missouri included a slight concession to the industry by creating an exception for cases of willful fraud. By 1915, twenty-two states had passed valued policy laws. Industry-friendly New York was not one of them, due in large part to pressure from the New York Board of Fire Underwriters and the large New York firms. In most states, however, insurers were unable to combat the momentum for valued policy laws. A committee of insurance company presidents presented Georgia's governor with "personal arguments" documenting the difficulty in complying with their proposed measure. But the *Baltimore Underwriter* glumly reported that the political climate was not favorable: "Notwithstanding this the Governor signed the bill and has expressed his approval of other restrictive measures pending."[61] In New Hampshire, fire insurers made good on their threat and withdrew from the state en masse in 1885 in response to its new valued policy law. Yet their bluff was not successful. New Hampshire maintained its law, and farmer and village mutuals began to gain market share. Conceding defeat, the companies relented and filtered back into the state over the next several years.[62]

Fire insurers preferred to keep the focus on fire waste, attributable to poor building practices, inadequate firefighting capacity, and general carelessness. There was a particular interest in arson. With an annual count of four thousand to five thousand arsons per year, wondered the *Baltimore Underwriter*, why was it that only about five hundred "firebugs" were serving time in penal institutions? "When the crime of arson shall be punished with promptness and certainty there will be much less of it."[63] Agents were accused of facilitating arson by deliberately insuring a property for more than it was worth. In extreme cases, organized schemes involved criminals who conspired with policyholders and corrupt insurance adjusters to share in the profits. This account of one famous ring in New York described the modus operandi of the leader, who had been convicted for setting fire to a bakery on East Fourth Street:

> Having gained a man's consent, Schoenholz would do his part without any personal danger. He would get a bladder and fill it with alcohol and benzene, and taking a candle and a match would go to the marked premises with an ordinary bundle under his arm and enter, without the necessity for any sneaking, by means of the key. He would attach the bladder to a gas fixture on the ceiling of the principal room, in which most of the goods had been placed, put the lighted candle on the floor under the bladder and go away; passing some of the other tenants on their way to their homes upstairs, where they would soon find themselves in the panic of a tenement-house fire—their lives jeoparded three for a dollar. . . . In a short time the heat from the candle would cause the contents of the bladder to vaporize and explode, scattering itself and causing a surface burning simultaneously in all parts of the room. The fire would be well under way before any effort could be made to stop it, Schoenholz having locked up the place; Schoenholz's adjuster, who had been notified by him, would be on hand; the loss would be adjusted and the insurance paid; and the conspirators would divide the money, the insured, now enmeshed so that he could not squeal, not getting any the better of the bargain.[64]

After a highly publicized trial, Schoenholz was sentenced to forty-eight years in Sing-Sing.[65]

Some regulators did acknowledge that arson loomed as a problem potentially made worse by valued policy laws. Maine's insurance commissioner reported in 1896 that reducing the cost of fire insurance would require a reduction in fire waste from "incendiary and unknown causes," which were facilitated by policies that permitted insuring properties for more than they were worth.[66] A Massachusetts report similarly made the connection between overinsurance and arson, with the cause of one fire being ascribed to "friction caused by a very small stock of goods rubbing up against a very large insurance policy."[67]

But antipathy toward fire insurers created strong momentum for policies seen as proconsumer.

Dissatisfaction was greatest in rural states, where dislike of the "fire trust" was mixed with sectional resentment of eastern companies. For example, in the 1890s Missouri had two rating bureaus, the local St. Louis Inspection Department and the Fetter Bureau of Kansas City. Both were disliked intensely for seemingly capricious and discriminatory rate increases. When the Fetter Bureau increased rates in Kansas City's packing house district by fifty percent, incensed packers considered forming their own mutual, but in the short run they either paid the increased rates, sought cheaper and potentially less reliable nonbureau coverage, or went without protection.[68] Lamented one Missouri merchant: "In portions of Europe the government conducts the insurance and does it successfully. Why cannot the government protect our property as well as protect our lives?"[69] As unhappiness grew, state regulators were pressured to act. In his 1897 report, Kansas superintendent of insurance Webb McNall appreciatively quoted a newspaper editorial expressing rural antipathy for insurers: "There is no greater, more arbitrary or unscrupulous combine in the country than the old-line fire insurance companies."[70]

The first phase of state attempts to control fire insurance rates took the form of antitrust action. Fire insurers were not monopolies but were perceived as colluding on prices. As a result of the Supreme Court's decision in *Paul v. Virginia* (1869), which had been instigated by the fire industry, insurance was not considered to be interstate commerce and was therefore exempted from new federal antitrust laws such as the Sherman Act. In an attempt to work around this, states began passing laws to try to outlaw collusion among insurers.[71] Ohio adopted the first "anticompact" law in 1885. By 1913, nearly half of states had such laws.[72] Most forbade participation in any type of organization that established rates. Some states, such as Mississippi, sought differential taxation, requiring underwriters that were members of alliances to pay a four percent premium tax versus two percent for others. Arkansas passed an extremely restrictive anticompact law in 1895, which had an "extraterritorial" aspect, in that it prohibited membership in any organization that was involved in rate setting, even if that organization was in another state. Texas followed suit, passing a law that led to the immediate disbanding of the Texas Fire Underwriters' Association.[73]

Yet fire insurers were so eager to avoid uncontrolled competition that they continued to find ways to collude on rates. Seeking to follow the letter but not the spirit of the law, they would disband rating organizations and establish new private rating bureaus or associations that would establish "advisory" rates.[74] For example, after the 1896 passage of Iowa's restrictive Blanchard Anti-Compact Act in 1896, the Fire Underwriters' Alliance disbanded their Field Club and formed the "Fire Underwriters Social Club." They spent a meeting "perfecting" the constitution and bylaws of this new organization: "No mention of insurance is made in them. Only special and state fire insurance agents are eligible, however."[75]

The antitrust strategy was legally challenging. For example, Missouri's antitrust statute, passed in 1891, was designed to be used against the two rating bureaus, but the attorney general's attempt to use it for that purpose failed in court. In 1895, another bill was passed that specifically extended the provisions of the antitrust statute to apply to fire insurance rating bureaus, but bureaus successfully lobbied to exclude cities with more than one hundred thousand residents, namely St. Louis and Kansas City. While this compromise dampened rural resistance, it preserved high rates in the most profitable markets. Rural rates were swiftly reduced, while the *Kansas City Times* lamented the outcome for the cities:

> Thanks to the lawmakers, the insurance combine still has the cities, where the bulk of the business is done and from which the big profits are obtained, by the throat. . . . The history of the fire insurance business in Kansas City has been that rates have constantly been increased. The improvements in the fire service and the city's inspection service have been constant. The class of buildings erected is better every year; in every way the chance of loss is being decreased, and yet, at the same time, the insurance rates have been going up.[76]

Reformist attorney general Edward Coke Crow tried again in 1897 and brought a suit before the Supreme Court charging that the Fetter trust violated provisions the 1895 antitrust act, and the city exemptions were unconstitutional. This action received strong bipartisan support, with newspapers throughout the state editorializing against the trust, which has "systematically plundered" Missourians. Yet once again the industry won the legal battle, as the court found that the rating bureaus were exempted from antitrust law. Amendatory antitrust legislation passed in 1899 explicitly prohibited combinations that set fire insurance premiums. In the aftermath, the two rating organizations dissolved, replaced by two new "advisory bureaus," ostensibly disconnected with any rating associations. While these actions were widely supported, the victory was partial at best. Most understood the advisory bureaus to essentially be the trusts in disguise, and there was episodic frustration with rates throughout the next decade.[77]

In Kansas, the legal course was initially more favorable. The state explicitly included fire insurance companies on their list of businesses to be regulated by its 1889 antitrust law, which was the nation's first. An "advisory" bureau quickly sprang up to replace the prior associations, but Populist commissioner Webb McNall successfully argued that using rating books constituted a restraint of trade. He issued an order that required firms to stop using these books or else risk having their licenses revoked. Yet after McNall left office and the Populists suffered a defeat, a new agency arose and employed many of the same practices, publishing a rate book that was allegedly "advisory" but soon followed by all firms in the state. After some years of indifferent leadership, a reformist attorney general attempted to use antitrust law to break up the trust but this time lost in court in 1907. Kansas ultimately got little relief from its antitrust strategy.[78]

In Texas, efforts to combat the powerful Texas Insurance Club began during the administration of James Stephen Hogg, who also initiated the state's first rail-road commission. A series of escalating antitrust actions beginning in 1891 failed to bring material relief, as the combination of "advisory" boards and legal losses over the period diminished any meaningful outcomes. Even the inclusion of the "extraterritorial" clause from the Arkansas anticompact law failed to have any im-pact, as underwriters signed an affidavit and quickly formed a "solely advisory" organization. Frustration with rates even led to a public protest in the town of Palestine in 1901 and a joint negotiation strategy led by a group of businessmen. But rates remained a problem, and the promise of the antitrust strategy was not realized.[79]

Some states sought to combat the power of the stock companies by aiding the competition, which in most cases consisted of invigorating the "home companies" or local fire mutuals. The importance of helping such companies was presented in stark sectional terms in 1897 by Commissioner McNall of Kansas, who noted an awareness of differential rates across the country and ac-cused eastern companies of subsidizing the New York customers at the expense of western states:

> I will say in this connection, that not only in Kansas, but in other Western states, prices are charged for fire insurance largely in excess of what it costs. To illustrate: In the city of New York insurance is written by companies transacting business in Kansas as low as ten to twenty-five cents upon the one hundred dollars' valuation. It is admitted that this is very much less than it costs to carry the risk, and an additional amount is charged by the same company in the West in order to make up for what they lose in the East. This is the kind of experience Kansas is paying for.

By then, Kansas had experienced disappointment with its anticompact legisla-tion, which had largely failed to prevent collusion on rates by the out-of-state stock companies. McNall criticized his predecessor for revoking the license of a local mutual and made a case for a more protectionist stance: "There is no good reason why responsible home mutual companies cannot be built up, if given a fair chance by the Insurance Department of this state, and thus retain the money at home that is now annually paid to the combine of foreign companies." The alternative was portrayed as subjugation, since legislation had not been successful: "Take away the protection of our home companies, and the combine will advance the rates." Yet, even in these protectionist comments lay an acknowledgment of the risks involved with mutuals and prior bad experience: "There is a large difference between honest home companies, properly and well conducted, and wildcat companies."[80]

Fire insurance mutuals were not new, but they received more attention as dissatisfaction with the cartels grew. Mutuals were smaller, limited geographically, and sometimes restricted to particular kinds of risks or establishments. They were sometimes financially troubled. While fraternal plans in life insurance struggled with inadequate rates resulting from the flawed assessment principle, an additional vulnerability for fire mutuals was the inadequacy of diversification. This was especially a problem in more urban areas, where conflagrations would destroy large portions of towns and sometimes cities.

The importance of mutuals varied geographically. They tended to be more common in rural areas, which were often not covered by rating boards. The Granger movement, with its emphasis on cooperative purchasing and selling arrangements, was conducive to the development of farmers' mutuals in the nineteenth century. The midwestern states, and Wisconsin in particular, had a culture that was more generally supportive of insurance mutuals, reflecting the German and Scandinavian heritage of many residents. An 1878 law amended their original 1859 mutual insurance statute to encourage the development of all kinds of mutuals for specific occupational groups, and many small mutuals arose to provide fire insurance. In 1887 a law was passed to permit fire mutuals for cities and incorporated villages. Many municipalities established these quasi-public mutuals. In 1889 another law authorized church mutuals, and in 1895 these mutuals were allowed to insure religious property outside of Wisconsin and also to take on other risks. In 1903 these mutuals were authorized to cover congregation members' private property.[81]

Even as anticompact and antitrust laws continued to be enacted, by the turn of the century there was also the beginning of a counternarrative that held that preventing companies from sharing information was not only futile but also not in the best interests of the insured. In part this reflected developments in the actuarial side of fire insurance. While to the public the activities of rating bureaus seemed largely a wanton exercise of market power, there was an increasing ability on the part of underwriters to analyze and share information relevant to fire risk.

Starting in the middle of the nineteenth century, some fire insurance companies began to make detailed maps of cities. Over time these maps became more complex, reflecting building characteristics as well as streets and water supplies. Increasingly complex color-coded keys provided a guide to interpretation. Daniel Sanborn, first employed by Aetna, started out making maps of the Boston area. Initially local, the mapping industry consolidated, with the Sanborn Mapping Company the undisputed leader by the early twentieth century. These maps provided insurers with a "common visual language" that required industry cooperation in both their production and consumption. By the early twentieth century, the Sanborn Mapping Company published maps for more than five thousand cities and towns.[82] Figure 5.3 shows fire insurance agents consulting Sanborn Maps.

Fire reporter services, such as *Whipple Fire Reporter* in St. Louis, produced a public record not only of fires, with estimates of losses and a list of companies that had taken positions, but also of fire hazards. The *Whipple Fire Reporter* inspected and reinspected properties, releasing public reports that detailed the presence of hazards and whether they had been removed. These reports created a degree of transparency about fire costs and their drivers. Additionally, the very public delineation of fire hazards created pressure on policyholders to remediate hazards or face the possibility that their claims would be disputed. Reports and maps created a body of common public information that was used collectively and helped to standardize practices.[83] The reporting of the Alfred M. Best

Figure 5.3   Insurance agents using Sanborn maps. Used with permission of the Insurance Library, Boston.

company, which had grown in popularity as the result of the Baltimore fire of 1903 and the San Francisco earthquake and fire of 1906, played an important role in informing consumers about the financial status of fire insurers.[84]

In addition to maps, advancements in schedule rating in the late nineteenth century helped to put the industry on a sounder empirical basis, but this too necessitated cooperation. Schedule rating represented an attempt to quantify the information about various internal and environmental fire hazards in a systematic way. A base rate was increased and/or decreased to reflect various features of the property and the environment. Cities and towns were grouped into classes based on characteristics like the adequacy of their fire departments and water supply. Two rating systems rose to dominance—the older Universal Mercantile system and the Dean Analytic Schedule. By the end of the nineteenth century, approximately half of the states used each.[85]

Schedule rating reflected a significant improvement in the systematic use of information about fire hazards and the fire environment, providing a mechanism through which the industry could apply pressure to property owners and public officials. Schedule rating also served to more tightly connect the industry to the business of fire prevention. In the late decades of the nineteenth century, the National Board of Fire Underwriters began to greatly amplify their fire prevention efforts. They issued recommendations for building codes and safety features of new technology, for example, proposing a national electrical code in 1892. They also began to systematically assess the quality of fire protection and make recommendations about city and town investments in their firefighting agencies. The board helped to create the Underwriters Lab in 1894. Originally developed to supervise electrical safety at the Chicago Exposition, the lab went on to more generally inspect the safety of consumer products and produce standards for fire protective devices.[86]

Yet the exploitation of these new tools necessitated some degree of cooperation between companies. To the fire insurance industry, the associations that the public saw as anticompetitive trusts were essential to sound rating and the avoidance of rate wars that threatened solvency. This critique of antitrust efforts started to soften the ground for a different regulatory structure—some kind of sanctioned cooperation between firms, which would lead to various forms of state regulation of the rate-setting process. This tension between whether it was better to combat or regulate market power anticipated the more general debate between Roosevelt's "New Nationalism" and Wilson's "New Freedom," which would be prominent in the presidential campaign in 1912.

In a speech to regulators in 1898, Alfred Dean, creator of the Dean Analytic Schedule, implored state officials to understand the folly of anticompact laws. Dean created an elaborate analogy between current state laws and "pin the tail on the donkey," a game he described as being "full of amusing absurdities and very suggestive of anti-compact laws." These laws, Dean argued, served to blindfold the companies as to what rates should be, to the detriment of all involved: "As a diversion the mule game is funny, but as business it is and always will be a dismal failure."[87]

Dean described the tension between the public and private aspects of fire insurance, suggesting the only rational choice for government was to allow insurers to share information:

> The fact is that the making of fire rates is a colossal work—a work that transcends the capacity of individual enterprise. Like fire departments, water works, public school systems and Panama Canals, it is an undertaking that can only be accomplished by united effort. If the public won't let the companies cooperate in making rates the public must eventually take charge of the work itself, and from a long and intimate knowledge of the subject I can most devoutly say: God help the public functionary who has to apportion rates among breweries, theatres, churches, schools, dance halls, distilleries and other natural enemies in our social fabric.[88]

Since the nineteenth century fire insurers have attempted self-regulation to protect themselves from the effects of competition. Yet perceptions of collusive behavior leading to high rates and unfavorable claims adjustment practices led to antipathy for the industry, and some state regulators pursued antitrust strategies to reduce insurers' ability to collaborate. However, the fragmented and nonuniform nature of state regulation, along with practical issues in underwriting, undermined attempts at coherent change. The San Francisco earthquake and fire highlighted collaborative insurer practices in an unflattering light but also revealed the potential collective power of policyholders in a massive loss event with major political and economic dimensions. By the early twentieth century, fire insurers were developing a more scientific approach to underwriting and used this as the basis for a new argument that their cooperative practices should be sanctioned by regulators. As the century progressed, the increasingly technical nature of their business gave insurers some leverage over their critics, but persistent concerns about collusion would remain.

6
Little Fires Everywhere

On July 30, 1916, Jersey City's fire department responded to the scene of a massive explosion, when a large shipment of munitions docked at Black Tom Island caught fire. The blast was felt in five states and resulted in a brief episode of mass pandemonium as people woke up in the middle of the night and had no idea what had happened. While there were only a few deaths, there was about $25 million in damages, creating major losses for marine, fire, and plate glass insurers. Ultimately, this incident was judged to be an act of sabotage, and years later Germany made reparation payments to the United States. Like the San Francisco earthquake and fire, the Black Tom Island explosion was a complex event, but this time the causality was reversed. In San Francisco, an earthquake led to a fire, whereas in the Black Tom Island incident, a fire caused an explosion. Since standard fire policies specifically excluded damages caused by explosion, and the "fallen building clause" would also potentially apply, the situation was open for debate.[1]

In a similar process to that which followed the San Francisco earthquake and fire, a committee of insurers met, initially arguing that losses caused by fire should be paid while those caused by explosion should not, and that subrogation should be sought against parties found responsible for the explosion due to their negligence.[2] Yet the group soon acknowledged that it would be very difficult to disentangle losses caused directly by explosion and those caused by fire. They chose to recognize their obligations to their policyholders in a "broad and friendly spirit" and offered a compromise in which they agreed to pay a large share of the losses and gave their policyholders a share of any future recovery against responsible parties. Many policyholders with losses from the Black Tom incident were important commercial customers, so there was a business incentive to settle on good terms. As in the San Francisco incident, some companies used the opportunity to advertise their generous adjustment in advertisements that touted their settlement rate and pointed out the similarity to their behavior after the San Francisco incident.[3]

Though only ten years had passed since the San Francisco earthquake and fire, much had changed in the relationship between fire insurers and their regulators. Insurer conduct in the San Francisco incident, along with the Armstrong hearings, had fed furious attempts to thwart the collusive behaviors of insurers. Yet despite their energetic pursuit by many state reformers, antitrust efforts had

Uncovered. Katherine Hempstead, Oxford University Press. © Oxford University Press 2024.
DOI: 10.1093/oso/9780190094157.003.0006

failed. At the same time, insurers were beginning to adopt new approaches to underwriting, such as schedule rating, which they argued made cooperation a necessity. As this chapter will show, most states ultimately ceded ground and accepted the need for industry collaboration but sought to exert some influence over the rate-setting process.

There was a regional pattern to state response. Midwestern agricultural states were more inclined to attempt to set rates or foster the development of mutuals. Some southern states persisted in fruitless antitrust efforts. Yet most other states would gravitate toward New York's more collegial approach of supervising the rate-setting process. There were no significant efforts at state fire insurance, although some western states became involved in providing crop hail insurance, a unique line where there was significant unmet demand, foreshadowing later federal involvement in crop insurance.

Insurers wanted permission to cooperate yet wished to minimize the level of state involvement, but a Supreme Court decision in 1914 affirmed state regulators' right to set rates, finding that insurance was an industry "affected with the public interest." Few states actually used their powers to effectively control rates, but by linking themselves more closely with the rate-setting process, regulators made themselves more accountable to consumers regarding the affordability of insurance and created a more interdependent relationship with insurers. Model laws created some unity in state response, but the fragmented and nonuniform pattern of state regulation along with the increasingly technical nature of underwriting gave insurers increased leverage, and cartel-like regional rating organizations that set prices and prohibited new entrants became well established. State regulators ultimately found that their control over rate setting was largely illusory.

The onset of World War I created new business opportunities for fire insurers but also caused anxiety. New lines of insurance that included both casualty and property risks disturbed the rigid structure of the business. The growing federal role in war-related insurance activities along with continued state activism caused insurers to worry about the potential for more government involvement in the postwar period, leading them to embrace a version of "Americanism" that implied an absence of government involvement in business.

The San Francisco earthquake and fire accelerated an already intensifying public scrutiny of fire insurance. The fact that some companies couldn't or wouldn't pay all of their losses was troubling, as was the variation in contract terms and the confusing role of reinsurers. The banking and credit industries began financial investigations, due to the importance of fire insurance to the growing mortgage market. The frequency of fires made fire insurance a top-of-mind issue to most people. Newspapers carried regular fire sections, and insurance information was often included in stories about fires.

A jump in premiums after San Francisco invited further attention from regulators and consumers, who were convinced that fire insurance cost too much. The persistence of rate wars created a general disappointment with the status quo and, to many, confirmed the failure of the antitrust approach. There was a general belief that agent commissions were too high, and rates differed arbitrarily for different kinds of consumers. Pre-existing angst about rates was now joined with new worries about reliability, as one newspaper editorial mused: "Everybody, from the mechanic carrying a $100 policy on his handful of furniture to the banker whose interest in fire insurance runs into the millions is asking himself: Is fire insurance on a business basis? Is it sound?"[4]

The necessity of fire insurance to economic life and the interrelatedness of insurance and credit markets led some to wonder whether the government may be a more reliable insurer. New Zealand at the time had state fire insurance, which was essentially a "public option," where the state offered fire insurance along with private companies. New Zealand had lower administrative costs, since it did not use sales agents, and a high degree of reliability, since "a policy underwritten by the Government of New Zealand has all the backing behind it of a Government bond."[5] Government fire insurance in New Zealand operated somewhat like the Wisconsin Life Fund, which would emerge several years later. Franklin Hichorn, a California journalist and a strong advocate for the public ownership of utilities, thought the New Zealand experiment was worth watching: "If it can point a way out of the uncertainties of an institution in which the interests of every other man one passes on the street are directly or indirectly wrapped up, the island government will have earned the gratitude of the business world."[6]

In the context of both the San Francisco fire and the recent Armstrong Committee investigation of the life insurance industry, many states began to consider new approaches to the regulation of fire insurance. As with life insurance, sectional economic and political imperatives drove the pattern of insurance regulation. Hatred for eastern companies was a key motivator in agricultural states, where some regulators began to set fire insurance rates themselves and took steps to bolster domestic mutuals and stock companies. Limited experiments with state insurance took place in some quarters, while in much of the South, antitrust efforts would persist well into the 1920s. In New York, where both confidence in bureaucracy and the desire to cooperate with the insurers were higher, state officials sought a more collaborative role and attempted to regulate the rate-setting process, a strategy that was ultimately adopted by many other states. Regardless of the approach taken, consumer pressure created a new level of accountability for regulators everywhere, which in turn led to an increased state focus on fire prevention and agent behavior.

Insurers sought to turn the regulatory process to their advantage and argued that regulators should accept and protect their need to collectively set rates through bureaus but should otherwise play a minimal role. Individual fire insurance companies were less powerful than the large life insurers, but the disciplined cartel-like behavior of the industry impeded the effectiveness of many reforms. The National Bureau of Fire Underwriters continued to point to the problem of fire waste as the most appropriate focus for state officials.

In 1908, the National Convention of Insurance Commissioners (NCIC) appointed a commission of state regulators to investigate fire insurance expenses. Commissioner Barry of Michigan, in comments that the trade press described as "more than merely suggestive," warned that "unless the fire underwriting expense is reduced companies will have to contend with burdensome and harassing legislation, possibly state insurance."[7] The *Indicator* sounded the alarm: "The natural sequence to investigation of this sort is legislation and this is undesirable from every point of view." The shadow of the Armstrong investigation was apparent. With a reference to the "ill effect of the legislation in New York," the companies were encouraged to "meet this committee halfway and by co-operation endeavor to arrive at a solution of the difficulty before state legislatures solve it for them with ill-advised laws."[8]

Due to the general ineffectiveness of antitrust efforts in preventing excessive fire rates, states turned to new regulatory strategies during the Progressive Era. Some insurance commissioners during this time were reformers and consumer advocates: Herman Ekern in Wisconsin, Charles Barnes and Ike Lewis in Kansas, Thomas B. Love in Texas, Frank Blake and Charles Revelle in Missouri, and William A. Hotchkiss in New York. Two timely examples for state insurance regulators contemplating a more active role were utilities and railroads. Especially in cities, Progressive reformers were devoting substantial energy to the regulation of streetcars, water, gas, and electrical power. Charles Evan Hughes, of Armstrong Committee fame, had successfully regulated utilities in New York City. In Cleveland, Mayor Tom Johnson took on street cars. In rural America, the regulation of railroads was an important model.[9]

While there was frustration with fire insurance rates in every state, the strongest initial responses came from rural states with a Populist tradition, where there was a strong antipathy for eastern corporations and a desire to appeal to farmers. The first state to begin setting fire insurance rates was Kansas in 1909, followed by Texas in 1910 and Missouri in 1911. Kansas superintendent Barnes invoked railroad rate setting to justify the regulation of fire insurance in 1909, and also commented on the failure of past approaches: "We have wasted too much time with anti-trust law." Working with the attorney general, Barnes convinced the legislature to pass the nation's first laws regulating the price of fire insurance. Barnes anticipated controversy but maintained that "the experience will demonstrate it is a solution of the vexatious problem about which the people of the state have been so much concerned in connection with the purchase of fire insurance."[10]

Barnes ordered many rate reductions on commercial and residential property. A major objective was to equalize charges to different kinds of customers, for example, tenant farmers versus owners. To Barnes, the antidiscrimination aspect was critical: "There is one feature of this law which is of greatest importance; that is, the dollar of the poor man buys exactly the same amount of protection against fire that is purchased by the millionaire or the man of wealth."[11]

Ike Lewis, who succeeded Barnes, continued these practices but wished he had more ability to determine what rates should be. Ultimately, Lewis requested an increased staff so that the department could do more rate review, and in this way the passage of rate supervision statutes led to the growth and professionalization of insurance departments around the country.

Insurers strenuously objected, likening state rate regulation to a government takeover. The German-Alliance Insurance Company went so far as to legally challenge the Kansas statute. They argued in part that government should only regulate the prices of goods in businesses that were "impressed with the public interest," such as railroads and telegraphs. Yet the insurance industry had many times claimed that they had a special quasi-public status, particularly when protesting taxes or arguing that they should be permitted to collude. In an important decision, the Supreme Court in *German Alliance Insurance Co. v. Ike Lewis Superintendent of Insurance* sustained the Kansas law in 1914, ruling that insurance was indeed an industry "affected with a public interest," and therefore states could regulate rates.[12]

Several other states followed the Kansas example and began to pursue rate-setting measures in their legislatures. In Texas, a somewhat similar process unfolded. In addition to a strong push for lower and more equal rates from small farmers and businesses, domestic insurers favored rate setting, since they were not able to compete with eastern companies. Support for antitrust had been stronger in Texas than in Kansas, and there was more resistance to the idea that government should be so directly involved in business. Yet the reformist commissioner, Thomas B. Love, pushed strongly for rate setting and was influenced by his conversations with other reform commissioners of the day, such as Barnes of Kansas and Reau Folk of Tennessee. Love established a three-person state insurance board with the power to raise or lower rates filed by companies. One member of the board was designated as the state fire marshal, who would conduct arson investigations and estimate fire loss for the state. By 1916 Texas had expanded their rate-setting methodology by establishing a set of "key rates," which were used to rate towns.[13]

The road to rate setting in Missouri looked quite different. Agents played a leading role in the passage of the Oliver Act, which set rates. Yet poor implementation doomed the effort, and after much controversy, there was a return to a very strict antitrust law, which led many companies to briefly withdraw from the state. There were some calls for state insurance and mutuals, but ultimately the dispute was resolved and firms re-entered. A commission was appointed and in 1915 a new insurance law was passed that established a rate-setting system much like that of Kansas and Texas. As we will see in a future chapter, difficulties in implementing this law would lead to a protracted legal battle that would ultimately make its way to the Supreme Court and have significant implications for the insurance industry.[14]

* * *

While some states tried to set rates, there was little appetite for state provision of fire insurance. One partial exception was crop hail insurance. Hail insurance was an early "side line" for fire insurers, with the first policies sold in 1876 in Wisconsin. Sold exclusively to farmers, hail insurance was initially offered primarily by county mutuals. These mutuals had a quasi-public aspect, since their creation was tied up in agrarian political ideology. The proliferation of farmers' mutuals was popularized by the Grange movement, which encouraged farmers to organize economically as well as socially. Deep-seated hostility toward "old line" stock companies in farm states drove support for economic cooperatives and preference for localism popularized by the Grangers and the Populists. As shown in Figure 6.1, farmers' mutuals depicted rural scenarios in their advertisements that illustrated the benefits of insurance.

In the twentieth century, the Non-Partisan League and other farmers' groups would expand on this theme and develop more expansive cooperative purchasing associations and successfully advocate for state-run enterprise, ranging from grain elevators to insurance, in an attempt to give farmers more power in the marketplace.[15] States became more involved in hail insurance than other lines of insurance due to the political and economic importance of farmers, market problems unique to hail and crop insurance, and the ethos of economic cooperativism that drove the creation of mutuals. Ultimately, state hail insurance proved to be an inadequate mechanism and the federal government would become involved in crop insurance in the 1930s. The private sector continued to play a role, but the business was often unprofitable, and farm mutuals that succeeded grew larger and adopted the underwriting practices of the commercial insurers.

In Iowa, Henry Wallace, known to his readers as "Uncle Henry," was the publisher and editor of *Wallace's Farmer*, an influential agricultural publication from the nineteenth century. Wallace was an early proponent of mutuals,

Figure 6.1 Advertisement for the California Farmer Mutual Fire Insurance Association from the late nineteenth or early twentieth century uses the common insurance advertising practice of visually depicting the consequences of being uninsured in the event of a fire. Library of Congress.

and *Wallace's Farmer* contained an insurance section. Wallace was the father of Henry C. Wallace, who served as secretary of agriculture under President Harding from 1921 to 1924 and the grandfather of Henry A. Wallace, who was secretary of agriculture under President Roosevelt between 1933 and 1940. The earliest farm mutuals operated at the township or county level, but in the late nineteenth century they expanded in terms of both scale and lines of business. In Iowa, the number of mutuals grew from about half a dozen in 1869 to 137 in 1894. The Iowa Mutual Insurance Association, formed in 1880, advocated for legislation to enable statewide mutuals. Initially restricted to life and fire, mutuals were permitted to insure against tornadoes, windstorms, lightning, and hail in 1884.[16]

Hail insurance was sold on field crops, namely wheat and corn, with policies that were in force during the relatively short growing season. A single premium for the season was payable in full for coverage to be in effect. As an insurable event, hail has some desirable properties, since it is exogenous and clearly measurable. However, there were a number of complicating factors that made the early hail business difficult. It was often difficult to assess the extent of damage from hail and to separate the impact of hail from other factors that may have impeded a crop's growth. Crops damaged by hail could often recover. Early policies based the amount of coverage on the market value of the crop, which increased farmers' incentives to overstate hail damage when prices were high, and increased risk for insurers. Fluctuations in market price and other crop conditions impacted volume significantly, so there was an inherent instability to the business. A final factor was that farmers often had cash flow problems and wanted their policies on credit.

Many of the early mutuals struggled due to their small geographical area and inadequate assessments. Some were forced to make partial payments, while others became insolvent. Storm coverage in particular did not lend itself to county mutuals, due to the uneven distribution of risk.

The Iowa Mutual Tornado Cyclone and Windstorm Association (IMT) was established in 1884 and became the first statewide mutual to insure against storms. In the 1890s, former Grange member and schoolteacher Walter Rutledge founded the Farmers Mutual Hail Insurance Association, the first statewide hail insurer. Rutledge was a staunch exponent of agrarian cooperativism and simultaneously published a monthly paper, the *Western Farmers' Institute*, devoted to "making the farm pay." The pages of the *Western Farmers' Institute* advocated economic cooperation as a response to the power of corporations and was motivated by a distrust of "bigness" reflected in this 1894 column: "The American people have done enough by the way of building up institutions to such enormous proportions and influence, that they are able to defy and make slaves of their creators. These companies as well as some other institutions that have been over fostered are now so far beyond the control of the people that the only human agency left to us to protect ourselves from this avarice is co-operation."[17]

While the *Institute* was fairly short lived, the Farmers Mutual Hail Insurance Association persisted. Despite the founder's disdain for bigness, scale proved essential for economic success, as did other standard business practices, such as the use of reinsurance, which commenced in the early twentieth century. A national trade organization was established when Rutledge and Henry Wallace founded the National Association of Mutuals in 1895. Just as many assessment and fraternal life insurance companies adopted actuarial methods, by the early twentieth century, farm mutuals selling property insurance began to practice the same kinds of adjustment and loss prevention practices that stock companies used. By the early 1920s, an estimated twenty-five percent of hail insurance was carried by mutuals, although this was distributed unevenly among farm states. Both the Farmers Mutual and the IMT persist to this day. The Farmers Mutual transitioned from an association to a company in 1941 and started charging fixed premiums rather than assessments.[18] Today Farmers Mutual is a large property and casualty carrier and one of the leading crop insurers in the nation, with more than $2 billion of insurance in force.

Early efforts in hail insurance by stock companies were not successful, and hail business was initially considered undesirable, as in this account from the St. Paul Fire and Marine Insurance Company of Minneapolis: "Nearly all loss adjustments ended in a wrangle, and if this did not make the business unpopular, the Mutual Companies usually closed up when a large district suffered hail losses."[19] Yet after some setbacks, the St. Paul managed to obtain some hail policies that had been used by the German government and adopted them for use in the United States.

The German approach was to provide less coverage and to calibrate the amount of coverage to the farmer's investment in growing the crop rather than the market price of the crop, with a monetary limit per acre. These policies also required the farmer to pay the first ten percent of any loss, in an early form of coinsurance. The St. Paul tried this type of policy first in Wisconsin and Minnesota in 1883 and then in Kansas, Nebraska, and the Dakotas in 1884. They became the first stock company to make a profit selling hail insurance on growing crops, and other companies soon entered. For example, Continental left the hail market in 1887 after heavy losses but re-entered in 1892.[20] Nevertheless, the business did not seem particularly lucrative. St. Paul president Bigelow described the line almost as a public service in 1900: "We have pursued the crop-hail business for many years with indifferent success and will probably continue it. Farmers need the insurance very much, and we are willing to assume the responsibility where we can be of so much benefit to them."[21]

Hail insurance was a volatile line of business. It was only sold during the growing season, so farmers whose crops had failed for other reasons did not have the incentive to buy. Demand for insurance also fell when market prices were low. Companies attempted with mixed success to require that premiums be paid in full.[22]

Adjustments were always a challenging negotiation with farmers. In the very earliest days, in an attempt to create some neutrality, policyholders were asked to choose neighbors that did not have hail insurance to assess their damage. Early adjusters engaged in a process that was described more as "horse-trading" than adjusting, in which they might "quote from the scriptures when that seemed desirable" or "swap dirty stories and drink corn liquor."[23] Later, the "hoop method" was considered to be a major advance. This was an attempt to randomly sample hail damage by throwing a wire circle, or sometimes the straw hats often worn by adjusters, into the field. Adjusters would then measure the extent of damage by calculating the percentage of stalks within the circle that were damaged. As in the case of fire insurance, companies formed underwriting associations to share information and jointly set rates as early as 1916. Companies started to hold "adjusting schools" in the 1920s to develop more standard approaches, although the hoop method remained common until the 1940s.[24]

The strenuous attempt to avoid competition that typified fire insurance underwriting was also evident in hail insurance. An unusual poem written by Walter Rutledge of the Farmers Mutual puts this business practice into verse:

> The word co-operation
> is one of mighty worth.
> And brings peace and contentment to
> The people of the earth.
>
> At the hail adjusters' meeting
> It pervaded all the place
> And plainly showed its presence
> On every happy face.
>
> Competitor met competitor
> With a warm and welcome thrill
> And recognized with pleasure
> The beginning of good will.
>
> The object of that meeting
> Was to change a foe to friend
> For men can work in harmony
> If all try to meet that end.[25]

Successful mutuals adopted the same practices that the stock companies used. For example, in the early twentieth century the Farmers Mutual started to use the same types of policies earlier introduced by the St. Paul.[26] Advertising was similar as well. The St. Paul Mutual Hail and Cyclone Insurance Company reported its size and investments much like a stock company in a 1914 brochure filled with testimonials from satisfied policyholders. They sought to differentiate themselves from the many failed mutuals: "The mutual insurance graveyard is a large one ... like a weak colt they stood up and nursed awhile, then passed quietly away. But we're 'Live Ones.'" Yet they nevertheless embraced what they claimed was positive about mutualism, describing themselves as a "MUTUAL and CO-OPERATIVE organization" where "everyone chips in his mite" in a business that was a "family game, not a skin game."[27]

A few states began to sell hail insurance in the early twentieth century, and Montana still sells hail insurance. Though mutuals and stock companies had become fairly successful in the business, state involvement reflected an unmet demand for insurance that persisted in some areas. As in fire insurance, stock companies limited their exposure by restricting the number of policies they would sell in each geographical area through use of detailed township maps. They also used a zone system and charged higher rates in areas considered to be at greater risk. County mutuals were not well suited to storm coverage, so where statewide mutuals were lacking, state insurance functioned to pool risk over a broader geographical area. The practice of state hail insurance may also have been imported from Europe, since Germany and France had compulsory hail insurance dating from the eighteenth century.[28] State hail insurance in the late nineteenth and early twentieth centuries functioned as a "public option," which existed along with private coverage offered by mutual and joint-stock companies.

North Dakota established voluntary state hail insurance in 1911. The county auditor collected assessments from participating farmers and the state paid losses based on a fixed value per crop. Unlike private insurance, the state paid on a pro rata basis, so losses were not always paid in full. Everyone was charged the same assessment rate, while the stock companies used different zones based on hail risk. The incomplete payment was unpopular, and the number of policies dwindled to less than five hundred in 1918. As early as 1914, North Dakota's insurance commissioner could see the writing on the wall:

> There is now general recognition of the fact that the present system of State hail insurance, which is simply mutual insurance with the Commissioner of Insurance as general manager without pay, is a pretty thorough-going failure. It will never be anything else, no matter how much or how long legislatures tinker with it. Experience has demonstrated beyond cavil that men will not solicit their own insurance; that the state cannot successfully compete with privately owned and managed enterprises; that every undertaking of that nature has been fraught with disappointment and ultimate failure. I am speaking of state managed schemes in which membership is voluntary. Compulsory insurance is another matter.[29]

North Dakota's Non-Partisan League ascended to power in 1918, when they scored a trifecta and controlled the governorship and both houses of the legislature. The league advocated for economic cooperation to oppose monopoly, yet they strongly favored government participation in the marketplace. The leaguers promoted a number of state enterprises, including a grain elevator and a bank. North Dakota also sought to insure its own buildings, as did Minnesota and Wisconsin, and implemented state-run workers' compensation. League ideas spread to neighboring states such as South Dakota, Minnesota, and Idaho, and to a limited extent as far as Texas, but they never achieved nearly the success elsewhere that they briefly enjoyed in North Dakota.

Advocacy for a more expansive role of government in the economy made the league vulnerable to charges of radicalism, and while admired by intellectuals like Sinclair Lewis and Upton Sinclair, they were viewed with suspicion by Uncle Henry and more mainstream rural advocates of mutual associations and organizations like the Farm Bureau. Leaguers were accused of disloyalty during World War I and sometimes attacked by angry mobs and even tarred and feathered and denounced as "rural Bolsheviks." Yet as insurance commissioner S. A. Olness argued, they were misunderstood. As he saw it, the league's agenda was simply to harness the power of government to give farmers a leg up in the marketplace: "Why call us Leaguers Socialists, Bolsheviks, free lovers and all such rot, when we simply ask for enough publicly owned resources and enterprises to make ... profiteering and the creation of private monopoly impossible?"[30]

The league implemented a compulsory hail insurance system modeled on a Canadian plan, which tried to solve the problem of inadequate payment by passing a constitutional amendment to permit an assessment on acreage. They levied a tax high enough to create a fund with which to pay claims and also provide for a surplus. Though described as compulsory, farmers were in fact able to opt out. This state system interacted awkwardly with private insurers, who didn't want to provide additional coverage on top of the state insurance, due to differences in loss adjustment practices. The state used county officials to make adjustments, and, given their alleged "fondness for the farmers," stock companies assumed their loss adjustments would be very liberal. Instead, the commercial industry only sold hail insurance to farmers who had opted out of the state system.[31]

This system soon confronted the problem of adverse selection, since areas with different risk were being charged the same premium. In 1923 Commissioner Olness argued that "this condition must be met by an adjustment of rates if we would retain the patronage and goodwill of the farmers of those sections where the average rate for the state, hitherto charged, was obviously too high." A zone system was adopted in 1925, but it failed to fully adjust for differential risk, and participation from farmers in the lower-risk eastern counties began to erode. The agricultural depression also contributed to the undoing of the state system, as farmers became increasingly delinquent on their acreage taxes. The result was that "the Hail Fund had to furnish free insurance—being unable to collect premiums except when loss occurred—year after year, resulting in hundreds of thousands of dollars of loss to the fund."[32] In an attempt to save the business, the state switched back to a voluntary system in 1932, available only to those who were not delinquent on taxes and could pay their assessment. But demand dwindled during the drought and depression.

The hail insurance business grew as crop prices rose during the "golden age of agriculture" in the early twentieth century. A particularly strong year was 1919, when wheat prices were extremely high.[33] The St. Paul alone had $19 million of hail insurance in force that year. But this was the end of the golden age; the 1920s saw the beginning of a severe and prolonged agricultural depression, as prices declined significantly, and the supply of agricultural commodities exceeded demand. Economic pressures were reflected in growing adjustment problems in hail insurance, where farmers sometimes tried to collect on their hail policy for a wheat crop that had been damaged by rust. One underwriter commented on their desperation, noting that "sometimes the only thing between a farmer and starvation was an insurance policy." The resistance to paying cash for premiums rose as the agricultural depression deepened. A 1922 industry update reported that "Conditions of the farmers are now not good. . . . [I]t is found quite impossible to obtain cash premiums from them."[34]

Wisconsin experimented with state fire insurance, although unlike the Wisconsin Life Fund, where the state sold life insurance to consumers, the state fire insurance fund was only for state, county, and municipal property. The development of the state fund grew less out of the hatred of the stock companies and more out of the state's longstanding tradition of insurance mutuals. During the nineteenth century Wisconsin had passed laws permitting county and village boards of supervisors to insure public buildings. A similar authority was extended to the state in 1903 during the LaFollette administration, making the state a self-insurer for its own property. This came in reaction to the perception that Wisconsin state government was being charged excessive rates by commercial insurance companies. Shortly thereafter, a fire in the capitol depleted the fund and required the state to draw on the treasury for approximately $80,000, creating some early criticism of state insurance.[35] But nevertheless, in 1911 the law was expanded to allow the state to insure the property of counties and municipalities.

The debate over state fire insurance became highly partisan during the administration of conservative Governor Phillipp, who, along with his appointee, Insurance Commissioner Cleary, made their disapproval of state insurance clear,[36] a position that Senator LaFollette claimed reflected the influence of the insurance industry.[37] The Phillipp administration sought to unwind both the state fire and life funds.[38]

The burning of the Normal School in Oshkosh in 1915 caused another furor.[39] The fact that the state insurance fund had to draw from the general treasury caused widespread disapproval. "What kind of fire insurance game are the people of this state permitting themselves to be buncoed with?" asked the *Wassau Daily Herald*.[40] The *Chicago Tribune* noted this indebtedness as well, arguing that while state insurance may appeal to "a certain brand of 'uplifters' who specialize in baiting the soulless corporations," the idea of state insurance had been experimented with for thirteen years and had been shown to be a failure, since the fund had allegedly been "in debt" since the burning of the capitol building.[41] Despite these criticisms, state fire insurance in Wisconsin persisted and ultimately became more popular. In 1917 the state began to reinsure, and in the 1930s the fund was expanded to cover all state risks.[42]

In southern states, the challenges for state regulators were greater due to a very powerful multistate rating association, the South-Eastern Underwriters Association (SEUA). This group comprised representatives of seventy-five companies and fixed rates in Virginia, North and South Carolina, Mississippi, Alabama, Florida, and Georgia. They were notoriously secretive and arbitrary in their business practices. Commissioner Young of North Carolina described how a legislative committee attempted to learn from the association how rates were made "but could get no very clear idea nor definite information." The lack of forthcomingness, evidence of arbitrary penalties for defects, and discrimination between types of risk led the committee to call for more state control, concluding that "the system of rate making imposed upon North Carolina is old and not modern, it lacks much of the elasticity of other systems, and the basis rate is comparatively and proportionately, on some classes of property, too high."[43]

In some southern states, support for antitrust strategies was tied up in antinorthern political rhetoric designed to appeal to small farmers. The *Weekly Underwriter* decried how in Mississippi, the "demagogic resort of stirring up among the poor and ignorant a hatred of organized wealth is injuring the good name of the state, crippling her finances, and putting evil men in her high offices."[44] James K. Vardaman and Theodore Bilbo were two Mississippi politicians who combined Progressive policies with virulent racism; both incorporated antibusiness rhetoric into their political appeal. An unsuccessful drive for state insurance in Tennessee was driven by hatred of eastern companies.[45]

Blacks were doubly disadvantaged as policyholders because they largely lived in the South, subject to the pricing power of the SEUA cartel, and additionally were discriminated against by companies and the courts, making them more likely to pay excessive rates and have difficulty prevailing in disputes about claims. The *Insurance Field* speculated in 1907 that "the negro must be careful of his property" because of fears he would "not have good standing in the courts if it were possible to question the cause of the fire or the fairness of the claim."[46] Members of Black fraternal orders felt the need for a fire insurance company exclusively for their members. For example, in 1910 a fraternal order member in Mississippi described the problem facing "the negro who depends upon the fire insurance companies solely controlled by whites" and called for the establishment of a Black-owned company: "As fast as the Southern Negro gets his property out of debt there seems to be a move to dispossess him of his insurance protection."[47] Racial violence in the postwar period, most notably the Tulsa massacre of 1921, may have increased interest among Blacks in having better in-surance protection. A few Black-owned fire insurance companies were formed, including the Bankers Fire Insurance Company, which was founded in 1920 in Durham with capital coming from the Black-owned North Carolina Mutual.[48] In 1921, the Mutual Fire Insurance Association was created in Arkansas.[49]

While southern and western states approached fire insurance rate regulation through a combination of tactics including rate setting, promoting mutuals, and antitrust, New York developed an alternative strategy of supervising the rate-setting process. The state had a more competitive fire insurance market than many other states, due in part to the concentration of industry in the area. While some of the antitrust issues that were popular nationally were raised during the 1890s, the persistence of competition and rate wars was a more common pattern.

In 1910, the New York legislature began a second insurance investigation by convening the Merritt Committee to investigate the fire insurance industry. It was initially motivated by Governor Charles Evans Hughes' desire to expose graft and corruption stemming from an elaborate set of payments from stock companies to politicians, revelations that, Hughes said, "have caused every cit-izen to tingle with shame and indignation." Most of the bribes related to valued policy and anticompact legislation. Complaints of "blacklisting" or refusing to write insurance for customers with a prior loss or in a high-risk area and concerns about claims adjustment practices were also part of the committee's focus.[50]

Despite these scandals, there were overall far fewer fireworks than the Armstrong investigation, and unlike that previous oversight investigation where the companies were constantly on the defensive, in the Merritt Committee in-vestigation, the discussion of rating issues was quite favorable to the companies. For one thing, the analysis of company financial statements led the Merritt Committee to conclude that profit rates in fire insurance were not particularly high. Companies were also able to convincingly make the case that compe-tition created instability and that regulated collusion was necessary for stable pricing. Despite the existence of rating bureaus, companies argued that it was still too easy for other firms to enter and undercut the board rates. The Merritt Committee accepted the industry view that competition was not the solution to the industry's problems and that the antitrust approach was not effective. They also accepted the argument that firms should be permitted to share data and col-lectively set rates through rating bureaus, with oversight from state regulators, to ensure that these rates were adequate but not excessive and not discriminatory.[51] The technical nature of the fire insurance rating issues and power of the insur-ance industry in New York resulted in an outcome of the investigation that was quite favorable to the insurers.[52]

In 1911 New York passed legislation that essentially sanctioned a process of supervised collusion, in which rate bureaus set rates and filed them with the superintendent of insurance. State review was designed to prevent rates from being excessive or discriminatory, ensuring that companies charged the same rates to the same types of property. So while New York did not opt to set rates, the state supervised the rating associations. A very important outcome of the Merritt Committee's hearings was the initiation of a data submission process, whereby firms were required to submit standardized financial data on premiums and losses. Small farm mutuals were also subjected to solvency standards and required to follow actuarial methods, a requirement that was helpful to the stock companies. So while agricultural states were taking steps to support the formation of mutuals, New York took steps to make the success of mutuals more difficult. As was the case with the Armstrong laws, New York fire insurance rating laws had national influence, and many other states would ultimately pass similar legislation.[53]

Wisconsin also adopted an approach to fire insurance regulation that supervised the rate-setting process. The state had a unique insurance environment due to both a strong Progressive reform environment and a significant presence of cooperatively owned fire insurance mutuals in many municipalities. Members of mutuals were generally satisfied with coverage. Yet those who depended on stock companies complained of excessive rates and discrimination. Wisconsin's insurance commissioner Herman Ekern convened the Fire Insurance Investigating Committee in 1912, which held fourteen weeks of hearings and concluded that antitrust methods had failed. The committee called for a system of state rate control, similar to that developed in New York, based on the concept of fire insurance as a public utility. Insurers could participate in a common inspection bureau that would be supervised by the insurance department. Board rates were required to be used. Wisconsin also called for increased regulation of the conduct and qualifications of agents.[54] Insurers lobbied hard against these changes, but finally, in 1917, a fairly robust system of rate review was passed in Wisconsin. Under the law, the commissioner could order a change in rates after establishing good cause.[55]

As states developed different approaches to fire insurance rates, a certain amount of interstate friction emerged. The San Francisco earthquake and fire had demonstrated that fire insurance was a national business, where rates everywhere needed to reflect some provision for conflagrations that could occur anywhere. Stable pricing required not only local but also interstate cooperation, and aggressive state rate-setting efforts could be problematic. Scheduled rating developer Alfred Dean noted the difficulty in 1911: "The citizen of Iowa or Missouri failed to see why he should contribute toward the Baltimore fire of 1904 or the San Francisco fire of 1906, not recognizing that his proportionate contribution was a mathematical application of the law of distribution." More frequent collection and dissemination of state-specific data was making it possible for regulators to see how underwriting loss varied geographically and how states that suppressed rates excessively were essentially free riding on other states. Companies that felt limited by the political climate in some states often resorted to making up their losses elsewhere, rather than face a "storm of protest which would be very shortly followed by drastic legislation."[56]

Some regulators pondered whether they should refuse to license companies operating in the low-rate states until "proper conditions were secured."[57] The president's address at the 1912 commissioners' meeting noted that state involvement in rate making created political pressure to reduce rates below sustainable levels, which was problematic because "all states should pay a ratable share of the fire losses of the whole country."[58]

By the NCIC meeting in 1914, there was evidence of a "marked unanimity" regarding the "value and utility of ratemaking bureaus" and the abandonment of the antitrust approach. Regulators had largely accepted the industry view that problems with the business stemmed from unrestricted competition coupled with conflagrations. Commissioners made liberal use of the utility metaphor in explaining their heightened regulatory stance, as in this report from Illinois, which "adopted the theory that the fire insurance rate is a tax" and would be treated as such: "It has come to be generally conceded that fire indemnity is not merchandise to be bought and sold in the open market, as flour or lumber, subject to the exigencies of trade and competition, but a public service, and as such subject to proper regulation, and at the same time that it is entitled to reasonable protection." Illinois regulators vigorously embraced their responsibility and made it clear that everything was on the table, at least in theory: "The State, in the final analysis, has and should have the right to say by what agencies its economic necessities are to be served, and if it should be discovered that some variety of the insurance business is not performing its proper function, why should it not either be reformed or eliminated?" California attorney general John Stetson in a welcoming address to the 1915 NCIC similarly alluded to "that legislation which treats insurance companies as quasi-public utilities," observing that the "general drift of economic life" was trending toward "recognizing the consumer's right to participate in the control of that which his money maintains," and maintaining that this movement constituted "an extension of democracy."[59]

The NCIC created four model laws that were based on the New York fire laws, and a number of other states adopted them.[60] These model laws sought to regulate bureaus rather than directly regulating rates.[61] The increased state role created the need for more data and expertise. The National Board of Fire Underwriters created an actuarial bureau in 1914, which was supported by the NCIC. This helped to advance the development of actuarial science in fire insurance and also increased the professional capacity of state insurance departments. By 1914 more than a dozen states had passed antidiscrimination laws and laws providing for the supervision of rate-making bureaus. By 1920, almost thirty states were regulating rates or supervising rate making in some fashion.[62]

As state involvement in rate supervision grew, so did regulators' awareness of their own accountability for the cost of fire insurance, knowing that "so long as the public have reason to believe—and do believe—that they are not obtaining the benefits and service for which they pay, there will be dissatisfaction and strife."[63] Regulators began to focus more on the drivers of fire insurance costs and how they could be reduced. The fire insurance industry had always emphasized fire waste and moral hazard in their trade publications and communications with legislators, and now emphasized the role that schedule rating played in incentivizing better behavior in the absence of stronger building codes and other laws. At their 1916 convening, state regulators acknowledged their growing interdependency with fire insurers and the quasi-public function of schedule rating, which "takes the place of missing cogs in our governmental machinery." The perennial unfavorable comparison to Europe now focused on the regulatory void in the United States in the area of fire prevention:

> In Europe schedules and rate making are not even discussed outside the insurance fraternity. This is for the reason that rates are so low that they are negligible; and the reason their rates are low is because their losses are small. The reason their losses are so small is because they have legislated against fires instead of legislating against fire insurance companies. . . . [I]nstead of dealing with fundamentals, we experiment with legislation that operates not at all upon the cause, but only upon the manner of distributing an appalling waste. Their laws fix the doctrine of personal responsibility, and we pass valued policy laws which encourage arson and reward the dishonest at the expense of the honest. . . . Our fire waste is largely a matter of mental attitude.[64]

Given their closer involvement with the rate-setting process, state insurance departments came to feel more responsible for fire prevention. Arson was still a significant problem in the early twentieth century, and some state regulators had long had their misgivings about the valued policy law, which required insurers to pay the full value of the policy in the event of a loss. Wisconsin commissioner Fricke had opined back in 1896 that it was "an indisputable fact that the valued policy law has raised the rate and increased the number of fires in all states in which such a law has been enacted. Of no benefit to the honest man, it invites carelessness and becomes a tempter to the dishonest." Governor Altgeld of Illinois made a similar observation and went on to note that while "fire insurance companies are not blameless and have invited much of the opposition," the legislation had proven to be "a detriment rather than a help to our people."[65]

Wisconsin repealed its valued policy law in 1915. In 1916, the Texas State Fire Insurance Commission, which sets fire rates, similarly recommended the repeal of the valued policy law and a related "anti-technicality act" (which prohibited the pleading of technicalities by insurance companies), arguing that the law "places a premium on incendiarism and provides no benefits for the honest insurer."[66] More states appointed fire marshals and had them work with their insurance departments. In Texas, the state fire marshal was part of the three-person commission that set rates and reported annually on fire loss.

As their own sense of accountability increased, regulators focused on agents. Agents were seen as sometimes complicit in arson but more generally indifferent to poor risk and overinsurance. In Portland, which in 1916 was reportedly "in the clutches of the greatest arson gang that ever existed on the Pacific Coast," a sting investigation targeted fire insurance agents who wrote policies for large amounts without inspecting properties. More of a "lashing with a wet noodle" than the prelude to a criminal proceeding, the commissioner's letter to agents reveals both a growing sense of responsibility to the public and the minimal level of control over agents at the time:

> Please do not go around now with a chip upon your shoulder and show that you were a poor loser because you were caught in the recent trap. You will probably recall that Fire Marshal Stevens openly stated that he could purchase insurance from some agents—any amount he wanted—without being questioned. These statements were commented upon, and resentful remarks were made. Then prominent citizens made inquiry of the department why a license should be issued to such a person, and I answered by stating that if the situation was as reported I would be justified in recalling the license. Fire Marshal Stevens has certainly placed sufficient information before me to justify the department in asking for the return of the licenses of certain agents, and right here, for the benefit of several agents, let me say that this can be done.[67]

The fact that agent compensation was directly related to the size of premiums created perverse incentives. The agent was described as a "juggler of bad risks, tossing them about from one company to the other, to the piping of the special agents, until fire ends the game by making some company 'it.'"[68] The commissioner of Texas argued in 1914 that "this character of underwriting" led to $3 million of the $8 million in annual fire losses in Texas and joined others in advocating for a different payment arrangement—"contingent commission"—where agent pay would be related to company profitability. The NCIC passed a resolution in 1914 endorsing a different payment mechanism "that gives the agent a financial interest in the loss experience of the business written by him," referencing the use of profit sharing by the Ford Motor Company as a similar concept.[69]

In his NCIC presidential address, West Virginia commissioner Darst spoke approvingly of the Armstrong reforms as a useful model where both the companies and the public benefited: The whole subject is one in which the public has a legitimate interest.... Is not the case of life insurance in point? These companies had increased their expenses, principally in compensation of various kinds of agents, to such an extent that the situation was no longer bearable. Then came statutory limitation of expenses. Can it truthfully be said that the action was not beneficial? Under these limitations life insurance has prospered as never before, and the savings to policyholders has been enormous.[70] Regulators also began to be more interested in creating higher licensing standards and potentially limiting the number of agents and the size of commissions. Consistent with their increased involvement in fire insurance rate setting, commissioners also sought to tighten up their financial oversight. In 1916, the NCIC acknowledged that since "public ratemaking has replaced or is replacing private ratemaking," the transition to a more scientific basis would be "abortive" unless the method for calculating reserves also changed. They advocated a change in the standard from an "arbitrary" share of the premium to a specified percentage of the risk, along with a conflagration reserve requirement.[71] Relatedly, they sought to crack down on "interinsurance" organizations, also known as "reciprocals," which sold fire insurance at below board rates but were often either intentional scams or otherwise prone to insolvency. Reciprocals appeared similar to mutuals but were not actually created within a homogenous class of risks with some level of reserve. Rather, as described by Texas commissioner John S. Patterson: The reciprocal idea was evolved from this plan by some American gentlemen with more brains than money, who brings together his subscribers by the thousands under an agreement to insure each other, but with few fully understanding the purport of the scheme.... Some are solvent, others are insolvent. Some reside in one State, some in another. Some have one class of hazard, some another. There is nothing in common save and except the attorney and the contract.... It is a one man underwriter. Patterson described his frustration with the lack of any Texas law to prohibit these reciprocals and the necessity of using federal mail fraud law to shut them down, but usually only after damage had been done. When he was finally able to insert a clause into Texas law permitting the commissioner to revoke reciprocal's certificates, he reported to his colleagues: "I proceeded to apply, not a pruning knife, but a stump-puller."[72] (Patterson, an avowed crusader against all kinds of fraudulent activity, may be the only insurance commissioner to be killed in the line of duty, as he was fatally shot in 1916 by an irate bank owner while he was in the process of affixing a closure sign on the bank's window.)

At the 1916 NCIC meeting, states shared their generally positive experiences with their new antidiscrimination laws. New York superintendent Phillips described how their rate-making regulation bureau responded to "a great many complaints," and "very frequently as a result of the hearing we find they are unfairly discriminating." When discrimination is found, the lower rate is adapted, but otherwise "we steer clear of State rate-making." On the whole, he felt the law worked well. Commissioner LaMonte of New Jersey told a similar success story about their antidiscrimination law, the Ramsay Act. Unlike New York, although there were "minor complaints which resulted in correspondence," there had never been a formal complaint that resulted in a hearing. While some of the companies "informed us in the beginning that their business would be ruined by the necessity of conforming with the filed rates," these fears were not realized and they now supported the law. And while there are occasional complaints each year—"some hue and cry about insurance matters"—there has been no call for repeal of the law. Yet LaMonte made clear there were winners and losers, since at the time the law was passed, "some people were getting insurance for less than it was worth and others were paying for it." All in all he felt the law worked well, although "I have sometimes thought that the law would be a better law if it went further and gave the department the right, upon complaint and investigation, to order the reduction of a filed rate. This power might not be exercised, but it would be 'the stick behind the door.'"[73]

Fire insurers accepted these new regulatory arrangements warily and sought to avoid state rate making at all costs. In 1916, the National Board of Fire Underwriters celebrated a semicentennial anniversary with a large gathering in New York City. The board modestly described their own role as an "active public service organization" and a "force for the development of our Nation's welfare." Complaining that the fire insurance industry was unfairly maligned and overly burdened with taxation, they opined that public relations should be predicated on "mutual understanding and a spirit of perfect fairness." They denounced the recent trend toward state rate setting and bitterly referenced the *German Alliance* decision. The board encouraged members not to meet state rate regulation with an excessive spirit of compromise, because "when it exists in any form, however mild, it contains the germ of state rate-making to which it may eventually arrive."[74]

By 1916, it seemed there was relative tranquility in the fire insurance industry. Many states had accepted schedule rating and the necessity of rating bureaus and were taking an active role in rate supervision. This was basically the change that companies had asked for, so they grudgingly accepted this new role, though remained vigilant for evidence of overstepping. The National Board of Fire Underwriters created an actuarial bureau with the partial support of the NCIC, signaling another level of industry-regulator cooperation. A column in the *Weekly Underwriter* in January 1917 forecast a profitable year and noted that the relations between the industry and the public were "on a more satisfactory basis than heretofore."[75]

In addition to providing some good public relations for insurers, the incident at Black Tom Island also showed how the beginning of the hostilities that led to World War I would create new opportunities for insurers. One month later, most of the major fire insurers were providing explosion coverage. By early 1917, the Explosion Insurance Conference had been established, and a full schedule of war cover rates were disseminated. Standard policies for damages due to bombardment, explosion, riots, and full war risk coverage were created, and laws were passed in the states permitting the sale of this coverage.[76] After the war, the war risk aspects of this coverage ceased, but some of the other risks such as riots and explosions were combined in standard policies that were sold in addition to fire insurance.[77] (At the time of the Tulsa racial massacre in 1921, the exclusion of riot coverage from standard fire policies was still common, which allowed insurers to deny claims across the board.)

War risk joined a growing list of "side lines" or other types of property coverage that fire insurers had started to write. By 1917, premiums from these lines amounted to $40 million, nearly half of which was auto, followed by tornado and hail. Additionally, some fire insurers wrote policies for loss of registered mail, sprinkler leakage, earthquakes, and tourists' baggage. Plate glass was generally its own specialty, and plate glass insurers had large losses in the Black Tom Island explosion, which shattered windows all over lower Manhattan. Fire insurers were also beginning to write coverage that related to the use of property— generally classified as "use and occupancy" policies.[78]

The lines between property and casualty insurance were increasingly blurred. Plate glass coverage was classified as a casualty line, and in the 1916 edition of the *Spectator Yearbook*, automobile coverage was reported along with other "miscellaneous" fields such as steam boiler and flywheel, where liability for injuries was combined with protection from property damage. Many fire insurers started casualty or accident and indemnity companies. The *Hartford* ran an ad called "The two Hartfords" in 1917 delineating their fire company from their new casualty company.[79] State associations of fire insurance agents began to drop "fire" from their name to include casualty agents, and agents began to sell both kinds of coverage, reflecting the fact that the casualty business was growing rapidly and provided new opportunities for agents to increase their income.[80]

From the outset, the insurance industry as a whole identified itself thematically with the war effort. Shortly after the United States entered the war, a "preparedness parade" was held in New York City. All branches of the insurance industry were well represented. Noted the *Weekly Underwriter*, the industry represents "the firm and vigorous poise of a people ready for every contingency," and the call for action will find "a hearty echo in the spirit of every true insurance man."[81] While fire prevention had long been a theme, during the war it took on a new urgency. Given shortages of many parts for machines, fires at factories could cause delays that could impede the wartime effort. The general emphasis on thrift, economy, and efficiency that imbued the domestic front of World War I manifested itself in rhetoric about fire prevention as a patriotic duty. In a speech given by Ohio's fire marshal, agents were exhorted to do their part and "keep the home fires burning but be sure the smoke is not a peon of joy for the Huns in Berlin!"[82]

One goal may have been to tighten the screws on agents. Advising policyholders on how to reduce fire hazards was described as a patriotic service, though it may "seem to reduce your premium returns." The business context, in which the withdrawal of foreign firms combined with higher prices had increased opportunities, made it reasonable to expect agents to do good while doing well: "The agent that does not do so now is unpatriotic."[83] The National Board of Fire Underwriters initiated a "fire Americanization" movement among agents, commenting on the "menace of the present situation" and expressing confidence that the "fire insurance fraternity represents a very high average of patriotism."[84] Preparedness campaigns by insurers took on an anti-Socialist edge that provided cover for attacks on the Non-Partisan League in North Dakota and other states, on the grounds that their advocacy of state insurance and other alliances revealed their disloyalty.[85]

The war created opportunities for fire insurers as new perils emerged but also catalyzed an expanded role for the federal government. Property insurance was an international business with foreign companies serving the U.S. market both as direct writers and as reinsurers. The war disrupted many of these relationships and resulted in a larger government role in insurance in most countries involved in the conflict. In the United States, the War Risk Insurance Bureau was created and initially assumed risk for shipping due to the threat of submarine attacks and the withdrawal of German insurance companies.[86]

The U.S. government assumed control of certain types of economic activity during wartime, which also had implications for the fire insurance industry. The Army Appropriations Act of 1916 gave President Wilson the authority to administer transportation systems for the purpose of helping the war effort. National control and regulation of the railroads had actually been a longstanding desire of Grangers and agricultural interests, and during the war effort, the popularity of the idea increased among Progressive reformers who sought more efficiency in the nation's supply chain. In December of 1917, Secretary of the Treasury William McAdoo assumed control of the United States Railroad Administration (USRA).[87] The government pledged to maintain all stock and infrastructure and return control to the private operators at some point after the war.

An early step taken by McAdoo was the cancellation of commercial fire insurance policies since ostensibly the government could pay for losses by fire.[88] Insurers reacted negatively to what they viewed as government encroachment on private business. In a speech to agents, the move was denounced by John Stone of Maryland Casualty: "Mr. McAdoo has squarely put the Federal Government into the fire insurance business . . . and there is not a shred of war winning justification for it." Urging his audience of agents to be vigilant, Stone placed the move in a broader context, raising concerns about a growing movement that "favors or apparently leans toward government transaction of insurance on its merits and independent of any war securing necessity."[89]

The incorporation of fire prevention into the war effort allowed the fire insurance industry to raise its profile. In a separate but related effort to better control domestic production, Wilson in 1917 created the War Industries Board (WIB) to foster collaboration between government and industry to maximize the efficiency of the supply chain. Originally created as part of the Department of War, the WIB became a separate agency in 1918. Business leaders from various industries saw the chance to participate as a critical way to lobby for their interests, and working largely through the chamber of commerce, they sought representation on the WIB.[90]

The insurance industry wanted its place at the table as well, being concerned about various governmental incursions into insurance and the potential for more to come. Henry Evans, president of Continental, chaired the fire prevention committee of the chamber of commerce and suggested to his friend, WIB head Bernard Baruch, that there should be a section of the WIB concerned with fire hazards in plants involved in war production. Accordingly, the board established the Fire Prevention Bureau, with Evans as the chair of the Advisory Commission. From this perch, Evans could more easily convince Washington officials that the federal government should not sponsor insurance for plants engaged in war work.[91] Evans was low key about the business objectives, suggesting that the insurance men were "merely good citizens having knowledge of a certain kind that we are putting at the disposal of the Government, and all idea of profit or loss to the insurance companies is put out of consideration."[92]

The insurance industry enjoyed having influence in the WIB but did not intend for it to become a two-way street. As the war grew to a close, fire insurers worried about continued government involvement in insurance. While understandable at the very beginning of hostilities, when the sinking of the *Lusitania* and several other events made marine insurance briefly very expensive, insurers argued that there was now "nothing apparent in the war emergency" that the private sector couldn't handle. The continuation of "some sort of a paternalistic insurance system" after the war's end was of great concern to underwriters expressing their views in the *Journal of Commerce* in 1918.[93]

In this context, the long-reviled state regulatory authority became an advantage. Insurance attorneys now argued that there was no power in the Constitution for the federal government to conduct or supervise the business, since "the authority to regulate, control, and license insurance companies has been assumed by the states." Yet state intervention deemed excessive was also decried. Patriotic preparedness efforts spearheaded in many localities by the business community had associated socialism with disloyalty. In the postwar period, business employed a rhetoric of "Americanism" to denounce state insurance and even state rate setting, arguing that business belonged in government, but the reverse was not the case.[94]

In the aftermath of the San Francisco earthquake and fire, California Representative Julius Kahn in an angry speech on the House floor acknowledged federal powerlessness vis-à-vis insurance but gave a nod to a potentially different future: "The splendid report emanating from the Judiciary Committee of this House and also the one from the Judiciary Committee of the Senate indicate that Congress has no jurisdiction on the question of insurance. It is perhaps unfortunate that such a condition should exist."[95] Since San Francisco, much had improved in the science of underwriting. Fire insurers had persuaded many state regulators that the collective nature of the rate-making process made it necessary for companies to share information, but state action had evolved in a nonuniform manner, driven by sectional economic and political imperatives. Many states had begun to regulate the rate-setting process but were beginning to find that their powers were limited. Southern states persisted in antitrust strategies that generally had little impact on collusive behavior. Regardless of the approach taken, consumers in most markets continued to believe that fire insurance rates were too high and arbitrarily set, and increasingly held their state regulators accountable.

World War I increased opportunities for insurers but also posed a threat by increasing federal involvement in business. To ward off a stronger public sector presence, fire insurers focused on preparedness and prevention and attempted to depict their conduct as beyond reproach, characterized by public spiritedness, patriotism, expertise, and a high degree of cooperation, with the "competition idea reduced to the minimum."[96] Yet as we will see, this self-portrayal would soon be tested and found to be sorely wanting. Internal and external pressures would invite the attention of the federal government and force the disruption of the status quo in an industry where a lack of competition would come to be seen as both a feature and a bug.

7

Accidents and Mishaps

When Horace Frederick Merwin of Brooklyn accepted a job as a messenger for the Butterfield Overland Dispatch (BOD) in 1865, he had not yet reached his twenty-first birthday. The short-lived BOD traveled the Smoky Hill Trail, which cut the distance from Kansas to Denver by one hundred miles, compared to other routes. Yet the shortcut came at a price. Also known as the "starvation trail," the route was poorly marked west of Fort Riley and there was little access to water in the hundred miles before Denver. West of Fort Ellsworth, the trail passed through the hunting grounds of the Cheyenne and Arapahos, and attacks on stages and at stations were common.[1] The BOD was established hastily in June and the first stage set off in September, before all of the intervening stations had been completed.

Merwin left Atchison for Denver in November. The stage had traveled about 350 miles, and was stopped at the recently constructed Downer's Station, when a group of Cheyenne attacked, and Merwin and several others took refuge in the little temporary hut that had been built at the station. According to accounts of the incident, one member of the party was Charles Bent, son of famed fur trader William Bent, who had joined a group of elite Cheyenne warriors known as the Dog Soldiers.[2] After some negotiations with Bent serving as an interpreter, Merwin and the others laid down their arms and emerged from the hut. However, the situation quickly unraveled and Merwin was shot with an arrow through the heart, dying instantly.[3]

Merwin knew that his new job was dangerous. As a "shotgun" messenger, he rode next to the driver and was responsible for guarding the cargo. Expecting that he might be killed, he "took the precaution of leaving messages for his friends." He took another precaution as well and invested in what was, at the time, a novel form of insurance: an accident policy from a new company called Travelers.[4]

When first introduced, accident insurance was a very small line of business that was not taken particularly seriously, but it evolved to form the basis of workers' compensation, arguably the first major example of social insurance in America. In doing so, it established a framework for the interaction of employers, employees, insurance companies, and the medical profession that has endured to this day.

To Progressive Era reformers, workers' compensation was an important part of a broader platform of social insurance. For a time, there was some momentum

Uncovered. Katherine Hempstead, Oxford University Press. © Oxford University Press 2024.
DOI: 10.1093/oso/9780190094157.003.0007

for broader measures including compulsory health insurance, old-age and disability pensions, and unemployment insurance. Government forays into insurance during World War I had left reformers hopeful for expansion, but the postwar retreat from activism derailed most of this agenda. The many gaps left by workers' compensation were partially filled, at least for some, by the expansion of voluntary workplace benefits. Yet for the majority of Americans who remained unprotected even by workers' compensation, life insurance and a very small market for personal accident and health insurance were the only ways to protect themselves and their families against the risks of illness, injury, and premature death.

Casualty insurance covers assorted accidents, mishaps, and disasters, providing both protection against being injured and liability protection against injuries to others. In the late nineteenth and early twentieth century, this included situations that ranged from injuries to pedestrians to plate glass breakage to the sinking of the *Titanic*. Early forms of casualty insurance fell between the cracks left by other lines of business but intersected with all of them. There was a clear overlap with life insurance, especially with industrial and fraternal plans that provided some coverage for disability resulting from accidents. Much of the approach to rating risks and collectively setting rates and the emphasis on prevention came directly from fire insurance. In its initial focus on travel, casualty insurance also borrowed from marine insurance but protected passengers rather than ships and expanded the types of conveyances covered. Casualty insurance evolved to cover a number of specific risks where property damage and liability were combined, for example, plate glass, fly wheel, steam boiler, and, most enduringly, automobile. As the twentieth century progressed, the overlap with property insurance increased and the two lines of business ultimately merged.

A widely retold origin story about the early days of the Travelers Insurance Company conveys much about how the company built its brand. In 1864, Travelers founder James Batterson met a local banker, James E. Bolter, in the post office in Hartford, Connecticut. Hearing of the new enterprise, Bolter teasingly asked how much it would cost to buy $5,000 worth of protection for his walk home to lunch. "Two cents," Batterson allegedly replied, and Bolter agreed. Batterson tucked the pennies into his vest pocket, and the banker made the four-block walk without harm. This two-cent premium has been preserved since as a totem of the company's roots. The anecdote is telling on a number of levels. It revealed contemporary incredulity about the concept of accident insurance, which at the time was a novel concept. It showed the company's nimbleness and willingness to quote a premium for any risk, a trait of the newly developing field of casualty insurance. But perhaps most of all, it revealed Batterson's great gift for self-promotion.[5]

Batterson founded Travelers in 1864 in Hartford, Connecticut, and served as president until his death in 1901. He had first learned about accident insurance on a trip to England and modeled Travelers after the Railway Passengers Assurance Company, which was founded in 1850 in London. His original petition to the Connecticut legislature was for a company with the express purpose of "insuring travelers against loss of life or personal injury while journeying by railway or steamboat." Just one year later the charter was broadened to include insurance against accidents of all kinds. The next year the company added life insurance, and Travelers continued to expand to other lines over the years, including workers' compensation, automobile, and even aviation insurance.[6]

Batterson was from the Hartford area, which was a hive of insurance activity. While the big life insurance companies were centered around New York City, Hartford was an insurance hub from the early nineteenth century. With its location on the Connecticut River near the Atlantic Ocean, Hartford was an important trade city, and soon came to be known as the "insurance capital of the world." The Hartford started out as a fire insurer in 1810 and added life and accident insurance in 1875. Aetna was founded in 1819 as a fire insurance company, added life insurance one year later, and issued its first accident policy in 1891. Connecticut Mutual Life was another notable Hartford company.[7]

Batterson, shown in Figure 7.1, was an omnivorous overachiever in the nineteenth-century tradition, and insurance was arguably not his primary vocation. He may have been known best as a stone designer and builder. One of twelve children of a poor stonecutter, Batterson left home early to become an indentured apprentice to a printer before returning to take over his father's business. Located on Hartford's Main Street, it grew from a maker of cemetery headstones into a large enterprise that constructed many government monuments and buildings including the National Soldiers Monument at Gettysburg, the U.S. Capitol, the Library of Congress, and the state capitals of New York and Connecticut. His firm also did the stonework for many important commercial buildings, such as the Waldorf Astoria Hotel in New York. Batterson also invented a lathe that created polished columns of stone.[8]

Batterson's pursuits were not limited to stone building and insurance. Though he never attended college, Batterson studied on his own and developed a great knowledge of languages and poetry, particularly the classics, publishing his own translations of the *Iliad* and the *Odyssey* and serving as president of the Greek Club of New York. Batterson also traveled extensively in Europe and Egypt and was an honorary secretary of the Egyptian Exploration Fund. Somehow he also found the time to be highly civically engaged. He was an ardent supporter of the Union cause and active in Republican politics, both locally and nationally. Reportedly, Batterson visited with Abraham Lincoln in Washington on the day of his assassination.[9]

Figure 7.1 Travelers Insurance founder James Batterson. Permission granted by Travelers Archives.

In the very earliest days of accident insurance, the focus was strictly on travel. Travel policies were sold as tickets that covered specific trips, which could be purchased at railway stations and steamship offices. The field quickly became very crowded. Seventy new companies were formed within a few months of the inception of Travelers in 1864. The multitude of travel companies competed to offer inducements to railroads to let them sell their policies, and for a brief time some of the railroads even experimented with entering the business themselves. Competition was frenzied and rate wars prevailed. Batterson ultimately consolidated all of these competitors and created the Railway Passengers Assurance Company, which was folded into Travelers.[10]

On the one hand, travel insurance might seem like a somewhat limited field for insurance, as many people did not travel, or did not travel often. Yet travel by rail and steamship was growing in the nineteenth century, and there were many accidents that were thoroughly covered in the popular press. The *New York Times* reported that more than three thousand people died from accidents on trains, steamboats, explosions of powder magazines, or falling buildings in a five-month period after the end of the Civil War. One notable example of many mass fatality incidents was the sinking of the steamboat *Sultana* in 1865. The steamboat was carrying 2,100 passengers, 1,500 of whom were Union soldiers recently released from Confederate prison camps. About seven miles north of Memphis on the Mississippi River, the boiler exploded, setting the ship ablaze. Only 600 passengers made it to shore alive.[11]

As a way to publicize the risks of travel and the benefits of insurance, Batterson started publishing *The Travelers Record* in 1865. The *Record* was distributed freely at hotels, libraries, and other public places and allegedly had a circulation in the 1860s that rivaled *Harper's Weekly* and other top periodicals. The *Record* provided thorough coverage of travel accidents and shared stories of fortunate policyholders who received prompt payments. An ongoing comic strip featured the mishaps of Bedediah Buttercup from Podunk, Pennsylvania, who is resistant to the idea of accident insurance but ultimately becomes convinced of its wisdom after a series of unfortunate events. Travelers advertised frequently in *Harper's* and other popular publications, as seen in Figure 7.2, with cartoons that showed the risk of travel, but also those that emphasized the risks of everyday life and the peace of mind that came with insurance.[12]

From its earliest days Travelers sought to broaden its accident coverage beyond the limited domain of travel. The first personal accident policy was written

Figure 7.2 Early advertisement for travel insurance, depicting accident scenarios involving different kinds of conveyances. Permission granted by Travelers Archives.

to Batterson himself. Other policyholders came from the ranks of the wealthy and famous, including John Wanamaker, P. T. Barnum, William Lloyd Garrison, and Henry Ward Beecher, celebrated life insurance advocate and uncle of Lieutenant Frederick Beecher. James Harper, the head of Harper Brothers and mayor of New York City, was another well-known early policyholder, who was thrown from a carriage and killed, resulting in a payment of $10,000.[13]

Another large payout that grabbed the headlines in 1865 was the death of young Fred Merwin. In the first chapter we learned the story of another unfortunate young man named Frederick—Lieutenant Frederick Beecher, who died in 1868 under somewhat similar circumstances in the same general vicinity. Beecher's family fought with an insurance company for several years over technicalities related to the payment of a war risk premium and potential policy lapse for a missed premium payment. A partial payment was received only after a very public airing of grievances in trade publications. The claims adjustment experience for Merwin's family was far smoother. Merwin's policy had cost him $70, and his mother received a payment of $10,000 in less than one month.

Much of the newspaper coverage of the incident emphasized the insurance angle, making use of copy supplied by *The Record*, which liked to publicize cases where the unfortunate person in question had purchased their policy shortly before death. Merwin fit the bill, since his policy was dated "but little more than one month previous" to his untimely demise. *The Record* also provided a strict accounting of the time lapse between certification of death and payment of benefits; in this case the claim was paid in seven days.[14]

The local paper, the *Hartford Courant*, covered the story and quickly pivoted to the insurance point, observing that Merwin, "a young man of good family, was insured in the Travelers Insurance Company, of this city, for $10,000, which amount the company will pay with their usual promptness. This is the second $10,000 loss the company has paid within three months, and both the gentlemen deceased were murdered."[15] Some newspaper stories concluded by listing the name of the local Travelers agent, so that readers could get covered.[16] Travelers made much of the Merwin episode from a publicity perspective, but from an underwriting standpoint they made some adjustments. Soon after, there was a West Coast version of the accident policy, which was more expensive and payable in gold coin. Injuries resulting from "Indian troubles" were classified as a war risk and similarly excluded by 1870.

The publicity around Merwin's death reflected how in the late nineteenth century, the concept of accident insurance was a novelty. As Batterson himself recalled: "For a while we were not in general taken seriously: we were more a subject of jeers and flat witticisms, and we heard confident prophecies of bankruptcy through the large possibilities of undetected fraud."[17] Many predicted the ultimate failure of Travelers and similar companies. Mark Twain, then a San Francisco reporter, wrote a jokey letter to the *Record* asking why the company "didn't make particular mention of taking risks on Blighted Affections. If you should conclude to do a little business in that line, you might put me down for six or seven chances."[18]

Yet while much of the publicity about early accident insurance emphasized unusual deaths and rich and famous people at risk of accidents from travel or recreation, there was a very conscious appeal to the everyday needs of working people. An item in the *Record* made the point directly: "An accident policy is a great convenience to the well-to-do, but it is a necessity for a man who lives by manual labor." Travelers competed directly with industrial and fraternal insurance by offering wage replacement for disabling injuries, for periods up to twenty-six weeks. This feature allowed policyholders to "keep the household going comfortably without the dread necessity of laying up debts." This part of the business grew rapidly, and by 1898, nearly half of the claims paid by Travelers were for injuries associated with "manual labor and trades."[19]

Travelers did not conduct physical examinations, but it did do a careful assessment of risk when writing accident coverage. Early policies promised to pay the owner for injury or loss of life for any accident caused by "outward and visible means" but did carve out some exclusions, such as "dueling or fighting ... or other breach of the law on the part of the assured, or by suicide, whether felonious or otherwise, or by war, riots or invasion, or happening while the assured is in a state of intoxication, or riding races, or by willfully exposing himself to any unnecessary danger or peril." Risks were classified into five categories, ranging from preferred to extra hazardous, and no claims were paid until a medical examination was conducted.[20]

An 1865 guide to agents encouraged them to target leading citizens of their communities, since "influence descends from the higher to lower classes." At that time the company offered both travel and general accident policies. Agents were told to promote general accident over travel policies by telling prospective clients that most accidents did not occur on modes of conveyance. Another drawback to a travel insurance policy was that "it may go to the bottom in the pocket of the person insured, and thus all evidence of insurance is lost." Accident policies, on the other hand, were registered with the home office. The policy purchased by A. C. Boyd in 1868 was typical. As an ordinary risk, he paid $22.50 annually for a $3,000 death benefit and a $15 weekly indemnity in the event of disabling injury, payable for a period of twenty-six weeks. Agents were advised to exclude potential policyholders with certain pre-existing conditions, such as epilepsy. A section titled "A word about the ladies" contained this interesting caveat: "Owing to the habits and occupations of the female sex, it is difficult in many cases to determine whether or not a bodily injury is a disabling one; it is therefore recommended that women should be insured for 'death only,' without compensation. In exceptional cases, the Agent will act according to his own judgement."[21]

Despite the success of Travelers, accident insurance was a niche field. Travelers reported sales of ten thousand policies by 1865, and seventy-seven thousand in 1889. Yet in that year there were nearly four million life insurance policies.[22] While Travelers was the industry leader, many other stock and mutual companies sold accident insurance, as did fraternal societies.[23] Disability coverage was also a part of many industrial and fraternal life policies. By the turn of the century, some accident insurers, such as Aetna, started to issue very small amounts of health insurance, which offered protection against illnesses not caused by accidents.[24]

The field moved increasingly away from a strict focus on travel, and the definition of what constituted an accident generally broadened over time, but a lack of standardization in the industry created difficulties for policyholders and regulators. A presentation at the National Convention of Insurance Commissioners (NCIC) in 1898 described the widening scope: "The tendency of American companies is to shut out fewer and fewer causes of bodily injury. They even pay for injuries which are in no wise accidental, such as those which are inflicted by burglars and highwaymen."[25] Underwriters tried to respond to technological change quickly and quoted premiums often without much empirical basis. For example, the early days of the bicycle "rattled the accident insurers," with many serious accidents caused by adult learners and poor integration with other forms of transportation.[26] As people learned how to ride, bicycle injuries declined sharply, and they constituted only about three percent of Travelers' claims by 1898.[27]

Accident insurance was inherently complex. The circumstances of individual accidents were varied, and claims adjustment could be time-consuming. Claims were often litigated over factors such as whether the cause of the accident was excluded or whether the policyholder voluntarily exposed themselves to danger, or at least to a risk not covered. The insurance industry followed important court decisions that were summarized in trade publications. Many cases revolved around the intersection between home and the workplace, and the legal system often sided with the policyholder. For example, when in 1900 a Kansas barber shot off his left hand while hunting rabbits, the state's supreme court did not agree with the Wildey Casualty Company that he was working in an occupation more hazardous than that in which he was insured. Hunting, the court found, was an incident in the plaintiff's daily life. An Indiana jury found that a man who was injured by riding his bicycle into a wagon during a heavy wind did not voluntarily expose himself to danger, even though he could have avoided the injury by looking ahead. Similarly, the court found that an Iowa house painter did not voluntarily expose himself to danger when he ascended by means of a rope sling to retrieve pigeons from a cupola in his barn to feed his family. He was experienced in working at great heights and had examined the equipment before the accident.[28]

By the late nineteenth century, a relatively small number of people had accident insurance or a fraternal life insurance policy with some coverage of disability. These were primarily attempts by workers to protect their income in the event of an accident that temporarily or permanently threatened their ability to work. Yet the vast majority of the population had no such protection. As the century wore on, Americans increasingly turned to the court system for compensation when injured. The rise in tort lawsuits in the late nineteenth and early twentieth century reflects broader changes in the public's interpretation of the cause of and responsibility for accidental injuries. The fact that injury lawsuits increased more quickly than the injury rate or the population suggests a broader social change, namely increased expectations about what it means to exercise care.[29]

These social changes, along with the increasing mechanization of workplaces and the accompanying rise in accidents, contributed to the emergence of employers' liability insurance at the end of the nineteenth century. Offered first by an English company in 1885, Travelers brought employers' liability coverage to the United States in 1889. A year later, they broadened the coverage to create a general liability policy to protect employers from accidents to nonemployees as well as employees. General liability premiums were based on payroll, with adjustments for the perceived hazardousness of the workplace. There was usually a limit for accidents that injured or killed one person and for those that injured or killed more than one person.

The Mather Electric Company in Boston applied for a general liability policy in 1893: "It is desired to cover our entire legal liability as to employees and the public on account of bodily injuries to our employees or the public at our above location or wherever employed in our service." They were quoted a premium of $165 on a $15,000 payroll. This would provide a maximum $15,000 of protection for injuries to either employees or the general public. In the application, the company's agent described the size and nature of the workforce.[30] Aetna created an accident and liability division in 1902. The development of liability coverage fostered an interest in accident prevention, and Travelers created a safety division in 1904. This was comparable in many ways to the prevention activities of the fire insurance industry.[31]

Unlike accident insurance, liability insurance grew quickly, at least at first. The 1900 edition of the *Spectator Yearbook* described the rapid and somewhat unruly growth of the field. In the rush for business, many new types of policies were being developed, with little sense of what was successful. The emergence of some industry self-regulation and standardization around policies and rates in the form of a liability conference was described as much needed "after five years of mad, and oftimes reckless, scrambling for premiums."[32]

By the end of the nineteenth century, employers' liability premiums had risen from approximately $150,000 in 1887 to $4.7 million by 1897, but growth had started to slow, and the business had become increasingly expensive and difficult. Complexities included difficulties in assessing the hazardousness of different workplaces, the "long tail" of injury claims that required adequate reserves, and some other difficulties that reflected the sociolegal environment of the late nineteenth-century workplace.

One was variation in the likeliness of workers to file claims and potentially sue their employers. A presentation to regulators in 1897 emphasized the importance of social factors, drawing a contrast between older states where longstanding ties between employers and employees and "kindly treatment" reduced claims and lawsuits, versus more "cosmopolitan" places where workers were largely immigrants and where "no such good feeling exists or is likely to exist," resulting in frequent and expensive claims: "The sums demanded assume proportions which if paid would be a menace to the successful continuance of a business or trade where mechanical labor is a chief factor; and in such communities when claims are resisted and carried into the courts unreasonable verdicts are frequently the result, presumably because the juries are to a great extent in sympathy with the working people as against corporations and capitalists."[33]

Lawyers were also thought to play a role in driving up costs: "Particularly since the advent of Employers' Liability Insurance, our court calendars have been filled with accident cases hunted up by a species of lawyer known as the ambulance runner." These lawyers monitored reports about accidents and encouraged injured parties to sue, with the result that "a person who has suffered a trifling injury will be visited by several such lawyers." Employers' liability coverage created an attractive target for these lawsuits.[34]

The increase in claims and litigation reflected important changes that were taking place in the legal treatment of workplace injuries. Throughout the nineteenth century, the legal system had developed in ways that served to shield employers from liability for workplace injuries. The concept of contributory negligence created a difficult initial hurdle. The injured party was required to prove both that they were not negligent and that the other party was. This already difficult requirement was complicated in the workplace due to several special laws that had no application elsewhere. One was the "fellow servant" rule, which was not a part of traditional common law but stemmed from an 1842 decision by Massachusetts Supreme Court Chief Justice Lemuel Shaw. This exempted employers from liability for the negligent actions of all other workers and supplanted the legal concept of *respondeat superior* or "let the master answer," which made employers far more liable in the event of injuries to the general public.[35] Another legal rule, "assumption of risk," further shielded employers by holding that workers could not hold their employers liable for injuries that resulted from risks they were aware of and therefore implicitly accepted by continuing to work. This concept undermined the employer's responsibility to create a safe working environment.[36]

This special workplace law had the result of making employers more liable to the public at large than to their own employees, yet it began to come under increasing pressure in the nineteenth century. Employers' liability insurance was one response to the increasing litigation around workplace injuries. Liability insurers also experimented with creating a standard "workers' collective" policy, which provided a fixed amount of no-fault coverage, "irrespective of the liability of the assured," for workplace injuries, yet these agreements were not honored in the courtroom.[37] In some workplaces, employers asked workers to sign waivers and created a relief fund, mostly through worker contributions.[38] Some employers bypassed insurance and relief funds and simply settled cases in an ad hoc manner, essentially self-insuring.

Yet in spite of these measures, as common law protections came under increased pressure, employers' exposure to litigation rose. A variety of forces contributed to the momentum for change. As workplaces increasingly mechanized, the number of accidents increased, as did public awareness and disapproval of unsafe workplaces. As was the case with fire, there was a growing unhappiness with the far higher accident rate in the United States compared to Europe. The relative safety of railroads in Britain versus the United States was a frequently raised comparison. While often ascribed to differences in the national character, the differences may have resulted from shortages in labor and capital that resulted in more slipshod construction methods in this country.[39] Whatever the cause, higher rates of accidents in the United States began to be seen as unacceptable. Progressive reformers and journalists detailed safety and working conditions in meatpacking and other industries. Publications such as Upton Sinclair's *The Jungle* helped to make the case for a number of reforms including the establishment of the Food and Drug Administration and passage of regulations such as the Pure Food Act. It also led to an increased focus on accident prevention through heightened safety requirements and inspections. Both federal and state governments began various forms of industrial safety regulation and inspection in the nineteenth century.[40]

Many large corporations supported these efforts. They stood to benefit from complying with regulations, which required expenditures that their smaller competitors may not be able to make. Establishing uniform requirements worked to their advantage. Workplace accidents and litigation were becoming increasingly costly and impaired labor relations. There were reputational benefits as well. U.S. Steel is an example of a large company that embraced the "safety movement" and became a leader in corporate efforts around workplace safety. They had begun safety work even before the publication of William Hard's exposé, "Making Steel and Killing Men," which appeared in *Everybody's* in 1907.[41]

The American approach to workplace injury was initially comparable to the legal environment elsewhere, but over the course of the late nineteenth century other countries started to make significant changes. Prussia led the world in the creation of social insurance. Under Chancellor Otto von Bismarck, the Employers Liability Law was passed in 1871, and Workers' Accident Insurance was established in 1884. This would be followed later by public pension insurance for nonjob illnesses, along with public assistance for those who could not work due to disability. Franz Kafka famously worked for years as a lawyer at the Austro-Hungarian Workers' Accident Insurance Institute.

In England, under Prime Minister William Gladstone, the Employers' Liability Act of 1880 had abolished common law, and the Workers' Compensation Act of 1893 established a no-fault doctrine similar to the German system. The "Friendly Societies" in England provided insurance rather than the state under a law passed in 1897.[42] These developments were watched closely in the United States. The Department of Labor authored a report in 1893 on "Compulsory Insurance in Germany."[43] The *Spectator Yearbook* in 1900 noted the growing outlier status of the United States, remarking that the U.S. Supreme Court and the British House of Lords previously interpreted things quite similarly, but lately "these two tribunals have been diverging more and more, the former in favor of the employer and the latter against him."[44]

The courts began to chip away at workplace laws that shielded employers, as judges and juries began to interpret them less strictly. The "vice principal" doctrine created an exception to the fellow servant principal, and the growth of safety standards and regulations heightened perceptions of the employer's responsibility for the creation of a safe workplace. State legislatures made important contributions. In 1887, Massachusetts limited the fellow servant defense. In 1902, the New York Employers' Liability Act weakened both the fellow servant rule and the reach of the assumption of risk by increasing employer liability for hazards in the workplace. Other states took similar actions—including Maryland in 1902, Massachusetts in 1908, and Montana in 1909. A 1905 decision in Washington essentially unwound the "assumption of risk" defense as a judge ruled that "reasonable" safeguards in the workplace essentially meant "all necessary safeguards." The federal Employers' Liability Acts of 1906 and 1908 softened common law doctrine of contributory negligence and provided no-fault coverage to federal workers. In 1908 another federal law protected workers involved in interstate trade. Additionally, starting in 1908, federal employees were protected by no-fault compensation, which had a major impact on the subsequent passage of workers' compensation laws in states.[45]

The erosion of the common law defense increased the cost and unpredictability of employers' liability insurance, as both the number of lawsuits and the size of losses to employers began to increase.[46] Some companies exited the market due to underwriting losses. Travelers' annual report of 1912 noted that liability insurance had experienced "a year of difficult problems," as courts were increasingly liberal and claims mounted: "It was impossible to advance premiums with equal rapidity, with the probable consequence is that every insurance company in America writing liability insurance will suffer a loss upon the business of 1911."[47]

Large employers were early advocates for transitioning to a no-fault system of workers' compensation, with the National Civic Federation, a Progressive Era organization of big business, labor, and civic leaders, giving an early endorsement. George Perkins, as president of International Harvester, was explicit about the imperatives of improving relations with labor in the modern economy: "Cooperation in business is taking and should take the place of ruthless competition." Organized labor was the last major stakeholder group to give up on employers' liability, hoping it could be reformed in a way that would be more generous to workers. Labor was concerned about agreeing to guaranteed but inadequate payments under a compensation system and also had general unease with the idea of government regulating the conditions of the workplace, believing that this would deprive unions of their independence. Samuel Gompers of the American Federation of Labor did not support workers' compensation until 1909.[48]

The transition to workers' compensation reflected the general consensus among a broad-based group of workers, employers, the insurance industry, and state officials that the current system of employers' liability was not workable. Workers' compensation, often referred to as "the great compromise," was tort reform. At essence it is an ex ante contract between workers and employers in which workers trade a cause of action—the right to sue—in exchange for coverage for compensable injuries. Workers' compensation is generally recognized as the first example of social insurance in the United States. As such, it set many important precedents for future programs such as unemployment insurance, Social Security, and Medicare. It also laid the groundwork for the application of no-fault liability in other contexts, namely auto insurance.[49]

Almost all states passed workers' compensation laws in a flurry of legislative activity between 1911 and 1919, with the first ten states passing their laws between March and July of 1911. Washington and Kansas were the first two states to pass their laws in March, but Wisconsin actually had the earliest effective date, May 3, 1911, the same day that their law passed. By 1915, thirty-three states had passed laws. The speed of passage was impacted by the influence of a broad group of stakeholders, including employers, organized labor, social reformers, legislators, and regulators, along with the insurance industry. Legislation tended to pass earlier in states where there were more large employers and more workers who would be affected. In general, agricultural interests opposed compensation laws, and passage came latest in southern states. By 1920, all but five southern states had passed workers' compensation, and Mississippi did not pass its law until 1948.[50]

Despite the general consensus, the passage of workers' compensation laws did not go smoothly. Battles over benefits took place in some states as employers sought caps on payments and tried to get workers to pay a share of the premium, while labor tried to increase benefits as a share of earnings and reduce waiting periods. Passage was delayed in some states as details were negotiated. Missouri argued over the specific aspects of its workers' compensation law for years, with disputes within organized labor and between labor and employers over the scope of benefits, before finally passing legislation in 1926. In Illinois, passage was delayed because organized labor did not initially unify in support of establishing compensation versus expanding the existing system of employers' liability. In other states, constitutional challenges impeded the initial establishment of compensation, reflecting dissenting views of interest groups.[51] For example, New York passed a compulsory law in 1910, but relatively quickly it was declared unconstitutional and reversed by the New York Court of Appeals in 1911. After a constitutional amendment, a permanent law was passed in 1913. That law represented a compromise between labor, the insurance industry, and employers, resulting in a system that combined a state fund with private companies.[52] Ohio faced a constitutional challenge originating from the insurance industry over the establishment of its state-run system. Nor did the passage of workers' compensation put an end to litigation. Huey Long spent several formative years as a compensation lawyer in Louisiana before running for railroad commissioner in 1918, burnishing his reputation as a defender of the underdog who claimed to have never "taken a suit against a poor man."[53]

Despite the fairly close timing of the passage of many states' compensation laws, they differed markedly, leading a 1920 Bureau of Labor Statistics report to lament "the refusal of most states to be guided by the experiences of other states." In part this may have been because and not in spite of the close sequencing, which may have served to "prevent the adoption of any one form of law as a type."[54] State differences extended to the two most fundamental attributes of compensation—the level of benefits and the extent of coverage.

In terms of scope, most states had some kind of exemption for domestic and farm workers and other types of casual workers and the self-employed. Agricultural interests lobbied hard for farm worker exclusions, and in farm states, compensation covered a much smaller share of the labor force, since fewer workers were employees, and many employees worked in agriculture. This resulted in large differences in the reach of compensation in different places. In 1920, for example, only about a third of Alabama's employees were eligible for compensation, as compared with over ninety-nine percent in New Jersey, where farmers and women's clubs had lobbied unsuccessfully to exempt farm workers and domestic workers.[55] The racial implications of state variation in workers' compensation laws are clear. Blacks, who disproportionately lived in the South and worked in agriculture, had far less protection than other groups.

Another important early issue was whether or not to make the program required for employers. A number of states, including Ohio and California, initially created a voluntary compensation program and then revised their laws several years later. In many states, compensation was theoretically voluntary, but employers going without would no longer have common law protections and would be exposed to liability claims.[56]

While in most states the compensation scale was approximately fifty to sixty-five percent of wages, this was usually combined with a weekly maximum, which made the actual payment usually well below fifty percent of wages. Most states had a noncompensable waiting period of at least one week, but for some it was ten days or as much as two weeks. Compensation for a fatality generally approximated three to four years of earnings, although states went about this in different ways. Most required three hundred to five hundred weeks of payment at the compensation scale, but some required that payments last until the death or remarriage of the worker's widow. In some states, payments were adjusted to reflect the number of dependents, with some variation in how long and at what level payments to minor dependents would last. For permanent disability, eighteen states and the federal government made payments for the remainder of the worker's life, three states made payments for less than 350 weeks, while others fell somewhere in between or did something else. For permanent partial disability, such as the loss of a hand, most states used a schedule of payments that paid a portion of wages for a fixed period of time.[57]

States also differed markedly in how they administered workman's compensation. Some housed their programs in industrial departments that were also responsible for workplace safety inspections and enforcement, while others used the court system to administer compensation claims. The level of involvement with state insurance departments varied, with some states making provisions for regulating premium rates and ascertaining the solvency of companies, while others did not. A few states, Washington being one, explicitly said they did not consider their compensation program to be insurance, but rather referred to it as a "first aid fund." States differed over whether workers should retain the option to sue if they thought they could prove negligence on the part of the employer.[58]

But perhaps the most controversial design issue in the early days of workers' compensation was over the role of the state. In some states workers' compensation was offered exclusively by private insurers, in some there was a state monopoly, while in others there was competition between the state and private insurers. Seven states set up a system where the state had the monopoly, initially Ohio, Washington, Nevada, Oregon, West Virginia, and Wyoming, and in 1919, North Dakota additionally adopted a state system. Some of these states permitted employers to self-insure and to even use a private insurance company if they could demonstrate sufficient solvency. Another group of states, including New York, California, Maryland, Michigan, Arizona, Colorado, Montana, Pennsylvania, Idaho, and Utah, created a system with both a state fund and private competition. In other states only private companies provided insurance. This was the case throughout the South. A few states took yet another approach and granted a monopoly to an employers' mutual. For example, in Massachusetts, organized labor wanted casualty companies to be barred from workers' compensation, so as a compromise the state established a mutual company—the Massachusetts Employers Insurance Association—which received some initial state funding. This company ultimately became Liberty Mutual Insurance. The state later amended this law to allow employers to use any stock or mutual company.[59]

Advocates for a state system made their case on the grounds of both social values and economy. By eliminating insurance company costs and profit motives and using some of the state's general revenue to administer compensation, benefits could be richer, and premiums lower. Organized labor strongly favored a state-run system, believing that insurance companies were biased in favor of employers. This suspicion reflected both a generalized dislike and distrust of the insurance industry and specific negative experiences with casualty companies under employers' liability coverage.

In Minnesota's unsuccessful attempt to create a state system, labor argued that casualty companies "should not make money off the crushed bones and mangled bodies of injured workingmen." Advocates additionally made the point that money not spent on insurance companies could be used to increase benefits and therefore bring compensation closer to meeting the unmet demand for more social insurance. In doing so, they explicitly raised an uncomfortable issue: that the benefit for a permanent disability was itself far from permanent, usually lasting between three hundred and five hundred weeks. After that, the outlook was bleak. *Minnesota Labor World* noted, "It is but a step from workingman's compensation as it obtains in Minnesota to a charitable institution." Labor argued that diverting the money currently paid to insurance companies to the state would allow workers to receive higher benefits without raising the cost to employers: "This is good economics. By doing so the state will solve a great social problem."[60] Progressive state reformers also emphasized the possibility for

savings if administrative expenses were paid out of the general budget. The potential for lower premiums made employers somewhat ambivalent about a state
system. While generally predisposed to oppose state involvement in business,
employers could be convinced to favor a state system if they thought it would
lower their costs.

Ohio was considered at the time to have the best functioning version of a
state monopoly but faced constant criticism from the casualty industry, especially at the beginning. Chair John Duffy recalled how the members of the
newly created Industrial Commission traveled around the state, attempting to
educate employers about the new coverage while being heckled by the casualty
companies:

> Hundreds of such meetings were held, and in almost all of them lively
> discussions took place between the members of the board and the insurance
> men. While this was very embarrassing at the time, yet I feel that the insurance
> men unconsciously contributed much to our success. By quizzing us at these
> meetings and calling attention to the defects in our rules and methods, they
> pointed out the things that it was necessary for us to learn, and the defects it was
> advisable for us to remedy. In other words, their opposition educated us and
> equipped us for our work more rapidly and more thoroughly than any other
> method could have done.

In Ohio, employers were able to opt out of the state system if they could demonstrate that they could self-insure. Duffy described how the insurance industry tried hard to peel off employers from the state system. "Some insurance
companies have had their agents working constantly to prevail upon employers
to get authority to carry their own risks with the object of insuring with the insurance company."[61] But by 1916 the state system was clearly dominant, with
about 900,000 employees covered by the state fund versus 225,000 that were not.
In a presentation in New York, Duffy described growing enrollment and declining premiums and was able to refer to a long list of testimonials from satisfied
employers. Since administrative costs were paid out of Ohio's general revenue,
benefits were relatively generous, and premiums were below those charged by
commercial companies. Ohio's system was considered the best-functioning example of state compensation insurance. Duffy himself became a national figure
and gave testimony in 1918 at a hearing about an unsuccessful bill supported by
the New York Federation of Labor that proposed to convert New York's compensation system to a state monopoly.[62]

The casualty industry was alert to the opportunity presented by workers'
compensation. As early as 1911, Travelers in its annual report described the liability business as "trying," adding, "Appropriate compensation laws are likely

to come soon to the relief of both employer and employee."[63] The International Association of Casualty and Surety Underwriters issued a lengthy statement in 1912 in support of compensation, noting that the current system was "inequitable and wasteful" and "unsuited to present industrial conditions." Yet due to the expanded scope of coverage, cautioned the underwriters, the transition to compensation would necessitate a "very considerable increase" in premiums.[64] The best way to establish these new rates would be through some form of state-sanctioned cooperation between the companies, so that they could share information. Travelers anticipated the growth potential in compensation, "which will materially increase the hazard and consequent losses of the employer, against which liability insurance will be more urgently required than ever before."[65] It was clear that compensation would be significantly more expensive than employers' liability. For example, consulting actuary Miles Dawson testified to the New York commission that it might cost on average two and half times more, and studies of European systems yielded similar conclusions. These concerns led employers' groups to seek to restrict benefits but created attractive opportunities for insurance companies.[66]

In fact, Travelers had been preparing for this transition for some time and had been teaching agents about workers' compensation in their famous training dormitory, Denniston Hall, since 1907.[67] Like the rest of the industry, they saw a new and greatly expanded role under compensation in helping employers prevent accidents. "Such service will be more than ever marked by methodical inspection, in which the Travelers is the admitted leader."[68]

Travelers had started a safety division as early as 1904, but the transition to compensation raised the safety stakes considerably. While under employers' liability insurers spent much of their time contesting claims, in the no-fault compensation system claims were generally paid, so preventing accidents became increasingly advantageous. In most states, experience rating was used at least to some degree, especially for larger employers, so a lower accident rate would help reduce premiums. Borrowing from fire insurance, many states used schedule rating as well, so safe equipment and practices also affected premiums. States reinforced these incentives through an increasing array of regulations and inspections.[69]

Casualty insurers played an important part in the safety movement that emerged during the Progressive Era, a movement that coincided with the heightened interest in fire prevention and the overall enthusiasm for all forms of efficiency, prevention, and "conservation."[70] Insurance companies were incentivized to develop expertise in safety. While big casualty companies like Travelers and Aetna created safety departments, smaller trade mutuals, such as the Lumberman's Mutual, developed highly specialized safety expertise and wrote compensation insurance for particular industries. This was comparable to developments in the fire insurance industry, where specialized employers' mutuals emerged in some industries like laundry and flour mills. The Bureau of Labor Statistics and various state agencies created and disseminated information about workplace injuries and their causes. Large companies like U.S. Steel developed in-house safety expertise, as did trade associations like the National Association of Manufacturers. The National Safety Council was formed in 1912 with representatives from government, manufacturers, railroads, and insurance companies. Its membership exploded from forty in 1913 to more than four thousand by 1920.[71]

The new occupation of "safety engineer" emerged from this movement. As Travelers saw it, this engineer was to be a scientist but also an evangelist, for the primary argument for safety to employers was "to the producer's heart, not his pocketbook." But if that were to fail, the safety engineer should be able to demonstrate "that his subject actually does touch the pocketbook as well as the heart. And he can do it if he knows the subject properly, because there is no doubt whatsoever but that in the present state of our industries, to diminish the number of industrial accidents is not only humane and merciful, but also distinctly profitable."[72]

Borrowing heavily from the world of fire prevention, where insurers also played a major role, the safety movement drew frequent unfavorable comparisons to safer European workplaces and ascribed the high American accident rate to remediable defects, which left room for significant improvement. A mainstream belief among casualty insurers was that most workplace accidents were traceable to managerial failures and were therefore preventable.[73] Travelers created a new publication for employers, the *Travelers Standard*, to provide the safety engineer's perspective. The *Standard* described causes of workplace accidents including factors such as ignorance, carelessness, poorly fitting clothing, and bad lighting. The publication sought to showcase the expertise of the casualty insurer, including photographs of safe versus unsafe conditions and discussions about how to install better equipment. The *Standard* suggested that the casualty insurer should be consulted before all major purchases.

Safety engineers communicated that the responsibility was with employers rather than workers to make conditions safer, and that changing the environment was a better strategy than hoping for changed behavior. For example, while women's hair was the cause of "a number of frightful accidents" involving rotating machinery, requiring head coverings was unlikely to be successful, since "women often regard their hair as one of their chief ornaments, and regard it as birds do their plumage." The suggestion instead was to change the environment: "It would no doubt be safer to see that all revolving machinery and transmission lines are protected so thoroughly that hair cannot be caught in them."[74]

Like fire prevention enthusiasts, Progressive Era workplace safety advocates gave great credit to Europeans for their more highly evolved approach, showing particular deference to Germany as being "foremost, thus far, in all matters pertaining to accident prevention."[75] Yet workplace safety in Europe was also a contested terrain, as seen in excerpts from the writings of Franz Kafka, who worked in the Workman's Accident Institute, the state-run compensation program in Prague. Kafka navigated often contentious issues related to the adoption of safety equipment and schedule rating. For example, in a carefully argued brief in favor of cylindrical shafts in woodplaning machines, he played the role of both the regulator and the safety engineer yet avoided an appeal to the heart by going straight to the pocketbook. Kafka took pains to show that cylindrical shafts were cheaper and more efficient, as well as safer: "Thus their adoption does not call on employers' sociopolitical judgement but is clearly advisable as a practical matter." Yet his matter-of-fact report included some carefully drawn pictures of hands with severed fingers.[76]

Insurers were bullish about the compensation business, so they naturally fought state insurance with all their power. The arguments they used varied by circumstance. One claim was that the state had an unfair advantage, since they could sell at cost and didn't have to compete for their customers. Another was that the state was incompetent, because they lacked insurance expertise. The Casualty and Surety Underwriters likened state insurance to a "proposition that all watches should be repaired by a state official that has no particular training along those lines."[77] Another was that a state-run system could be politicized in a way that would harm workers and employers.

In 1911, as compensation legislation began to pass in the first cohort of states, the trade publication *The Indicator* asked sourly: "Whither are we drifting?" They answered their question by asking another: "If the State enters the field of insurance for the purpose of selling at cost, why can it not conduct the growing of grains, fruits and vegetables, and their distribution?"[78] By this argument, state insurance was "encroachment," and permitting it created a slippery slope that could lead to the ultimate government takeover of every branch of commerce. When James Hoey, Eagle Insurance president and former New York deputy superintendent, addressed the Brooklyn Brokers Association in 1916, he criticized the New York State Insurance Fund as an example of "a situation that confronts us today which may have disastrous results. I refer to the constantly growing tendency on the part of the State to engage in private business."[79] In the postwar period, state insurance was frequently linked to the dangers of socialism. Endorsements of "Americanism" served as shorthand for the advocacy of limited involvement of government in business.

Insurers were sensitive to their many critics who accused them of profiteering and heartless treatment of injured workers, arguing they were unfairly being blamed for the "odious conditions" of the flawed employers' liability system.[80] Travelers complained how "some people seeking a scapegoat" chose to blame insurance companies for the problems with employers' liability, noting that "unjust and untrue claims" were made about their profits, even though "for many years the business was underwritten at a loss."[81] Labor had a very different perspective, with clear bad memories of casualty companies using tactics that "smelled to Heaven," such as pressuring injured workers to sign release waivers in exchange for small payments.[82]

A. M. Best, the insurance rating publisher, included state funds along with stock companies and mutuals in the annual *Best Insurance Reports*. Best described the characteristics and management of state funds in the same way that he assessed stock and mutual companies, as in this summary of California's fund: "The personnel of the organization is made up of capable and experienced insurance men who are chosen entirely upon personal merit with no regard to political favor."[83]

In the design of workers' compensation, there was a tension between the relatively straightforward idea of wage replacement and a somewhat more amorphous concept of social need. One way this is seen is the decision of some states to adjust benefits to reflect the number of dependents and/or the marital status of widows. The question of for how long to make payments in the event of a permanent disability similarly flirted with the border between the responsibility of the employer and the broader society. On the other side of compensation payments lay charitable institutions and little else; where should the line be drawn? To social reformers, workers' compensation was an important but incomplete component of a broader social insurance agenda that included maternal, old-age, and disability pensions as well as universal health insurance and unemployment insurance. Yet while many European nations were adopting these reforms, the political climate in the United States had not evolved sufficiently for these solutions to be seriously considered in most places.

Reflecting this, the use of public funds in workers' compensation was in general not an option, although this created some difficult situations. Nothing illustrates this better than the perplexity caused by "second injuries," an early example of a pre-existing conditions problem. The second injury problem was seen as an unintended consequence of workers' compensation. The example of a man with one eye was frequently used to illustrate the dilemma. Under compensation there was a reluctance to hire such a man, because he may "lose the other eye and thus be a burden upon the employer for life."[84] Individual accident insurance addressed this issue through underwriting, but this was neither possible nor desired for workers' compensation.

The result was an incentive to discriminate against workers with disabilities, which became exacerbated after World War I when injured soldiers began returning to the workforce. The issue was not addressed consistently by states. By 1920, about fifteen states explicitly excluded compensation for the prior injury, thus undercompensating disabled workers who became permanently disabled. In some of these states this position was the result of lobbying by the disabled, who felt otherwise they would not be hired. Some states found a way to split the difference between ignoring versus fully counting the prior injury. A few states had a version of a pre-existing conditions exclusion and required disabled workers to sign waivers restricting their rights to compensation. This made it easier for a disabled worker to be hired, but as the Bureau of Labor Statistics noted in an assessment of state compensation systems, "as far as he is concerned the compensation law is to a great extent a dead letter, and in case of injury he will be thrown upon public charity or the generosity of his employer."[85]

In another fifteen states, the full disability payment was required, which potentially fostered discrimination, but in a subset of those states that problem was addressed with the creation of a "second injury fund," generated from an assessment on employers. The assessment was applied to cases where there was a fatality with no dependents, creating a windfall for employers. The existence of the assessment also kept employers from discriminating against workers with dependents. New York was the first to establish such a fund, and several other states took similar actions. A Bureau of Labor Statistics report notes approvingly that these special funds provide "substantial justice" to both employers and employees and provide the best solution, even while acknowledging that the actual incidence of second injuries is "infinitesimally small."[86]

The incremental response to the problem posed by second injuries reflected the line between workers' compensation as a limited response to workplace injuries and a broader system of social insurance. The great degree of state variation did reflect a spectrum of views about social responsibility, and in general second injury funds were more likely to be found in states with state monopolies or at least a state fund. Ohio's Duffy noted that while lower administrative costs was one argument in favor of a compulsory state fund, another was to arrive at a "different method of distributing loss" that was consistent with the idea of a social insurance program. The case of the "one-eyed man" was his example: "To be fair about it we can hardly blame an employer for taking all reasonable precautions to protect himself against the cost of a permanent total disability. But that is no consolation to the workman whose unfortunate condition hinders him from getting employment and subsequently inflicts suffering upon himself and his family." Yet the compulsory state-run insurance fund solved this problem and "protects the employer against the embarrassment of having to meet the cost in such cases and at the same time removes the condition that prompts employers to refuse to employ such partially disabled workmen. This certainly gives us a more desirable social condition, no matter whether we view from the standpoint of the employer or the employee."[87]

While it solved many of the issues associated with employers' liability, workers' compensation retained the fundamental complexity that is inherent to accident and health insurance. States developed divergent approaches to program design and compensation scale. There were also difficult questions about what was compensable and what forms the nonmonetary aspects of compensation take. Over time, the scope of compensable injuries grew to include some diseases, starting with California in 1915, and here again states made different determinations. The issue of pre-existing conditions was again raised in this context, as workplace injuries that exacerbated underlying medical conditions became compensable in some circumstances, and some injuries that resulted from sustained exposure, such as "housemaid's knees," were also increasingly considered to be compensable.

Compensation programs expanded to include some diseases reluctantly and not particularly logically. A tortured legal logic allowed the Supreme Court of Minnesota to rule that a case of typhoid fever resulting from drinking water supplied by an employer was not compensable,[88] while a case of sunstroke was, since the latter met the definition of an accident because the symptoms came on suddenly while those of the former did not.[89] In the early twentieth century, the United States lagged behind Europe in its attention to and compensation for occupational disease. A casualty insurance textbook noted that "it is bitterly ironic that the very gradualness, the very inevitability of many industrial diseases have operated to retard public interest and knowledge. We act principally on what we see and what is dramatically and horribly obvious."[90]

As a wider range of injuries and illnesses came to be compensated, the nonmonetary aspects of compensation, medical treatment and rehabilitation, rose in prominence. Initially, rehabilitation had been an area of neglect, a problem pointed out in a 1920 U.S. Bureau of Labor Statistics report: "Disabled workers have been paid their compensation benefits and then allowed to shift for themselves exactly as they would have done prior to the enactment of compensation laws." However, the war experience and the growth of the Veterans Administration greatly increased interest in rehabilitation, and some states started to create new agencies that were devoted to the emerging fields of occupational and physical therapy.[91]

The medical aspects of the workers' compensation benefit grew in significance and quickly emerged as a pain point, establishing a pattern of dysfunctional relationships between employers, insurance companies, medical providers, and workers that persist to this day. Initially, not all states even included medical benefits as part of workers' compensation, and for those that did the benefits varied greatly, some placing limitations on length of time, dollar amounts, both, or neither. There were also vast differences over what types of services were covered and how the medical providers were chosen. As the Bureau of Labor Statistics notes in their 1920 report on state compensation laws, early battles over physician choice and provider rates revealed how "the interplay of these various and sometimes conflicting interests constantly causes friction and creates innumerable difficulties."[92]

In the case of physician choice, there were worries that employees would choose unqualified family physicians who attempt to inflate payments from employers by "prolonging treatment, making unnecessary calls, padding their bills, and overcharging generally, and because of their incompetency are an actual menace to the patients themselves." Yet alternatives proved problematic as well, since while some employers maintained high-quality medical facilities, many did not. In particular, there were quality problems with "contract physicians" hired by insurance companies, a practice that was more common in western states. A report by the California Industrial Accident Commission in 1917 expressed concern about the system, since "the contracts are frequently made with men of poor judgement and some whose only equipment seems to be a willingness to work for little money."[93]

The use of contract physicians had grown due to friction over provider rates. Physicians generally wanted to maintain the rates they had received prior to compensation laws, while insurance companies sought to strike a bargain where the increased volume and security of payment was taken into consideration. An extreme version of this took place in hospitals, where we can see the roots of today's "cost-shifting" issue, where hospitals try to get some patients to pay higher rates, allegedly to make up for losses suffered on other patients. Many injured workers would have been charity cases in the absence of compensation laws, and insurers argued that the price for their care should be discounted to reflect that counterfactual. Hospitals disagreed, and the Bureau of Labor Statistics report observes, "As might be expected, such a condition immediately resulted in numerous and acrimonious disputes, between the medical profession on the one hand and the employers and insurance carriers on the other, as to medical fees."[94] More than one hundred years later, these disputes are far from being resolved.

The wartime effort created an unprecedented level of government activism and involvement in the economy, including the temporary takeover of the nation's railroads, the management of an emergency shipping fleet, and widescale partnership with business through the War Industries Board. The government collaborated with experts from the insurance industry as well as social progressives, many of whom were advocates of improved labor conditions and the expansion of social insurance. Lee Frankel of Metropolitan Life was recruited to work on the War Risk Insurance Act, along with Julia Lathrop of the Children's Bureau. Grace Abbott of Hull House and Florence Kelley of the National

Consumer League advised on working conditions for women. Organized labor was brought on board as well; a no-strike pledge was reached early on with the American Federation of Labor, and Samuel Gompers was appointed to an advisory commission to the National Council of Defense.[95]

Many were hopeful that this wartime collectivism would carry over into a postwar expansion of social insurance. The word "reconstruction" began to be used as shorthand for this opportunity to remake society after the war, and a number of states and cities established reconstruction committees. Old-age pensions, health insurance, unemployment insurance, and expanded federal labor standards were among the priorities to social reformers, and the expanded role of government raised hopes that the postwar period would see the completion of this unfinished agenda.[96] Before the war there were efforts in a number of states to broaden social insurance. Theodore Roosevelt's platform in the 1912 presidential election included a proposal for national health insurance. Commissions on social insurance were established in a number of states including Ohio, Massachusetts, and New Jersey to study the feasibility of creating broader programs, mainly health insurance and protection for old age and disability. In California, Governor Hiram Johnson established a commission in 1915 to investigate a system of universal health insurance.[97] The American Association of Labor Legislation, with some cooperation from the Committee on Social Insurance of the American Medical Association, developed legislative proposals, and there were legislative initiatives in a number of states.

Yet the hoped-for "reconstruction" did not take place. Though the war effort led to government activism on a large scale, paradoxically, the war itself countered some of the momentum toward reform. Germany, an early model for the design of workers' compensation, was now the enemy, and their system of state-run social insurance began to be viewed with disfavor. The postwar period was one of disillusionment for labor, with a series of protracted strikes followed by injunctions and other repressive actions, which were increasingly justified by references to the threat of socialism.

Workers' compensation became an important remaining avenue for improvement of conditions, and labor increasingly advocated for state insurance and the expansion of benefits. Due to wartime inflation, the real value of benefits had fallen, making the need to raise compensation standards generally accepted in most states, but the issue of state insurance became a flashpoint.[98] In New York, the American Federation of Labor supported the unsuccessful Gilchrist bill that would have prohibited the casualty companies from workers' compensation, giving a monopoly to the New York State Insurance Fund.[99]

In Illinois, the Federation of Labor advocated for both a state compensation system and compulsory health insurance, creating what the *Weekly Underwriter* described as "disquieting conditions" on the eve of a state constitutional convention.[100] In Minnesota, labor had fought for years for state insurance and larger benefits for permanently disabled workers. In 1921, after a long study and multiple hearings, the state increased benefits and regulated rates, but the plan for state insurance was defeated.

Domestic wartime efforts elevated the prominence of business organizations such as the chamber of commerce, along with industry trade associations like the Insurance Federation.[101] In the postwar period, these groups used patriotic rhetoric to advocate for the noninterference of government with business and denounced state insurance as a steppingstone to socialism. The Americanism League was a public relations outlet for the insurance industry that lobbied state legislatures against state insurance. The reformist insurance commissioners were by then largely gone, replaced by regulators that sympathized with business. Compensation programs were not administered by state insurance departments in any case, so it was unsurprising when then NCIC issued a resolution condemning state insurance in 1919. The *Weekly Underwriter* reported on the development with a deference not usually shown to the commissioners, noting that they "look after the interests of their constituents and are independent of the private companies," and linking the issue to the pervasive theme of "Americanism": "The private companies should be given at least a fighting chance to write compensation in every State. That is true Americanism applied to a question which is of vast import to thousands of employers and workers."[102]

Embodying the wariness about social insurance typical of the postwar cohort of commissioners, New York superintendent Phillips testified in 1920 that a state monopoly in compensation was an "opening wedge for other socialistic experiments."[103] In opposing the Fitzgerald bill, which would have created a federally run workers' compensation program in Washington, DC, the *Underwriter* channeled the current political zeitgeist by noting that the bill contradicted Warren G. Harding's campaign slogan: "more business in government and less government in business," warning that if it did pass, "it will only be a time before the government goes into other insurance branches."[104] Aside from North Dakota, where the ascendant Non-Partisan League was in control, efforts to create additional state-run compensation programs did not succeed.

Progressive ideas with a European pedigree could not defend themselves against the wave of nativist and reactionary sentiment, when the fear of ascendant communism, in the wake of the Bolshevik revolution in Russia, caused deep misgivings about most proposals for social or economic reform. While state compensation insurance was the most imminent threat, health insurance was also a casualty to the forces of Americanism. The attempted substitution of England for Germany as a model was not sufficient to resurrect the cause of health insurance, especially when the medical community inveighed early and often against "state medicine."[105]

The expansion of workers' compensation to include compulsory health insurance had taken place in European countries, and before the war many thought it was an inevitability for the United States as well. On the eve of the war, compulsory health insurance was under consideration in a number of state legislatures. At the 1917 meeting of the Casualty Actuarial and Statistical Society, the general view was that were it not for the war, "we would, without doubt, find ourselves much further advanced in the throes of socialistic propaganda, and thus be dealing more intimately with the question of state insurance, especially compulsory health insurance. It remains to be seen whether the war will increase or decrease these socialistic tendencies." The risk was considered great enough that it "behooves actuaries and statisticians to inform themselves thoroughly on the subject."[106]

A report by the U.S. Department of Labor described the recent experience of Austria and alluded to the difficulty of strictly distinguishing between occupational and nonoccupational contributions to sickness as an explanation for the inevitability of adding health insurance to compensation. One main takeaway was that all sicknesses and injuries were traceable in some way to the worker's basic station in life, making the distinction less critical:

> While sickness or other temporary disability may be due to causes other than industrial, the policy of making compulsory insurance against sickness a feature of the industrial organization of a country is now regarded in Austria as the only practicable solution of the problem. Although the causes of sickness arise in part from the physical and mental constitution of the individual workman and in part from general living conditions, both causes are strongly influenced by occupation, by influences connected with occupation, and in particular by the general standard of life of the individual as fixed by his occupation and the income derived therefrom.[107]

The powerful alliance between business and government helped to shape the nature of the response to labor unrest and activism that marked the immediate postwar period. Concerns about "labor conditions" and the potential for radicalism led not to the expansion of social insurance, but rather to the voluntary expansion of workplace benefits via group insurance. Life insurance companies had entered the group business to a limited extent before the war, although the practice was far from widespread. A few large companies, including U.S. Steel, had tried to provide accident and health insurance to employees in the advent of compulsory compensation. Former New York Life president George Perkins was an early exponent of the practice, instituting what was referred to as a "welfare" program at International Harvester that provided sickness and accident benefits, disability pay, and a pension, motivated, he argued, by "pure business spirit."[108]

Group insurance grew substantially in the postwar period, and the range of benefits expanded to include life, health, disability, and old-age pensions. Speaking to a group of casualty actuaries and statisticians, Edward B. Morris of Travelers described welfare capitalism as an American solution to a social problem: "We are learning as a nation that it pays to take care of the human unit—to conserve this unit in life, limb, efficiency and freedom from worry. Our problem, as a democracy, is to achieve this without interfering unduly or unnecessarily in any respect with the individualistic principles upon which our political life is planned. Group insurance points a way."[109] The expansion of employee benefits was covered in the press in glowing terms. Under the headline "Employees Insured Free," a New Jersey newspaper in 1920 described how "More than $13,000,000 in old line insurance policies has been presented to its employees by a Seattle shipbuilding concern. All workers, from the heads of departments to the boys and women, have received the $1,000 policies."[110] In the same year, the city of Schenectady received approving media coverage for being the first municipality to provide insurance for all city employees, when they took out a group policy with Travelers that included disability benefits and a pension.[111]

Travelers, with its existing life business in addition to accident, health, and compensation lines, was particularly well positioned to sell group insurance. It established a group department in 1915, with $8.5 million of insurance in force, a number that by 1920 had grown to $400 million.[112] The company reported that premiums for group life, accident, and health insurance rose from less than $900,000 in 1913 to $7.9 million in 1923.[113] In a 1921 discussion of group insurance, William Chamberlain of Travelers ascribed its particular salience in the postwar period given the "subject matter on the first pages of the daily paper," that is, "strikes, unrest, and dissatisfaction among workers." Chamberlain memorably explained how, during a difficult period of social and economic readjustment, group insurance offered a modern solution to an age-old problem: "There have always been panaceas sought to establish confidence between those who work and those who find work for others to do."[114]

The Travelers Yearbook in 1923 described the addition of accident and health benefits to group life as a growing component of their group business, part of a modern trend toward "amplifying wages" with good working conditions.[115] They were by then the largest company offering group coverage. The 1925 annual report notes the importance of illness versus accidents as a reason for missed work and lost income: "This insurance takes up the accident protection of the workers where compensation insurance leaves off and supplies an income during illness, which causes more physical incapacity than industrial and non-industrial accidents together."[116] And while this insurance provided reimbursement for medical expenses, the indemnity clause that offered wage replacement, much like workers' compensation, was the most important feature.

Health insurance was challenging from an insurance business perspective. Mortality patterns were well known, standard accident tables were emerging for various industries, and even the patterns of automobile accidents were starting to be understood, yet reliable data on morbidity was lacking. The steadily rising premium rates in European countries was a subject of concern at the American Casualty Actuarial and Statistical Society meeting of 1917. The subjective nature of illness made it conducive both to "malingering and camouflage" and to trends in medical practice:

> Very often the man in his anxiety to be a faithful worker may insist that he is not sick enough to stay away, but his physician may insist that he should, and that is the main reason why in the European sickness experience the number of sick cases has been constantly rising, which was in some people's opinion an indication of camouflage. It isn't; it is because the physicians' opinions are becoming more liberal; and a man is compensated not only when he wants to stay home, but when he should stay home.[117]

In the individual health insurance market, competition created unsustainable downward pressure, as new and poorly capitalized firms, complained the *Weekly Underwriter*, "refuse to make rates that will place health underwriting on a real business basis."[118] The absence of a standard policy contributed to the disorganization of the business. Travelers survived due to its long experience, but it engaged in careful underwriting and had explicit pre-existing conditions and a number of other exclusions on their policies. However, Equitable exited the individual accident and health business in 1922.

Other companies limited coverage and contested claims, to the exasperation of state regulators. A discussion at the 1921 NCIC meeting revealed broad agreement on the existence of "fool freak" health and accident policies but lack of unity about what action should be taken. Minnesota's commissioner advocated for a standard policy. North Dakota's commissioner Olness, affiliated with the Non-Partisan League, advocated for state insurance. Honorable James F. Raney, commissioner of Kentucky, felt that less involvement would be better. Speaking at a meeting of health and accident insurers, Commissioner Raney encouraged them to regulate themselves: "By keeping your ear to the ground and recognizing silent forces you can correct evils that spring up in your business and leave our legislative bodies to apply their time and talent to more important matters of state. Very few more laws are needed in the insurance business."[119] Yet the view was different in neighboring Tennessee, where the commissioner noted in his 1921 report that many personal health and accident policies were of little value: "It is extremely difficult for any benefits to be derived from these policies, so limited is their coverage, and it is recommended that their issuance in Tennessee be forbidden."[120]

Out of what initially appeared to be a somewhat frivolous branch of casualty insurance evolved first employers' liability coverage and then workers' compensation, arguably the first example of social insurance in the United States. The establishment of compensation was one of the most significant state accomplishments in insurance supervision and was achievable because it primarily required regulation rather than public funds. Compensation reflected a consensus among stakeholders that the existing system of liability coverage and litigation was not adequate to address evolving conceptions of responsibility for injury. The establishment of compensation programs marked an explicit attempt to change the distribution of loss between workers and employers.

Despite this common basic understanding, compensation programs were established in fifty different ways with a nearly four-decade interval between passage in the first and last state. And while it was an important achievement, the coverage gaps left by compensation were large. Many workers did not benefit because they were self-employed, worked in a small business, or worked in agriculture or domestic service. The slow and limited implementation of workers' compensation in the South, along with the occupational exclusions in most states, meant that Black workers were less likely than others to be protected. Benefits for permanent disability were generally inadequate, and many accidents and illnesses that caused loss of income did not fall under the category of a compensable workplace accident.

Progressive reformers had sought a broader set of social insurance programs, and there was some momentum for the establishment of unemployment insurance, health insurance, and old-age, maternal, and disability pensions. Yet in the postwar period the country turned away from the expansion of government and embraced a probusiness type of "Americanism" in which state insurance was viewed as a steppingstone to socialism. The provision of voluntary benefits to employees—welfare capitalism—began to emerge as the uniquely American solution to the unmet needs of workers. Yet while group insurance spread to large manufacturing plants and public employees, the vast majority of workers had no access to these benefits, and the tiered system that we live with today began to take shape. The small individual market for health insurance offered little protection as it was highly variable, poorly regulated, and not available to individuals with pre-existing conditions, much as it was before the passage of the Affordable Care Act in 2010.

8

Private Governments

When sentencing famed Kansas City political boss Thomas Pendergast in 1939, U.S. district court judge Merrill Otis noted that until the current case, the "Boss" had never been indicted or even charged with a crime, yet his criminality was known to be extensive: "It was believed that the tentacles of his octopus-like power reached into every nook and cranny of the city and into every enterprise— legitimate and illegitimate, good and evil. Over and over again for a score of years it was whispered that he must be particeps criminis in a hundred different offenses against the laws of state and nation."[1] Even by the standards of political bosses, Prendergast, shown in Figure 8.1, was legendary, with vast control over all kinds of political and business enterprises in Kansas City, most particularly its vice district and gambling operations. Yet his seeming invincibility was undermined by his mounting debts. Known by the code name "Sucker" among New York bookies, Pendergast sometimes lost $100,000 in one week. By the late 1930s, his chronic indebtedness was weakening his grip on power, making him take unwise risks and bringing his activities to the attention of the federal Bureau of Internal Revenue.[2]

Prendergast was convicted along with his crony, machine politician and former state director of the Department of Insurance Robert Emmet O'Malley. O'Malley was a former Kansas City cigar manufacturer and Pendergast loyalist with no obvious qualifications as an insurance regulator. Judge Otis denounced him for betraying his state for "30,000 pieces of silver."[3] The two had taken a large bribe from a group of fire insurance companies and agents in exchange for reducing a court-ordered settlement that was supposed to have provided Missouri policyholders with millions in refunds. The legal wrangling over this refund had lasted more than a decade and reflected the repeated legal challenges to the state's rate-setting law, which had been enacted in 1919. Missouri residents had yet to benefit from the state's enhanced regulatory powers.

What might have been just another sordid story of political machines and state corruption was amplified by the involvement of the federal government. The U.S. Treasury Department investigated Pendergast and O'Malley and charged them with tax evasion. They were tried and convicted in federal court. And the federal government was far from finished with the fire insurance industry.

In the beginning of the twentieth century, the federal government and the insurance industry had relatively little to do with one another. The Supreme Court

Uncovered. Katherine Hempstead, Oxford University Press. © Oxford University Press 2024.
DOI: 10.1093/oso/9780190094157.003.0008

Figure 8.1 Tom Pendergast Sr. (center) during his trial for tax evasion with his son Tom Pendergast Jr. (left) and nephew James Pendergast (right). The three men are seated at the defense counsel's table after the judge has passed the sentence. May 22, 1939. International News Service, Harry S. Truman Library and Museum.

had ruled in the *Paul* decision of 1869 that insurance was not commerce, placing regulatory authority with the states. Disappointed, insurers had made a few attempts to challenge *Paul* and replace state with federal oversight, but they did not prevail. Accordingly, the federal government played almost no role in insurance, with the exception of a few marine insurance issues. Yet as the century progressed, there were increasing points of intersection, and interactions with the federal government increased dramatically during the twentieth century in ways that property and casualty insurers could not control.

During World War I, the government developed ambitious life and property insurance programs to help meet the emergency. While most of these efforts were temporary, insurers resented them greatly and strenuously resisted any type of partnership with government. Insurance would also become an important tool of Depression-era federal policy. Subsidized crop insurance was included in the Agricultural Adjustment Act, and the Social Security Act created an old-age pension, disability, and unemployment insurance as well as Aid to Families with Dependent Children (AFDC). The New Deal also brought with it an increased focus on economic concentration and the behavior of corporations, and during the 1930s, the federal government became involved with the property and casualty insurance industry through new judicial and legislative pathways. Most notably, an antitrust investigation of a fire insurance rating organization led to a momentous Supreme Court decision that overturned the precedent set by *Paul* and threatened the industry with federal regulation.

As this chapter will show, the impetus for federal scrutiny arose from unresolved problems with fire insurance rate setting that date to the nineteenth century. The failure of state antitrust efforts and the acceptance of collaborative rate making in most states during the Progressive Era had solidified a cartel culture ruled by a small group of executives, who fended off efforts to reduce rates through increased competition and opposed calls to establish multiple lines of coverage and other business innovations. The property and casualty insurance industry of the early twentieth century was ossified and bureaucratic, resisting both internal and external pressure for change.

Insurers sought to limit their interactions with the federal government to areas where in their view "mutual interest requires cooperation," mostly concerning the war and related issues, such as risks at nuclear power plants, while resisting government incursion into "traditional private areas of the economy."[4] Yet much to their dismay, as the century progressed, the federal government not only expanded its use of insurance as a policy tool but also increasingly saw the insurance industry itself as a potential trouble spot. Congressional oversight hearings would become the new public square for an industry that resisted both the increased scrutiny and growing economic role of the federal government.

One early twentieth-century example of the relationship between insurers and the federal government comes from agriculture. Inspired by wartime experience, hopeful supporters in Congress and the U.S. Department of Agriculture (USDA) investigated a potential federal role in providing crop insurance in some type of partnership with the insurance industry. There was some precedent for government involvement in insurance for farmers, with a history of state activity in hail insurance, both in the United States and Europe. Federal policymakers turned to insurers for advice and potential collaboration, yet they encountered an impassive and uninterested industry that had no desire for a peacetime partnership and did not seem to think that the quasi-public role of insurers required them to show any interest in the plight of the farmer.

Disinterest in assisting the government was clear from insurers' testimony at a Senate Committee hearing in 1923. John H. Griffin, president of Northwestern Fire and Marine Insurance Company, provided information about the company's hail business but gave a "drop dead" response to questions from the chairman, Senator Charles McNary, Republican from Oregon.

THE CHAIRMAN: Have you thought, Mr. Griffin, of going into insurance on other crops?

MR. GRIFFIN: No.

THE CHAIRMAN: Are you interested in that subject?

MR. GRIFFIN: Why, I would like to see a plan worked out. I would not like to work it out myself.

THE CHAIRMAN: What would you advise this Committee to do in order to help along the line which we desire to render assistance?

GRIFFIN: Well, I presume a crop policy could be written safely over a large distance, if you could get all the farmers to contribute. You cannot do that, of course.... It seems to me to be a hopeless job.[5]

Insurers did not see all-hazard crop insurance as a profitable line of business and had no interest in brainstorming about it with federal officials. Federal crop insurance would await the passage of the Agricultural Adjustment Act in 1933, and the government would act on its own.[6]

At the same time, the practices of fire insurers were increasingly subject to attack by the states. For example, in New York State's Lockwood Committee hearings, famous consumer lawyer Samuel Untermyer accused the city's fire insurance industry of being run by a "small group of millionaires" who operated as a monopoly and contributed to the high cost of living in New York City.[7] The Lockwood hearings surfaced many examples of anticompetitive behavior by the members of the city's rating organization, the New York Fire Exchange, such as preventing mutuals from paying dividends, compelling brokers to only place business with firms that belonged to the exchange, and discriminating against certain sprinkler companies that did not belong to a "combine."[8] Insurance publisher Alfred M. Best testified that profits were systematically understated and competition from nonbureau companies was virtually impossible.[9]

From a pure business perspective, the postwar period was promising. As was the case with the life insurance industry, the government's role during wartime had seemed to be threatening but was instead a catalyst. The industry had even managed to pass off a ten percent war "surcharge," based on higher prices and taxation. The war had provided opportunities to develop new lines, such as explosion, aviation, riot, and strike coverage.[10] The year 1919 had broken all records in volume and variety of insurance. Travelers initiated aviation passenger insurance at a splashy 1919 event in Atlantic City where Woodrow Wilson and Secretary of War Newton Baker were presented with "aero tickets."[11] Profit insurance of all types grew in popularity, as commercial clients sought coverage for when fires and other mishaps left their businesses idle. Rain insurance had the potential for "unlimited expansion and adaptation" and was sold by the day on Coney Island. The New York market grew to the point that the Weather Bureau issued a special daily report for "the insurance men."[12]

But after the war, attention began to focus once more on the fairness of rates. The national organization of commissioners summarily rebuked the continuation of the wartime surcharge in 1919, on the grounds that it had become "offensive to the people generally."[13] Some states required that carriers issue partial refunds. The issues raised by the Lockwood Committee surfaced in different ways around the country. A 1920 letter to a North Carolina newspaper could have come from anywhere: "Our fire loss has been very low, and we might keep it low, but it makes little difference, if any, in the rates. Will someone please tell us what is necessary to get a lower rate and one that will stick?"[14]

In many southern states, antitrust activity had never ceased and was tied to political demagogy by politicians like Mississippi's James P. Vardaman and Louisiana's Huey Long who combined virulent racism with hatred of northern corporations in their appeal to upcountry "redneck" farmers.[15] The Kansas attorney general, in a 1922 report, described the fire insurance business in his state as a "combination to fix prices" and called for greater state rate-making power, adding that it was a "crying evil" that such competition that did take place was for agents and brokers, "rather than service to the public."[16]

The National Board of Fire Underwriters continued to promote itself as a public service organization, advocating for laws to increase personal liability for fire and attributing the high cost of insurance to the nation's deplorable level of fire waste and nothing else. The board converted some of their talking points into a patriotically themed children's textbook on fire prevention in 1921. In *The Flame Fiend*, a genie makes an unexpected visitation to a group of boys playing carelessly with an oil lamp and tries to both terrify them and use their patriotism to enlist them in a new war against an old enemy—fire waste—caused by carelessness and a failure of individual responsibility in American culture and law.

The genie made sure the boys understood that fire waste was exclusively to blame for the cost of insurance:

"Skinny, how could the rate of insurance tax be lowered in your state?" asked the Genie.

"By having fewer fires, I suppose," answered Skinny.

"Correct," said the Genie. "And Skinny, that is absolutely the only way it could be lowered too. The amount of insurance that you and your father pay each year depends directly on the fire loss in your state each year. Will you remember that for me?"

"Yes," murmured Skinny.

And when it came to carelessness, the genie did not believe in second chances:

> "People who are careless about causing fires," said the Genie, "are traitors and criminals. They destroy the property of their country, they make the burden of tax heavier for rich and poor alike, and they betray their countrymen into the hands of a cruel merciless enemy that was never known to give quarter. Such a traitor and murderer should be treated as traitors and murderers have been treated since the beginning of time—he should be put to death!"
> "Oh," said Tom, sobbing, "they don't all think. I know I didn't."
> "But that is no excuse," said the Genie, mercilessly.[17]

But outside the bubble of the board's propaganda machine, real-world problems were mounting. The seeming prewar understanding between regulators and insurers that caused momentum to shift away from antitrust action and toward state rate setting and/or greater state supervision of rating bureaus had not translated into greater consumer satisfaction with insurance rates.

There were increasing discussions about acquisition costs and appropriate levels of profit. In 1921 the National Convention of Insurance Commissioners (NCIC) defined underwriting profit and set a benchmark for a reasonable amount of profit, five percent, and in the event of a conflagration, three percent.[18] In 1922, the NCIC even proposed the creation of a national rating and supervising bureau, making a presentation to an National Board of Fire Underwriters committee in which they described the essence of the problem: "Regional rating associations are a prolific source of misconception . . . and have presented conditions which the companies have been unable to justify." The National Board of Fire Underwriters itself was forced to acknowledge "manifest evidences of dissatisfaction and distrust . . . mutterings of unrest, ominous clouds threatening a coming storm."[19]

The growth of automobile use accelerated pre-existing pressures for the integration of property and casualty lines of business, so that single policies could cover multiple kinds of perils. At the NCIC meeting in 1924, a committee on "multiple lines" reported on the rigid and illogical divisions between property and casualty insurance: "In many lines, the difference between what is a fire insurance risk and what is a casualty insurance risk is extremely vague," with the result that many customers instead turned to the less regulated British insurance companies, particularly Lloyds of London. Noted the committee: "The so-called American System has tended to encourage the growth of branches of foreign companies until at the present time about 40% of the fire business and about 23% of the casualty business of the United States is written either in the United States branches of the British companies or in British-owned domestic companies. Contrasting this with the fact that

American companies have been unable to make any inroads in Great Britain furnishes cause for reflection."[20]

The American property and casualty insurance industry at the time was painstakingly organized and tightly regimented. "Perhaps no business is so addicted to organizations as is insurance," observed professors Albert Mowbray and Ralph Blanchard in a mid-century analysis.[21] It was somewhat paradoxical that while the government played a larger role in the provision of insurance in Britain, where social insurance was far more developed, the private sector was far more flexible in terms of pricing and lines of business. This contrasted sharply with the United States, where companies resisted government intervention but had a high degree of self-imposed regulation via rating bureaus and trade organizations that were designed to enforce uniformity.

The fire insurers set the standard for industry orthodoxy. The National Board of Fire Underwriters from its inception in 1866 was devoted to uniformity in pricing and commissions and avoiding competition at all costs. Failing in their attempts to set rates nationally, the board exerted their control over a set of regional rating organizations. Though the casualty business was inherently less rule bound and bureaucratic, it soon established a counterpart organization— the National Bureau of Casualty and Surety Underwriters—which similarly tried to control the approach to pricing and commissions.

Ruling over the combined industry was a special group, the Insurance Executives Association, atop of which was perched an elite "committee of fifteen" composed of executives from the largest companies. This small group of chief executive officers controlled the entire property and casualty industry and ostensibly "ruled like monarchs."[22] Retribution came swiftly to those deviating from organizational norms. Uncooperative companies found themselves unable to obtain reinsurance and without access to agents, two fatal business problems. The lack of reinsurance alone was a crippling blow since few if any companies could self-insure against all risks without risking insolvency.[23]

Slowly this system started to come under pressure. One agent of change was the Insurance Company of North America (INA), ironically one of the oldest companies in the country. With its origin in the relatively free-wheeling marine line, the INA maintained a more flexible outlook and obtained a size that permitted them some leeway. In 1925, President Benjamin Rush made a pitch to the industry for multiple lines and for "a greater flexibility in the rating of each individual risk," praising Britain's more competitive model.[24]

Another source of competitive pressure came from mutuals, especially in rural areas, where new companies formed to sell auto insurance to farmers. A new kind of company emerged, the "direct writer," which largely bypassed the agency system by selling directly to customers. One example was State Farm Mutual, which was formed in Illinois in 1922 to sell auto insurance to farmers. By 1942 it was the nation's leading auto insurer. Nationwide similarly started out in 1926 as an Ohio farm mutual specializing in auto insurance and expanded its geography before changing its name in the 1950s. Allstate started in 1931 as a subsidiary of Sears, taking the name of a popular brand of tires. It initially sold policies directly to consumers through mail and in the Sears catalog. Allstate also sold policies from a booth at the 1933 World's Fair in Chicago and then set up counters within Sears stores in the auto parts department.

By 1929, the INA resigned from the National Casualty and Surety Association after that organization resisted the company's attempt to offer "merit pricing," an early form of good driver discounts in auto insurance. That year the president of the NCIC cautioned that the industry should be mindful that its business model continues to evolve: "Insurance retains its rightful place in the economic history of a country only as it meets the public needs. It should not be embarrassed in its development by statutory or other requirements which have not kept pace with the times."[25] Yet control over the business only tightened during the Depression. Rush tried again, in a 1932 speech arguing that insurers needed to give customers what they needed, "as cheaply and with as little red tape as possible." For this to happen, "it must change some of those laws and practices adopted many years ago which are no longer applicable to modern business conditions."[26] But with investment income plummeting and fire premiums declining during the Depression, the industry chieftains sought to tighten their grip and doubled down on their established practices.

This was seen in the response to the threat posed by the rapidly growing "inland marine" line of coverage. Designed to cover goods in transit, inland marine expanded beyond rail and river transport with the growth of the automobile and the trucking industry. Inland marine grew in ways that cut across the rigid pre-existing lines dividing property and casualty insurance, covering things like bridges, racehorses, jewelry, and art. Incensed by the encroachment, fire insurers complained to state commissioners, resulting in the appointment of a committee with representation from all lines of business to study the problem. The outcome was a treaty of sorts, the restrictive 1933 "Nationwide Definition," under which inland marine was compelled to cede business to fire and casualty. Before retiring in 1939, Benjamin Rush once again called for multiple line charters, praised the British system, and complained about high agent commissions. Criticizing the industry for its "obstinacy," Rush issued what turned out to be a prescient warning—the continuation of these practices would invite "a political investigation of the cost of fire and casualty insurance."[27]

This investigation was in fact slowly taking shape. At the same time that the rigid structure of the national fire and casualty bureaus was being internally challenged, a sequence of events was slowly unfolding that would ultimately escalate far beyond the control of the initial participants and threaten to upend the entire regulatory structure of the insurance industry. The entire episode lasted more than two decades.

It began in Missouri, where a long-fought battle for state rate-setting authority had finally been won in 1919. A prolonged disagreement began in 1922 when the state insurance superintendent Ben Hyde, who was the brother of the governor, sought to use that authority to reduce fire insurance rates. The insurance companies sought an injunction and the case went all the way to the Missouri Supreme Court, which upheld the insurance commissioner in 1926.

With Charles Evans Hughes as their representative, the insurers successfully petitioned the U.S. Supreme Court to hear the case, but in January of 1928, the court refused to set aside the Missouri verdict. "Get your refund!" proclaimed the *Dexter Statesman*, and it appeared that after six years of litigation, the approximately $10 million in contested premium reductions was on the verge of being paid to policyholders.[28]

Yet it was not to be. The next month, the fire insurance companies took to the federal courts again and obtained temporary restraining orders, then filed 137 individual lawsuits seeking injunctions to prevent the state from implementing the reduction. In April 1929, the state filed a motion to quash the injunctions. Public discontent grew over "a suit that cost Missouri taxpayers thousands of dollars and that was heralded as a great accomplishment of the former Hyde administration [but] has benefitted nobody."[29]

In January of 1933, Missouri attorney general Roy McKittrick initiated proceedings to order the distribution of the impounded funds.[30] It was time, editorialized the *St. Louis Post-Dispatch*, for the state to "make an example of these recalcitrants."[31] After another round of appeals to the Missouri and U.S. Supreme Court, it finally seemed that in 1934, twelve years after the beginning of the episode, the refunds, now estimated to exceed $10 million with interest, were on the verge of being distributed. Yet a method for calculating and disbursing the refunds needed to be created and would be established by the courts in the absence of a voluntary agreement.

At this point the story takes a criminal turn with the involvement of the legendary political boss Thomas Pendergast, a former saloon bouncer who controlled the Kansas City Democratic Party during the 1920s and early 1930s and launched the career of Harry Truman when he backed him for a judgeship in 1922. Even by the standards of machine politicians, "Boss" Pendergast was exceptional, due to his close alliance with criminals, his undermining of the democratic process, and his opulent lifestyle, as well as a large and increasing gambling addiction, primarily to horseracing. This latter trait resulted in Pendergast's chronic indebtedness and motivated a vast array of illicit business activities. At Pendergast's insistence, Governor Guy Park in 1933 appointed party hack Emmett O'Malley to the position of state insurance supervisor.[32]

In January of 1935, a set of meetings took place involving Pendergast, O'Malley, and two representatives of the insurers, at which it was communicated that a settlement could be reached, but a payment would be necessary. Charles R. Street, former president of Fidelity-Phoenix, was at the time vice president of the Great American Insurance Company. He also served as the head of the Subscribers Actuarial Committee, based in Chicago, which represented the 137 involved companies. A. L. McCormick represented the Missouri Insurance Agents Association.

O'Malley initially suggested to McCormick and Street that a favorable set-tlement could be arranged for a payment. Pendergast followed up several weeks later at a meeting with the two at Chicago's Palmer House to work out the logistics. A sum of $750,000 was agreed upon and an initial payment of $350,000 was transferred by McCormick, who toted an enormous satchel of bills on a train from Chicago to Kansas City, then took a taxi to Pendergast's mansion. Pendergast, after taking a large share, instructed McCormick to split the remainder with O'Malley. Meanwhile, O'Malley and Street publicly went through the motions of a negotiation and announced a settlement on May 14, the day before legal arguments were scheduled to begin. Under their agreement, policyholders would receive only twenty percent of the escrow fund, while the companies and attorneys would get the rest.[33]

The settlement was announced in May of 1936, but quickly the situation started to unravel. From the start, the agreement had an "unsavory ring" that aroused suspicion, since the state seemed to have made so little effort to defend the interests of policyholders. Democratic governor Lloyd Stark, who took of-fice in 1937, withdrew his support and favored legal efforts to reverse the set-tlement, infuriating O'Malley.[34] When O'Malley publicly referred to Stark as a "polecat" for questioning the settlement, Stark fired him immediately and named a successor with no ties to the machine. The rift between Stark and Pendergast widened, and Pendergast quickly had O'Malley appointed as water commis-sioner for Kansas City.

A search for evidence of impropriety began almost immediately. The first crack came when Treasury agents questioned Street about the tax treatment of a large number of checks he had cashed from insurance companies. Street responded that he had simply been a disburser of funds, cryptically alluding to the involve-ment of Pendergast by mentioning the *Queen Mary*, on which Pendergast was known to be a passenger. Street never made the remaining payment and died in 1938. Correspondence between Street and McCormack that referred to "our friends" in Kansas City and Jefferson City was found and introduced as evi-dence, and all the details of the bribery were revealed.[35]

Secretary of the Treasury Henry Morgenthau saw the insurance settlement as an opportunity to bring down the Pendergast machine and gave his agents carte blanche to prioritize the investigation. Missouri governor Stark also saw the insurance settlement as an opportunity to weaken the machine and apparently implored President Roosevelt to bring the full force of the federal government to bear on the investigation. Worried about a disruptive internal war among Missouri Democrats, FDR allegedly slow-walked a promise to Stark that he would double down on the investigation. But nevertheless, the Bureau of Internal Revenue widened an ongoing probe and publicly announced a criminal tax investigation of Pendergast in 1938.

Meanwhile, U.S. Attorney Maurice Milligan opened an investigation into Pendergast's banking transactions. Milligan and his small staff began a painstaking study of Pendergast's finances, much of which remained unknown due to the Boss's preference for cash, use of assumed names, and multiple corporate entities including a concrete company and a liquor distributor. Nevertheless, it became clear that Pendergast had received large amounts of untaxed income. One sum received in 1936 corresponded to the payment in the insurance settlement.[36] Both O'Malley and Pendergast pleaded guilty to tax evasion and were sentenced to Leavenworth, with their terms beginning on May 29, 1939.

The prosecution of Pendergast and O'Malley reflected the growing role of federal financial investigation and prosecution to combat organized crime. The famous conviction of Al Capone on tax evasion charges was another contemporary example. But the sentencing of O'Malley and Pendergast did not end the insurance story. The behavior of the companies attracted attention as well, and once again the federal government would be important, with a result that would impact the entire industry. Missouri attorney general Roy McKittrick filed suit against the companies that had participated in the bribery, seeking to bar them from doing business in the state. In doing so, he charged them with defrauding policyholders, fixing prices, and restricting competition. But given that the rating bureaus to which they belonged operated in multiple states, McKittrick sought help from the federal government.

McKittrick's case dovetailed neatly with federal antitrust aspirations. New Deal economic policy combined centralized economic planning with attacks on corporations and the idea of bigness, a sometimes chaotic assemblage that represented the impulses and shifting priorities of those who were close to Roosevelt rather than the execution of a carefully thought out master plan. The anticorporate agenda was a sustained part of New Deal thinking but is seen as a quixotic campaign that ultimately accomplished little of substance.[37] One manifestation of that focus was the creation of the Temporary National Economic Committee (TNEC) in 1938–39. While in practical terms the committee accomplished little, an investigation of the life insurance industry was one of its activities. That investigation will be the focus of the next chapter.

Additionally, prosecutions increased substantially under Thurman Arnold, who led the antitrust division of the Department of Justice between 1938 and 1943.[38] In 1942, Attorney General Francis Biddle agreed to take the Missouri case and convened a grand jury to investigate alleged violations of federal antitrust laws. At the same time, a hotel and a department store in Georgia had been complaining to the Department of Justice that they were unable to buy fire insurance at competitive rates. Their dissatisfaction was centered on the South-Eastern Underwriters Association (SEUA), one of the strongest cartels of insurers in the nation. The SEUA controlled rates in Georgia and five other southern states. Biddle decided to use the case as a test of the *Paul* decision, which had granted the insurance industry immunity from federal antitrust law. The focus of the federal prosecution shifted from the bribery case in Missouri to an investigation of what were ostensibly the normal business practices of a rating bureau, but the underlying issue was the same: potential restraint of competition in fire insurance.

A grand jury was convened to investigate alleged violations of federal antitrust laws, and in 1942 they returned an indictment, charging the SEUA with violations of the Sherman Act. Their report detailed how the SEUA controlled ninety percent of fire insurance and allied lines sold by stock insurance companies in the five southern states. The SEUA effectively set premiums and agent commissions and employed boycotts and other forms of coercion and intimidation to maintain uniformity. For example, reinsurance was denied to nonmember companies. Customers who bought from nonmember companies were threatened with boycotts. The government further charged that inspection and rating bureaus as well as agents' associations were also part of the conspiracy.[39]

To the members of the Insurance Executives Association, the indictment was earth-shattering. The business practices that they had followed for decades had suddenly been classified as criminal. Even the INA, an industry critic, banded together with the other companies to fight back. In the white shoe country club world of insurance executives, a federal indictment was unimaginable. "To think that it was done by a Biddle!" one old Philadelphia executive was said to have exclaimed indignantly, referring to the Main Line origins of the attorney general.[40]

An article in *Fortune* well described the incredulity of the insurers: "The great men of the fire and casualty insurance business are, without exception, unspectacular citizens who rarely get their names in the newspapers, never, if they can avoid it." But the indictment had changed all that: "None but the crème de la crème, the real churchgoers of the fire insurance business, were brought up on the Washington carpet. They couldn't have been more surprised than if they had been arrested on suspicion of being Episcopal vestrymen." Now they were being indicted for "conspiratorial practices in which they had openly and even piously engaged" for decades.[41] Even Biddle was cognizant of the culture shock, observing that it was "pretty hard" on the companies to suddenly deem their business practices criminal after seventy-five years of taking no action, noting that it would be "unfair to send a man to jail for something he considered legal."[42]

The industry's legal defense was to fall back on the *Paul* decision. Since insurance was not commerce, they reasoned, it did not need to conform to the Sherman Act. Initially, the federal court in Georgia agreed and dismissed the indictment. However, the Department of Justice appealed the decision to the Supreme Court. There was much to make insurers uneasy about the potential ruling. The world had changed greatly since *Paul*. During the 1930s alone, the federal government had become far more involved in the economy, with federal insurance of bank deposits, the establishment of the National Labor Relations Board, the set of commodity price supports and federal crop insurance in the Agricultural Adjustment Act, the passing of the Social Security Act, the establishment of the Securities and Exchange Commission and the Tennessee Valley Authority, and passing of the Rural Electrification Act. In 1938–39, the TNEC had investigated the state of competition in a number of industries, including insurance, and identified the need for further scrutiny. Antitrust prosecutions were a federal priority. Between 1938 and 1943, Thurman Arnold initiated nearly half of all antitrust activity undertaken since the Sherman Act was passed.

It was not a complete surprise, then, that in 1944, in *United States v. South-Eastern Underwriters Association*, the Supreme Court reversed *Paul*. In a four-to-three decision, the court held that Congress could regulate insurance under the commerce clause. Writing for the majority, Associate Justice Hugo Black argued that there was nothing in the Sherman Act that indicated that Congress did not intend it to be exercised over the interstate insurance trade, referencing the long history of state anticompact activity as evidence that "combinations of insurance companies were not exempt from public hostility against the trusts."[43]

Industry analyst Alfred M. Best, known for holding the industry to account, described the new world succinctly in the *Fire and Casualty Report*: "Insurance is now commerce, the rules have been changed, and it is up to the insurance business to adjust itself to the altered situation with as good grace and as great benefit to itself as it can." Yet the chieftains of the insurance industry were far from sanguine. To the National Board of Fire Underwriters, which of course had originally brought about the *Paul* case in the hope of obtaining federal supervision for the industry, the decision was not only "a threat to insurance specifically but also to our theory of government generally." They wished desperately to return to the world that existed before the decision. The Association of Casualty and Surety Executives also sounded the alarm and advocated finding a way to "restore the status quo ante as soon as possible," since "practically our whole structure of rates, uniform policies and commissions is condemned by the antitrust laws."[44]

The industry was joined by state commissioners in their quest for reconsideration. State officials worried about the status of their authority and ability to regulate and, not insignificantly, the tax revenue that came from the insurance industry. Judge Jackson in his dissent had expressed a common concern that the Roosevelt administration might seek to oversee the insurance industry: "I have little doubt that if the present trend continues federal regulation eventually will supersede that of the states."[45] Forty-one state regulators unsuccessfully petitioned the Supreme Court to rehear the case. An industry-sponsored effort to obtain a complete exemption from federal antitrust laws "blew up in its face" under questioning from Senator O'Mahoney, a staunch antimonopolist from Wyoming.[46]

But there was some sympathy for the insurance industry's situation. Even Biddle had appreciated the suddenness of the reversal implied by the Supreme Court's ruling and proposed that states and companies be given time to revise their practices. "I have not asked, nor has anybody in the Department of Justice considered, taking any action against the insurance company or group of insurance companies until the states have had an opportunity to consider to what extent they may wish to amend their laws, or until the Congress has had a full opportunity to decide if it wishes to amend a federal statute."[47]

Insurers and state regulators proposed a limited exemption to federal antitrust regulation, contingent on state regulation. This proposal became the McCarran-Ferguson Act, passed in 1945. The act gave states three years to pass laws that would bring the industry under effective control, after which federal antitrust laws would apply only to the extent that state law did not regulate, except in the event of "boycott, coercion, or intimidation," in which case the Sherman Act would apply. The McCarran-Ferguson Act essentially was a type of reverse preemption, but Roosevelt when signing the bill made it clear that states needed to do more than simply go through the motions of regulating. If they failed to be effective, they risked further federal involvement, since Congress would not tolerate "private rate fixing." There was no desire to allow the "private governments" created by insurers to retain power.[48]

To Senator Joseph O'Mahoney, Democrat from Wyoming and staunch opponent of monopoly, it was important that the act not be interpreted as a nullification of the *SEUA* decision, but rather as an "invitation to the insurance industry and the states to set up a formula of state regulation that will preserve a free economy in insurance by preserving competition and banishing the evils of monopolistic central control."[49] There was support in Congress for the continuation of state control and concern about an overly active federal government, as seen in this statement by cosponsor Senator Homer Ferguson, Republican from

Michigan, in an address before state insurance regulators in 1946: "There is a domination today by the bureaucracy and there were a few people, I am satisfied, in Washington that were licking their chops when they knew that the United States Supreme Court declared that the insurance business of America was interstate commerce. What a great bureau could be built if we had them all down in Washington regulating the insurance business of America and putting out of business these 48 Commissioners here!"[50]

For the national organization of state commissioners, which had adopted new bylaws in 1936 and changed its name to the National Association of Insurance Commissioners (NAIC), the McCarran-Ferguson Act was a major turning point. Initially set up as a voluntary organization for state regulators, the group had thus far had relatively little to do with the federal government. Going forward, a major focus of the NAIC would be to represent the interests of states to Washington and advocate for state autonomy whenever possible. This led to an increase in the professionalism and importance of this national organization of state regulators and drew the state regulators closer to the companies. For political as well as fiscal reasons, no state wished to relinquish its ability to supervise and tax this large industry.[51]

The state of affairs that had led to the *SEUA* decision and the subsequent McCarran-Ferguson Act had caused doubt about whether states could adequately regulate the business of insurance. Now states would be required to work with the industry and craft rating laws that would preserve the exemption from federal antitrust regulation. This would require standardizing a higher level of state oversight. At the time of the *SEUA* decision, there was considerable variation in state practices, with a few setting rates, others supervising rating bureaus, and still others engaged in some type of antitrust strategy.[52]

The NAIC set up a process to create model legislation, establishing the All Industry Committee (AIC) with representation from both insurers and regulators. A leader was New York's superintendent of insurance, Robert Dineen, whose basic objective was to increase the power of state regulators while supporting the desire of rating bureaus to be shielded from competition. The model legislation that resulted sought to strike a balance between uniformity and independence. It prohibited rates that were "excessive, inadequate, or unfairly discriminatory." While it permitted cooperative action among insurers for the purpose of rate setting, it explicitly did not "prohibit or discourage" competition; nor did it either "prohibit or encourage" uniformity in rates. Companies would have "the privilege" of following the patterns of others but also "complete freedom to make patterns of their own."[53]

With regard to the power of regulators, there was a split within the committee on the issue of rate regulation between whether regulators should have the power to grant prior approval or whether rates should have some version of a "file and use" status. The model bill ended up with a form of prior approval, recommending that commissioners would have fifteen days in which to disapprove a rate, and a disapproval would require a rate hearing. Rating organizations would be licensed by the state and could file for all members. Deviations could be granted if an individual company made a separate filing and defended its separate rate. The model rating laws were designed to increase the power of both the regulators and the rating bureaus.

The model rating laws were considered a compromise and as such did not please everyone. By 1951, all states had passed some version of these laws, but they did not all go about it in the same way. California adopted a system where bureaus, though legal, were not permitted to set rates. Market competition determined rates, which were "file and use"—that is, not subject to approval by commissioners. Texas, which had set rates prior to the SEUA, would continue to establish rates separately from industry. Life and health insurance were exempted from these laws, since they had no history of collusion, and so was marine insurance, which was generally not subject to state regulation.[54]

During this time, internal pressure on the business continued to build. In 1942, John A. Diemand, who succeeded Benjamin Rush as president of the INA, continued his company's critique of the industry in a widely publicized speech in which he advocated for integrating multiple lines of insurance and taking steps to increase competition, identifying excessive commissions and "self-imposed red tape" as key contributors to the current stagnation of the fire business. Diemand argued that complacency and attachment to a glorious past were the bane of the industry. *Time* observed the crossfire of criticism: "From both directions the charge was the same: that insurance rates are too high."[55]

In June of 1944, the same month as the SEUA decision, an NAIC committee chaired by Diemand issued a report recommending the establishment of multiple lines for comprehensive auto, aviation, and "personal property" floaters. While most committee members supported a comprehensive homeowner's policy as well, that recommendation was seen as too controversial at the time. The Insurance Executives Association (IEA) and the Association of Casualty and Surety Executives reacted strongly and negatively to the recommendations, arguing that "there would seem to be no reason for disturbing the business of those companies now adequately meeting public demand."[56] Yet despite this opposition, the NAIC accepted the recommendations and laws permitting multiple lines began to spread throughout the states.

The *SEUA* decision and the subsequent state regulation played into the ongoing internal strife in the insurance business, between an entrenched bureaucracy bent on uniformity and a growing impetus to develop new products and pricing methods. One appraisal saw a split between "a few choice mossbacks" and a group that recognized the "momentous importance of recent events" and was trying to avoid the development of a "state-blessed monopoly."[57]

Reflecting this tension, Diemand resigned from the IEA shortly after the *SEUA* decision, signaling that the INA intended to strike out on its own. This move caused a painful rift in the clubby culture of the property and casualty business, where "business and fellowship were mingled" and competitors were friends.[58] Field agents from different companies called on customers together, socialized with each other, and participated in occupationally specific fraternal organizations like the Honorable Order of the Blue Goose. It was considered "ungentlemanly" to take business from one another.

The decision to leave the rating organization led to the ostracism and social shunning of INA employees. Employees from other companies would cross the street to avoid INA representatives. Challenging the norms of cooperation and stability was an unforgiveable breach. Just as competition was a dirty word to the leaders of the IEA, field agents had been trained to believe that "rate cutters were not fit to associate with, and no honorable man would buy insurance from them." Friendships were strained and broken. To some at the INA, the costs were too high, as acknowledged in one resignation letter: "I can't work for a company which is not friendly to its competitors and wants to be independent of the rest of the industry."[59]

In various ways, the INA and other companies tried to take "independent action" in the post-*SEUA* period. One example was an attempt to market an auto policy with a different type of premium payment structure. The "Installment Premium Endorsement," first proposed in 1951, would allow policyholders to finance a multiyear policy by paying in installments rather than by taking a bank loan. When regional rating organizations opposed, the INA filed forms independently. Although the coverage was ultimately approved in most states, opponents used the structure of state rating laws to create impediments by requiring lengthy hearings.

Other examples of independent action included alterations in the commission structure that resulted when a company wanted to charge rates that were lower than the bureau rates. In many states, the rating laws required that rate "deviations" be filed and approved each year, a process that inherently complicated the path to independent action. Even when commissioners approved the lower rate, rating bureaus would often be able to create a legal challenge. So when the INA filed a deviation in Illinois in 1951, the Cook County Inspection Bureau contested it and requested that the state hold a hearing. When the state commissioner approved the deviation, the rate bureau filed a series of legal challenges, which, while unsuccessful, were time consuming for both sides and took up the entire year, at which point the INA needed to file the deviation once again.

Despite the *SEUA* decision and the creation of new rating laws, the orthodoxy that still controlled the property and casualty industry did their best to maintain uniformity in pricing and prevent the creation of new products, including comprehensive homeowners coverage.[60] When this new coverage was first proposed in 1950, it was considered a major advance: fire, lightning, hail, windstorm, explosion, riot and civil disorder, aircraft, land vehicles, smoke and smudge on the home and its contents, residence theft insurance, legal liability for accidents, and medical care for injuries to guests and others—all covered in one policy. While commissioners around the country approved it and *Business Week* described it as "revolutionary," the IEA argued it should be prohibited, opposing it on the grounds that the premium was indivisible into the separate lines. This indivisibility, of course, eliminated the usefulness of the rating boards, whose statistics were based on the premise of separate lines of coverage.

Yet comprehensive homeowners coverage could not be derailed. It was immediately very popular, and premiums written grew one-hundred-fold from about $750,000 in 1951 to more than $750 million in 1960.[61] The establishment of multiple line coverage was more than thirty years in the making, with the resistance coming from within the insurance business. It was not until 1955 that multiple lines were approved in every state.

In 1953, the struggle within the industry was ratcheted up another notch when the INA announced their resignation from the rating bureaus for the homeowners lines but signaled that they intended to maintain their membership for other lines of business, thus attempting to become a "partial subscriber." This led to a mass rejection of their business by agents, including boycotts from state agencies. In New York, the main rating organization, the New York Fire Insurance Rating Organization (NYFIRO), unsuccessfully took the INA to court, filing a series of appeals in which they argued that rates should not be based on the experience of one company.

By this time, it was becoming clear that the National Board of Fire Underwriters was spearheading a coordinated effort to maintain uniformity and status quo business practices. The president of the Hartford, John A. North, was tasked by the board to run a special strike force of chief executives with the goal of stifling competition. Also involved were the NYFIRO, the Pacific Fire Rating Bureau (PFRB), and the Eastern Underwriters Association (EUA), as well as a number of local rating organizations.

The so-called North Committee attempted various legislative strategies to try to raise the cost of independence. One was to lobby states to prevent partial subscribership in rating bureaus. Another was to try to get states to amend their laws to require universal membership and uniform pricing. A third was to prohibitively raise the cost of partial subscribership. While the NYFIRO tried to suppress independent activity in New York, the PFRB and other members of the

North Committee attempted similar strategies elsewhere. The INA was singled out as a particular target because of its size.

The machinations of the North Committee did not escape the notice of Congress. The Senate Subcommittee on Antitrust and Monopoly, a standing judiciary subcommittee established in 1951, added the insurance industry to a wide-ranging investigation of competition, including meatpacking, steel, automobile manufacturing, and pharmaceuticals. Senator O'Mahoney, who had previously investigated competition issues in insurance while chairing the TNEC between 1938 and 1940, presided over the investigation. Senator Estes Kefauver, Democrat from Tennessee, chaired the subcommittee between 1957 and 1963.[62] Insurance industry hearings were held in the summers of 1958, 1959, and 1960 and included the testimony of more than seventy-five witnesses. The result was two reports and ten volumes of materials, totaling nearly seven thousand pages.

In his opening statement, O'Mahoney noted that in 1957 Americans spent $26 million in insurance premiums, representing more than eight percent of national income. Insurance affects "the pocketbook of every businessman in the land" and in "one way or another touches the lives of all the citizens of the United States."[63] In the context of the Cold War, the old saw about insurance being affected with the public interest got a new twist. Subcommittee member Senator Alexander Wiley of Wisconsin noted that while the "Commies" might provide "cradle to grave" security, Americans were free to acquire it on their own, making the operation of the insurance business "one of the most important adjuncts of the free enterprise system."[64]

O'Mahoney, who had been one of the architects of the McCarran-Ferguson Act, made it clear that the investigation was "keyed from its very inception to an appraisal of the effectiveness of competition under the State laws within the broad framework of the McCarran Act."[65] Called to testify first were various aggrieved parties, including INA president John Diemand; Vestal Lemmon, who represented independent agents and direct writers; representatives of mutuals; and an executive from Allstate Insurance. All gave accounts of rebukes and obstacles placed in their path by those set on maintaining the bureau system. The subcommittee's counsel Donald P. McHugh requested internal documents from the National Board of Fire Underwriters and the regional rating bureaus and heard testimony from industry executives involved with the North Committee along with state commissioners. The subcommittee questioned whether states were regulating adequately and whether "any revision should be made" to the conditional exemption granted by the McCarran-Ferguson Act.[66] States were under strong pressure from the industry to preserve the bureau system, as observed by Kentucky commissioner Spalding Southall during an NAIC meeting in 1951. This comment was read into the testimony to illustrate how "advocates of the status quo" used the machinery of state regulation to maintain power:

> Knowing human nature, we must understand that although the SEUA decision required a change in some of the practices of the business, it could not change the fundamental desire of those who one way or another, want to bring about a restriction of competition. It would be only natural to expect to find a continuation of efforts to restrict competition, using whatever devices and channels that might be available: and it would be especially probable that the devices and channels of greatest interest to those desiring to restrain competition would be those as to which State supervision under Public Law 15 could provide an apparent cloak of immunity from federal prosecution. We must recognize that much of the machinery by which restraints upon competition in insurance were enforced in the pre-SEUA days is still around. We still have the boards and the bureaus and the associations.[67]

Commissioners tended to side with consumers in supporting the introduction of new products such as homeowners' coverage, but the resources and expertise they brought to bear on regulatory questions were often inadequate, and they rarely questioned bureau rates. This was even true in New York, which was, relatively speaking, a very proficient regulator yet tended to be protective of the established rating organizations.[68] In many other states, departments were underresourced and lacked the technical ability to productively examine rate filings. A study of the Utah Insurance Department, for example, observed that the staff of nine people had a total budget of less than $35,000 and no trained actuary. This situation led the commissioner to "rely heavily on the rating bureaus."[69] As a result, rates were sometimes approved without review or might be changed as a result of political pressure or other nontechnical reasons. The capacity to regulate fire insurance rates in Wisconsin was improving but not yet able to escape involvement in political and personal controversy.[70]

Yet greater state involvement in rate regulation was not necessarily synonymous with good government. Texas was one of the strictest states in terms of rate regulation, but in practice this enabled myriad loopholes and facilitated a culture of official corruption. For example, Lloyds companies and county mutuals were not subject to the rate laws, so other insurers began to buy or create them to circumvent regulation. The SEUA decision and the subsequent rating laws did nothing to reform the regulatory culture, and the postwar period came to be referred to as the "bad old days." Bribery and influence peddling were normalized, contributing to a number of celebrated financial collapses of insurance companies that were created using fabricated sources of capital. The sorry state of affairs reached the point where the new commissioner in 1957 felt it necessary to announce: "There will be no more private meetings, secret persuasions, or surprise decisions."[71]

The second subcommittee report, released in August 1961, documented a "bleak picture of concerted efforts on a nationwide basis to restrain competition which not only went unchallenged by the states but virtually unnoticed."[72] This included "impressive" attempts to "pervert the state regulatory process" in order to impede competitive threats.[73] In detailing the machinations of the North Committee, the subcommittee sought to demonstrate that the participants were "well aware that their activities constituted a conspiracy and a possible restraint of trade in violation of the anti-trust laws." In fact, the committee observed, "the bureaus *were* the companies in different form."[74]

The subcommittee recommended that states modify their rating laws to promote competition by permitting deviations, independent filings, and partial subscriptions. On the topic of mandatory bureau membership, they made a strong suggestion: "It is earnestly hoped that those States still retaining in their rating laws such vestiges of pre-*SEUA* thinking will accept this invitation by the Congress to modify their laws accordingly."[75] The NAIC came under criticism for its lack of leadership. The subcommittee derided the association's claim that each state should have the freedom to choose their own regulatory system, claiming the NAIC was "simply closing its eyes to its responsibilities" and has not "faced up to the hard task of challenging State laws which violate the spirit of the McCarran Act."[76]

Senator O'Mahoney, in one of his last acts before retirement, introduced a bill repealing the insurance laws of the District of Columbia and creating a new set of regulations that incorporated the subcommittee's recommendations regarding competition. Senator Kefauver reintroduced a modified version of this bill in January of 1961.[77] The subcommittee's endorsement of the California style of open rating laws was reflected in this bill, with the modification that insurers should be required to file rates, "since insurance remains a regulated industry," but that they would become immediately effective—that is, "file and use."[78] In place of perfunctory rate review, state regulators were urged to more carefully monitor advisory associations and double down on examinations of solvency. The practice of charging companies for the cost of examinations, standard in many states, including New York, was deplored for creating perverse incentives.[79]

Writing for the minority, subcommittee member Senator Everett Dirksen, Republican from Illinois, authored "Individual Views" at the end of both subcommittee reports. Some of the contours of postwar disagreement about the federalist structure of economic regulation can be seen in the differences between the minority and the majority views. In the 1960 report, Dirksen laid bare a longstanding fundamental difference with O'Mahoney over the federal role in the supervision of business, accusing O'Mahoney of having supported federal charters for business since his time with the TNEC. Dirksen argued that state supervision of insurance was adequate, if not perfect, and that the industry demonstrated "flexibility and elasticity."[80]

In the 1961 report, Dirksen critiqued the majority for taking too long to release their findings, claiming that they were largely out of date and irrelevant. He further objected to the subcommittee's inquiries into the details of state regulation, which he argued were intrusive to states and their sovereignty. Dirksen argued that the majority employed a type of "straw man" argument to castigate the current state of regulation, which painted the "old guard" as more resistant to change and more powerful than they actually were. As partial evidence he cited North's own assessment of his lack of progress:

> With the decision in the Arizona Supreme Court on partial subscribership and the results of action taken in New York State, I am wondering now whether our special committee of chief executives can serve any further useful purpose. We have actually accomplished very little. Whatever moves were inspired by us have practically all failed so that now there is a question in my mind as to the future of this committee.[81]

While agreeing with the merits of increased competition, Dirksen argued that the majority had become "diverted into many inconsequential details" and found it "regrettable that the majority's report, in an effort to impugn the motives of particular companies and segments of the insurance industry, diverts attention from the problems of the American people today to activities that are no longer relevant."[82] More broadly, Dirksen began to criticize the antitrust investigations as a whole for attacking free enterprise and burdening corporations while turning up "little of value."[83]

The report received relatively little public attention. In the pages of the *Journal of Insurance*, the assessment was that the recommendations covered no new ground, and the hearings and report were, even by their standards, "dull beyond expectations."[84] But even Dirksen and insurance insiders who critiqued the subcommittee for indulging in "nostalgic oversimplification" supported the basic recommendations. The current regulatory system had resulted in an overemphasis on bureau rates and vested too much power in advisory associations. There was little disagreement that mandatory bureau membership was inconsistent with a competitive market and that deviations, independent filings, and partial subscriptions should be unencumbered.

Some speculated that a transition to a system where all companies filed their own rates might demand a degree of "executive ingenuity and imagination" not currently found in insurance. In fact, a "daring and fertile sort of mind" was not thought to be a hallmark of the insurance industry, which had "traditionally attracted more conservative career types."[85] According to *Fortune*, conformity was prized as a virtue: "Indeed, the soaring imagination is suspect in insurance. It was considered a mark of statesmanship for an executive to keep his company in line with the 'right practices' in the way of policy forms, rates, and commissions, and an honor to be an officer in one of the cooperative organizations that enforced stabilization among the companies."[86] While allowing that "one does not expect the GPO to turn out best sellers," a reviewer for the *Journal of Insurance* nevertheless panned the hearings for a lack of "snappy and exciting dialogue."[87] Yet the testimony, though not explosive, revealed how deeply ingrained the cultural norms were that maintained the bureau system. Kenneth Black, president of the Home Insurance Company, described his participation in the work of the North Committee. Under questioning from counsel Donald P. McHugh, Black admitted that one of the group's legal strategies was to try to "tighten up" the deviation section of the model rating law. McHugh asked Black how he thought that might affect competition.

MR. BLACK: I don't know as it would open up competition in the sense that you mean it, but if we could talk about utopia in this business, it might be a good idea if everybody belonged to a rating organization and there was no escape hatch.

MR. MCHUGH: If I understand your suggestion, if all companies were in a single rating bureau, that means you would have a single rate on behalf of all companies who were in that bureau and selling insurance.

MR. BLACK: I am not suggesting that; I am suggesting it would be utopia.

MR. MCHUGH: And you suggest that the public would be better served—

MR. BLACK: I would be inclined to think so.

MR. MCHUGH: (continuing)—if all the companies were in the same rating bureau?

MR. BLACK: Yes, sir.

MR. MCHUGH: Would you say, Mr. Black, that the effect of such a method of determining rates at which insurance is sold would have the effect of discouraging innovation and preventing companies who wanted to pioneer and to take risks that others may not wish to take and deterring that type of thinking in the insurance industry?

MR. BLACK: Please do not misunderstand me, sir. I am not proposing that. I merely say that it would be utopia, and I recognize that practically and from the social standpoint, it is impossible. I recognize that.[88]

Peter Drucker observed, "Some theories of the business are so powerful that they last a long time. But eventually every single one of them becomes obsolete."[89] Based on experience with urban conflagrations, the fire insurance industry became convinced in the nineteenth century that restricting competition was necessary to preserve stability. The National Board of Fire Underwriters was originally established in 1866 for the purpose of standardizing rates nationally. A price-fixing approach based on regional rating bureaus became widespread by the early twentieth century, with varying degrees of oversight and accommodation by states. Yet federal intervention, the development of new insurance products, and competition from direct writers all combined to put pressure on these long-established business practices.

While in one sense the rating laws that states adopted after the *SEUA* decision enshrined the collusive norms of the fire insurance industry, it also may be argued that this marked the beginning of the end of this longstanding system.[90] By the mid-1960s, the disintegration of the bureau system was well underway. States moved to change laws to promote competition and make it easier to deviate from board rates. Many eliminated prior approval and transitioned to open rating.[91] Direct writers and mutuals increased their market share.

The National Board of Fire Underwriters celebrated its centennial in 1966. By then this iconic organization, the nation's oldest business association, had merged with its casualty counterpart. The combined group had in turn been absorbed by the American Insurance Association, itself an organizational replacement for the ultimate symbol of stasis, the IEA. Presumably without irony, the board observed in a commemorative history, "The business of insurance is never static."[92]

The orthodox theory of the business also had a proscribed role for government. The worldview of the fire insurance establishment was that it was a quasi-public entity of its own creation and should be able to set the terms of its engagement with government, much like a sovereign nation. The National Board of Fire Underwriters consistently described itself as a public service organization. The fact that it was "so successful in developing its *own* program of public services quite independently of government" seemed to justify the fact that it "places great importance on preserving its traditional freedom." Even as late as 1964, when the board was virtually no more, the last president saw fit to express this preference as a demand: "But we must insist that those in government recognize that private enterprise properly conducted must not be unduly restricted by big government."[93]

As government became more active, the quasi-public worldview of the insurance industry became less central to its identity. This is seen in the tone struck by the St. Paul Fire Insurance Company in describing the status of crop insurance, which had slowly developed in the private sector, facilitated by largely publicly funded advances in agricultural science and better data. In 1968, the St. Paul reported they were experimenting with covering other perils such as insects, disease, and excessive moisture. In their telling of the history, the federal government was the interloper, whose involvement was nothing but a nuisance:

> Our toughest competition is the federal government. They entered the market during the depression because some farmers were experiencing difficulty obtaining all risk crop policies from private companies. For over 30 years the government has vigorously extended their crop insurance program. Their plan is heavily subsidized. Rates are computed to cover pure losses only, with administration and other expenses absorbed by the general taxpayer, that's you and me. In 1967 they had a 25% increase in business compared to an increase of about 12% for all companies. We're working to curb their growth by offering better products and better service, although it's tough to compete with federal giveaways.[94]

We will see that the dismantling of the bureau system and the transition to more competitive rate making did not eliminate persistent consumer discontent. Problems in insurance markets would continue, but their characteristics would change, and they would become in many ways more difficult to solve. In the next several decades, controversies would emerge over the cost and availability of auto and property insurance that involved challenging issues of gender, age, and racial discrimination and complex distributional questions. Insurers would seek to retreat from their quasi-public role as it created new constraints and obligations. A new cohort of reform-minded state commissioners would reflect the growing wave of consumer activism. At the same time, the willingness and ability of states to adequately address these issues would continue to be questioned. The federal government's involvement in insurance, both as watchdog and as participant, would only deepen, though the ability to make substantive change would prove to be elusive.

9

A Squirrel Cage Operation

When James Rancher tried to buy life insurance in 1949, he didn't expect to find himself at the center of a controversy. Rancher was a student who was working at a shoe repair shop in Milwaukee. He was also a young husband and new father and had recently returned from service in World War II, where he had been stationed in the Philippines. He was twenty-four years old and in good health, but his application to the Wisconsin State Life Fund for a $1,000 policy was rejected. Rancher was Black and listed his nationality as "Negro American" on his policy application. The Wisconsin State Life Fund claimed they couldn't sell Rancher a policy at standard rates, due to the higher mortality of Black people, and they were forbidden by law to write policies at substandard rates. The only option the state could see was to deny his application.[1]

The experience of James Rancher was an important episode in a long history of racial discrimination in life insurance. Rancher was trying to buy an ordinary life policy; however, much of this history concerns industrial insurance. Industrial insurance is a type of life insurance developed in the late nineteenth century for low-income workers. Industrial insurance differed from "ordinary" life insurance because the policies had lower face values and had weekly premium payments that were collected in person. The "Big Three," Prudential, Metropolitan Life, and John Hancock, dominated the industrial business from its inception and had about eighty percent of the market in 1900.

In the earliest days of industrial insurance there were no differences in premiums based on race, but in 1881, Prudential started to charge higher rates to Blacks on the grounds that their mortality was higher. Metropolitan Life followed suit. Massachusetts soon responded by passing a law forbidding race-based premiums, and a handful of other states passed similar laws.[2]

In response, Prudential stopped selling to Black customers altogether. Metropolitan initially responded by withdrawing from states with antidiscrimination laws while continuing to use raced-based premiums elsewhere. But by 1894, they had come to believe that with careful underwriting, the race differential was negligible, so they returned to the states they had formerly abandoned.

In 1896, Prudential's chief statistician, Frederick Hoffman, published what would become an infamous study of race differences in mortality. "Race Traits and Tendencies of the American Negro" sought to prove that higher mortality

Uncovered. Katherine Hempstead, Oxford University Press. © Oxford University Press 2024.
DOI: 10.1093/oso/9780190094157.003.0009

among Black people stemmed from innate biological inferiority and that the race was essentially doomed.[3] Frederick professed to be motivated by science only and even argued that his foreign birth left him free from "personal bias" that might otherwise cloud his judgment.[4] And while "Race Traits" was intended as a response to state antidiscrimination efforts in life insurance, its influence spread far beyond the insurance industry.[5]

Standard mortality tables for industrial insurance were adopted for the first time in 1907 and showed the differential mortality by race. Previously, industrial rates had been set based on individual company experience. The publication of the new tables prompted Metropolitan Life to change their policy and stop selling to Black people once again. As Marquis James noted in his 1947 history of Metropolitan Life, to continue writing insurance at the same premiums would have been "discrimination against the whites."[6] Metropolitan analyzed its industrial policyholders and published its own study of mortality by race in 1919, concluding there was a "true difference in the vitality of the two groups" but avoiding Hoffman's broader interpretation and making no mention of "Race Traits."[7]

Trying to stay within the language, if not the spirit, of the antidiscrimination laws, the company created a set of "special tables" for extra mortality. They were largely intended to be used with Black policyholders. If a Black policyholder was enrolled in a policy where the premium was based on the ordinary tables, an adjustment was made by withholding the agent's commission.[8] In this way, companies were able to continue race-based discrimination even in states that tried to prohibit it. The 1907 mortality table for industrial insurance remained in use until the 1940s, when a new industrial table was adopted, along with a new "substandard" table, the latter intended largely for use by companies with many Black policyholders.[9] The racial discrimination practiced by life insurance companies gave rise to Black fraternal societies and, later, separate legal reserve companies. These companies sold both industrial and ordinary policies and competed with the Big Three. The largest of these was North Carolina Mutual, which was founded in Durham in the late nineteenth century.

There were initially relatively few Black customers for the more expensive ordinary policies. But by the 1920s, Metropolitan Life became concerned that the growing share of Black policyholders in their "intermediate" ordinary category ($500 policy) was pushing up the overall mortality experience of the group. Reverting to the same playbook used in the industrial branch, the company sought to adjust by paying partial agent commissions on policies sold to Black policymakers. However, the state of New York broadened the scope of their antidiscrimination law in 1935 to include a prohibition on differences in commissions. In response, Metropolitan stopped soliciting any kind of life insurance to Black residents of the state, insisting that the antidiscrimination laws had the unintended effect of restricting access. In his account, Marquis James took a defensive if not slightly exasperated position: "Time and again it has been demonstrated that the mortality of colored lives is sizably greater than that of whites. Where possible Metropolitan has tried to write insurance on colored lives, but at rates commensurate with mortality experience."[10] Thus, race discrimination in life insurance was still a standard practice in the late 1940s, though it was coming under increasing pressure from civil rights groups. Rancher challenged the decision of the Wisconsin State Life Fund and in September 1949 filed a civil suit in U.S. district court that alleged that the current and former insurance commissioner, the manager of the Wisconsin State Life Fund, and the treasurer had violated the Fourteenth Amendment. The *Capital Times* supported the suit, expressing "surprise" on behalf of state residents "who are now told we have a law that sets up second class citizens in Wisconsin."[11]

Wisconsin insurance commissioner John Lange, who had been at the insurance department since 1921, contended that the Wisconsin State Life Fund was only authorized to issue policies using rates based on the standard American Experience Table. Since Blacks had higher mortality than Whites, they were classified as substandard risks. His outlook showed the persistence of Hoffman's "Race Traits" in actuarial thinking about mortality risk as a group rather than an individual trait. In what he may have thought was an encouraging comment, Lange acknowledged recent improvements in Black mortality: "in the future—maybe in 50 or 100 years—the colored race will eventually be classified as part of the class of 'standard risks.'"[12]

The trial court accepted Lange's version of events, despite considerable testimony that the higher mortality of Blacks arose from environmental and social rather than biological differences. But the federal district court had disagreed, and on appeal, the Wisconsin Supreme Court held six to one in *Lange v. Rancher* in 1953 that the state had failed to make the case that the racial classification used was the "only one which will achieve the purposes for which the state fund was created."

Writing for the majority, Justice Grover Broadfoot found: "The plaintiff (Lange) offered no proof in support of his inference that the higher mortality rate among Negroes is the result of some inherent difference between them and white persons. The defendant (Rancher) on the other hand, produced expert testimony, which is not controverted, that physically and biologically white and Negro persons are essentially the same." The fact that race-based underwriting was used in the insurance industry was not relevant. The majority found that the practices of private insurance companies were "not controlling" of the operation of the Wisconsin State Life Fund.[13]

The *Capital Times* agreed with the decision in an editorial that also took a swipe at standard actuarial practices: "Our Constitution does not recognize differences between citizens because of the color of their skin or the manner in which they worship their God. Nor does it recognize the existence of the fictitious average man, which is the basis of the insurance companies' operations."[14]

Since *Rancher* pertained to the particularities of the Wisconsin State Life Fund and explicitly did not engage with the practices of private companies, it was not considered to be far reaching. The case did not garner an enormous amount of publicity. An article in the *Chicago Tribune* observed that *Rancher* meant that "a Negro must be considered as an individual rather than as a member of a race."[15] But the story was buried on page thirty-five. The case was not mentioned at the annual meeting of the National Association of Insurance Commissioners (NAIC).

In part this was because private industry itself had already begun to change. Companies had started to unwind race-based practices in the postwar period, in response to pressure from civil rights groups. In 1948, just one year after Marquis James's iconic *The Metropolitan Life* was published, and one year before Rancher filed his complaint against the Wisconsin State Life Fund, Metropolitan Life equalized the death benefit for Black and White policyholders and eliminated the use of substandard tables prospectively. In 1951, the company began soliciting both Black and White customers. By 1954 most rules about race-based commissions were gone, and by 1958 the majority of race-based practices had ceased.[16]

In 1961, a new "race-merged" industrial mortality table was adopted, which did not include a separate substandard table, although margins were created to allow some adjustment for experience.[17] This change accelerated the decline of industrial insurance, which was already a shrinking line of business. The Big Three stopped writing new industrial policies by the end of the decade, ceding the ground to smaller companies, and by 1970 they had only thirty percent of industrial insurance in force.

This chapter addresses the transitioning perspective of the life insurance industry in the twentieth century. The collapse of industrial insurance, which is central to that story, was seeded in the Depression, though the end of race-based underwriting was a final blow to profitability. Before the Depression, life insurers had an expansive view of their place in society and spoke of their business as a public service. Those companies that sold industrial insurance described it as a social welfare program.

Yet as the century progressed, the perspective of life insurers changed. The role of the federal government increased, both as a provider of insurance and as a critic and potential regulator. The insurance industry's outlook accordingly narrowed. The creation of Social Security and the travails of the industrial business during the Depression illustrated the inadequacy of voluntary collectivism, especially during hard times. The withdrawal from industrial insurance was replaced with the enthusiastic pursuit of group insurance sold to employers, including life insurance, pensions, and health insurance. This exponentially growing "private welfare" system became the object of whatever remained of the "social" outlook of life insurers.

Industrial insurance was a low-value product that was a commercial response to the demands of low-income people who could not afford ordinary insurance. In the absence of public intervention, this product remained on the market until it was no longer profitable. The federal government filled some of the gap with the creation of Social Security, and the judicial system complicated profitability by prohibiting race-based underwriting, but nevertheless industrial insurance was left to die on its own.

State regulators largely ignored both the industrial business and the unmet demand that made it possible, with the exception of sporadic regulatory efforts and limited forays into savings bank insurance and kindred efforts in a few states. One of these was the Wisconsin State Life Fund, which was earnestly created in 1911 as a public alternative to commercial insurance and ironically became a defender of the status quo industry practice of race-based underwriting in the Rancher case. The unmet demand for insurance was greatest for Black people, who were systematically overcharged or excluded from coverage.

The life insurance industry entered the Depression in an exuberant if not grandiose frame of mind. During the 1920s, sales soared for ordinary, industrial, and the nascent group business. The total amount of life insurance in force increased from $36 billion in 1919 to $100 billion in 1929.[18] Despite initial concerns about government encroachment, the efforts of the War Risk Insurance Board had been a tremendous source of free advertising and an accelerant for demand. As one Metropolitan Life executive who had been an artilleryman in World War I observed: "When Uncle Sam put a value of $10,000 on the life of a buck private it worked a lot of people up."[19]

Life insurers continued to speak of themselves as though they were primarily engaged in public service. The companies' well-publicized "compassionate" handling of farm mortgages during the agricultural depression only burnished their image as largely charitable agencies.[20] They could afford to be charitable, because business was booming. Between 1920 and 1929, Metropolitan Life reported growth in ordinary life insurance from $2.6 to $8.6 billion. The industrial business grew nearly as much, from $2.6 to $6.7 billion. Still smallest, but growing exponentially, was group insurance, which increased nearly twenty-fold, from $136 million to $2.6 billion.[21] Throughout the industry, interest was gravitating toward group business, and there was a shared conviction that workplace benefits along with industrial insurance would solve all problems for the "laboring classes." As the prosperous 1920s unfolded, concern about socialism and state insurance was a receding threat.

In the postwar period, both life insurers and fire insurers described themselves as being primarily engaged in the performance of a public service, but their businesses differed in some important ways. The fire insurance business was structured around the industry rather than the individual company. The National Board of Fire Underwriters, the main trade association, had been active since the 1860s. Important trade associations for life insurers were not formed until the twentieth century. Property and casualty insurers avoided competition and sought uniformity. Life insurance rates were based on a common set of mortality tables that was jointly used by the industry, but there was less need to cooperate with competitors in the way that property and casualty insurers did to produce maps or schedule ratings. The life insurance business was driven by the cultures of the individual companies. Due to the lengthy time horizon of policies, the largest life companies achieved enormous financial scale. The size and related excesses of the largest companies were the focus of the Armstrong investigation. And while many lasting reforms resulted from that investigation, the massiveness of the largest firms and their accompanying sense of grandeur remained very much intact.

Another factor that differentiated life from fire insurance was that to a much greater extent, the former had to be actively sold. This led to a major difference between the two lines of business with regard to the importance of sales and the role of agents. In property and casualty insurance, demand was more routine. Although direct writers were gaining market share, agents generally were not employees and placed risks with multiple insurers. Life insurance was discretionary in a way that fire insurance was not. This placed a premium on sales and the role of the agents, who were more likely to be company employees.

Company leadership often emerged from the ranks of agents. This was true, for example, at New York Life, where Presidents Darwin Kingsley and George Perkins both started as agents, worked to establish the branch office agency system, and rose through the ranks of leadership. Educating agents and motivating them to sell was perhaps the most crucial part of the life business. This required a system of financial rewards and group activities to build morale. Much of the culture of the major life firms revolved around their approach to sales.

Business historian Thomas Cochran has written of the social personality of the business enterprise.[22] These distinct personalities are very evident in the large life insurance firms of the early twentieth century. What is common to all is a celebration of their largesse, a magisterial worldview, and a messianic belief in life insurance as a public service. In terms of sheer grandiosity, New York Life was a standard bearer. Then-president George Perkins, on the occasion of the sixtieth anniversary in 1905, modestly observed that "To attempt a review of the work of the New York Life Insurance Company would be to attempt a review of the progress of the world during the last half century; for one is safely within bounds in saying that our great Company has, in several notable respects, been a leader in the most potent influences that have been working for the betterment of humanity."[23] The next president, Darwin Kingsley, kept this tradition of rhetorical flourish alive, in 1927 likening the company to a country, comparing its "population" to that of Switzerland. Here the fact of the firm's mutualization—a consequence of the Armstrong investigation—is used to strengthen the metaphor of New York Life as a "constitutional democracy," a literal unit of governance, an entity unto itself. On a per capita basis, he found the comparison impressive: "Take Switzerland for example. The population of that prosperous country is about four million souls. The population of the New York Life, if we regard its policy-holders as its population, is something over two million. The federal revenue of Switzerland in the year 1927 was $66,263,227, and the expenditures were $66,580,056. . . . The revenue of the New York Life for the year 1927 was $325,475,914.64."[24] In addition to policyholders, Kingsley notes that New York Life's "inhabitants" include nearly 3,800 employees, for whose benefit the company has adopted the most modern principles of "welfare work," such as pensions and sick benefits.

And New York Life was not just talking to itself. Calvin Coolidge, like presidents before him, was an important validator. In 1929, Coolidge accepted an invitation to serve on New York Life's board of directors, commenting that "Life insurance is the most effective instrumentality for the promotion of industry, saving and character ever developed" and that "the New York Life Insurance Company may justly be called a Public Service Institution." When an injury prevented him from attending a gathering of agents, Coolidge expressed regrets and extended his best wishes to these "missionaries of sound and enduring prosperity."[25]

To Metropolitan Life, welfare work was the key to their corporate culture. They too luxuriated in their sheer size and quasi-public status, describing themselves as a mammoth "trusteeship" that in 1922 encompassed one-sixth of the population of the United States and Canada, and one in three residents of New York City.[26] But as the largest of the companies selling industrial insurance, Metropolitan's persona derived from what it perceived to be its social mission to the poor. Metropolitan had a philanthropic and almost governmental outlook toward the improvement of the health of the "laboring classes." President Haley Fiske described the sweep of the company's social vision in 1927: "The desire that we have for the future is not aggrandizement. We are distributing all the money we have. It is not power, except to be used as men with power should use it. No, it is for the bettering of human conditions; it is for a reaching out a heart as big as Mother Metropolitan to better the condition of working men, to lengthen their lives, to improve their domestic relations, to bring up children better, to educate them, to make them live longer lives, to make happiness."[27]

Unique among the companies, they had a designated welfare department, led by Lee Frankel, who had been recruited from the United Hebrew Fund. This department funded nurses to visit policyholders and produced copious quantities of public health literature, translated in multiple languages and handed out by the thousands. Metropolitan also invested in affordable housing and made significant commitments to large-scale research projects, including an effort to reduce infant mortality in Quebec; an experiment to reduce tuberculosis in Framingham, Massachusetts; and an ambitious and wide-ranging intervention in a rural community in Tennessee. Metropolitan funded improvements in vital statistics and the practice of public health. The welfare department studied trends in social insurance, and Frankel and colleagues visited Europe to keep abreast of developments there. Fiske, who was president from 1919 to 1929, was such an enthusiast that he often spoke as if the welfare work was the primary mission, sustained out of necessity by selling insurance: "The wherewithal came from the man on the debit."[28]

Metropolitan's closest competitor for industrial business, Prudential, was more hard-nosed in its outlook. While the intellectual and philanthropic Frankel embodied the public face of Metropolitan's thought leadership, Prudential's most visible emissary was the statistician Hoffman, author of "Race Traits." While Metropolitan had "hosts" meet arriving relatives of industrial customers and shepherd them through customs, Prudential described similar activities as an opportunity to promote "Americanism."[29] Yet these differences may have been more superficial than substantive, and Metropolitan watched their largest competitor closely.[30]

Life insurance companies may have had different corporate cultures and personalities, but they were all concerned with growth.[31] For companies that sold only ordinary insurance, there was a concerted attempt to broaden the base of policyholders economically. New York Life issued a new basic policy written in "plain language, which could be understood by a person of average intelligence." Yet in a swipe at industrial insurance, they pledged to never swerve "from the path of standard lines which only tend to befuddle the insuring public into believing they are getting something for nothing."[32]

For Metropolitan, which had an industrial and an ordinary business, there was an attempt to attract ordinary policyholders of more modest means but also to try to bridge the gap between the two lines of business. One change that helped to accomplish both goals was the creation of the monthly premium. This was something that Metropolitan had been trying to do for years, but the administrative costs were initially too high. First introduced in ordinary insurance, monthly payments attracted new customers and allowed some existing policyholders to "graduate" from industrial to ordinary insurance. Monthly payments were then introduced within industrial insurance, permitting premium reductions of as much as fifteen percent. By 1939, the combined amount of monthly ordinary and industrial insurance in force exceeded the weekly industrial totals, a development the company saw as a "milestone in the economic progress of the laboring man."[33]

Another route to expansion was to increase underwriting to a broader class of enrollees. Metropolitan Life expanded their coverage of women and liberalized the terms.[34] New York Life claimed to be the first to stop charging higher premiums to women at around the turn of the century; this became an industry practice. Offering coverage to people with health problems, which the companies called "impaired" or "substandard lives" and what we might now call "pre-existing conditions," was another important strategy to increase sales. In the late nineteenth century, New York Life studied a group of "rejected lives" and measured their mortality. This led to the development of a numerical system that calibrated the estimated mortality of different categories of substandard lives as a ratio of the standard. This ratio was used to establish higher premiums for those with various health conditions.[35]

This expanded coverage became a big business. In 1896, when the first of these policies was issued, "substandard business" made up less than one percent of life insurance in force for New York Life. By 1928, ten percent of insurance in force was substandard. President Kingsley touted the broader social benefits with his characteristic lack of reserve: "This contribution to Life Insurance has taken an innumerable army of men and women out of the Purgatory of the impaired and put them into the Paradise of the insured."[36] This practice became widespread, with different companies having similar, but not identical, ways of assessing substandard lives. Metropolitan added a "special class" policy in 1899, which accommodated those with estimated mortality risk twice as high as the average. In 1920, a new "Special Class B" extended the range up to 250 percent of the standard mortality risk.[37]

But nothing could compare with the opportunity presented by group insurance sold to employers. For Metropolitan Life, their group business increased nearly thirty-five-fold between 1919 and 1929, from $60 million to $2.25 billion. Major contracts included General Electric in 1920, Southern Pacific Railroads in 1923, and General Motors in 1926. News of the latter deal was shared with President Haley Fiske, who was visiting London at the time, through a dramatic overseas telephone call.[38]

Group insurance had obvious appeal: lower administrative costs and the opportunity to sell multiple kinds of coverage. The biggest category was group life insurance. Another was group annuities, or retirement pensions, which

Metropolitan tried first on their own employees in 1925 before making the product more broadly available in 1927.[39] Less common initially, but growing quickly, was group accident and health insurance, which Metropolitan first offered in 1914, along with separate coverage for accidental death and dismemberment. Fiske saw the group business as the next phase of industrial insurance, sharing the views of Progressive Era advocates of employee "welfare benefits" for employees: that it would provide increased security to working people and promote a more harmonious relationship between labor and capital. Accordingly, the services of Metropolitan's welfare division were extended to group insurance.[40]

Continued growth for life insurers depended on sales, and therefore the training of agents was paramount. As New York Life's Darwin Kingsley noted: "No life insurance company has ever achieved anything worthwhile without driving its principles home through men." Each company developed their own approach, but to Kingsley, the industry efforts were more similar than different: "The great companies are all akin, in their methods, to the aggressive churches. They have followed the same methods, and in their determination to reach the people, they may even be said at times to have been as undignified and as useful as the Salvation Army."[41] New York Life was famous for its cultivation of agents. Perkins and Kingsley developed an elaborate system of compensation that became known industry-wide as the "NYLIC" system of benefits. A primary goal was to dignify the profession and create a culture based on friendly competition, reverence for company tradition, and love of life insurance. The annual multiday convention of agency directors was described as a good way for a "visitor from Mars" to get a sense of the corporate culture. An early company history describes the following scene for this potential extraterrestrial observer:

When the enthusiasm over some special achievement, or for some favorite officer, or about some newly announced plan of the Company reaches an irrepressible stage, all present—even the youngest and most conventional—under the rhythmic direction of an accomplished cheer-leader burst into the well-known Nylic slogan:

> Nylic! Nylic! Lic, lic, lic!!
> When you write 'em, make 'em stick.
> Do we write 'em? Well I guess!
> Nylic! Nylic! Yes! Yes! Yes![42]

There was also a special company song at North Carolina Mutual, an iconic Black life insurance company headquartered in Durham. Every Saturday

Figure 9.1 "The Forum" Meeting, 1920s, North Carolina Mutual Insurance Company, President C.C. Spaulding seated in Front right, David M. Rubenstein Rare Book & Manuscript Library, Duke University.

morning at eleven, employees left their desks and gathered in the basement cafeteria for the Forum, "as seen in Figure 9.1." Accompanied by a piano, they sang to the tune of "Old Time Religion":

> Give me that good ol' Mutual Spirit,
> It was good enough for Merrick,
> It was good enough for Moore,
> And it's good enough for me . . .

The persona of North Carolina Mutual was centered on religion, reverence for the founders, and commitment to racial progress. Founded in 1898 by a group of businessmen, the Mutual was first established as a mutual benefit association. After some financially difficult early years, it officially became a legal reserve life insurance company in 1913. Its triumvirate of early leaders consisted of John Merrick of the True Reformers, a famed southern fraternal society; Durham physician Dr. Aaron McDuffie Moore; and the youngest, Charles Clinton Spaulding, who rose from within the ranks. By 1923, Merrick and Moore had died, and Spaulding would lead the Mutual until his death in 1952.[43]

Spaulding devised the idea for the Forum in 1921, basing the structure on a devotional ceremony he had observed at an Arkansas fraternal society. Different in many ways from the NYLIC's secular pep rally, the Forum emphasized religion and ideology as well as ritual, with hymns interspersed with company songs, and "sufficient prayer to qualify each session as a church service." The Forum was also a time for employees to showcase their talents through music, drama, and competitive events such as spelling bees and debates. Outside speakers, including luminaries like W. E. B. DuBois and Adam Clayton Powell, would visit the Forum when passing through Durham.[44]

North Carolina Mutual, like other life insurance companies of the time, for example the National Benefit Mutual Life Insurance Company, shown in Figure 9.2, viewed themselves as largely engaged in public service, though with the additional mission of operating a Black business. Like Metropolitan Life, they engaged in welfare work with their policyholders, although they did not describe it as such. The company's Life Extension Department, created in 1925, included public health education but also provided medical treatment in a hospital created in the home office. The biggest health concern was tuberculosis, which earlier in the century had led some other life insurers and fraternal societies to create sanitariums for policyholders.

Religion was the driving force behind Spaulding's interactions with employees and his overall approach to the business of the Mutual. Known as "Papa," Spaulding was described as taking an almost pastoral approach to his duties: "His office door, along with his Bible, was always open, and he customarily read an appropriate verse as prologue to his advice."[45] The sense of mission extended to the home office. Spaulding had a stern but protective attitude toward

Figure 9.2 Employees at the National Benefit Mutual Life Insurance Company in Chicago. Library of Congress.

his employees, insisting on punctuality, forbidding whisky and indebtedness, and warning about the difference between recreation and dissipation. The company had a dormitory for female employees, complete with a housemother.

The other driving force was racial pride. The Mutual's newspaper responded with outrage to the news of Metropolitan Life's 1907 decision to stop selling to Black customers but used the opportunity to reinforce the point that Black people should support their own businesses.[46] Stories about disrespectful behavior by White agents from other companies were similarly circulated to make the case for the superiority of Black enterprise. Spaulding, speaking to the National Negro Business League in 1915, argued that though more expensive, the Mutual was a worthy investment in racial progress: "We are just a little bit higher . . . but there are many advantages which accrue to our race to more than offset the slight difference in rates."[47]

While the 1920s were generally a period of limitless growth and profitability for life insurance companies, Spaulding shepherded the Mutual through a difficult period of retrenchment and belt tightening. While growth had been rapid in the postwar period, claims experience was increasingly poor. The Mutual sold off some their territory in other southern states and focused on improving their risks and reducing overhead expenses. The company struggled competitively against Metropolitan Life, which, even though they charged Blacks higher premiums, was often priced lower.

The Mutual lacked an actuary until the 1930s and found it difficult to improve their risk selection. A major challenge was the large urban-rural mortality differential. The U.S. Public Health Service estimated a death rate of 14.2 per 1,000 for Blacks in the rural South versus 19.8 per 1,000 in cities.[48] While urban business was much easier to get, the experience was far worse, with tuberculosis the leading factor. Yet these austerity measures would permit the Mutual to survive the challenges of the Depression.

Despite its overall feeling of imperviousness, the life insurance industry did keep a wary watch on the activities of the government. Concern about war risk insurance and the potential for government encroachment generally had become enough of a common cause to foster the growth of a trade association, the American Life Conference (ALC).[49] Life insurers cheered as talk of social insurance receded and the War Risk Insurance Bureau and subsequently the Veterans Administration encountered significant logistical problems.[50]

Even the confident Haley Fiske occasionally looked over his shoulder, as he argued that while he saw a role for government in making things better for the working masses, insurance was better off in private hands. He kept a close eye on the Wisconsin Life Fund and the Massachusetts Savings Bank Life Insurance, despite their insignificant size, and had a rough personal benchmark. If Metropolitan Life could reach twenty million policyholders, Fiske reasoned, state insurance would never gain a foothold. When that was achieved in 1923, his worries about state insurance subsided, but ongoing concern about the potential for government action doubtlessly fueled Fiske's enthusiasm for the welfare work, which was predicated on the idea that the company's responsibility to society did not end with the collection of premiums.[51] But even though many aspects of this welfare work had a quasi-governmental nature, and in fact included a number of activities that came to be carried out by the government, to Fiske, this work was a corporate version of the voluntarism that was key to the life insurance worldview.

Fiske's unsuccessful quest to create private unemployment insurance is revealing of his unmitigated confidence in voluntarism as an approach to solving social problems but also shows the limitations of that approach and how the company's view of its "public" role began to evolve. Metropolitan Life was long interested in unemployment in the context of their welfare work. In 1914, Lee Frankel assisted the U.S. Department of Labor by reportedly surveying the staggeringly large number of six hundred thousand industrial policyholders, finding that ten percent were jobless and another fifteen percent lacked regular work. This intrigued Fiske, who then got interested in the idea of insuring against the risk of unemployment.

Fiske struggled unsuccessfully to convince others that unemployment was an insurable risk. New York's insurance superintendent Jesse Phillips opined that permitting Metropolitan Life and other companies to sell such coverage would be an "entering wedge" to socialism. Fiske purportedly responded: "Why my dear fellow, Socialism is the taking over by government of the functions of private corporations and individuals. This is a private corporation. Whatever else unemployment insurance is, it is not socialism."[52] While possibly apocryphal, the sentiment well represents Fiske's sense of the broadness of Metropolitan's purview.

Fiske had his actuaries develop a prototype for the product. But the results were sobering. When constructed with a sufficient underwriting safeguard, private unemployment insurance provided a relatively small level of protection for the cost. While Fiske maintained some enthusiasm, his colleagues were dubious: "The problems of extended unemployment, of the chronically unemployed, and of unemployables were recognized as objects for government relief. This is not insurance."[53] In any case, during the prosperous last few years of 1920s, the risk of widespread unemployment seemed like a distant concern. Looking back, Metropolitan statistician and historian Louis Dublin notes that by restraining Fiske, the company dodged a bullet: "In spite of Mr. Fiske's solicitude for men and women threatened with this hazard, the Company did not underwrite unemployment insurance, and thus it saved itself an unhappy experience in the depression which was to develop only a few years later."[54] Fiske died suddenly in 1929. James described his legacy as a fierce advocate of the power of voluntarism to create prosperity: "The ruling passion of his life was to evolve machinery by which the millions by their own efforts, could create for themselves a comforting degree of security, and, what was almost as great an accomplishment, to persuade them to use that machinery."[55] The other major advocate of Metropolitan's welfare work, Lee Frankel, died in 1931. Neither lived to see how the Depression exposed the limitations of this work and the critiques that hardship would unleash. In a major transition of focus, what was left of the welfare department was moved into the group insurance division. Dublin, with some circumspection, described the "end of an era": "The solid accomplishments of that period will remain a valuable contribution to our way of life; but here, as in all times of rapid growth, there were excesses and dislocations. It became the task of the administration which followed to retain the accomplishments and to correct the errors."[56]

New York Life's Darwin Kingsley leaned into the pending economic catastrophe with his characteristic bravado, daring his audience of agency directors in a January 1930 speech to indulge him in his almost manic exuberance about the future: "If I now claim the recent discoveries in science anticipate the evolution of a form of society higher in its aims, more splendid in its ideals and achievements than the forms of society now existent, will you think I am a dreamer?" Kingsley envisioned an interconnected but free modern world based on new technology and held together by the "master machine": the voluntary collectivism of life insurance: "Life Insurance is a declaration of interdependence; a declaration of freedom. There is no such thing as complete independence possible in our world and in our day. Freedom is possible and it is coming through the use of physical and social machines and the master machine which applies all production and efficiency to the solution of the greatest of all problems, sociology, is life insurance." The stock market crash only reinforced the point:

In the midst of this recent cataclysm, when even strong men lost their heads and panic ruled, did anyone question the soundness of life insurance? Did anyone suggest that life insurance policies would shrink like common stocks and even bank stocks? No one made such a suggestion. No one even thought of it. Why not? Because the life insurance agent has taught a majority of the people that there is a section of Society from which the financial incantationist and the financial witch doctor have been banished. Back of all the follies of speculation, fighting all get-rich-quick schemes, stood and stands this great machine called Life Insurance. It has gathered the money of the people, put it in to sound and creative enterprises, holds it outside the world of speculation and is today, as never before, the herald of a new order—an order based not on the independence but on the interdependence of men.[57]

Kingsley died in 1932. His prediction that life insurance would be a safe haven during the Depression was in many ways correct. In part because of the conservatism imposed by the financial regulations that came out of the Armstrong investigation, life insurance companies were relatively immune to the economic downturn. In 1932 alone, thirty-two thousand commercial enterprises failed, but during the entire course of the Depression only thirty-nine legal reserve life insurance companies failed, and they represented only two percent of life insurance in force.[58] However, the Depression, along with the growth of the group business, served to permanently disrupt the business of fraternal and assessment insurance, which saw insurance in force decline by half between 1930 and 1937.[59]

Sitting outside the imposing New York Life building at Fifty-One Madison, E. B. White reflected on Kingsley's legacy for *The New Yorker*, while "cold and afraid, hunched in our coat ... looking upon the perpendicular and vasty halls of life insurance." The company had recently announced their largest ever number of new policyholders in a single day. To White, that made sense: "That was it— everybody was scared; people were timid birds running to cover under Mr. Kingsley's wing."[60]

Yet the Depression created a critical shift in the "publicness" of life insurance. The crisis elevated two longstanding issues—unemployment and the financial needs of the aged—with the result that the federal role in these areas was greatly expanded through the passage of the Social Security Act in 1935. At the same time, the social and economic role of life insurance was changing. There was also a literal changing of the guard, as some of the most enthusiastic proponents of the quasi-public worldview of life insurance died and were replaced by others with a more narrow commercial orientation. The increased role of government in social insurance and criticism of some aspects of life insurance also changed the reputation and self-perception of the industry.

In the areas of unemployment and old-age assistance, reformers and state governments had been developing social insurance approaches to these problems during the 1920s. This preparation, combined with the urgency of the Depression, created the necessary momentum for change. Public solutions were feasible in part because private markets hadn't developed. By the 1920s, a number of European countries had developed unemployment insurance, including Britain, which had adopted a system in 1911. The American Association of Labor Legislation, the leading advocacy group for social insurance, endorsed the British system in 1914.[61]

Lack of work came to be seen as a risk that needed protection, just like injury. But casualty insurers judged the underwriting to be difficult, since unemployment, unlike accidents or illness, was more difficult to "establish" conclusively, creating a concern about moral hazard.[62] To Isaac Max Rubinow, a Russian immigrant and social insurance advocate who was both a physician and an actuary, the coverage was inherently not commercially viable: "For here appears again the central principle upon which social insurance is based—the inability of the wage-earning class to meet the cost of insurance based on ordinary commercial principles."[63]

To organized labor, the connection between unemployment insurance and workers' compensation was clear, and it made sense for both to be the employer's responsibility. By that logic, the funding structure should be similar, as labor leaders argued in 1920: "There is no reason why the industry which pays a permanent tax to the various insurance companies in order to indemnify the employee in case of emergency should not likewise have a permanent fund for the indemnification for lack of work."[64] This distinguished unemployment insurance from charity or government relief, which was important to labor.[65]

While the concept of unemployment insurance as an employer's responsibility drove some initial policy efforts, other reformers, such as Rubinow, argued instead for a more insurance-like approach, based on a pooled fund. These advocates argued that individual employers could not really prevent unemployment, because they had little control over broader economic slowdowns, and a pooled fund created a better safeguard against more systemic business cycle issues. During the 1920s, state legislatures around the country considered a variety of unemployment insurance bills, most of which were based on either a framework of individual reserves or pooled funds.[66]

With the onset of the Depression, the urgency of the issue increased, and it became clear that federal action was needed, since private provision was not possible and purely state responses were unsustainable, due to concerns about interstate competition. When FDR issued an executive order in 1934 creating the Committee on Economic Security (CES), unemployment was the top priority. The name was later changed to Social Security in the House Ways and Means Committee in 1935. Chaired by Secretary of Labor Frances Perkins, the committee also included Secretary of Agriculture Henry A. Wallace, Federal Emergency Relief administrator Harry Hopkins, Attorney General Homer Cummings, and Secretary of the Treasury Henry Morganthau Jr. It was assumed at the time that the federal government would also play an important role in supplying jobs to the unemployed. Work "assurance" was originally to be part of the CES legislation, but in 1934 this activity was transferred to Harry Hopkin's public work program. The Emergency Relief Administration Act of 1935 included funding for work relief, but this effort was temporary.[67]

While many on the CES wanted to create a purely federal response, there was a concern about opposition from states' rights advocates and potential constitutional challenges. This prospect was particularly an issue with southern Democrats, who worried that federal control would jeopardize their social system based on racial hierarchies.[68] To get around this, Congress used a federal tax offset, levying a federal payroll tax that could be offset by the creation of a satisfactory unemployment insurance program.

Some discretion was allowed in the design of state unemployment insurance programs, but compared to workers' compensation, there was considerably less variation and a much shorter implementation timeline. By 1937, all states had established unemployment insurance, and ultimately all had adopted the approach of pooled funds and experience rating. Like workers' compensation, unemployment insurance disproportionately excluded Blacks and women who were more likely to work in industries such as agriculture and domestic work that were not covered.[69]

Though unemployment was initially the top priority, the old-age pension provision of the Social Security Act, known simply as "Social Security," is the best-known component of the legislation. The economic problem of the aged preceded the Depression. With the growth of wage work, it was increasingly difficult for older adults to support themselves when they were no longer working. In 1934, nearly half of those over age sixty-five were dependent on family members for economic support. An estimated one million received some form of charity.[70]

Means-tested pensions had been adopted in a number of states and funded out of general revenue. This approach followed, though in a piecemeal way, developments in England, where a noncontributory means-tested pension had been enacted. By 1934, there were nearly thirty state-based old-age pensions, which differed significantly in benefit levels and eligibility. They provided relief to an estimated 180,000 people.[71]

In the conservative postwar period, when European policy ideas were associated with socialism and regarded with suspicion, the concept of "prevention" was enlisted as a rationale for social insurance by some U.S. reform advocates. This was one of the prime arguments for workers' compensation, that compulsory insurance and experience rating would motivate employers to try to prevent accidents. Indeed, expertise about prevention was a major selling point for insurers in the compensation business.

The concept of prevention was also behind initial approaches to unemployment insurance that sought to place responsibility on the employer to establish a reserve fund. In the context of old-age dependency, prevention translated to savings, insurance, and contributory pensions. Yet to others this approach obscured the broader objective of social insurance. Abraham Epstein, for example, rejected the notion of "prevention" in the context of pensions, likening it to the "equity" principles of private insurance that equate benefits to contributions. Social insurance represents a broader contract, "a social guarantee against the results of emergencies or accidents." The most important goal of social insurance was income maintenance, and noncontributory state pensions served that purpose.[72]

Yet pensions were a highly controversial concept in the early twentieth century. The strong disapproval of the Civil War veterans' pension still resounded; the entire structure of life and disability insurance for World War I veterans was predicated on the imperative of avoiding a revisit to military pensions that were seen as a handout.[73] Pensions threatened to eliminate the fear of old-age dependency and destroy the motivation to work and save. Opponents argued that pensions would make "thriftlessness and laziness genteel" and that it was the threat of the "poorhouse over the hill" that drove effort and ambition.[74] The twentieth-century anxiety about pensions echoed antebellum concerns about life insurance itself as a deterrent to thrift.

The strenuous objection from the life insurance industry to any attempt by state government to create even extremely incremental public life insurance opportunities such as the Wisconsin Life Fund and the Massachusetts Savings Bank Life Insurance came from the worry that these programs would ultimately be used to offer state pensions or old-age annuities. Even more than state life insurance, the concept of government pensions constituted a major threat to advocates of voluntarism. The inception of the Massachusetts Savings Bank Life Insurance, the source of such consternation to the life insurance industry, was in fact itself initially motivated by concerns about old-age dependency. Yet the state resisted creating a pension, on the grounds that thrift and the filial obligation to care for parents were key to family cohesion. As a compromise, voluntary "savings bank insurance" was established instead in 1907, with the hope that thrift would be increased and dependency prevented.[75]

Old-age dependency posed a challenge to exponents of a prevention approach to social insurance, since aging could not be prevented. Yet dependency could be prevented through voluntary collectivism. Frederick Hoffman of Prudential was not alone in his worry that state-sponsored old-age pensions would threaten the American character. Life insurance was popular with political leaders because it represented a form of collectivism that seemed well suited to the times, not rugged individualism, but rather the voluntary use of modern institutions. These values were expressed through strong vocal support of life insurance by contemporary leaders such as Herbert Hoover and Calvin Coolidge. Hoffman came out strongly against state pensions, preferring instead "mutual aid of the right kind," namely insurance, fraternal societies, and the growing field of "industrial pensions."[76]

Compared to unemployment insurance, there were more private sources of old-age pensions, such as unions, fraternal societies, and, increasingly, workplace benefits provided by employers. There was also a very small market for annuities offered by legal reserve companies. Yet this supply was wholly inadequate to the need. Private pensions offered through unions covered an estimated 150,000 workers in 1930. Workplace benefits were similarly in short supply. On the eve of the Depression, not more than one in five workers was covered by group life insurance, and fewer than one in eight had any type of retirement benefits. Workplace benefits were not reliable. Many pensions at the time were informal and discretionary, meaning they could be withdrawn, suspended, or abandoned at any time.[77]

But in the 1920s, retirement pensions started to become a more common feature of the American workplace and were evolving into a contributory form that was financed on an actuarial basis. The life insurance industry began to solicit the pension business to employers. Pensions were becoming standard for municipal employees such as teachers and fire and police departments. In 1920, the Sterling-Lehback Act extended pensions to the entire U.S. civil service.

The National Industrial Conference Board, a coalition of large employers, made the case for pensions as a modern necessity as early as 1925. While old age was not "essentially" a problem of industry, it had become one, since workers depend on wages and prevailing habits of thrift are generally "inadequate." It was an issue that employers needed to address, for the alternative would be a government pension, an outcome that was described as "socialistic and mischievous," a scenario in which "the danger of waste, extravagance and corruption in the disbursement of pension funds is too real to be ignored."[78]

Describing with concern the proliferation of state pension bills around the country, the board argued that it would be far preferable if private industry assumed this responsibility voluntarily. The stakes were clear. If industry "fails to afford to its employees the means to livelihood after they have lost the power of productive labor, then this burden will be passed on to the state, and the cost will become a charge upon the public purse or met in other ways."[79]

At the time, most industrial pensions were discretionary. The board described approvingly a trend toward a more formal and contractual pension, which was based in part on employee contributions and funded using actuarial methods: "Gradually pension schemes are being freed of arbitrary and discretionary features and are outgrowing their paternalistic character."[80] Pensions were here to stay.

The board produced another report on industrial pensions in 1931. In just a few years, there had been considerable forward momentum. The board now counted 420 plans, covering an estimated 3.8 million workers. The Depression had elevated the issue.[81] The stakes remained high. Positive action by employers would "counteract agitation for legislative proposals to provide universal state pensions for the aged, which are opposed generally by employers as unnecessary, expensive, and harmful in their effects on individual thrift, independence, and self-reliance." Employers needed to demonstrate that "industry can take care of its worn-out workers through pension plans resting on voluntary initiative and cooperation."[82] Employers were responsible for the continuation of voluntary collectivism.

Yet advocates were highly dubious about industrial pensions, claiming that a small share of workers allegedly covered would actually receive benefits. Many employees were not vested. Advocates likened informal and discretionary pensions to charity, which was offensive to workers and interfered with their efforts to attain greater security.[83] Organized labor initially viewed pensions with suspicion. Their implicit promise of future payments reduced wages in the present and bound workers to their employers. They were also offered, sometimes very explicitly, as a tactic to prevent strikes.[84]

Epstein saw a big difference between the "equity principles" of private insurance as embodied in contributory industrial pensions and true social insurance, which "did not seek individual protection according to the ability to pay, but rather a socially adequate arrangement which will protect all the workers as well as society from certain social hazards."[85] Despite the protests of employer groups and some in the life insurance industry, there was the general recognition that current voluntary efforts were inadequate. And while individual employers may have been motivated to create pensions by a desire to smoothly offload older workers who were no longer at their peak productivity, the Depression created a broader macroeconomic rationale for shifting older workers as a group out of the labor force.

Political pressures during the Depression also helped tilt the shape of the policy toward social insurance rather than assistance. There was growing concern about the large amount of emergency relief. By the mid-1930s, millions were dependent on New Deal relief programs such as the Federal Emergency Relief Administration, the Civil Works Administration, and the Civilian Conservation Corps, which provided work and cash relief. The size of these programs raised questions about the continued proliferation of stopgap measures and increased demand for more structural long-term solutions. Pressure from the Left made action imperative.[86] Contributory social insurance met that need better than a federal means-tested pension, which sounded like another relief program. These factors raised the appeal of a social insurance solution.[87]

As finalized, Social Security was a contributory pension that also had a redistributive element. There was the recognition that many low-wage workers would be unable to finance their own retirement through savings. Therefore, Social Security was designed in a way that it was not completely dependent on payroll taxes. Those who were closest to retirement at the time of the program's creation would similarly get benefits that would far exceed their contributions. Social Security was also pitched as a system of forced savings. Proponents argued that many people would not save sufficiently for their retirement, even if they had the means. And investing was not without risk. By transferring the risk to the federal government, the retirement funds would be assured. Said Senator Robert Wagner: "I do not think any greater contribution could be made to the happiness of our people than to give them security in old age."[88]

The Social Security Act attempted to combine "voluntarism"—that is, the equity principles of private insurance—with the income distribution of social insurance. Epstein and Rubinow, who felt sidelined by Frances Perkins and her team, both believed it tilted excessively to the former. Subsequent revisions to the act in 1939 would redress this to a certain extent by reducing the reserve and increasing expenditures while holding contributions constant. The benefit formula was also altered in a way that favored lower-income workers. Ensuing debates over Social Security would revolve around tradeoffs between solvency and redistribution.[89]

Initially, Metropolitan Life had expressed concern about the growing role of government. Reacting to the concept of unemployment insurance, counsel Leroy Lincoln, who chaired a committee of the U.S. Chamber of Commerce, spoke for both the chamber and the life industry in 1932: "We consider government insurance a mistake, and almost sure to become a political football."[90] Yet just a few years later, Metropolitan's position and that of the industry changed once again, tracking closely with public opinion. Given the depths of the Depression, noted Marquis James in his history of the company, "The country came to believe that the government should provide self-respecting citizens some protection against unemployment and old age." Metropolitan Life supported both unemployment insurance and old-age pensions that were proposed in the Social Security Act. They had learned from their experience with war risk insurance that government insurance was a complement to and not a substitute for private coverage. In fact, sales pitches were developed around the concept that life insurance should be built upon the edifice of Social Security. Since the government benefits provided for "subsistence only," "it was up to the individual to protect himself beyond that point."[91]

The Depression created financial pressures for policyholders that affected the life insurance business in a variety of ways. Policy loans and surrenders rose as desperate people tapped into their last resources. Overall, however, relatively few companies went out of business, and the industry emerged in the 1930s with more insurance in force. There was also an increase in disability and accident claims. A number of companies were already having trouble with the disability income benefits clause in the ordinary life policy. When the Depression started, claims increased sharply. By 1931, for example, Metropolitan was already $9 million behind in this line and subsequently eliminated this provision.[92]

But the biggest Depression-era problem for the life insurance industry came from industrial insurance. People applying for relief were often found to be carrying multiple industrial insurance policies, for which premium payments made up a high share of their income. One study found that approximately seventeen percent of the income of families applying for relief went to insurance policies.[93] Welfare workers felt that many applicants were overinsured and wanted to use some of the value of their polices to defray the cost of relief. Due to the volume and complexities of the interactions between relief agencies, clients, and insurance companies and the fact that many of the policyholders had insurance with multiple companies, in 1929 Lee Frankel of Metropolitan Life worked with his counterparts at Prudential and John Hancock to establish the Life Insurance Adjustment Bureau (LIAB). The bureau was designed to serve as a type of clearinghouse between relief agencies and the Big Three and assisted with insurance adjustments, which usually consisted of cash payments and conversions of endowments to smaller burial policies. The LIAB was run by Edward Eklund, who had come from a long career at charitable agencies, including the American Red Cross.

Once the Depression started, the volume of these transactions exploded, and most involved the federal Emergency Relief Bureau. Practices of relief agencies varied locally. Sometimes insurance policies were converted to cash payments that were given to clients as a lump sum. In other cases, the welfare agencies controlled the payments and doled out the money to policyholders "so the worker may supervise spending of the money." After the insurance money was exhausted, policyholders became eligible for relief. Relief agencies were incentivized to adjust insurance to a minimum, exercising "vigilance in avoiding excessive funeral costs that sometimes keep families on relief longer than they should be."[94]

This arrangement was not without controversy. Some relief officials found themselves responding to "rumors" that applicants were required to surrender their life insurance policies to be eligible for relief. Despite his "vigorous contradiction" of these rumors, the director of the Emergency Relief Bureau in Kingston, New York, acknowledged their general truth when explaining that adjustment was for the "conservation of purely protective insurance at minimum premium and in an amount necessary to cover the actual cost of a burial."[95]

Some outrage was directed at the relief system. A letter to the *Brooklyn Daily Eagle* recounted the experience of a destitute old couple forced by a "pert young insurance adjuster" to liquidate two burial policies to which they had been contributing for many years. They were told to subsist on the proceeds before receiving any assistance. "Can you imagine the dejection of these old people— one is now 73—now facing a pauper's grave because of an asinine system?"[96] In Wisconsin, the legislature even sought to ban the practice of adjustment, but Governor Philip LaFollette vetoed the bill on the grounds that the alternative would be even worse, since it would leave more money in the hands of the despised insurance companies.[97]

Publicity around adjustments resurfaced longstanding criticisms of industrial insurance as a low-value product that was aggressively oversold to low-income families. Disgruntled industrial policyholders turned to the emerging field of insurance counselors, who offered to "adjust" their policies for a fee. The first and most famous of these counselors was Morris Siegel, who had initially been a Metropolitan Life agent and then a broker before becoming an industry critic.[98]

Siegel was a skilled publicist who used multiple channels to air his grievances with the insurance industry and advertise his services. He had a radio program that he devoted to cynical invective about the motives and practices of the insurance industry, warning potential clients not to trust their insurance agent: "If you go to your agent you will be skinned alive before you get out of his hands. He will bamboozle you from here to Halifax and back, take the gold fillings out of your teeth, talk you deaf, dumb and blind until you're dizzy, and then tell you lies about us to keep you tied down to your present heavy premium payments, on weekly policies at that."[99] Siegal publicized the sensational case of the "unfortunate Fortune family," who collectively held forty-three separate policies, creating a combined annual premium bill of nearly $1,000 on a longshoreman's modest salary.[100] He reserved his bitterest attacks for his former employer. Metropolitan Life fired back on the airwaves and in the courtroom, suing Siegel (successfully) for libel.[101]

All this publicity attracted unwanted attention from New York State and the federal government. The state had an unfinished regulatory agenda relating to industrial insurance, which had escaped sustained attention during the Armstrong hearings. This was not because "serious evils" were not recognized; in fact, Charles Evans Hughes had commented on the "excessive premiums, enormous lapse rate and the hardships of the agents" as inherent problems of the system.[102] At the time there had appeared to be no better solution, but now the legislatively appointed Piper Committee in New York held hearings that focused on excessive cost, and in particular on industry practices that led to overselling. Federal attention would soon follow.

The idealistic mission of Metropolitan's welfare work seemed very distant. Companies that sold industrial insurance were subject to widespread rebuke for a product that seemed to have so poorly served the low-income customers for whom it was designed. A new kind of industry critic, the insurance counselor, represented consumer discontent. Agents at some companies were unionizing. And the growing size and power of the federal government was a recognition of the limitations of voluntary collectivism. While Calvin Coolidge had called New York Life a "public service agency" in 1929, ten years later the Roosevelt administration launched a federal investigation of the life insurance industry.

The Temporary National Economic Committee (TNEC) was established to investigate the concentration of economic power as part of the late New Deal focus on antitrust. The committee had twelve members—three from the Senate, three from the House, and six from the agencies—and conducted investigations of multiple industries. The Securities and Exchange Commission (SEC), headed at the time by future Supreme Court justice William O Douglas, was the agency responsible for the investigation of insurance. Wyoming senator Joseph O'Mahoney was the TNEC chairman. Other notables were Assistant Attorney General Thurman Arnold from the Department of Justice and SEC economist Leon Henderson. A twenty-eight-year-old Gerhard Gesell, who would later preside over the Watergate trials as a U.S. district court judge, was the lead attorney for the SEC.

There were three sets of hearings about life insurance, as seen in Figure 9.3. The first one started in February 1939 and followed themes raised in the Armstrong investigation, focusing on size, acquisitions, and investments. Senator O'Mahoney raised concerns about the overall size of life insurers' financial assets, likening their accumulation to a "snowball rolling down an endless hill."[103] The second set of hearings began in June of the same year and focused on anticompetitive behavior.

Figure 9.3 Securities and Exchange Commission officials provide testimony about life insurance for Temporary National Economic Committee investigation, February 6, 1939. Library of Congress.

Industry fears about federal aspirations were amplified after the testimony of Judd Dewey, director of the Massachusetts Savings Bank Life Insurance program. Dewey's presence likely reflected the influence of recently retired Supreme Court justice Louis Brandeis, who had played an instrumental role in the creation of the Massachusetts program at the beginning of the twentieth century. Gessell recalled that Brandeis, who "of course, had a fetish against bigness," followed the hearings closely and "commented by a note or a suggestion when I should come out for a talk."[104] Brandeis told Gessell that he considered the establishment of the Massachusetts Savings Bank Life Insurance program to be one of his most important accomplishments.

The goal of the Massachusetts program had been to create a public substitute for industrial insurance. Probably also reflecting the influence of Brandeis, a subcommittee on industrial insurance was established and held hearings during the summer of 1939. The Armstrong Committee had not acted on industrial insurance but had left some breadcrumbs for future reformers: "The Committee is not prepared to make recommendations with reference to industrial insurance further than to say that the subject is one deserving of special investigation." And despite the fact that New York's Piper Committee had recently held hearings on the subject, the SEC quickly asserted a federal prerogative, though they had no particular authority: "Industrial insurance is not the peculiar problem of any state, and it is fitting that operations of the industrial business be examined from a national point of view."[105]

Gessell opened by calling out the industrial business as a "squirrel cage operation," a money machine fueled by a cycle of sales and resales to the same customer base of poor families, who would lapse their policies, take up new policies, and lapse again.[106] Called to testify was Edwin Eklund of the LIAB, who reported that they handled nearly six hundred thousand cases of families on relief between 1932 and 1939 and returned approximately $25 million to relief agencies from policies either lapsed or in force. Morris Siegel testified about the families he encountered in his work as an insurance counselor, describing the case of the Fortune family as "unusual with regard to numbers but not unusual with regard to the principal behind it."[107]

Gesell sought to show that overselling was inevitable, as agents "on the debit" were paid on commission and constrained to a fixed geographical area. While agent behavior had also been a focus of the Armstrong investigation, the TNEC subcommittee assigned blame further upstream and argued that agents themselves were victims of an abusive system. As Marquis James recounted the hearings from the perspective of Metropolitan Life, "Each session seemed like a prize fight."[108] Gesell tried to get Leroy Lincoln to concede that overselling was a problem, asking him to react to the Piper Committee's conclusion: "The pressure exercised on the agents in the sale of industrial policies has driven them to the point where they have been forced to depart from the ethics of their calling." Lincoln characterized the statement as "entirely unwarranted."[109]

Gesell read into testimony letters from Metropolitan field agents, recounting browbeating from management and intense pressure to sell: "It is hard to describe in words the suffering and humiliation forced upon the men by these so-called Managers and Assistant Managers. Here are some expressions used by them in their daily 'pep talk' meetings: 'Why don't you go on relief, you are too old to be useful?' 'I will give you two weeks to make good or get out.' 'You are yellow.' 'You are a coward.'"[110] While Lincoln conceded there was "some discontent" reflected in these letters, he maintained they were exceptional cases. But his attempt to transition the conversation to the subject of the company's venerated welfare work fell flat. Lincoln was forced to concede under questioning that improving the health of policyholders was financially beneficial to Metropolitan Life, though he vaguely claimed a higher social purpose: "I do feel that there is a bigger and broader angle to it." Yet the commission was having none of it, asking Lincoln whether the welfare work was something "from the 'king's largesse' over and above what you are obliged to do" before wondering out loud whether policyholders might not rather have lower premiums.[111] A newspaper published a cartoon called "Light on a Sacred Cow" that depicted a statue of a cow labeled "Life Insurance Companies," with a beam of bright light ("The Investigation") shining upon it.[112] The days of Mother Metropolitan seemed very far away.

Industrial agents themselves provided the most incendiary testimony. Bert B. Cohen, agent of the Equitable Life Insurance Company of Washington, DC, told the subcommittee that sometimes his entire debit was in arrears, requiring him to make the payments himself and creating a desperation for new sales from any source. This created a predictable cycle, where frequent lapses lead to aggressive sales followed by more lapses. Cohen described largely Black policyholders on his debit paying far too high a share of their income on insurance: "I have colored families who pay more for insurance in two or three or four different companies than they get in a week, and how they do that I sometimes don't know."[113]

Yet this awareness did not lead to restraint. Cohen described how he tailored his approach to customers' fears and did whatever was required to make a sale: "Well, it will largely depend on what kind of person the policyholder is. Since the bulk of mine are Negroes, I will metaphorically draw up a hearse in front of his door and park it there until he signs." Cohen's description of how he handled a lapse captured the essence of the "squirrel cage operation" that was industrial insurance: "I re-hire the hearse again."[114]

A final set of hearings focused on financial misdeeds, providing the SEC with the opportunity to criticize the poor quality of state supervision and hint at the need for federal intervention. The absence of participation from state regulators in the entire TNEC proceedings was notable. Aside from the Piper Commission, state regulation was scarcely mentioned, except to note its inadequacy.

State regulators at the time seemed primarily focused on defending the industry and their own regulatory authority. Aside from New York and a few other states, there was little interest in the problems of industrial insurance, and the conferees at the NAIC were instead agitated by the activities of "insurance counselors" and others who criticized the life insurance industry, forming a publications committee to monitor anti-insurance literature. Despite a clear danger to consumers from unauthorized insurance companies that used the mail to send materials across state lines, concern about potential federal encroachment caused the commissioners to oppose federal legislation and pursue "the elimination of this evil through state enactment."[115]

Proceedings of NAIC meetings during the 1930s were thin and filled with asides about golfing events and other recreations. The general tenor was not that of an assemblage of thoughtful and dedicated public servants. The Alabama commissioner, who was also NAIC president, opened his 1938 address with a racist joke, then followed with this observation: "I want to take this occasion to say here, too, that the Irish got me last night. In going back to the Southern vernacular, I just ain't in no fix to do no oratin' this morning."[116]

By the time the TNEC hearings concluded in 1940, some life insurers suspected that the federal government might try to abolish the agency system and replace the industrial business with government insurance. Out of these concerns, nearly two hundred companies signed on to a statement in 1940, which pushed back on some of the TNEC findings and emphasized the "safety" of life insurance.[117] Leroy Lincoln of Metropolitan Life authored the statement and adopted a bellicose air throughout much of the TNEC hearings, refusing to comply with a final request for documents.

The pugilistic spirit of Metropolitan executives was admired within the company.[118] But four of the leading life companies chose not to sign on to the statement, feeling that they had been fairly represented in the hearings. A mid-century text on life insurance marketing chided those who were uncooperative, observing that government investigations were both a fact of modern life and a public relations opportunity, in which "a surly, balky, recalcitrant attitude gains life insurance nothing with either the public or the administration." Increasingly, the author noted, people view government as their champion. If by "fighting federal government regulation the companies succeed only in making themselves look like the traditional unregenerated economic royalist in new dress, then it cannot be expected that the public reaction will be favorable."[119]

The SEC released a series of reports, which were very critical of the life business. There was a proposal for a "federal insurance advisory council" that would cooperate with state regulators. Another idea was for industrial insurance to be turned into a government service—either through the extension of Social Security or by sales through the post office.[120] But the final TNEC report, released on March 26, 1941, made more moderate recommendations. It proposed that states should strengthen their supervision and that some relatively minor federal controls be established. There was a statement about industrial insurance that was stronger than that of the Armstrong Commission but similarly vague: "A fundamental change in the conduct of industrial insurance should occur. Otherwise, its eventual elimination may be necessary."[121]

Gesell recalled that Brandeis had hoped for much more: "He was very disappointed when the government did not take over the life insurance business or alternatively come forward with legislation breaking up what was then believed to be mammoth concentrations of economic power reaching $5 billion assets. But World War II was creeping into reality and Congress had no taste for new approaches."[122] In 1941, Brandeis died, and Gesell entered private practice.

The TNEC investigation put the industry on the defensive and hinted at the potential power of the federal government. From a financial standpoint, the federal footprint had grown quickly. In 1944, of the estimated $3.5 billion paid to individuals for death benefits, annuities, dividends, matured endowments, and the like, $1.5 billion came from various federal and state programs including Social Security, workers' compensation, veterans' programs, and federal and state employee benefits.[123] The rest came from private life insurance companies. While the private sector had the lead, the boundary was clearly shifting. A mid-century text noted: "The very existence of the companies might depend on the action of the federal government someday; they might need to be supported and revived by that government."[124] Increasingly, the life insurance industry associated their "public service" persona with the growing field of group insurance, giving less and less thought to the world beyond. At Metropolitan Life, Lee Frankel's welfare work was reorganized into the group division, and Metropolitan statistician and historian Louis Dublin credited this line of business with helping to shape Social Security into "practical and useful channels," commenting on their joint development with some satisfaction: "There has always been the closest cooperation, which has ensured the harmonious development of Social Security plans side by side with voluntary Group insurance as its partner and supplement, to the great benefit of both."[125]

Stripped of its welfare veneer, the industrial business was reputationally problematic, as the Depression and the subsequent TNEC hearings illustrated. The Big Three knew this and were quietly attempting to "graduate" their industrial policyholders into ordinary policies whenever possible, and draw the two lines more closely together, all the while maintaining that nothing was amiss. They were not willing to drop the line altogether, because even in the 1930s, industrial business constituted a meaningful share of life insurance in force.[126]

In 1939, Charles Williams, president of the Western and Southern Life Insurance Company, gave a speech to his managers with a simple title: "More Ordinary." In it he argued that industrial insurance was doomed, besieged by critics, new regulations, and competition from Social Security. Even aside from that, "to a certain extent it appears to have outlived its usefulness, one reason being that a few hundred dollars is no longer the important money that it used to be; it doesn't go so far or buy as much." His reading of the situation called for a pivot: "It appears to the company, as it should to every man in the field, that the future rests entirely with the development of Ordinary. The real purpose of this meeting is to impress upon the managers individually and you in turn to impress upon your superintendents and see that they impress upon their agents the necessity of switching to Ordinary."[127] Industrial insurance was collapsing under its own weight but was doing so in slow motion. By mid-century, industrial still made up about fifteen percent of insurance in force and two-thirds of the policyholders of legal reserve companies. The Big Three now accounted for about two-thirds of the industrial business, reflecting their attempts to slowly edge out of it and cede the territory to smaller companies that sold only industrial. Increasingly, industrial insurance was not intended for the primary breadwinner, since improved economic circumstances made many industrial wage workers able to afford a minimum ordinary policy, and a growing number also had the "additional protection of group insurance."[128]

The conversations about industrial insurance and racial discrimination in life insurance were taking place separately. The TNEC hearings incidentally surfaced some information about Black policyholders, but neither the disproportionate impact of industrial insurance on Blacks nor the broader issue of racial discrimination in life insurance was an issue in the hearings. For example, despite the fact that Metropolitan Life seemed to be a primary target of the investigations, the fact that they had stopped soliciting insurance of any kind to Blacks in New York in 1935 was not raised by the TNEC, even though the investigation ranged freely into many aspects of life insurance and, as Dublin noted, "no opportunity was lost to seek out matters for criticism."[129]

Yet racial discrimination in insurance was a growing public issue, and the James Rancher case would shortly bring it to the fore. And in fact, industrial insurance and racial discrimination were closely related. The industrial business was increasingly composed of Black policyholders, and companies that solicited Black business relied on the substandard mortality tables. Were Blacks and Whites to be offered insurance at the same rates, the attractiveness of industrial business would sink even further. Racial discrimination was key to profitability.

For North Carolina Mutual, surviving the Depression was a major accomplishment. Like other companies, they saw an increase in policy loans and surrenders. This increased administrative costs at a time when mortality was high, new business was hard to find, and investments were growing slowly. Black life insurance companies depended on industrial business; in 1930, it constituted sixty-three percent of revenues for North Carolina Mutual, as compared with seventeen percent for the industry as a whole.[130] But while industrial business was subject to a very high lapse rate, it was also relatively resilient. After the first few years of the Depression, the Mutual saw a gradual return in volume, and their assets stayed fairly constant at approximately four million throughout the Depression.

Risk selection was a longstanding problem, so the arrival of the first actuary in 1933 was an important development. Asa Spaulding, a distant cousin of the president, worked at the Mutual initially before receiving degrees in accounting at New York University and in actuarial science at the University of Michigan. Of his fellow students and professors, he wrote, "I think they are beginning to feel that I am not a 'quitter,' consequently they may as well resign themselves to the idea of a Negro actuary."[131]

Once at the Mutual, Spaulding embarked on a revamping of all aspects of the company's underwriting, changing the terms of policies and training agents. While mortality was generally improving, there was a growing impact from fatal automobile accidents, which usually required double or triple indemnity payments. Negative experiences with disability claims led the Mutual, like many other companies, to abandon this coverage altogether during the 1930s.

As a beacon to the Black community, the Mutual's role during the Depression went far beyond insurance. The company fielded innumerable requests for jobs, loans, help for the destitute, and credit references. Spaulding began a set of thrift clubs for local children, encouraging savings, endowment insurance, and church attendance. And while Metropolitan Life viewed the Social Security Act with "friendly eyes," the involvement of the Mutual was far greater. At a time when the quality of vital statistics data was poor in southern states, the company became a major resource for age verification for their own policyholders and many others attempting to apply. Spaulding went further and created materials for Black newspapers that provided instructions for how to apply for the new federal benefits.[132]

The Mutual emerged from the Depression in a greatly strengthened position. Assets had risen to $5.4 million. At a 1939 meeting of the National Negro Insurance Association there were reports of sound finances and increased dividend payments, signs of "a growing confidence on the part of the American Negro in life insurance companies owned and operated by members of the race."[133] In 1938 the Mutual expanded to Pennsylvania, following the patterns of Black migration. Philadelphia was the first district to have over $1 million in premiums, and during the war female agents made major inroads. The first payment of dividends in 1944 was a milestone, responding to long-expressed desires by Spaulding for the Mutual to become the "Black man's Metropolitan."

This rapid growth changed the culture of the company, replacing the old "Mutual spirit" with something more corporate and technocratic. The Saturday employee gathering called the Forum became a perfunctory monthly meeting. Spaulding doubled down on business growth until his death in 1952. The Mutual continued to expand into states like New Jersey and Illinois, where it acquired a smaller Black firm, Unity Mutual Life, shown here in Figure 9.4.[134]

But the growth of economic opportunity for Blacks that fueled the Mutual's growth would also prove to be its greatest challenge. Integration created economic opportunity, but integrated mortality tables were an existential threat. As Walter Weare writes in his history of the Mutual: "After decades of sustenance from a market protected by segregation, the Black entrepreneur looked to integration as the warrior looked to peace." Competing with White firms that were now charging Blacks standard rates put the Mutual at a distinct disadvantage, as seen in Figure 9.5. To stave off the inevitable, the firm began to pursue group business, and in the late 1960s it secured large contracts with General Motors and IBM. These contracts increased their business enormously. In 1971 the Mutual

Figure 9.4 Meeting of agents at Unity Life Insurance Company, Chicago, 1942. Library of Congress.

Figure 9.5   L. B. Frazier, Maceo A. Sloan, and employees, North Carolina Mutual Insurance Company, 1960s. Debit account statistics are written on the blackboard in the background. North Carolina Mutual Insurance Company Archives, David M. Rubenstein Rare Book & Manuscript Library, Duke University.

had more than $1 billion in life insurance in force, but at a cost to their historic identity as a Black company. The company now had many White policyholders, who were, strictly speaking, part owners, given the mutual status. Now "Black managed" rather than strictly "Black owned," the Mutual was also obliged to become an "equal opportunity employer" and employ Whites.[135]

The large group contracts faded away as consolidation in the industry eroded the Mutual's competitiveness. Michael Lawrence, the president and chief executive officer, acknowledged in a 2017 interview that desegregation had "priced us out of the market to a certain extent" and that competition with companies that could spread risk over a broader group of policyholders was very challenging. He noted that the number of Black life insurance companies had declined from forty-three in 1973 to twenty-three in 1993 to fewer than five in 2017. Lawrence's attempt to save the Mutual was one that C. C. Spaulding would have endorsed, a rebranding that emphasized the company's history and legacy, partnership with churches, and an appeal to customers on the basis of racial pride.[136]

But it would not be enough. A company that boasted a thousand employees in 1938 had only forty in 2017, when they sold their famous headquarters and removed their iconic signage from the roof. Reduced to one floor, they held their staff meetings in a church across the street. In another ironic twist, they entered into short-lived and unsuccessful distributing agreements with Metropolitan Life and Prudential. That year the mutual was downgraded by A. M. Best to a C++ due to large losses.[137] Their problems multiplied in 2018 when the funds for a reinsurance transaction were misappropriated by a financial advisor, who is currently facing charges of wire fraud and perjury.[138] Since then, the company has been in receivership with the North Carolina Department of Insurance, its few dozen employees still working on the twelfth floor of its historic headquarters, its future uncertain.[139]

In 2020, North Carolina insurance commissioner Mike Causey described the plight of the Mutual as "a sad situation which I inherited."[140] This serves as an apt metaphor for the racist practices that defined the historical experience of Blacks with life insurance. Most Blacks were relegated to the industrial branch where, due to race-based underwriting, they paid even higher prices for what was already a poor product. State regulators were largely indifferent or ineffective, and companies responded to state antidiscrimination laws by finding other ways to differentiate or by exiting markets.

In response, a separate industry rose to serve Black customers against great odds, but many of these companies struggled and failed. The most successful among them, North Carolina Mutual, was a storied company that was the hub of Durham's Black Wall Street and a source of racial pride throughout the South. In the early twentieth century the Mutual, like other life insurers, saw itself as a public service agency where mission was central, but with the additional burden that came with serving a clientele that was subject to widespread discrimination. The postwar economic growth and civil rights movement led to a more strictly commercial focus for the Mutual, but rapid expansion was followed by a painful collapse, as integrated mortality tables eliminated their fundamental reason for existence and made successful competition virtually impossible.

But the end of a racially segregated life insurance industry by no means erased the cumulative economic impact of discriminatory pricing and exclusion. In the early years of this century, Metropolitan Life, Prudential, and John Hancock settled a series of multi-million-dollar class action lawsuits acknowledging that race-based underwriting practices caused Blacks to pay more than Whites for life insurance. Another set of lawsuits involved a host of smaller companies. While the Big Three adjusted their underwriting practices in the 1950s and exited the industrial business by the late 1960s, many smaller companies, mostly located in the South, continued selling industrial insurance. Some of these companies did not change their underwriting practices until the late 1970s, and not all previous policies were retrospectively adjusted, creating the possibility that policies created using racially based underwriting rules remained in force into this century.[141]

The Depression created the necessary momentum to advance the case for social insurance in two areas where private industry had not made sufficient inroads: unemployment and old-age assistance. With the passage of the Social Security Act, the federal government quickly created an enormous insurance footprint. The Depression also brought some aspects of the life insurance business into sharp relief and provoked a long-delayed critique of industrial insurance. Yet despite a prolonged federal investigation, that business was allowed to collapse of its own weight several decades later.

The industry that emerged was defensive and circumspect and increasingly thought of itself as a business rather than a public service agency. In response to mounting pressure, by mid-century life insurers finally began to wind down their longstanding practice of race-based underwriting and exit the industrial business. By then, the "public service" mindset had long been confined to the ever-growing area of workplace benefits, while ordinary policies were largely marketed as additional coverage or investments to middle-class customers. The life insurance industry had ceded its mantle of quasi-publicness, and as the twentieth century progressed, its outlook would narrow further.

10

Stuck in the Age of Containment

A series of well-known television commercials features a duck who quacks an insurance company's name in ads that vaguely describe a product that "pays the bills that health insurance won't" or "pays cash when you're hurt and can't work." Commercials featuring this duck are ubiquitous and are frequently aired during popular events like the Superbowl. The ad campaign has won numerous awards.

The duck represents a type of coverage that fills gaps created by health insurance, which is sometimes referred to in the ads as "major medical" and represented by a bedraggled pigeon. Scenarios portrayed in ads show how this coverage helps with high out-of-pocket costs or pays bills that might otherwise accumulate during an illness or injury. The speed with which payment comes is emphasized. In some ads, the duck proffers wingfuls of currency to injured people. Forgoing this protection is equated with foolhardy exposure to financial ruin. The duck encourages viewers to ask for this coverage at work.

The name the duck quacks is "AFLAC," short for the American Family Life Assurance Company, the largest supplemental insurance company in the United States. Founded in 1955 on a shoestring, today it has more than $130 billion in assets and more than fifty million policyholders worldwide. Its history and business model provide a narrative that is helpful in understanding both the development of health insurance in this country and the persistence of unmet demand.

Health insurance emerged innocuously as a small and unimportant-seeming subcomponent of the broader category of disability insurance. Disability insurance itself grew from the narrow line of travel insurance that was popularized in the nineteenth century. Disability insurance was designed to cover lost income due to illness or injury; the cost of health care was initially an incidental afterthought. But over time health care costs became the most important component of disability insurance, and by the middle of the twentieth century, premiums for health insurance exceeded premiums for coverage to replace lost income. Health insurance had become a separate and rapidly growing line of business.

Though it originated in the casualty branch of insurance, disability insurance was soon offered by life insurers, which came to dominate the business, especially in the group market. The "double indemnity" policy clause, popularized by the early days of the automobile, was a gateway into disability coverage for life insurers. The double indemnity clause doubled and sometimes tripled the death

Uncovered. Katherine Hempstead, Oxford University Press. © Oxford University Press 2024.
DOI: 10.1093/oso/9780190094157.003.0010

benefit for certain types of accidental deaths. Casualty insurers added double indemnity clauses to accident policies, and life insurers added them to life insurance policies, then expanded into disability coverage in both the individual and group markets.

A consistent and defining characteristic of health insurance that sets it apart from other lines of insurance business is the general unaffordability of health care for most people. This has created a longstanding challenge for hospitals and physicians, who have historically been incentivized to find ways to finance the cost of care yet have been very concerned about how much they will get paid. During the Depression, hospitals and physicians devised an approach to financing patient payment through the creation of Blue Cross and Blue Shield plans, which were initially a competitor to indemnity insurance products offered by life insurers.

While the federal government expanded its insurance footprint significantly with the passage of the Social Security Act in 1935, the inclusion of national health insurance as part of that legislation was omitted in the face of opposition from physicians as well as southern Democrats. The rapid growth of group benefits created a relatively generous private welfare system maintained by employers and workers and subsidized by a federal tax incentive. Yet the sizable excluded population could ultimately not be ignored as it included the elderly, whose demands for health care increased as life expectancy grew.

The threat of greater public involvement bound insurers and health care providers together in a futile attempt to demonstrate that the private sector could meet the nation's demand for coverage, an effort that forced insurers to consider public need in order to avoid a government takeover of their business. Insurers sought to contain the federal role in insurance by providing more coverage privately. This involved increasing the generosity of group coverage and experimenting with some ill-fated strategies to attempt to cover the elderly.

The passage of Medicare and Medicaid in 1965 was in one sense a refutation of this effort, but it also showed that the federal government had no intention of displacing the private insurance industry. Medicare was modeled after the structure of group plans, and both Medicare and Medicaid were designed to fit around rather than replace the existing group market. Insurers quickly found that once again government involvement created new opportunities and began to sell Medicare supplemental policies and functioned as fiscal intermediaries in Medicare. Medicaid was designed as a program for the poor to be administered with considerable discretion by states. Southern resistance to racial equality would lead to significant geographic variation in eligibility and benefits. Medicaid would also ultimately prove to be an important business opportunity for insurers.

After the passage of Medicare and Medicaid, the focus shifted from containment to cost containment. Self-insurance grew among employers, and insurers were increasingly charged with attempting to manage the cost of care. High costs and adverse selection effectively doomed the individual market, and low-value supplemental products proliferated for those for whom comprehensive coverage was unavailable or unaffordable. Even many with insurance sought supplemental coverage due to high out-of-pocket cost exposure or lack of protection for their income in the event of an injury or illness.

Ultimately cost pressures led to the rise of health maintenance organizations (HMOs) and the birth of managed care. Life insurers largely exited the health insurance business in the 1980s and 1990s, ceding ground to these new entities. At around the same time life insurers introduced a new disability product, long-term care insurance, which in some ways marked a return to their early twentieth-century focus on disability coverage for individuals. It would similarly prove to be an underwriting disaster.

Health insurance is arguably the most high-profile line of insurance business in the United States today, generating a steady stream of policy debate and consumer complaints. There are several things that set health insurance apart from other kinds of insurance. One is its relative complexity. While home and auto policies have become more standardized and universal over time, at least at the state level, health insurance is fragmented into many mutually exclusive market segments with different benefit designs and financial structures. Another difference is that while costs in other major personal lines of insurance have generally fallen relative to income, health insurance costs have only risen. A final and important difference is that while the amount of home or auto or even life insurance a person needs is at least somewhat related to their income, the same does not apply to health insurance. These last two points, as this chapter will show, have led to persistent unmet demand and an inconsistent yet historically increasing role of government. It has also created a constant market for supplementary insurance, of which AFLAC is an important example.

The commercial origins of health insurance come from accident insurance, which was initially designed to protect against risks from public conveyances, specifically railroads, but also steamships and other types of transit.[1] Over time, coverage broadened to include all kinds of travel and accidents from all causes. The Travelers Insurance Company was the first to popularize the coverage and pioneered the more general form of accident insurance in 1863.[2]

The purpose of early accident insurance, as shown in Figure 10.1, was to protect income from the loss of productive time that would result from a disabling injury. The ultimate loss of time was death, and early policies generally paid a "principal sum" in the event of death and a weekly indemnity payment for

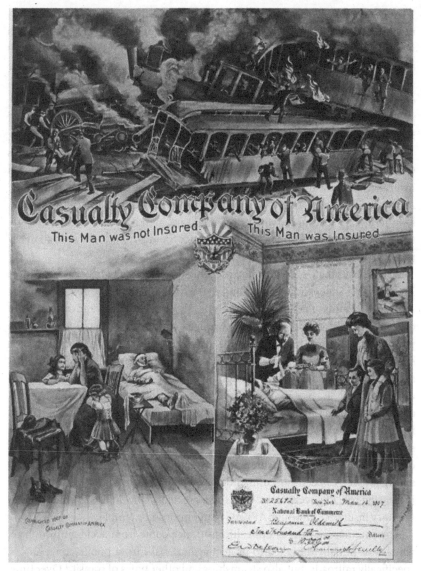

Figure 10.1 Early twentieth-century advertisement for the Continental Casualty Company contrasts insurance versus uninsurance in the event of an accident. Library of Congress.

permanent or temporary total disability, with maximum weekly amounts and time periods for payment. A fraction of the principal sum would be paid in the event of certain serious injuries resulting in permanent disabilities such as dismemberment or loss of sight.

While travel insurance was conceptualized as a hedge against a specific time-limited activity that was considered inordinately dangerous, the broader form of accident insurance was designed to protect income more generally. Premiums were rated based on the hazardousness of policyholder occupation, and there was a reluctance to sell policies to those who were not in the labor force. This is one of the reasons that policies sold by Travelers to women paid a death benefit only.

Coverage in these early policies was for total disability only, although there was some consideration of how the concept varied by occupation. For example, Travelers defined total disability in their agents' manual as "physical incapacity for business" yet created some wiggle room on the topic of "usual" versus "any" occupation, noting that "a spirit of fairness added to a discriminating judgement will determine certain cases." An accountant with a "trifling" hand injury, for example, might be completely disabled, while a merchant or salesman with the same injury would be only partially disabled (and therefore not covered).[3]

In a classic mid-century work on casualty insurance, Wharton professor C. Arthur Kulp described the early days of accident insurance as the "Age of the Promoter," where policies were "brief and loosely phrased." They were also priced too low, resulting in an ever-increasing list of restrictions and exclusions, as companies "promised liberally on the initial page and on its reverse side reconsidered the generous impulse."[4] The list of excluded injuries grew from dueling, fighting, and other "voluntary exposure to danger" to include playing sports, riding a bicycle, getting on or off conveyances, and even "lifting and over-exertion." The line of business quickly fell into ill repute, with the agent, according to another early analysis, turning into "more or less of a sharper, ducking in to town, securing what applications he could and departing as he had come, before any losses occurred to embarrass him."[5] Development of the field during this period was largely negative, as companies increased restrictions on coverage, yet many firms failed, in part because in the event of legal challenges, courts often ruled in favor of policyholders and invalidated technical restrictions.

Out of this climate arose the next phase of accident insurance, dubbed by Kulp "the Era of the Salesman." From the 1890s until the Depression an opposite trend prevailed: competition to liberalize coverage. An early and long-lasting example of this development was the double indemnity clause, which doubled the death benefit, or principal sum, in the event of death due to a railroad accident.[6]

The double indemnity clause was a marketing ploy, designed to appeal to the fears and speculative impulses of potential customers. The clause also referenced the original motive for travel insurance. Since the number of deaths due to railway accidents was very small and declining, it was an easy benefit for companies to offer. As evidence of its durability, this was the same policy provision exploited in the famous film *Double Indemnity* in 1937, where casualty agent Walter Huff and

Mrs. Nirdlinger murdered Mr. Nirdlinger, then dragged his body onto the train tracks in an attempt to make the death look like a railway accident.[7]

The double indemnity clause was an initial foray into a world of benefit liberalization, and it was also an early bridge that would ultimately help to connect accident and life insurance. By the late nineteenth century, some casualty companies that also sold life insurance started to incorporate a broader double indemnity clause into their life policies, doubling the benefit in the event of death by accidental means. Travelers was the first major company to do so, adding a double indemnity clause to their life policy as early as 1892.[8] The impetus was competitive pressure and the increased interest in accidental death that stemmed from the growing use of automobiles. Some limited accident policies were sold that only covered accidents associated with automobiles.

Double indemnity clauses became standard in life insurance policies by the 1920s, even though the practice was deemed gimmicky and sensational by some. An insurance textbook from 1930 noted that "keen competition" was the reason for the clause, which "appeals to the imagination and is often an attractive selling point." If it led to the purchase of more life insurance, the practice was acceptable, though its appropriateness in a life insurance policy was considered "debatable."[9] Edwin Faulkner, who was president of the Woodmen Central Life Insurance Company and would go on to lead one the earliest health insurance trade associations, described the practice at mid-century with a bit of disdain: "The best that can be said for the double indemnity provisions is that they add a little sales glamour to the contract that may appeal to the speculative instinct of the applicant and induce him to buy the other coverage that is important to his personal security."[10] The fictional Walter Huff described the provision as a "come-on."[11]

Benefit liberalizations multiplied during this new age of the accident business. Companies began to expand the definition of disability—increasingly covering partial disability, waiving the requirement for home confinement, and lengthening the period during which indemnity benefits could be collected, with some adding lifetime coverage.[12] Companies introduced noncancellable policies with guaranteed renewability, liberalized claims adjustment practices, and offered a greater variety of policy forms. By 1931, ninety companies offered approximately eight hundred different accident policies.[13]

During this period, life insurance companies entered the accident business in a variety of ways.[14] As we saw in the last chapter, in the early twentieth century, life companies seeking to grow sought to extend more coverage to women, to "sub-standard lives," and to people of more modest means. They also became increasingly interested in covering additional risks related to accidents and illness. To life insurers, disability coverage fit into the context of a broader interest in the protection of income. Travelers was the first to add a disability benefit to life insurance in 1904. New York Life added a premium waiver in 1910, and this practice quickly became ubiquitous. Many companies additionally offered a small monthly payment in the event of a total and permanent disability before age sixty.

At Metropolitan Life, disability coverage fit into President Haley Fiske's interest in the overall protection of income, the same impulse that had led him to seek to insure against unemployment. As early as 1909 Fiske had expressed interest in the area, and by 1912 Metropolitan offered its first disability benefit, a waiver of premium in the event of disability. In 1914, Fiske established a disability department as part of the welfare division, under the supervision of Lee Frankel. Frankel, well versed in social insurance, had traveled to Europe to learn about accident and health insurance. Yet with little solid actuarial information to go on, experience data from a Manchester fraternal society became the basis of the company's early disability underwriting. Metropolitan offered a weekly disability indemnity benefit in 1918 and a year later added a double indemnity clause.[15]

Among both casualty and life companies, the early twentieth century saw a steady liberalization of disability benefits.[16] In theory, disability coverage was a sensible addition to a life policy. As Mowbray noted in his mid-century textbook, real permanent disability was, "in a sense, a living death," and could create similar threats to income. Yet the devil was in the details.[17] Underwriting in accident and health insurance was based on a far less secure empirical framework than was life insurance. Disability coverage quickly became problematic. There was a creeping growth in claims. At the turn of the century, Travelers expressed some misgivings about their accident experience: "The additional features and increased terms of liability which have been introduced in the past few years for the purpose of competition have doubled the necessary reserve for the indemnity part of our accident policy over the reserve required for our death loss."[18]

At about this time, health insurance, which at the time meant coverage for disability resulting from illnesses, was introduced. While there had been several small unsuccessful attempts in the mid-nineteenth century, commercial health insurance was first introduced by casualty companies at the end of the nineteenth century. The Fidelity and Casualty Company of New York introduced the first combined accident and health policy in 1898. The next year, Travelers introduced similar coverage. While selling a combined policy, Travelers intended to monitor their accident and health experience separately, and acknowledged in a bit of prescient foreshadowing that in both areas, underwriting was driven by competition and was largely based on guesswork, as the company noted in an internal publication: "We have availed ourselves of the English experience covering disability from disease and our own experience of thirty-five years as to accidents, and yet we are without sufficient data to find a scientific basis for a class of risks which are being freely written without any experimental knowledge of whereunto we are driving."[19] At approximately the same time, Aetna and a number of other casualty companies added health to their accident coverage.

Initially health (or sickness) insurance was considered to be a "frill" benefit added to the accident policy, as part of the overall liberalization of benefits. (The coverage was interchangeably referred to as either "health" or "sickness" insurance.) The risk being covered was still income loss from disability, with limited instances of disability resulting from disease now included with disability from injuries. At first, health coverage was restricted to a limited number of diseases, with strict time limits and waiting periods for benefits. Yet over time, health benefits liberalized as well, with expansions in diseases covered and reductions in the waiting period. While coverage was initially restricted to disability that required home confinement, this definition also loosened and the time period for benefit payment expanded. By 1915, noncancellable and guaranteed renewable health and accident policies were being developed. In some policies the payment period was extended to the length of the policyholder's life.[20]

Accident and sickness policies began to include some benefits related to medical costs, including surgeons' fees, medical treatment for nondisabling injuries, and even travel costs borne by family members. Travelers included surgical benefits in their accident policies beginning in 1900. Often policies included a schedule of common surgeries with listed prices. By 1905, indemnity benefits were increased in some policies if the policyholder was hospitalized. Medical treatment outside of the hospital began to be covered in some policies by 1910, and by 1916 some policies even included coverage for nursing care.[21] Yet in the early twentieth century the cost of medical care was still considered incidental compared to weekly indemnity payments and the principal sum.

Life insurers soon ventured further to offer group accident and health insurance. This effort started experimentally at Metropolitan Life with a group policy for Metropolitan employees. Metropolitan soon expanded their offerings to other groups. A major contract was for the eight thousand employees of the Delaware and Hudson Railroad. During the 1920s, permanent and total disability became separated from accident and health coverage and was also offered to groups as accidental death and dismemberment coverage, thereby separating the simpler principal sum component of the coverage from the weekly indemnity payments.

With the general success of the group accident and health business, some life companies tried to provide similar coverage to individuals. While by then many life companies had added disability benefits as riders to their life policies, they did not offer separate accident or health coverage. Fiske was eager to provide this coverage. Yet as Metropolitan historian Marquis James noted, the company entered the field with trepidation: "Fiske knew that this would be an experiment not free from risk. Individual accident and health insurance was a department of underwriting in which countless well-meaning amateurs had gone bankrupt and in which professionals had sustained heavy losses."[22] To increase their chance of success, Metropolitan recruited a casualty expert from the Insurance Company of North America to run the new line, since, as Professor Kulp had observed, there were "inherent characteristics in accident and health insurance that make the relative precision and solidity of life insurance impossible."[23] While life companies started offering accident and health coverage to groups before selling to individuals, casualty companies sometimes approached the market from the opposite direction. Travelers, for example, sold accident and health coverage to individuals before attempting it in the group market in 1913, also experimenting first on their own employees.[24]

As benefits liberalized and sales of accident and health insurance grew, problems began to emerge. It quickly became clear that sickness accounted for a higher share of disability claims than did accidents. Writing in 1942, Kulp estimated that only eight to nine percent of nonoccupational disability resulted from injury; the rest were from illness, most of which were chronic conditions.[25] But the underwriting in health insurance was far more difficult. Albert Mowbray's classic insurance textbook from 1930 described some problems with this line of business: "The companies have found the moral hazard in the health business serious, and the business has not, in general, been profitable." Lack of standardization and poor understanding led to frequent policyholder complaints, requiring the involvement of state regulators: "Far more complaints to the state authorities concern claims under health and accident policies, than perhaps any other type of insurance, complaints generally arising from failure to realize the limited coverage granted under the policy."[26]

Even worse were the problems arising from a secondary subprime market, in particular policies sold through newspaper subscriptions, or industrial insurance policies with health and accident coverage. Mowbray commented on the problems created by deceptive advertising: "The publicity describing it is usually couched in such general terms as to lead the reader to believe it furnishes reasonably complete coverage, though a comparison of the premium charged with those quoted on standard policies should rouse some suspicion as to its probable incompleteness. This suspicion will be confirmed by an inspection of the policy. The restrictions of the coverage compensates for the cheap rate."[27] Mowbry observed: "There is much misunderstanding of these contracts, and no little friction in loss adjustment."[28]

The Depression would serve as a reckoning for the frothy disability business. Life insurers were hit particularly hard as claims skyrocketed. A mid-century lecture on disability benefits in life insurance identifies the hard lessons of the

Depression as pivotal: "The losses incurred by many companies were such as to call for an entirely new appraisal of the situation."[29] What followed was a period of retrenchment. Kulp, in his casualty text, labeled this third phase the "Era of the Home Office" or the "Era of the Actuary." This was a corrective to the Depression experience where by 1932 the average loss ratio for stock companies had plunged to −7.6 percent for accident insurance and an even grimmer −12.2 percent for health insurance.

From his vantage point, Kulp saw the change as a welcome one, since absent some form of external pressure, companies seemed unwilling to sacrifice their individual interests for the benefit of the business as a whole. Kulp alluded to the historic role of conflagrations in his assessment: "Depression, national or local, has its uses and in no area more markedly than in insurance, where many of the major reforms of the business date from calamities."[30]

In life insurance, a line of business that had become so unfamiliar with financial stress, the disability experience was chastening. To the National Convention of Insurance Commissioners (NCIC), these changes were long overdue. As early as 1916 the commissioners had expressed concern about the introduction of disability benefits, seeing this as an attribute that would diminish life insurance: "When a provision for health and accident coverage is incorporated in the life contract, the health and accident feature is not raised to the level of the life contract, but the life contract is brought to the level of the health and accident business; in other words, a contract is no more certain than its most uncertain feature."[31] A. M. Best saw it fit to issue a special publication compiling the double indemnity and disability provisions offered by life insurers, including this note of remonstrance in the introduction: "Because of the emphasis given to these clauses by soliciting agents, it is highly important, if these liberalizations of policy contracts are to endure, that extravagant statements or misrepresentations should not be permitted."[32] The NCIC created a special committee to investigate disability and accidental death benefits in life insurance in 1925, but it failed to take action and was disbanded in 1927.[33]

In 1928 the issue was raised once again, and the commissioners sounded the alarm, issuing a statement suggesting that the matter called for immediate action: "Competition has been the sole agent in the development of the disability benefit from a relatively unimportant position in the life insurance contract to one which overshadows the principal benefit itself." As a result, "Large and persistent losses in surplus are being experienced, a condition which Insurance Commissioners will soon be asked to explain."[34] By 1931, little had changed:

> Underwriting losses have continued, the class of undesirable "pensioners" has increased enormously, while controversies between companies and assureds as to the interpretation of the disability contract have not subsided to any

appreciable extent if at all. Insurance Commissioners are still compelled to explain to disgruntled policyholders the difference between total and permanent disability on the one hand and accident and health insurance on the other; to listen to the oft-repeated wail that the agent who sold the contract represented it as the latter; and to admonish assureds to do what we all know is seldom done even by the insurance intelligentsia—that is, to read their policies before filing them away for safekeeping. That life insurance suffers by reason of such controversies may be accepted as axiomatic.[35]

Commissioner White of West Virginia described how far the benefit standards had drifted:

A man had to be practically dead to get any benefits. He had to be totally and permanently disabled for all time. But the bars have been lowered. One company says that they will interpret total and permanent disability to be the ability of a man to earn only one-fourth of his former earnings. And so each company tried to get a little more favorable total and permanent disability benefit, so they could meet the competition of the other companies, and it has grown and grown until today it has become the burden of the life companies instead of a means of profit.

At this point, any attempt to modify or standardize the benefit seemed palliative rather than corrective. White believed that the best thing for the commissioners to do was to stand by and watch, since "whatever we do may only interfere with the final settlement."[36] And while the companies did not eliminate all aspects of the disability coverage, changes came quickly. The indemnity benefit was generally eliminated, the eligibility age restricted, and the definition of disability tightened.

By the 1940s, conditions had stabilized, and companies were feeling pressure to liberalize benefits once again. But now there was a different problem, one that foreshadowed the unmet demand that has continued to characterize this line of insurance. An analysis from 1948 acknowledged that the sharply reduced income benefits were too low and not "realistic" in light of current economic conditions. Consumer demand for enhancement was understandable, yet so far companies had resisted. In fact, there was a significant amount of unmet demand in the accident and health market. Despite the fact that the business had grown from $49 million in 1920 to $215 million in 1940, it seemed to Kulp that "Accident and Health cover remains greatly undersold." Companies generally concentrated on accident insurance, a "selected and minor part," and avoided much of the rest: "The fact remains: the unsold disability business is largely business the companies do not want."[37]

While life insurers struggled with disability insurance, a new model of financing the cost of medical care was being developed. As hospitals developed more expertise and technology, demand increased, but so did payment problems, particularly during the Depression, when occupancy rates fell and some hospitals had to close.[38] In an attempt to address the rapidly worsening financials at the Baylor University hospital, Justin Ford Kimball created the earliest version of a Blue Cross plan, an approach to prepayment. A monthly payment of fifty cents covered twenty-one days of hospital care, with a discount on additional days. Experience data from a cash disability program for Dallas teachers was used to establish the rates, and the plan was first offered to Dallas schoolteachers in 1929.[39]

Combining principles from group disability insurance and the practice of contract medicine used to hire company doctors for workers' compensation plans, Blue Cross was a "service" plan, offering a fixed amount of services rather than the fixed amount of dollars offered by the indemnity disability insurance policies. Initially the financial arrangement was between individual hospitals and groups of patients, but it quickly became apparent that local hospitals needed to jointly offer services to avoid competition and financial instability. Early Blues plans grew by marketing directly to employees using radio and newspaper advertisements. The prepayment movement grew quickly, from six plans with 11,500 members in 1933 to in seventeen plans with 215,000 members by 1935. By 1938 there were 2.8 million members.[40]

At a time when commercial insurers were relatively uninvolved in the medical expense part of disability insurance, the Blue Cross plans filled a void. They had the support of the American Hospital Association (AHA), but the American Medical Association (AMA) had historically taken every effort to oppose any kind of third-party interference in the delivery of medical care, whether governmental or private.[41] Yet the increasing problem of unmet demand and the looming threat of government interference made the AMA's position ever more difficult. The AMA accepted the Blue Cross model but was far more wary of the companion Blue Shield organizations that emerged in the late 1930s to provide a similar method of prepayment for physicians' services.[42]

Hospital prepayment plans were a novel type of organization. From a regulatory perspective, they were not considered insurance companies. They were given a quasi-public role as nonprofit tax-exempt groups with some supervision from the state insurance department, but without the reserve requirements imposed on licensed insurance companies. In 1933, New York developed the first special legislation in response to a request from the United Hospital Fund. But a certain degree of state supervision did not prevent financial misadventure. Plans did not always carefully adhere to the requirement of at least seventy-five percent participation in order to enroll a group, resulting in adverse selection.[43] The National Association of Insurance Commissioners (NAIC) created a committee on group hospitalization in 1938 and sought to tighten supervision.[44]

Sound actuarial data on hospital use was absent, and the presence of prepayment potentially affected utilization. This risk grew as plans sought to cover more inclusive services. One important decision a number of plans made was to offer maternity coverage, at a time when the majority of births still occurred out of the hospital. Insurers were lukewarm on the idea of prepayment and preferred fixed indemnities, to the extent to which they were involved in health care expense reimbursement at all. Yet insurers definitely felt the competition from the Blue Cross plans.[45]

At mid-century, what we think of as health insurance today was still usually referred to as "disability" or "accident and sickness" insurance and consisted of a number of different types of coverage. The term "accident and sickness" insurance was used both to describe the overall line of business to refer to one specific aspect of it—weekly indemnity coverage to replace lost wages. The rest of the line consisted of separate types of coverage for the expenses of major categories of health care—hospital, surgical, and medical. Yet another component, coverage for accidental death and dismemberment—that is, the "principal sum" of the original accident policy—was provided separately.

Accident and sickness indemnity coverage was still the most common disability benefit. In 1948, ten million workers had this coverage, compared with seventeen million that had group life in 1948. The indemnity insurance paid a weekly cash benefit to employees who couldn't work due to a nonoccupational accident or illness. There was a waiting period and a time limit for these benefits. About eight million workers and dependents had hospital expense insurance, seven and a half million had surgical insurance, and only about one million had the newest line, "medical" coverage.

The hospital, surgical, and medical benefits reimbursed employees for a portion of the health care expenses from an accident or illness. They were also limited in both the amount and the duration of payment. For example, a typical hospital benefit in 1948 would reimburse up to $6 a day for a maximum of thirty-one days. Surgical plans usually had a schedule with specific fees for different procedures, often with a maximum of $200. The newest coverage, "medical," was for doctors' visits at the office or at home and related services. This coverage also had a maximum amount for any particular episode of illness and a maximum time period over which benefits would be paid. Patients were responsible for the balance.

Employees who were offered these accident and sickness benefits were encouraged to think of them as a cohesive whole, and in most cases were required to either opt in to all of them or none of them. Aetna vice president George Beers advised that the employee would "grasp the essence of group insurance more clearly if he reads the employee booklet as a single whole. It is one group plan, even though it provides several different benefits." Employees generally paid about half of the costs. In 1948, family coverage for this group of benefits cost workers an average of $4.17 per month. In the early days of group coverage, employees would report claims to their employers, and in many cases employers would pay them. Employers were referred to as the policyholder, and employees were described as "claimants."[46] At mid-century, the individual market was still larger than the group market but was more focused on weekly cash indemnity insurance and had seen less growth in hospital, surgical, and medical coverage. Between 1945 and 1955, annual premiums for the overall line of business grew from $372 million to $2.2 billion—an increase of six hundred percent.[47] Growth was particularly rapid for hospital, surgical, and medical coverage.

By the mid-1950s, two important milestones were reached. Premiums for the various health care cost coverages exceeded those for cash indemnity payments to replace lost wages. In part this reflected the fact that more workers were receiving paid sick leave directly from their employer. Also, the group market surpassed the individual in terms of enrollment and premiums. By the end of 1954, more than sixty percent of the population had hospital coverage, fifty percent had some coverage for surgical expenses, and twenty-five percent were covered for the relatively new category of medical insurance.[48]

A third milestone illustrates the meteoric growth of group accident and sickness insurance relative to life insurance. By 1952, premiums for the various types of accident and sickness coverage combined had reached nearly $1 billion, exceeding premiums on group life insurance by a considerable amount.[49] Though fairly recently considered a relatively unimportant "side-line," accident and sickness insurance by mid-century was the largest line of casualty business. Life insurers quickly dominated the group market, with about eighty-five to ninety percent of premium volume versus about half of premiums in the ever less important individual market.[50]

The growth of group health insurance was fueled by the growing importance of benefits to workers, particularly organized labor, a trend amplified by a number of federal policies. In 1943 the National War Labor Board permitted the substitution of benefits for up to five percent of wages to control inflation. The 1935 National Labor Relations Act (the Wagner Act) required management to bargain over "wages and conditions of employment." The Taft Hartley Act in 1947 retained this language about "conditions of employment" as a subject for collective bargaining.[51] This was found by the Supreme Court to include employee benefits in the *Inland Steel* decision in 1949. Unions began to play an important role in the expansion of benefits. In some instances benefits were jointly management by industry and labor through equal representation in a Taft-Hartley trusteeship.[52]

Changes in the labor movement itself also fostered the focus on benefits. While the Taft-Hartley Act enabled collective bargaining for benefits, it also contained many antilabor elements such as right to work laws, exclusion of certain occupations and industries (including hospitals), and proscription of communists. These provisions slowed the momentum of organized labor, particularly in the South. A general purge of suspected radicals during the McCarthy era affected labor unions profoundly. This resulted in an increasingly insular and parochial union culture that prioritized member benefits, rather than a broader labor movement that represented the working class as a whole.[53]

Collective bargaining by unions with large memberships accelerated the overall growth of accident and sickness insurance as well as the expansion of private nonprofit hospitals. By the mid-1950s, unions negotiated an estimated one-fourth of the health insurance purchased. Reflecting higher costs, general prosperity, and the growing power of labor in collective bargaining, employers' share of health care costs rose during this time, from an estimated ten percent in 1945 to closer to forty percent for workers and twenty percent for dependents by 1950.[54] In 1954, the federal government provided a further accelerant to the growth of the employer system by providing important tax benefits. This privatized system of group benefits developed its own inertia and became very difficult to disrupt, even as costs rose and huge segments of the population were excluded from its protections.[55]

Another factor propelling the growth of health insurance was the fear of government intervention. Campaigns for public health insurance had a long history. The Progressive Era movement for compulsory health insurance led by the American Association of Labor Legislation ran into multiple buzzsaws, including organized labor and organized medicine. The final blow was World War I and the reactionary period that followed, where social insurance was associated with "bolshevism" and contrasted unfavorably with an "Americanism" defined by minimal government involvement with business. During the 1920s, the substantive investigation of the CCMC kept the issue of health insurance on the public agenda, but the group's work, particularly their endorsement of prepaid group practice, also began to strengthen and organize the opposition, namely organized medicine.

The Depression amplified concerns about the affordability of health care, but the combination of a conservative resurgence and the beginnings of World War II pushed the issue to the side.[56] Despite the high levels of public support for health insurance, there was also an organized opposition that was not present for other New Deal social insurance programs such as old-age pensions and unemployment insurance. Chief among them were organized medicine and, somewhat later, insurers. Another important force was the southern members of Congress, largely Democrats, who strongly opposed measures that threatened to disrupt racial segregation.[57]

Truman supported a single national plan that would include a broad range of the population, even those from occupations that were excluded from Social Security. His plan was intended to interfere minimally with physician and hospital payment and patient choice of provider, and Truman even claimed that physician income would rise. The AMA famously tagged the proposal as one that would lead to "socialized medicine" and empower government bureaucrats to interfere with the doctor-patient relationship. Their efforts included advertising and a strong grassroots campaign that enlisted physicians and their spouses. In the climate of anticommunism, the opposition campaign found support from conservative groups like the American Legion.[58] Truman's widening divisions with southern Democrats in Congress over civil rights issues also doomed progress toward health insurance.

Under the moderate Eisenhower administration, the threat of national health insurance was at least temporarily in retreat, but the potential for any reemergence led insurers to double down on the voluntary model. To Professor Kulp's famous delineation of disability insurance into the eras of the Promoter, the Salesman, and the Home Office, some proposed to add a fourth. The era that had begun with the passage of the Social Security Act was described by an economics professor with a repurposed Cold War metaphor: "This period in the history of disability insurance might well be labeled the 'Era of Containment' because of the efforts of the commercial companies to prevent any further extension of either the state or Federal governments into the disability insurance field." Success in this endeavor would require a steady expansion of coverage.[59]

The insurance industry was divided over Truman's proposal. Established life insurance companies from the Northeast were sensitive to federal criticisms of the industry expressed in the Temporary National Economic Committee (TNEC) hearings and were reluctant to adopt a position that appeared overly obstructionist. Smaller southern and western firms had a more antagonistic attitude toward government. There were also casualty companies, represented by two trade associations, the Bureau of Accident and Health Underwriters and the Health and Accident Underwriters Conference, which also tended to have a more conservative outlook.

Out of these differences a new trade association emerged. In 1956, the two accident and health organizations dissolved and were replaced with the Health Insurers Association of America (HIAA), which dedicated itself to the prevention of government health insurance and the promotion of voluntary insurance. The first president of the HIAA was Edwin Faulkner, who had been president of the Nebraska-based Woodmen Accident and Life Company. Faulkner was a far more strident foe of government intervention in health insurance than moderate presidents of northeastern companies such as Aetna's Henry Beers.[60]

To counter national health insurance, insurers emphasized the positive aspects of the voluntary system rather than adopting the negative posture of the AMA. Insurers would sometimes argue that national health insurance was unaffordable for society. A mid-century underwriter expressed the concern: "If we drastically change the balance, if we give everyone access to such services as a matter of right, we will find that we have increased our costs decidedly, and, it is quite conceivable, to the point of being a burden on the economy that is unsound and unwise."[61] This was a tacit admission that there were haves and have-nots: the benefits employees received through the private welfare state could not be made available to all.

To strengthen this argument, the runaway costs of British national health insurance were often invoked. Insurers argued that national health insurance would be bad for doctors. A life insurance president, describing the quandary, noted, "I cannot see how it is possible to have compulsory health service without having outside controls imposed on doctors' fees."[62] The AMA found it necessary to publicly support private health insurance. A "strange bedfellows" alliance developed between the AMA and the HIAA as they pursued their common interest in the preservation of the voluntary system. Eisenhower sympathized with these concerns, in a 1952 speech likening compulsory health insurance to a bad sort of economic collectivism where patients would be subjected to "regimented assembly-line treatment" from disinterested physicians, promoted by seniority instead of skill, while an "army of Government clerks" handled the voluminous paperwork.[63]

The Era of Containment was decidedly not an era of "cost containment," a term that had not yet been applied to American health care. On the contrary, the implicit pressure to stave off national health insurance placed pressure on the voluntary system to liberalize benefits as much as possible. The expansion of benefits was held up as proof that the system was working. Connecticut General Life vice president Eddy reflected that tension in his enthusiasm about the system's potential to meet society's demands. "Certainly, the continued and substantial extension of benefits that has taken place on a voluntary basis speaks eloquently of the full opportunity available for voluntary means to function."[64]

Protection from the risk of high health care costs was increasingly seen as separate from and more important than indemnity benefits. Concern about these costs had led to the creation of the Blue Cross model and accelerated its growth in the postwar period. By the mid-1950s Blue Cross accounted for an estimated thirty percent of hospital patient revenue.[65] The choice between commercial insurance and Blue Cross was described as a tradeoff between coverage for the "first dollar" versus the "last dollar" of health care costs. Insurers groused about the greater popularity of the service plan model and thought that policyholders wanted insurance to cover too large a share of their costs. HIAA president Faulkner supported the use of the deductibles, which at the time were measured in days, not dollars, and were sometimes called the "elimination period." Faulkner lamented consumer resistance to deductibles and their preference for "first dollar" coverage as shortsighted: "Unhappily too few applicants appreciate that first day coverage in sickness insurance borders on being a dollar swapping proposition."[66]

Metropolitan Life's vice president Gilbert Fitzhugh alleged that there was a "general unsettled question" as to whether health insurance should be primarily for catastrophic losses or should encourage early diagnoses and care. But the question was not unsettled for consumers. They wanted first dollar *and* last dollar coverage. Insurers viewed this as a collective character flaw that might bring on socialized medicine. Fitzhugh wondered out loud why policyholders would not dig deeper to pay for their care: "Why is it so much worse to go into debt to meet a medical bill, or pay it on the installment plan, than it is to meet the cost of an automobile or a television set—in fact, so much so that we are told the government must step in and provide the means for furnishing health services and for financing them?"[67] In a scolding tone somewhat reminiscent of fire insurers' discussions of safety, he called for consumer education about how medical expenses should be valued in the household budget: "Perhaps one great need is a continuing educational campaign to put the cost of medical care in a preferred position on the priority list of more of our citizens."[68]

Insurers thought Blue Cross jeopardized the prospects of the voluntary system. The service plans were faulted for driving up utilization and hospital construction, and for tilting hospital financing and consumer expectations toward first dollar coverage. Blue Cross plans covered most hospital expenses up to a limit defined in terms of days or dollars. The plans paid hospitals directly, a structure that many said was conducive to overuse. A hospital director in Detroit warned that Blue Cross plans were "endangered by abuses which have caused excess utilization of its benefits. Specifically, such factors as unnecessary admissions, unnecessary use of diagnostic and treatment aids and unnecessarily long length of stay have brought this about until today the danger is very real and widespread." The list of guilty parties was unfortunately quite inclusive: "In analyzing the situation, we find that abuses of Blue Cross stem from four major sources: Physicians, hospitals, patients themselves and Blue Cross itself."[69] Dr. Paul R. Hawley, who led Health Service Inc., a national enrollment agency for Blue Cross plans, contrasted hospital treatments and procedures for an uninsured patient versus a Blue Cross enrollee. For the former, "some degree of caution is usually exercised, but the Blue Cross patient is fair game."[70]

Rising hospital costs led to rapid premium increases for Blue Cross plans, since they covered a fixed amount of services at no cost to patients. Indemnity plans were able to raise premiums more slowly, allowing patients to absorb more of the cost at the time of use. This permitted more control over the relative cost of benefits as a share of wages. For this reason, employers often preferred commercial insurance. Another advantage was that commercial insurers used experience rating, versus the community rating approach of the Blues, so they could often be more competitive. Commercial insurers were also better able to serve national employers, while Blue plans were still very local, and commercial insurers were also able to offer other group products as well, such as life insurance.[71]

Commercial insurers had competitive advantages over the Blues, but by the mid-1950s their indemnity benefit designs were growing less popular, and there was growing pressure for more first dollar coverage. Over time, the similarities between service plans and indemnity plans grew, as the former started to require more patient payment, and sometimes used experience rating, while the latter increased benefits, and for some categories imposed coinsurance only after covering a fixed initial amount. By 1952, enrollment in indemnity plans for hospital expense coverage was slightly higher, about 52 million as compared with about 43.5 million in Blue Cross.[72]

Outside of hospital care, coverage for other kinds of medical expenses was fragmented and piecemeal, reflecting, as an Equitable actuary noted, the "ever-changing questions of what areas in the cost of health care are important enough to ensure and are theoretically and practically insurable."[73] Coverage was provided by Blue Shield organizations as well as life and casualty companies. The most common category of coverage was for surgical expenses. Medical insurance provided reimbursement for doctors' visits, with much variation between policies—some providing coverage for a fixed number of visits, much like a service plan, and others reimbursing for visits only when the policyholder was unable to work because of disability.[74] In addition to medical and surgical, there were plans offering coverage for diagnostic expense and other miscellaneous benefits, as well as plans covering specific "dread diseases," including polio, typhoid, smallpox, and meningitis.

Yet despite this explosion in coverage, there was an acknowledgment that the most common forms of accident and sickness insurance did not provide adequate protection against truly catastrophic illness, which was considered essential for the survival of the voluntary system. The development of a catastrophic coverage or "major medical" began in the 1950s. The basic design was based on the notion of a "blanket" of aggregate coverage with a high maximum that could be used for various categories of expense related to serious illness. These plans borrowed cost-sharing features from auto insurance, using both monetary deductibles and coinsurance.

A lack of solid experience data inhibited the creation of a major medical plan. Part of the difficulty was that much of the expense that families incurred in the context of major health episodes could occur outside of medical settings. A child with rheumatic fever, for example, could be confined to home and require nursing care for a lengthy period of time. Liberty Mutual debuted the earliest form of major medical insurance in 1949. Prudential surveyed their own employees about their medical expenses to develop rates. They presented their findings at the 1951 Society of Actuaries meeting and released their own major medical plan that year. Aetna also offered major medical in 1951, and Cigna did so in 1954.[75]

In 1955, New York Life offered GE workers one of the first examples of "comprehensive" medical insurance, which blurred the line between the separate categories of hospital, surgical, medical, and "major medical," combining aspects of first dollar and last dollar coverage. The popularity of comprehensive coverage grew, with seven million enrolled in the next four years. A similar approach that became increasingly common was to combine major medical with Blue Cross coverage.[76] Major medical plans were not always popular with workers. For example, steelworkers in 1956 demanded a completely noncontributory plan using a prepaid group, while management responded by proposing major medical coverage with its associated cost sharing.[77]

The Federal Employees Health Benefit Program provided an opportunity for workers to choose between different forms of coverage. Employees could select between Blue Cross and Blue Shield, commercial indemnity insurance, and locally available prepaid groups, including Kaiser in the West and the Health Insurance Plan of New York.[78] Although it was the most expensive, more than half chose Blue Cross and Blue Shield and the great majority elected the highest category of three potential benefit levels, further standardizing comprehensive health benefits.[79]

There was also pressure on companies to enhance indemnity coverage to replace lost wages, which was increasingly referred to as "temporary disability insurance." One motivation was to demonstrate that need could be satisfied by the private market.[80] The major thrust of liberalization was increasing the size of benefits and the length of the period during which benefits would be paid. There was also a trend toward more liberal disability definitions in group contracts and noncancellability in the individual market.[81] Liberalization was seen by the insurance industry as a social responsibility that needed to be shouldered by the private sector. However, private industry was better able to liberalize benefits than to increase the number of people covered.[82]

In 1955, three brothers started an insurance company in Columbus, Georgia. John, Paul, and Bill Amos had little experience in the insurance business and a very small amount of seed money. By any meaningful definition of the term, they were a startup, but before the existence of a venture capital market. To meet Georgia's capital requirement, they borrowed some money and raised more by selling stock door to door. Initially they also sold policies door to door and struggled financially. They named their new enterprise the American Family Life Insurance Company.[83]

The Amos brothers believed that despite the great expansion of health insurance benefits, many people felt unprotected in the event of a major illness. The coverage they offered was shaped by the footprint made by the standard market and reflected the nature of unmet demand. As major medical was rolled out in the group market, American Family offered a supplemental hospitalization policy that would provide a cash payment in the event of hospitalization. A formative early experience was when their father died from cancer. Seeing how much of the cost of his care was left uncovered by health insurance, in 1958 the brothers developed what became their most profitable product, cancer insurance. This coverage paid the policyholder a lump sum upon diagnosis. They also offered other accident and sickness policies with a similar design. American Family prided themselves on simple claims adjustment and extremely rapid payment.

In one sense, what the Amos brothers offered was a throwback to nineteenth-century health and accident policies with double indemnity features, in that they made a lump-sum payment in the event of a specific type of illness or injury. Even the concept of a policy on a single "dread disease" was not new. But the American Family product was designed around the shortfalls of the mid-century health insurance market, which excluded many and left even those with coverage feeling unprotected. Despite the appeal to consumers, the value of cancer insurance policies was questionable and would come under increasing scrutiny by regulators.

The growing cost of health insurance was finally becoming a concern. Though by today's standards they seem naïve, insurers were beginning to notice certain aspects of provider behavior that seemed to affect costs. Equitable's J. Henry Smith observed "significant and puzzling differences in the financial results of insurance of similar groups of people."[84] Smith had identified something that would forty years later be called "practice style variation" by the Dartmouth Atlas of Health Care: "It appears that doctors in some areas send more of their patients to hospitals than in other areas and they may use more laboratory examinations, therapeutic aids, and may even perform more surgery. It is not at all clear why these important differences occur, and one large question is, how much effect does the presence of insurance have in influencing medical practice?"[85] Smith suspected insurance did play a role. "Moreover, it is sometimes a little obvious that some hard-pressed hospital administrators have found ways to rearrange their charges to get the most out of the benefit provisions of an insurance plan."[86] Though insurers and physicians joined forces as lobbyists, as business partners they often tangled. Faulkner described the problem with considerable understatement: "To date it cannot be said the insurance companies and those persons who provide medical care are seeing eye to eye on all matters affecting disability insurance."[87]

The need to raise rates was a recurring problem. Smith noted that Blue Cross plans, with their first dollar benefit design, felt these increases "to a very important degree and have been forced to raise their charges again and again." Even insurance companies with fixed indemnities "have found their rates gradually becoming inadequate."[88] At this stage, rate setting in the different components of health insurance lacked uniformity. Due largely to a lack of common experience data, each company approached rates in their own way, with Prudential actuary Edward Neumann observing that only accidental death and dismemberment fell into the "stereotyped mold" preferred by insurers, where premiums were fairly uniform and competition centered on net costs, benefits, and administrative practices.[89] For the most recent and potentially most expensive category—major medical—the least information was available.

Competition, rising costs, and the threat of self-insurance created narrowing margins and a state of flux where at any time a number of carriers were showing losses.[90] Ohio State economics professor Edison Bowers harkened back to the experience of the Depression and wondered whether recent good times and the quest for new business had not "lulled to sleep some persons connected with this segment of the profession."[91] Professor Kulp made a similarly ominous comment in an address to the Bureau of Health Underwriters in 1949:

> Expansion of business has been accompanied and in part accomplished by a widespread liberalization of policy provisions and a general relaxation of underwriting controls without corresponding increase of premium. The result is the creation of an important and even dangerous source of deferred and hidden liability, not reflected in loss ratio figures when times are good and jobs are better than benefits, but bound to show up in the number and size of claims when the tide turns.[92]

John Hancock's William Green described business conditions with a metaphorical underwriter's nightmare: "He finds himself out on a tightrope, stretched between the tops of two tall buildings, with only a pole for balance. More recently, as margins between gross premium and net cost have narrowed, the balancing pole in the hands of the dreamer has become shorter. As business has grown and benefits have continued to expand, the buildings have grown taller and taller. At the same time the winds have grown stronger. Fortunately it is only a dream."[93]

By the 1950s it was clear that the individual market was developing underwriting problems. Equitable's J. Henry Smith described "serious problems of anti-selection."[94] John Miller of the Monarch life Insurance Company shared a well-known quip about the perceived tendencies of this market: "To collect on life insurance the insured must be dead, to collect on accident insurance he must have had an accident, while to collect on sickness he must have a policy."[95] Yet given the great amount of unmet demand and the desire to defend the private system, insurers felt the need to extend coverage as much as possible. Armand Sommer of the Continental Casualty Company invoked the vestiges of insurers' quasi-public role to describe this responsibility as "an obligation in the economic life of the nation to conduct its business so that with comparatively few exceptions everyone may share in its security."[96]

Under this pressure, noncancellable individual coverage began to make a comeback in the 1950s. Alfred Perkins of the Union Mutual Life Company . cautioned that "no line of accident and sickness insurance has experienced more problems."[97] After the negative experiences during the Depression, the reversion to cancellability was helpful financially for companies but reputationally damaging. In the context of social concern about uninsurance, there was pressure on the private system to change its practices. Equitable's Smith explained the change: "There is a growing feeling of responsibility among insurers as to the necessity of employing the cancellation clause judiciously and tactfully so as to merit public good will."[98]

Yet the only way this would work would be through the exercise of extreme caution at the point of application. Wendell Milliman noted the importance of the agent's role: "In order to guard against impaired risks tipping the scales, the insurer must ask many questions about the health history of the applicant."[99] One guide to agents listed three qualities to look for in a risk:

1. The physical ability to qualify
2. The mental attitude to regard his insurance fairly
3. The moral stamina to stand upright in the face of adversity[100]

The last point was considered the most important yet also the most elusive: "No company expects its agents to be psychologists. But if an agent is lucky, he may have heard of something in the prospect's past life that would either tend to qualify or disqualify him." Agents were told they should be "just without being generous and must always take time to be kind." It was all part of a new approach to claims administration, a movement away from that "great stumbling block in the thirties when companies had the reputation, justly or otherwise, of terminating the claim the first day they had knowledge of any business activities or even of a short visit to an office."[101]

An extremely difficult issue for the defenders of the voluntary system was the plight of older Americans. Survey data from the 1950s show that only about one-third of those over sixty-five had coverage, compared to two-thirds of those under age sixty-five.[102] For racial and ethnic minorities, the coverage rates were far lower. Only about seventeen percent of older males and females categorized as non-White had health insurance, according to data collected by the Social Security Administration in 1956. The HIAA published a resolution in 1958 that commercial and Blue Cross and Blue Shield plans would collectively take every possible measure to "enable voluntary health insurance to meet the problems of financing the cost of medical care."[103] This included increasing offers of individual coverage to the elderly, increasing the availability of renewable coverage, and including retiree coverage as part of group coverage. Yet insurers acknowledged that the bigger problem was affordability. John H. Miller of Monarch Life Insurance testified before an Eisenhower administration commission to this effect: "The ultimate problem is not its availability but the adequacy of personal income at older ages."[104]

With regard to the poor or "medically indigent," insurers had fewer suggestions and certainly offered no hope that the voluntary system could be helpful. Insurers did not support the idea of the public sector purchasing coverage for the poor but preferred that the public sector subsidize care rather than coverage, arguing that insurance itself would raise costs to a level that was societally prohibitive. Equitable's Smith acknowledged the structural inequality imbedded in the system of employer-based insurance, observing that it could never be affordably scaled to cover everyone: "Perhaps a more serious problem is that there is not enough state money available today, nor likely to be provided in the near future, to pay premiums necessary to support proper and complete medical care of the indigent, much of which is now being provided on a free basis."[105]

The reform effort that resulted in the establishment of Medicare in 1965 began as early as 1950 when Truman unsuccessfully campaigned for a program of national health insurance. Efforts to establish national health insurance date to the 1930s. Much of the opposition to Truman's plans for national health insurance came from southern Democrats concerned about disruption of established racial hierarchies and the potential for the integration of medical facilities. While defeated by the combined force of the AMA's lobbying campaign and opposition from southern Democrats and Republicans, the pressure for coverage for the elderly persisted.[106]

Serious efforts to create a federal program started with the Forand Bill, a 1958 proposal from a Rhode Island congressman to cover hospital costs for the elderly in Social Security. The Forand Bill was initially squelched fairly easily in committee through the combined effects of Republicans, local medical societies, and southern Democrats. Arkansas Democrat Wilbur Mills, chairman of the House Ways and Means Committee, played an early role in stopping the Forand Bill, then cosponsored a weaker alternative, the Kerrs-Mill Act of 1960, which provided federal funds to states. Yet this approach limited assistance to the poor elderly and depended on state action. Proponents of Medicare castigated Kerrs-Mill for "pauperizing" the elderly by subjecting them to dehumanizing means testing. The rejection of means testing was a key issue among Medicare's proponents.[107]

The political significance of the issue continued to escalate. The rising cost of health care was a critical factor in growing support for coverage for the elderly, who used hospitals far more than the rest of the population. With the price of hospital care doubling in the 1950s, health insurance became a grassroots cause and a source of constant pressure for members of Congress, as shown in Figure 10.2. A newly created Senate subcommittee on the aging held hearings around the country, where health care coverage consistently rose to the top as a constituent concern. Members of Congress reported receiving "bagfuls" of mail on the issue.[108]

The insurance industry took a number of steps to attempt to demonstrate that they could adequately cover the elderly, including encouraging retiree coverage in group contracts and increasing sales of noncancellable individual coverage. In the late 1950s, companies petitioned state insurance commissioners for enabling legislation to permit a joint approach to the elderly population. The result was "State 65" plans, developed in a handful of states, where companies jointly

Figure 10.2 Senior citizens protesting for health insurance. Library of Congress.

offered major medical and hospital and surgical coverage to the elderly. The first State 65 plan began in Connecticut in 1961. Texas 65 and California's Western 65 started several years later.

The structure of State 65 plans was based on standard hospital and major medical coverage sold in the individual and group market. Adult children were permitted to purchase coverage for their senior parents and in some states could also buy coverage for themselves. The plans required enabling legislation to circumvent antitrust concerns. The result was that State 65 plans were a public-private collaboration and had a quasi-governmental feel since they were marketed in each state by a single nonprofit association with no individual company branding.

State 65 plans were a business strategy motivated by insurers' efforts to prevent federal involvement in health insurance, but in some states, they were co-opted by state officials and portrayed as a state policy offering. In Texas, for example, Governor John Connally embraced Texas 65, publicly purchasing the very first policy for his mother and the second two for his wife's parents.[109] He made frequent public comments about the plan, particularly around open enrollment periods.[110] A young George Bush campaigning unsuccessfully for Senate in 1964 opposed Medicare, preferring "the effective and efficient system now operating in our State."[111]

The motivation to champion a state approach to health insurance problems came in part from a "states' rights" sentiment linked in no small part to southern desires to preserve racial hierarchies, and also from a broadly held view among insurance regulators and companies, coming from the *United States v. South-Eastern Underwriters Association (SEUA)* decision and the resulting McCarran-Ferguson Act, that perceived state failure could result in a federal takeover of insurance markets and the premium tax revenue that came with them.

State 65 plans were not profitable for the companies that participated, and they were derided in Congress by supporters of Medicare as halfway measures with high premiums and insufficient benefits.[112] Their inadequacy, along with shortcomings seen in the AMA's proposed "Eldercare," weakened the case that the voluntary insurance model could provide meaningful coverage to the majority of the aged. Kennedy supported the federal approach based on Forand, represented by the King-Anderson bill. The passage of the Civil Rights Act of 1964 blunted some of the southern opposition, and a landslide Democratic victory in 1964 created a unique political opportunity for Johnson.[113] Due to concern about vociferous opposition from the AMA, the initial approach had excluded doctors' visits. But by co-opting aspects of the AMA's alternative "Eldercare" plan and a Republican alternative based on a voluntary insurance model, the final act consisted of the famous "three-layer cake" of hospital care (Part A), physicians' visits (Part B), and Medicaid, which provided federal aid to states for the care of the poor. Creating Medicaid as a separate program for the poor also helped to fend off concerns that Medicare could be used as a platform to create national health insurance. Lyndon Johnson signed the Social Security Amendments on July 30, 1965, enacting Medicare and Medicaid as Titles XVIII and XIX, respectively. The programs became effective on July 1, 1966.[114]

The AMA famously lost their pitched battle against Medicare, enlisting Ronald Reagan and others in the process. They emerged with their reputation lastingly damaged. The Blue Cross Association assisted from the beginning with the design of the program, and the AHA was also supportive. There was a range of views among insurers about how strenuously to oppose Medicare, with leaders of life insurance companies in the Northeast more inclined to be supportive than the small life and casualty companies in the South and West. The HIAA adopted a quietly negative posture, with most lobbying done in a low-key fashion by individual companies.[115] Yet this did not rule out activities such as a joint press conference given by Connecticut insurers to local media to explain the "crisis" Medicare posed to the industry, or the twenty thousand letters sent by Travelers Insurance Company president Sterling P. Tooker to managers and agents around the country, warning them that with the passage of Medicare, "the Federal Government would be in direct competition with our coverages" in a way that would "seriously hinder our growth."[116]

Medicare was modeled on standard group coverage of the time, with separate parts for hospital and physician care. Part A, the hospital component, was financed by a payroll tax, split between employers and employees. It covered inpatient hospital care up to ninety days, outpatient hospital diagnostic care, and some postdischarge home care. There were separate cost-sharing provisions associated with each type of covered benefit. The medical component, Part B, was financed through premium payments that were split between enrollees and the federal government. Initially, premiums were $3 per month for enrollees. Part B had an annual deductible and covered eighty percent of costs. Insurance companies and Blue Cross plans served as fiscal intermediaries between the federal government and providers of health care. Thus, the commercial model became enshrined in this new form of social insurance, as insurers performed a version of their role in the group market, but this time with government as their customer.[117]

The Medicaid program followed a more traditional public assistance model rooted in the concept of local responsibility and control. While there was joint state and federal funding, and some federal requirements, there was also the opportunity for significant local variation. Participation was voluntary for states, and eligibility requirements and benefit levels were determined at the state level. However, if states chose to participate, they were required to include all program categories: Aid to the Blind, Aid to Families with Dependent Children, and Aid to the Permanently and Totally Disabled. States also had to cover a set of required benefits including inpatient and outpatient hospital, laboratory, nursing home, and physician services. Medicaid would later become an important opportunity for insurers.

Medicare provided Blue Cross and commercial insurers with the opportunity to serve as fiscal intermediaries and relieved them from the pressure of trying to serve an unprofitable market. And while the State 65 plans had failed to prevent the passage of Medicare and led to underwriting losses for participating companies, they positioned insurers to instantly jump into the profitable world of Medicare supplemental policies. Even before Medicare became effective, Continental Casualty Company was running ads for "Golden 65," offering an indemnity plan that promised "cash to use for those medical expenses not covered by Medicare—and the bills at home!"[118]

The elderly were initially important customers for the American Family Life Insurance Company, but in 1964, the company developed a new distribution strategy of "cluster sales," selling their policies at the workplace and collecting premiums through a payroll deduction. Through this collaboration with employers, they greatly reduced their distribution costs. This allowed employees to increase the generosity of their benefits, albeit at their own expense. That year the Amos brothers changed their company's name to AFLAC. By 1970 the company was licensed in thirty-seven states, and in 1974 they were listed on the New York Stock Exchange and had started selling insurance in Japan.[119]

In 1970, the federal Department of Health, Education, and Welfare published a study on the status of private health insurance. They acknowledged that growth had been dramatic, yet pressed on: "But how broad and deep is this protection?" Scouring over benefit designs from hundreds of plans, they arrived at their answer: neither broad nor deep enough. Coverage was not standardized, it was often inadequate, and too many people did without. The obstacle was cost. The report concluded with a sobering observation: "Considering the distribution of the population by income level, it is apparent that a significant portion of the population is unable to afford comprehensive health insurance, or, for that matter, adequate health care, if the entire cost must come from their own current incomes."[120]

Mounting concerns about rising health care costs combined with weak economic growth in the following decades would lead to increased pressure on insurers in the group market, the rise of managed care, the proliferation of supplemental insurance products, and a retreat from further progress toward national health insurance. High and rising costs had been a concern since the early days of group insurance, but starting in the mid-1960s, health care cost growth began to exceed gross domestic product (GDP) growth by a significant amount.

As a share of GDP, spending on health care more the doubled from 5 percent in 1960 to 12.1 percent in 1990.[121]

While state regulators reviewed rates and forms to assess the relationship between premiums and benefits, increased costs were largely passed on to employers and employees with little interference. The third-party insurance mechanism was never designed to be a cost control device. The original design of the Medicare program, in a concession to providers, made little attempt to control prices and essentially paid hospitals what they charged for services, and additionally covered their cost of capital. Medicaid programs generally did pay providers lower prices but initially made no effort to manage the use of care.[122] But by the late 1960s, public and private payers began to try to control cost. In 1970, California initiated "prior authorization" within their Medicaid program for hospital admissions and some other procedures. In 1972, the Professional Standards Review Organizations (PSROs) were created to review the "appropriateness" of care in Medicare. At around this time, HMOs emerged.[123]

An HMO is an organization of providers that agrees to payment terms that at the time were commonly called "prepayment" (and would later be called "capitation") to receive a fixed amount for each month for each member. While HMOs were a disruptive entry to the health insurance market, their payment model was not completely new. Examples of group practice using a "prepayment" or capitated model had been in existence since the late nineteenth century, when certain kinds of employers in remote areas established "contract doctors" that would treat workers for a fixed sum. The Kaiser Foundation Health Plans emerged from contract medicine programs established in the 1930s for workers in California involved in large infrastructure projects. By 1977 this plan had six locations and served 2.5 million people. Others emerged later in the twentieth century, including the Health Insurance Plan of Greater New York, established in 1947, and DC's Group Health Association in 1937.[124]

Prepaid group practice was intensely opposed by the AMA; in the early twentieth century, participation in a prepaid group practice could result in loss of medical society membership. Yet the size of prepaid groups had never grown to the point where they were an existential threat to the medical establishment. One reason for this was that in most states, their growth was stymied by laws, usually proposed by the state medical society, which forbade the practice of medicine in "corporate form." The Federal HMO Act of 1973 appropriated $375 million over five years to encourage HMO formation, providing access to capital through grants and contracts as well as loans and loan guarantees. The act also allowed the pre-emption of state laws that otherwise would have made HMO formation difficult. This included requirements in some states for medical society approval; "any willing provider" laws, which prevented the exclusion of providers from networks; or the requirement that plans meet risk-based capital requirements meant for insurance companies.

HMOs were a significant disruptor to a health insurance market that at the time was based on either an indemnity model of the major insurers or the service plan coverage offered by Blue Cross and Blue Shield plans. These two models had become more similar to one another, but neither was directly engaged with the management of care. Commercial insurers at the time did not contract with providers or create networks. The HMO model offered consistently lower costs, about fifteen percent less than standard indemnity plans, by directly contracting with doctors and hospitals and also through the management of utilization. In addition to lowering premiums, HMOs reduced out-of-pocket costs to consumers by using low copays rather than coinsurance. A key feature of HMOs was that primary care physicians served as "gatekeepers" and needed to provide their approval for use of specialty care.[125] This feature was particularly disliked by consumers and contributed to a backlash against HMO management practices in the 1990s.

In the 1970s, HMOs were local and geographically tied to doctors and hospitals, but during the 1980s they began to proliferate rapidly. In 1970 there were fewer than fifty HMOs nationwide, largely limited to Seattle and California. By the mid-1980s, there were many HMOs, a mix of standalone organizations and others that were owned by health insurers. Some plans failed, while others were acquired. The largest had initial public offerings (IPOs), including U.S. Healthcare in 1983, Maxicare in 1983, and United Health Care in 1984. HMO membership skyrocketed from ten million in 1982 to ninety-one million in 1996.[126]

During the 1980s and early 1990s, share prices of leading HMOs increased tenfold. In response, the national Blue Cross Blue Shield Association, which had been formed in the 1970s, permitted its member plans to convert to for-profit status. Blue Cross Blue Shield plans, whether for profit or not, became increasingly indistinguishable from commercial health insurers. Health systems began to consolidate to increase their bargaining power. Enrollment in traditional indemnity plans declined as managed care became more prevalent.

The traditional health insurance business model was already under pressure from a growing trend toward self-insurance by employers, a move that was driven by costs. This transformed the insurer role into that of an administrator and forced them to become more involved with care management. As a vice president of American General Life noted, "If you are not directing health care delivery, there may be no role for you in the future." Even relatively small employers could self-insure and run their own claims administration. "And if you take away administration, and you take away risk, what's left?"[127]

But many traditional health insurers had little taste for care management. The cautious and bureaucratic culture of insurance companies was ill-suited to manage the spiraling cost crisis that was emerging. An unflattering 1970s profile of the insurance industry featured this comment from a New York state insurance regulator: "This is a hothouse industry just like the railroads ... not the environment bright young men thrive in." Life insurance in particular was depicted as a leisurely, incremental business, with layers of bureaucracy creating, as one agent put it, "perfect insulation from urgent problems or emergencies." A former president of a life insurance company was blunt about his former colleagues: "Most of these fellows could play golf three or four times a week and it wouldn't make any difference at all."[128]

As costs increased, life companies began to struggle with their health insurance business, especially in the individual market. The research director from Mutual of Omaha said inflation and rising health care costs had made traditional coverage "obsolete" in that market by the early 1970s as a result of "exploding" physician and hospital fees. Prudential tried to market a comprehensive individual market plan using zip code–based community rating but withdrew by 1978 due to rising costs. In some states, problems were compounded by insurance mandates requiring specific covered benefits or policy provisions. In the wake of the Employee Retirement Income Security Act of 1974, the self-insured market was not constrained by these state laws, placing the individual market at a further disadvantage. HIAA head John Hurley noted in 1984 that while any one of these mandates is miniscule on its own, "together they kill us."[129]

As the individual market continued to deteriorate, access to health insurance became more and more difficult for those who did not receive coverage from their job. The proliferation of unstandardized products, combined with significant medical underwriting, made the market bewildering, unaffordable, and many times completely unavailable for those with health problems. This was the essential problem that would later be addressed by the Affordable Care Act (ACA) in 2010. The ACA standardized the coverage in the individual market and required community rating and the guaranteed issue of policies. These reforms were coupled with a system of income-based tax credits to increase affordability.

As costs rose and coverage became less available in the individual market, various types of supplemental plans proliferated to fill the gaps.[130] Supplemental policies were not new, but some of the markets and methods had changed. There was a large new market for selling "Medigap" plans to seniors, and supplemental plans were also sold to the uninsured and those with inadequate employer insurance. Increasingly, supplemental health insurance was sold through direct mail or advertised in newspapers or magazines, often with sensational claims and endorsements from celebrities like Art Linkletter and Roy

Rogers. Supplementary hospital policies had become bestsellers. Newspaper advertisements for these policies stoked fears of catastrophic scenarios and promised seemingly limitless benefits.[131]

Another kind of supplemental policy that rose to prominence was cancer insurance. By 1979, the Federal Trade Commission (FTC) estimated there were 4.5 million cancer policies in force, covering 13 million Americans.[132] The leading seller of cancer insurance was AFLAC, which had originated the coverage in 1958. In the late 1970s, AFLAC ranked first among insurance companies on every financial performance index. Earnings per share rose from $.38 to $2.26 between 1970 and 1977. One equities analyst observed in 1978, "When the business history of the 1970s is written, American Family Corporation will in all likelihood be ranked among the top half dozen or so growth stocks of the decade."[133]

AFLAC was enormously popular, particularly in the South, where the company was hailed as a hometown enterprise. An Alabama newspaper columnist recounted the ubiquitousness of the policies in the rural community of his childhood, recalling that when his mother was diagnosed with cancer, "she had numerous American Family cancer policies. A lady named Maggie Allen had sold everybody in Pike County a policy or two. It seemed like my mother received a check a day for years without ever filling out a claim form."[134]

Yet increasingly, cancer insurance became a source of concern to consumer advocates and regulators. The average loss ratio of these policies was about forty-one percent, compared with ninety-five percent for a standard Blue Cross plan. In a 1980 report prepared for Congress, the FTC discredited cancer insurance as a concept, finding it a "questionable element in a financially sound plan of insurance."[135] The American Cancer Society issued a statement saying they did not endorse the concept of cancer insurance. Many insurers that sold comprehensive health insurance criticized cancer insurance, with an Aetna executive quoted in a 1979 *Business Week* article describing the coverage as "garbage." That same year *Changing Times* published a highly critical study of cancer insurance. An undercover exposé on television revealed high-pressure sales approaches.[136] The FTC report similarly referenced "promotional literature which uses misleading statistics to overemphasize cancer incidence and cost data and exploit people's fear of cancer" and, in comments that echoed the earlier TNEC investigation of industrial insurance, called out the role played by agents, who "were not trained to assist consumers, and given substantial incentives to make sales no matter how appropriate."[137]

The Senate Subcommittee on Antitrust and Monopoly held a set of hearings on cancer insurance in 1980. In part the motivation was to put more pressure on states. Much of state regulation prioritized solvency, an "opposite concern" from low payout ratios. An actuarial assessment from the FTC noted that most performance measures in state regulation were designed to assure financial soundness: "It would be surprising if the same measures were suitable to judge the actuarial value of the coverages to consumers."[138] The NAIC established a task force to make recommendations about cancer insurance. Nonindustry advisors to that task force protested that their views were not sufficiently incorporated.

The contrast between the 1980 subcommittee hearings and the TNEC investigation of life insurance in the 1930s is notable. While Metropolitan Life's Leroy Lincoln had been somewhat bellicose in the face of questioning, American Family chief executive officer John Amos was in a different category altogether. Amos had reacted very forcefully to his company's critics, filing lawsuits against Kiplinger's, ABC, and former Pennsylvania insurance commissioner Herb Denenburg, and vowing that his company was "prepared to return malicious stone throwing with cannon fire." American Family also unsuccessfully sued Governor Teasdale of Missouri when he declared that cancer insurance was a "rip-off" and banned sales of dread disease policies in 1982. Amos refused to testify voluntarily at the hearing and had to be subpoenaed.[139]

At the hearing, significant differences among senators were clear. Subcommittee chair Howard Metzenbaum (D-OH) was highly critical of cancer insurance and supported more federal oversight of insurance. Senator Orrin Hatch (R-OR) used his opening remarks to signal his support for states' rights by mentioning the McCarran-Ferguson Act and the fact that regulation of insurance was a state function. Sectional issues were at play too. Strom Thurmond (R-SC) was clearly partial to American Family, which was very popular in the South. He asked Amos softball questions and sought to introduce favorable testimony from his constituents into the record.[140]

To the FTC, the persistent popularity of cancer insurance signaled deeper problems. The agency estimated that seventy percent of the population lacked true catastrophic coverage. Many yearned for the cash payments that cancer coverage seemed to offer, leading the agency to conclude, "The phenomenal popularity of such a limited product suggests that many people feel their basic coverage to be inadequate against catastrophic cancer expenses. The continued rapid sales growth of cancer insurance despite these failings suggest serious imperfections in the health insurance markets."[141]

Researchers at the RAND Corporation believed the relationship was bidirectional: supplemental insurance was a sign of a defect but also posed a threat to the standard market. They feared that the tendency for people to buy supplemental coverage whenever their cost sharing increased would thwart efforts to contain the growth of health care costs through benefit design, and argued that the death of the supplemental market may be necessary for the main health insurance market to work: "Ironically, 'market failure' in the market for supplemental health insurance may be the only way in which another market—that for health care itself—could function in a fashion more closely approximating that portrayed by an economics textbook."[142] The negative publicity associated with the hearings caused a temporary hit to American Family's stock prices. The company settled their libel suit against ABC to avoid further disclosures and weathered the negative news cycle. American Family adopted the name AFLAC in 1989. John Amos died of lung cancer in 1990. Senators Strom Thurmond and Orrin Hatch were among the honorary pallbearers at his funeral.[143]

When the Clinton administration tried to establish national health insurance in the early 1990s, the AMA objected to the prospect of national spending limits and cost containment measures. The insurance industry was split, with larger companies seeing benefits from increased volume and subsidies, while smaller companies feared they could not be competitive. Reflecting the tension, the major life insurers, Cigna, Aetna, MetLife, Travelers, and Prudential, resigned from the HIAA, while those remaining sponsored the infamous "Harry and Louise" commercials, in which a beleaguered middle-aged couple sat at their kitchen table and pondered the bureaucratic complexities of the proposed health reforms. These ads were considered to be extremely influential in turning public opinion against the Clinton proposal.[144]

The Clinton plan would be defeated, and many of the large life insurers would soon sell off their health insurance assets, while some multiline insurers shed other lines of business to focus on health. There had been many bad years during the 1980s, with the loss ratio for the industry as a whole as high as 107 in 1988.[145] In the 1990s, waves of mergers aggregated HMOs and the health insurers that sponsored them. For example, in 1995 United Health Care acquired MetraHealth, the combined health insurance business of Travelers and MetLife. Cigna, formed by the 1982 merger of Connecticut General Life Insurance Company and property and casualty insurer Insurance Company of North America (INA), shed its nonhealth business and acquired HMO Healthsource in 1997. Aetna sold off their property and casualty business and acquired U.S. Health, then the second-largest HMO, in 1996. Aetna then went on to acquire the health insurance business of two of the original "Big Five" of the life insurance industry, New York Life's NYLCare in 1998 and Prudential Healthcare in 1999.

By the early twentieth century, the remaining companies in the HIAA had merged with a trade association representing the managed care companies and renamed themselves America's Health Insurance Plans (AHIP). In 2010, AHIP, the Blue Cross Blue Shield Association, the AHA, and the AMA supported the ACA, as did the pharmaceutical industry, acknowledging that any further coverage expansion must be publicly financed.[146] In fact, ACA supporters resurrected the Harry and Louise characters to make an ad in support of the proposed reforms. In designing individual market coverage, the ACA too built upon the well-entrenched system of public and private coverage centered on the group insurance model. Along with the individual market reforms, the

ACA included significant expansions in eligibility for Medicaid, to include low-income adults. These reforms, which have increased the covered population by roughly twenty million, have also created significant opportunities for the insurance industry.

Managed care companies have made increasing incursions into health care delivery, acquiring physician practices and building clinics. In 2021, AHIP rebranded itself by keeping its name but dropping its meaning. "AHIP" no longer stands for anything, perhaps representing an effort to further blur the line between insurance and care delivery and create some distance from the word "insurance." While often at odds, AHIP and the AMA still join together to oppose certain health reform proposals that would threaten their business interests, such as public options or single-payer health care, sometimes called "Medicare for All."

While life insurers largely left health insurance, they did continue to sell supplemental and short-term disability insurance. One example is long-term care insurance, which emerged in the late 1980s. Long-term care insurance is disability insurance that covers home health and nursing home care, which is generally excluded from Medicare or commercial health insurance.

There are many parallels between the long-term care insurance and the initial foray of life insurers into disability coverage before the Depression. Long-term care policies are generally sold to individuals and are underwritten. The policies are usually designed to make indemnity payments for approved expenses, such as home health or nursing home care. Like the original disability policies, they have an elimination period and a waiver of premium once the elimination period is reached. Travelers started offering long-term care policies to groups in 1986, then to individuals in 1988. And like the disability policies sold during the Depression, long-term care insurance is an underwriting disaster. As in the past, many insurers are attempting to withdraw from this market and view their existing policies as a closed and deeply unprofitable book of business.

Despite the significant coverage expansion that has resulted from the ACA, supplemental disability insurance products with deep historical roots are still successfully marketed. AFLAC continues to lead this segment, selling coverage that provides cash payments in the event of accident or illness. Their millions of customers feel ill prepared for a catastrophic event due to a lack of paid leave, high deductible plans, or no health insurance. One of their most popular products is cancer insurance.[147]

11
Clean Risks

When the National Association of Insurance Commissioners (NAIC) kicked off their winter meeting in Miami in December of 1957, camaraderie and pleasantries prevailed. Reflecting close ties with industry, a welcome to the regulators was given by the vice president of Prudential for Florida. A giant key to the city changed hands. Yet in his presidential address, Robert Taylor Jr., commissioner of Oregon, reflected a wartime mentality and a preoccupation with the states' vulnerability to federal incursion. Taylor painted a picture of a persistent adversary looking for an entry point: "Our dikes of state laws designed to hold back the pressure for federal regulation were in many instances constructed like sandbags on a levee and now need to be replaced in order to stop the erosion that is occurring because of the constant pressure of men in federal bureaus to seek and enlarge any opening through which a flood of federal regulation can penetrate." Increased activism on the part of the NAIC was one response to the perceived federal threat. An enhanced committee structure, including a new special committee on the "preservation of state regulation," was created, and Taylor encouraged members to participate actively in meetings and follow through with action in their individual states. In the struggle against federal domination, Taylor emphasized the common interests of state regulators and the companies: "In this regard it is reasonable that we should expect the support of the industry when these matters are presented for consideration in the state legislative assemblies."[1]

Taylor's comments reflected the uneasy state regulatory climate that prevailed after the passage of the McCarran-Ferguson Act in 1945. The act had been passed in response to the decision in the *United States v. South-Eastern Underwriters Association (SEUA)* case in 1944, in which the Supreme Court upended more than seventy-five years of legal precedent and declared that insurance was interstate commerce and therefore could be subject to congressional regulation. In response, Congress passed the McCarran-Ferguson Act to provide the insurance industry with a limited exemption, conditional on state regulation.[2] States were given several years to pass appropriate legislation, and the NAIC, working with industry, had drafted model all-industry bills, some version of which was passed in each state, designed to comply with McCarran-Ferguson by establishing state regulation of the rate-setting process.

Uncovered. Katherine Hempstead, Oxford University Press. © Oxford University Press 2024.
DOI: 10.1093/oso/9780190094157.003.0011

The McCarran-Ferguson Act was itself a compromise, forged rapidly in conference committee, which attempted to reconcile the interests of a contingent in the House that preferred a broader exemption and those in the Senate that advocated for more active federal regulation. The limited antitrust exemption in McCarran-Ferguson was conditioned on state regulation, yet it was not clear what level of state regulation would be considered adequate. Signing the bill, FDR expressed the view that the state role should be substantive: "Congress intended no grant of immunity for monopoly or for boycott, coercion or intimidation. Congress did not intend to permit private rate fixing which the anti-trust act forbids but was willing to permit actual regulation of rates by affirmative action of the states."[3]

State regulators were concerned that perceived inadequacy on their part could lead to federal intervention. In response to ongoing concerns about anticompetitive behavior, the Senate Subcommittee on Antitrust and Monopoly was holding hearings on various aspects of the insurance business. The Federal Trade Commission (FTC) was taking an interest in potentially unfair trade practices of insurers. In *FTC v. National Casualty* (1958), the agency argued that since Alabama did not actually enforce its deceptive practices law, there was effectively no state regulation, and the McCarran antitrust exemption should not apply. The court had ruled against the FTC, in a decision that was interpreted as suggesting that the standard for state regulation under McCarran-Ferguson was very low. Yet undeterred, the agency continued to pursue cases of deceptive practices involving insurers, a practice that led states to increase their own regulation.[4]

At the same time, the Securities and Exchange Commission (SEC) was attempting to regulate how insurance stock companies interacted with their shareholders, another incursion into what states considered to be their domain. The SEC was, of course, the agency that had organized the investigation of the life insurance industry under the New Deal–era Temporary National Economic Committee (TNEC), effectively starting a fairly uninterrupted twenty-year regime of federal investigation of insurance that persisted through the *SEUA* decision and its aftermath, up to and including the 1957–1961 hearings of the Senate Subcommittee on Antitrust and Monopoly.[5]

Federal scrutiny of regulatory issues involving insurance prompted outrage from state regulators but at the same time led them to attempt to fortify their own structures to ward off any potential critique. This put states in the somewhat paradoxical position of angrily denouncing the regulatory agenda of federal agencies while trying to quickly replicate it. Therefore, President Taylor at the 1957 NAIC meeting was able to with one breath castigate the SEC for trying to regulate the way in which stock insurance companies dealt with their shareholders as "an attempt on the part of the Federal Agency to pry open the door to invoke their regulation over the business of insurance" yet in the next call for his fellow commissioners "to immediately take steps to see that this regulation and policing are forthcoming." More broadly, Taylor advised his audience to be sure that "proper regulation is being applied to every facet of the insurance business so that the specialists in Washington DC cannot pick out some point for attack.... We must match wits with the most astute and imaginative minds in the country."[6]

In 1960, the NAIC convened in Miami once again, this time at the famous Fountainebleau Hotel at Miami Beach. The uneventful completion of the antitrust and antimonopoly hearings was imminent. Yet any relief was overwhelmed by the sense of ongoing danger. That year's president, Nevada commissioner Paul Hammel, in his address warned that "the battle may be won, but the war is far from over. Those who make federal control of every aspect of our lives their god will not repent and clamor for mass baptism in our faith."[7]

The commissioner was prescient in his view that the potential for increased federal scrutiny had not come to an end. The rest of the twentieth century would see an escalating series of episodes in which the ability of state-regulated insurance markets to meet the needs of the public would be repeatedly questioned and found wanting, leading to calls for increased federal involvement of various types. These episodes arose from issues within specific lines of business as well as more general questions about the industry as a whole and variously involved all three branches of federal government. As this chapter will show, unmet demand, high prices, and a rash of insolvencies in auto insurance were a major source of trouble. As the next chapter will show, others included the availability of flood insurance, homeowners insurance in some markets, and, in the 1980s, the price and availability of many types of commercial liability insurance.

Many thought the *National Casualty* decision had set the bar for state regulation artificially low. The 1960 *FTC v. Travelers Association* decision was seen as an important clarification of the federal interpretation of the antitrust exemption. In this case, the court found that the presence of an antideceptive practices statute in the state of domicile for the Travelers Association, an accident and health company, did not constitute a sufficient level of state regulation to preempt the FTC's jurisdiction in all states in which the company did business. The case was seen as a corrective and an affirmation of the intent of Congress that the exemption granted in McCarran-Ferguson Act was conditional on adequate state regulation.[8]

The greatest point of vulnerability for states was rate regulation. Concerns about anticompetitive rate fixing permitted by passive state regulators had led to the *SEUA* case. Insurance professor Spencer Kimball believed that the ability to regulate rates effectively was critical: "Unless the commissioner is able to perform his statutory duty of regulating rates well enough to prevent effective pressures for federal regulation, he may cease to have any role to play in our society."[9] While state insurance regulators may have feared for their professional relevance, the fiscal stakes for states were higher. Premium taxes were an important source of state revenue, of which only a small share was spent for the regulation of insurance.

The NAIC had worked with industry to create model all-industry bills, which authorized supervised rate setting and were passed in some form in every state. Commissioners used the threat of potential federal intervention to increase their regulatory authority. Legislatures were motivated to maintain state regulation and taxation of insurance. The insurance industry was generally allied with state regulators in wanting to maintain the antitrust exemption, although they were somewhat disappointed with the all-industry bills, as they were with the McCarran- Ferguson Act itself, hoping for a broader exemption and more flexibility.[10]

Not all states dramatically changed their practices after McCarran-Ferguson. Many states required "prior approval" from regulators, while others adopted a "file and use" policy, where regulators could disapprove or question rates within an established time period. In Texas, the state continued to set rates. California opted for open competition with no rate regulation.

An analysis by Spencer Kimball of the rate-setting environment in Wisconsin and Utah found that "Real regulation is only partially the result of improved statutes." In Wisconsin, there had been a long trajectory of progress toward more effective rate regulation, and the aftermath of the *SEUA* decision was not a watershed. Utah, on the other hand, had new statutes but little else in terms of regulatory expertise; therefore, they relied heavily on bureau rates, meaning that rates continued to be set by "a private body not responsible to the public, and not effectively regulated by a public agency." Kimball concluded that overall, effective state regulation was the exception rather than the rule, "if by effective we mean that public officials actually scrutinize and either approve, or with knowledge of the facts, fail to disapprove the rates filed by rating bureaus." This created a vulnerability for all states: "Unless state regulation is sufficiently stringent to prevent the development of substantial and organized consumer pressures, an attitude favorable to federal intervention may develop."[11]

And while the all-industry bills might have seemed to enshrine a supervised version of the antiquated cartel-like system of the property and casualty carriers, in the years after the McCarran-Ferguson Act, the amount of competition in property and casualty markets began to increase. Local rate-making bureaus began to consolidate. By 1960, there was one bureau for the fire industry—the National Insurance Actuarial and Statistical Association. For casualty insurance there were two: the National Bureau of Casualty Underwriters for stock companies and the Mutual Insurance Rating Bureau for mutuals. In 1967 the

National Bureau of Casualty Underwriters merged with the National Automobile Underwriters Association to become the Insurance Rating Board. By 1971 the six national rating bureaus for individual lines would merge to form the Insurance Services Office—one statistical bureau for all property and casualty lines of insurance. These consolidations eliminated the power of local rating bureaus.[12]

The direct writers bypassed the agency system and had lower operating costs. These companies, including Allstate, State Farm, and Nationwide, became large enough to file independent rates. As the 1960s progressed, there was a gradual movement toward open rating. A survey of commissioners in 1966 found that about half felt that the all-industry laws were no longer necessary. In 1967 Florida and Georgia transitioned to a "no file" system. Wisconsin followed in 1968, and New York also adopted competitive rating; by 1969 nineteen states had open competition for at least some lines of property and casualty insurance.[13]

While the development of automobile insurance had generated new business models that were critical to breaking down the bureau system, serious problems with this market would threaten trends toward greater competition. In states with open rating laws, there was little ability for regulators to respond to increasing premiums. In states with prior approval, commissioners were better able to hold down rates, but this impacted supply. A nascent consumer movement pressured commissioners, state legislatures, and Congress for solutions to problems with the affordability and availability of home and auto insurance. As the second half of the twentieth century unfolded, a series of issues involving these lines of business as well as commercial liability coverage would attract sustained and critical federal attention to the insurance industry, its antitrust exemption, and the system of state regulation.

The rigid divisions between property and casualty insurance were ill-suited to the multiple property and liability risks entailed in operating a motor vehicle. Drivers needed at least five separate kinds of coverage: property damage liability, bodily injury liability, collision, fire, and theft. Additionally, separate personal accident policies were needed to protect against bodily injury to the driver or driver's family members. Initially, property coverage was provided by fire/marine insurers, while liability insurance was sold by casualty companies. Rules about the overlap between property and casualty insurance varied from state to state in the early days of auto insurance.[14] Motorists in most states didn't need to deal with multiple companies, although the lines were still divided between fire/marine and casualty insurance. The consumer experience was made relatively seamless thanks to the growth of multiline companies or "fleets," in which casualty companies added property lines and vice versa. Comprehensive policies became standard in the 1950s.[15]

While multiline companies sold a large share of auto insurance, there were other participants in the market. These included some new companies, including mutuals and some divisions of established multiline insurers that emerged to sell only auto insurance, as well as "reciprocal exchanges" or "interinsurance exchanges," which were not, strictly speaking, insurers, but associations that collected premiums and additional assessments as needed. But most important were the "direct writers," which bypassed the agency system and sold directly to consumers. One of these was Allstate, which was started in 1931 by the Sears Roebuck Company. The idea to create the company was reportedly hatched during a bridge game on a commuter train, and the company was named after a line of tires that Sears sold. Allstate sold insurance directly at Sears stores and through the mail. The direct mail approach was also adopted by State Farm, which had started in 1922 as a farmers' mutual.

The importance of automobile liability coverage was recognized early on, with a 1924 guide to agents observing that "the owner or operator of a car may have the misfortune at any moment to kill or seriously to injure some other person."[16] Indeed, as the number of cars grew from fewer than 100 in 1897, as seen in Figure 11.1, to 125,000 in 1909 to more than 25 million by 1925, so too did accounts of

Figure 11.1 First automobile policy written by Travelers was in 1897. The policyholder paid $7.50 for a $1,000 liability policy. Permission granted by Travelers Archives.

the related carnage.[17] A Massachusetts report in 1920 described the sea change created by "a new mode of locomotion that has arisen within a few years that has rendered our highways places of extreme danger." The automobile had created a condition of "constant risk," where "a reasonably careful man, perhaps we might say the most careful man known, is not always in the exercise of due care. There are bound to be moments when attention is diverted and vigilance lags. In the days of pedestrians and horse-drawn vehicles, the mind might rest and attention halt without danger; with a motor vehicle a second of inattention may easily result in fatalities."[18] By 1930, one insurance text noted that "Use of the auto by all but the poorest has resulted in serious congestion on the streets and highways; its speed has raised problems of safety and of indemnity to the injured."[19] The rising toll of deaths from auto accidents became a major public issue; the death rate rose more than five hundred percent between 1913 and 1930, at the same time that the rate of deaths from other types of accidents was declining. Just to provide some perspective, thirty thousand people were killed in auto accidents in 1930, which translates into a fatality rate more than twenty times higher than today. Secretary of Commerce Herbert Hoover convened the first meeting of the National Conference on Street and Highway Safety in 1924 to begin to assess how the safety infrastructure could be improved.[20]

Inadequate standards for licensure and an absence of road signage and other safety measures led to an environment that became increasingly dangerous as the number of drivers grew. Fewer than half of states had drivers' license laws in 1932, and some of those that did had no examination requirements.[21] Within states there was significant local variation in standards, as acknowledged in a Virginia assessment from 1931:

> The requirements for licensing vary considerably and unhappily are in some places of little apparent value. Usually, however, some age requirements must be met, and physical deformity or incapacity must not be too evident. In Charlottesville and Suffolk, this is true; it is usually true in Petersburg. In Newport News there is no drivers' requirement at all. In some cities, such as Roanoke and Norfolk, a written test concerning rules of the road and the law must be passed, a practical demonstration of ability to drive given, and in Roanoke, a test of vision is added. In Richmond, it is only necessary to pass a written test. In Petersburg, there is the requirement of a practical demonstration if the applicant is underage or there is no one to vouch for his driving ability. The effectiveness of the city licensing laws is somewhat negated by the fact that there are many car-owners whose residence is in the counties, but who use the city streets without having imposed upon them the restrictions placed on those living in the city. Here again is the difficulty of keeping a check upon

those who have had their drivers' license revoked and then move to another city or into the country.[22]

The insurance status of the driver was the main determinant of what compensation an injured party might receive. A study by Columbia University in 1932 found that the chances of collecting was nine in ten if the driver was insured versus one in five if not. With rates of liability coverage well below twenty percent in the 1920s and less than thirty percent by 1942, recovery was extremely difficult. Yet liability coverage grew far more slowly than collision, fire, and theft insurance. Liability premiums were higher than other types of auto coverage, which was a deterrent. Insurance agents tried hard to increase the volume of liability coverage but, as Professor Kulp recounts, met with little success: "Lacking the pressure of compulsion on the one hand and requiring a large premium on the other, it is hardly surprising that the liability hazard is so largely uninsured." In 1939, only one in five autos was estimated to have either bodily injury or property damage liability coverage. In comparison, half of autos had property coverage for fire and theft, which was more likely to be required by lenders. Kulp argued that the growing importance of the automobile placed the issue of liability insurance in a special category "rapidly approaching workers' compensation as the object of special attention by legislature and court."[23]

An extensive consideration of how to increase liability coverage began in earnest early in the twentieth century. One idea borrowed from marine insurance would confiscate the vehicles of drivers involved in accidents, to be released only after the payment of damages. A variant of this was the "personal responsibility" standard, sometimes called "every dog is entitled to one bite," which required drivers found at fault in a serious accident to demonstrate adequate financial resources, either through insurance or otherwise, before being permitted to regain their license. Versions of this were first implemented in Connecticut in 1926 and in Minnesota, Vermont, New Hampshire, and Rhode Island in 1927, with support from the insurance industry and the American Automobile Association. Although a number of states had enacted compulsory liability requirements for commercial vehicles as early as 1916, only Massachusetts had a compulsory policy requiring liability insurance, which they implemented in 1927.[24]

Related to the issue of compulsory insurance was concern about the functioning of the liability system. A team of researchers at Columbia University in 1932 examined the issue of auto accidents and the current method for victim compensation, rendering a highly critical assessment of the status quo. The concept of negligence was ill-suited to the realities of auto accidents, where fault was often difficult to determine. The current legal process was slow, expensive, and deeply unfair: "The result of a jury trial in the ordinary automobile accident is largely a matter of chance. To a great extent, the verdict and the amount of damages depend on who secured the best or the most witnesses, or who has the best lawyer, on the personal prejudices of the jurors, on the so-called 'breaks of the trial,' and on the intangible human element; they do not depend on a scientific ascertainment of the facts."[25]

Plaintiffs' lawyers tried to remove those with driving experience from the jury pool and "with the skill of an actor, play on the emotions of the jurors."[26] A young Richard M. Nixon in a 1936 law review article warned of the outsized influence of juries, which "in an increasing number of cases have gained the power of determining whether the plaintiff has been at fault." In other words, negligence is what the jury says it is.[27] The Columbia team recommended the implementation of a compulsory state-administered system modeled on workers' compensation that would pay for accidents regardless of fault according to a schedule of costs.[28]

The self-named committee of nine, the leaders atop the Association of Casualty and Surety Executives, released a deeply critical commentary on the Columbia study, arguing its suggestions were mere "palliatives" and did not address the real problem, which was the prevention of accidents. Very much in the tradition of the National Board of Fire Underwriters, they argued that the main problem was excessive carelessness, and the only thing policymakers needed to do was to reduce losses. "Cocaine cannot cure a cancer; and no compensatory scheme can provide a real remedy for the ills which result from the negligent operation of automobiles."[29]

It might seem counterintuitive that insurers would oppose the concept of compulsory liability insurance, since mandating the purchase of a product would clearly increase demand. Yet insurers resisted being put in the role of assessing what was essentially a private tax on the right to drive. Their preferred solution was the "safety responsibility law," an enhancement of the Connecticut law made into model legislation by AAA in 1930. This bill would require evidence of financial responsibility as a condition of licensure after a serious accident. It would also put the state into the position of suspending the driving privileges of those who had unsatisfied judgments.

Another concern was that making insurance mandatory would put downward pressure on its price, since, as an insurance textbook noted, when "the state establishes any prerequisite to a right which it has previously freely granted its citizens, there is an implied obligation to see that the prerequisite is obtainable at the lowest possible expense and trouble."[30] This would compress commissions as well, so agents also generally opposed compulsory insurance. Insurers argued that compulsory insurance would do little to remove dangerous drivers from the road, and it would make people less cautious if not "claims-minded." Insurers also feared that compulsory insurance would interfere with risk selection, since the presence of a mandate would induce demand from potential policyholders who were undesirable risks, and there would be pressure to cover nearly everyone.

Finally, there was a concern that a mandate could be a slippery slope that could give way to a state fund, especially when combined with proposals to reform the fault-based tort system. While the committee of nine was willing to acknowledge that the prevalence of uncollectible judgments was a "grave evil that cried out for correction," they preferred an approach that tasked the state with the job of weeding out bad drivers who could not pay for their mistakes and kept the insurance system voluntary.[31]

A compulsory insurance law created a different level of accountability for insurance regulators. In Massachusetts, insurers complained of a chronic inadequacy in rates, while drivers saw things differently. As Professor Kulp described the early days of the law, politics held full sway:

> As long as car owners are not statisticians and have hundreds of thousands of votes, the political factor in the rating problem is inevitable. All sorts of influence ranging from the governor of the Commonwealth down through minor executive officers and others, brought pressure to bear on the Commissioner to lower the rates. . . . [T]he commissioner was in a very difficult position, realizing that from one viewpoint he would be accused of being an emissary of the insurance companies if he insisted on increasing the rates, and on the other hand if he did not decrease the rates he would be subject to removal by the chief executive. . . . He chose to extricate himself from that dilemma by resigning.[32]

Disagreements over rates aside, the Massachusetts law was considered to be successful. In speaking to fellow commissioners, Massachusetts' Wesley E. Monk was emphatic: "Has the main object of the law been satisfied? How often have I been asked that question and how often have I said yes?" The ratio of serious accidents to registrations decreased after passage, and while the number of claims rose, because more were worth pursuing, their average size declined.[33]

Insurer objections to compulsory insurance were met with criticism from business school professors and regulators. In 1930, Alfred Mowbray chastened insurers for abandoning their ostensibly public role: "Those in private insurance should look on their business not as a private enterprise but as a trust committed to them for the service of the public. . . . [T]hey should seek to extend their facilities to meet the needs of the public as rapidly as those needs develop and are recognized."[34] A discussion at the 1935 NAIC meeting led a Wisconsin regulator to threaten mildly that "fire, automobile, and compensation will be written in state funds if and when the private companies cease to service their policyholder in a satisfactory manner at reasonable rates."[35] Professor Kulp chided insurers for their claim about the risk of increased moral hazard, judging it a "dangerous argument, as it suggests that insurance is hostile to safety."[36]

As early as 1938, one executive acknowledged that insurers' "short-sighted policy of blind opposition to compulsory insurance, in lieu of a whole-hearted effort to contribute toward a solution to one of our most serious social problems, has brought private insurance face to face with a grave danger" as discontent with the system of auto insurance grew.[37] The financial responsibility laws that insurers promoted did not eliminate the problem of undesirable risks and assigned risk pools developed in nearly every state in response to the problems of licensed drivers who were unable to get insurance. A mid-century critique of the liability system identified insurers as part of a serious problem: "Plaintiff's attorneys clamor for higher awards to injured clients, the motoring public bewail increasing premiums, and insurance counsel shun reform. Meanwhile the automobile, in the brief period of its existence, has created a serious crisis of the administration of justice which endangers the very fabric of our democracy—the people's confidence in the law."[38]

Ultimately, there was a split among insurers, as some of the larger stock companies that belonged to the American Insurance Association (AIA) came to accept compulsory liability insurance. In the early 1960s, Bradford Smith, chief executive officer of the Insurance Company of North America (INA), in a comment that echoed how life insurers were feeling about the pressure to provide health insurance, acknowledged that insurers must play their quasi-public role to maintain their private business: "If it is to remain in the realm of private enterprise, it is up to us to find a way to satisfy the public interest even if it means compulsory insurance."[39]

Yet Vestal Lemmon, head of the National Association of Independent Insurers (NAII), which represented small mutuals and the direct writers, opposed all movement toward compulsory insurance. When New York became the second state with a compulsory insurance law in 1956, Lemmon urged repeal, arguing it was "unneeded," "impossible to enforce," and a "colossal failure." J. Dewey Dorsett, of the Association of Casualty and Surety Companies, claimed the law did not prevent accidents, had thrown consumers into a "snake pit of red tape," and distracted resources from what was needed most, "a really effective highway safety program."[40] By the 1960s, most states had passed some kind of compulsory auto insurance requirement. The number of registered automobiles rose from twenty-five million to seventy-five million between 1940 and 1960. Four out of five households owned at least one car by 1960, and the trend toward suburbanization increased car use and miles traveled. As volume on roads increased, so did accidents. While many improvements in road safety had occurred, the highway and traffic infrastructure was not calibrated to the level of traffic. Road signs were not uniform in all states, and licensing requirements were often lax.

Drunk driving was common, and there were no car inspections and very little speeding enforcement. By 1966, motor vehicle fatalities were the sixth leading cause of death in the United States. (By comparison, in 2019 it was the thirteenth leading cause of death.) Both the number and cost of claims increased significantly during the 1950s and 1960s, driving auto premiums up an average of thirty-five to fifty percent between 1957 and 1967.[41] Rising health care costs were one factor. Car repair costs rose, and the number of car thefts doubled. The costly tort system also played a role, with jury awards increasing nearly fourteen percent a year during the 1950s. The size of the average claim rose from $623 in 1946 to $1,143 in 1963. And while premiums were rising to levels that most consumers found unacceptable, many auto insurers were losing money. The industry reported a net underwriting loss between 1957 and 1967.[42]

In the face of rising complaints from consumers, companies sought to demonstrate their willingness to write insurance and tried to increase risk selection to make that feasible. Merit rating was an early tactic that insurers used to try to improve their selection. The INA instituted the "Champion Auto Policy" in 1959, which offered discounts for good driving and prepayment. The Continental introduced direct billing to reduce costs and compete with the direct writers.[43] Travelers touted its rating policy and knocked competitors, which, though they might "trumpet that they do not use convictions in rating, they nevertheless do use them in underwriting." Agents were pressured to apply the company's underwriting rules "to each case with acumen, candor, and honesty. By doing that, and only that, can he preserve his own integrity, the integrity of his client, the integrity of Travelers underwriting and, of course, the ultimate integrity of the private insurance market, itself."[44]

Yet complaints bubbled up around the country about insurers withdrawing completely from certain geographic areas or refusing to cover people for reasons unrelated to their driving record. Companies exposed themselves to public criticism by maintaining lists of "uninsurable" risks.[45] Some imposed arbitrary rules such as dropping all single policyholders under age thirty, regardless of driving record, or canceling insurance when policyholders turned sixty-five.[46] The availability of insurance became a problem for many, especially older and younger adults, non-White drivers, and those living in low-income neighborhoods.

While the state structure of insurance regulation would have once relegated accounts of these problems to local news, the existence of national consumer organizations amplified the stories for a broader audience. For example, the AARP created a stir by surveying two hundred thousand members, of whom forty percent reported an arbitrary increase in their auto premium and ten percent found themselves forced into the state's assigned risk pool upon reaching age sixty-five, despite having a clean driving record. The AARP's advocacy of a system of rating based only on driving record led several insurer organizations to propose "major computer studies" to examine the issue.[47]

While insurers made no attempt to hide their age-related rating policies, other underwriting practices were designed to be less transparent. In an explosive set of hearings in New Jersey in the early 1960s, it was alleged that agents for the Allstate Insurance Company drew circles on policy forms of Black, Puerto Rican, and Asian applicants. These applications would then be rejected. The company was accused of refusing to sell policies to Blacks applicants, with the exception of schoolteachers. At the same hearing, Nationwide acknowledged they had instructed agents to give non-White applicants an extra three points toward disqualification on their thirteen-point uninsurability scale, regardless of their driving record.[48]

Testimony from agents exposed more of the underbelly of auto underwriting practices in New Jersey. The push and pull between underwriters and agents had persisted since the earliest days of fire insurance. Fire insurers had historically sought to depict agents as craven and short-sighted, willing to sacrifice sound underwriting practices for personal gain. But with the companies themselves on the defensive, the agents appeared as the frustrated representatives of the hordes of cancelled or rejected would-be policyholders. Agents claimed that companies "pushed them around," tried not to write insurance, and did not accept risks that they should take. One testified that he could not write any auto liability insurance for immigrants, since the companies "claim these individuals would be ineffective witnesses in court." Another complained that companies routinely refused to write policies in "sub-standard neighborhoods." All reported fearing reprisal for their testimony.[49]

As large companies withdrew from parts of the market, the inadequacy of supply was filled by a secondary "voluntary" market of high-risk auto insurers. These companies specialized in drivers who been characterized as nonstandard risks. These companies had varied pedigrees. Some were owned by the major auto insurers. The Progressive Insurance Company initially specialized in nonstandard risks before moving into the standard market.[50] Some high-risk companies were small and financially unstable mutuals started by frustrated agents who could not get policies for clients. Others were deliberately fraudulent enterprises.[51] Many of these used the mail, an area of weakness for state regulators. According to a Department of Transportation analysis, failures among them resulted "from intentional management ineptness, bordering on fraudulent behavior, rather than impersonal market forces."[52] This rash of insolvencies further deepened the sense of crisis in the auto industry.

The other destination for drivers unable to find standard coverage was the "involuntary" market—also known as an assigned risk plan. The earliest assigned risk plan was established in New Hampshire in 1938, and by the late 1960s they existed in most states. State regulators required insurers to accept a certain number of nonstandard risks, usually in proportion to their share of overall premiums. Rates in the assigned risk pool were often set by the state, and while insurers consistently complained that they were too low, many consumers found them too high.

The size and characteristics of assigned risk plans varied by state. In North Carolina, almost twenty-three percent of drivers were in the assigned risk pool in 1968, compared to less than one percent in New York. In 1967, there were nearly three million vehicles in assigned risk pools around the country, and while this represented less than five percent of drivers nationally, the pool served as a barometer of the quality of the voluntary market. As underwriting tightened around the nation, there were increasing complaints that consumers were discriminated against for various reasons and placed in these plans without regard to their driving record. The voluntary market generally targeted the better risks among those denied coverage in the standard market. However, in some states, such as New York, New Jersey, and Pennsylvania, the assigned risk plan was partially subsidized, with the result that the voluntary high-risk market was smaller in those states.[53]

A 1970 Department of Transportation report noted the clash between public and private priorities, explaining that assigned risk pools reflected the "unwillingness of insurers to deal with all licensed drivers on a basis that does not fully consider loss potential and business risk." Widespread driving privileges, combined with compulsory insurance laws or other financial responsibility requirements, made it necessary that coverage be provided to "persons who are licensed to drive but considered undesirable by insurers." Insurers believed that standard rates were too low in most states due to the "poor image of the insurance industry" and the power of well-organized groups such as "labor unions, associations of attorneys, state legislators, and members of the general public." The situation was intensified by the annual rate filing process, which meant that big increases happened all at once and were hard to hide. Requisite public hearings ensured that the proposed increases were widely discussed. Even in Texas, where the state set rates, consumer protest had led to the establishment of a citizen's committee in 1969 to investigate the basis of the increase.[54]

Assessing the potential of an auto risk involved consideration of the loss potential—a function of the individual's driving record and other things that might be related to the likelihood of having a claim. Additionally, insurers considered the applicant's "defendability," in the event that a policyholder was sued in court. The Department of Transportation's analysis conceded that the criteria could be subjective and based on a "wide range of information, some of which is of a very private and delicate nature." This led to situations where applicants with no history of motor vehicle violations or accidents were nevertheless denied coverage in the standard market. Insurers referred to these individuals as "clean risks" and recognized that they posed a serious public relations problem: "Clean risks have been a concern for insurers because it is difficult to justify, at least to some elements of the public, why a driver with a clean driving record should be unable to secure insurance outside of an assigned risk plan."[55]

In response to consumer complaints, insurers tried to focus attention on safety issues and rising costs. Much of this came right out of the fire insurer playbook, with an emphasis on driver carelessness, combined with the unwillingness of state motor vehicle agencies to suspend the licenses of poor drivers. Just as the National Board of Fire Underwriters had developed the Underwriters Laboratory, auto insurers began to invest in car and highway safety research and established the Insurance Institute for Highway Safety, which conducted low-speed crash tests and reported on the cost of repairs. Insurers also became involved in sponsoring driver education, another parallel with fire safety activities.[56] Travelers even briefly established their own auto repair shop in Worcester, Massachusetts, to try to better understand what was driving costs. The rising cost of medical care was another factor affecting auto premiums, along with something that would become a growing theme to insurers, "skyrocketing liability judgements." Added to all this was an inflationary climate. Travelers summarized the combined effect in a set of talking points for agents: "Not all drivers have accidents; indeed, most of them don't. But the sorry record of those who do has helped elevate auto premiums to their present record-high levels and has forced many insurers to initiate drastic underwriting restrictions."[57]

As *U.S. News and World* reported in 1967: "A crisis seems to be developing in the field of auto insurance. . . . Screams from drivers reach Congress as insurance premiums rise." Members of Congress reacted to stories from constituents, many of whom were "clean risks." The reaction was bicameral and bipartisan. Representative Pete Rodino (D-NY) said, "Congress has a clear and direct obligation to protect the public from overcharges and abuses," while Representative William Cahill (R-NY) complained that liability insurance was priced "out of reach of the average man." In the Senate, Warren G. Magnuson (D-WA), chairman of the Commerce Committee, called the auto insurance problem "a blistering national issue." The McCarran-Ferguson Act was top of mind to the federal legislators, as newspaper accounts reported that the adequacy of state regulation was being questioned: "Many states have neglected this job, some Congressmen believe, in the 22 years since Washington gave them a 'free hand.'"[58]

Meanwhile, the hearings conducted by the Senate Subcommittee on Antitrust and Monopoly, which had started a broad investigation of the insurance industry in 1957, continued. In 1965 the members focused on high-risk auto insolvencies, under the leadership of Senator Thomas J. Dodd. That year, the highway death toll crossed fifty thousand—a meaningful marker. Ralph Nader had just published *Unsafe at Any Speed*, igniting a conversation about whether cars were unsafe and launching a new set of federal activities in the Department of Transportation. That same year, two law professors, Robert E. Keeton and Jeffrey O'Connell, released *Basic Protection for the Traffic Victim*, which introduced a new approach to auto insurance, the basic protection plan. This plan proposed a shift away from the current tort system toward a compensation model.[59]

In July of 1967, Emanuel Celler (D-NY), chairman of the House Judiciary subcommittee, called for a study of the auto industry. The report, released in October of 1967, was highly critical of both insurers and state regulators and called for a full investigation by the FTC. In his letter of transmittal to Judiciary Committee members, Chairman Celler noted that "a broad cross section of the American driving public was gravely disturbed by allegedly unfair and arbitrary insurance company action." Oversight activities were also mounting in the Senate. Senator Philip A. Hart (D-MI), chairman of the Senate Judiciary antitrust subcommittee, announced in October that the subcommittee would hold hearings on auto insurance in 1968. Congress also requested that the Department of Transportation conduct a study.

The Judiciary Committee report was a treasure trove for the industry's enemies. Its overall assessment was that "by any objective standard, performance of the automobile insurance business . . . is unsatisfactory. The system is slow, incomplete and expensive." The staffers surveyed companies and rating organizations, investigated complaints, and analyzed data on regulatory practices. They found that the cost of automobile insurance in many areas rose more than thirty percent between 1960 and 1966, while the consumer price index rose only ten percent during the same period.[60]

The Judiciary report also found that auto insurance was often inadequate in the event of an accident—covering on average one-half of losses. The tort system was costly and inefficient, resulting in backlogs and long delays, which often induced low-income plaintiffs to settle for small payments. Studies indicated that the average delay in bringing cases to trial in major urban areas was more than thirty-one months, with average delays of more than sixty-nine months in Cook County, Illinois.[61]

Information collected from companies on their underwriting practices proved highly damaging. Each company had a unique "risk list" of potential customers to avoid. One insurer included members of the clergy and doctors on their list of "undesirable occupations": "Both appear to drive when preoccupied with problems. The clergyman may drive with the attitude that the Lord will provide. With doctors, there is the possibility of the use of the car in emergencies." Wealthy celebrities were a danger: "May be target risks if income is high." Other exclusions included musicians, barbers, bartenders, farm laborers, waiters, and wrestlers, along with members of the military and men who married at a young age ("an indication of emotional problems"). The basis for many of these exclusions was uncertain, as the Continental Insurance Company acknowledged in their questionnaire: "We cannot statistically support all of our underwriting judgements."[62]

And while companies had different underwriting restrictions, nearly all had practices that worked to the disadvantage of poor and non-White drivers. Some referred to the use of a "secret code" by agents to indicate the race of the applicant. In general, low-income drivers were to be avoided: "Appearances and manners of such persons may prejudice a jury against them." All used zone systems to charge higher rates in low-income neighborhoods, and many companies prohibited coverage to residents of so-called blackout zones. Some rural areas were restricted as well, with a Kentucky congressman reporting that insurance company representatives had told him that the entirety of Appalachia was blacked out in his state, with the explanation: "We don't have time to underwrite those people individually." Another member of Congress was told by a constituent that his company cancelled his policy because they said his neighborhood was "going downhill."[63]

The business practices of auto insurers became a punchline, but also a source of consumer anger. Underwriting practices seemed prejudicial and arbitrary and worked in many instances to classify people with perfect driving records as substandard risks. Chairman Hart of Michigan summarized the widespread frustration with how capricious private business decisions seemed to restrict the opportunity to exercise an important public privilege that many viewed as a right. At the same time his comment made clear why auto insurers had historically resisted compulsory insurance laws: "Auto insurance, far from being a luxury, is regarded by most drivers as a necessary protection. But can we legitimately request that drivers carry insurance without taking some measures to see that it is available at something resembling reasonable cost?"[64]

The insurance industry employed various strategies to respond to the onslaught of negative public attention. They pledged to try to be more thoughtful about underwriting, particularly with regard to cancellations. The NAII promised to give "individual consideration" to insurance applicants and to provide "continued coverage to each policyholder" whenever possible. Allstate and several insurer groups announced new policies on cancellations.[65] Representatives of insurance companies and agents promulgated talking points that focused on safety issues and the rising costs of medical care, auto repair, and litigation.[66] Insurers also contended that they were losing money, claiming widespread underwriting losses. However, this opened up a broader discussion that insurers did not want to have about whether investment income should be considered in assessing their financial condition.

Yet auto insurers did not speak with one voice. The larger "bureau companies" that belonged to the American Insurance Association (AIA), including Travelers, Aetna, and the INA, acknowledged that the status quo was unacceptable. They had accustomed themselves to the inevitability of compulsory insurance and were open to some type of federal involvement including potentially a guaranty fund or no-fault regulation. The AIA released its own no-fault proposal in 1968. Travelers and other companies published individual statements of support for limited versions of no-fault. These companies were also more willing to criticize state regulation.

The NAII adamantly opposed compulsory insurance, no-fault, guaranty funds, and any type of federal involvement in the auto insurance business. While there were larger companies that belonged to the NAII, the group prioritized the perspective of smaller insurers, which feared that federal standardization would place them at a competitive disadvantage. This division among the trade associations paralleled the fairly contemporaneous split between health insurers. In both cases the older and larger companies, many of which dated from the nineteenth century and had multiple lines of business, were more willing to cede ground to what appeared to be the public interest, whether it be government provision of health insurance or greater regulation of auto insurance.

The negative attention being showered on the auto insurance industry very quickly spilled over into broader questions about the competence of state regulators. Chairman Celler told his colleagues in Congress that he hoped his study would be helpful in "your consideration of appropriate Federal-State relationships in regulation of automobile insurance." The Judiciary Committee report observed that state agencies, hampered by low salary levels and inadequate personnel, placed "too great a reliance on an industry that is all too willing to assist in the processes of its own regulation."[67] Dean Sharp, assistant counsel of the Senate Subcommittee on Antitrust and Monopoly, described how an initial probe of insolvencies among high-risk companies had led to recognition of broader problems with the auto insurance industry, chief among them that "state insurance departments are primarily engaged as spokesmen for the industry that they should be regulating."[68] Senators Magnuson and Frank Moss (D-UT), in their letter to the Department of Transportation, also described a widening focus: "Our attention was first drawn to the serious problem of insolvencies among so called 'high risk' auto insurers. But such insolvencies seem to be symptomatic of fundamental defects, both in automobile insurance underwriting and in our underlying common law and statutory system of fault liability."[69]

Chairman Hart in antitrust subcommittee hearings suggested that insolvencies among high-risk companies raised broader questions about the antitrust exemption: "Why is the high-risk market and the assigned-risk population constantly growing in an industry which speaks glowingly of competition? Does the kind of competition prevalent in this industry cover the spectrum of the automobile insurance market or does it only extend to a certain segment of that market? Do the criteria for qualification within this segment make sense within the context of a free enterprise society?"[70] The INA in their response to the questionnaire in the House report referenced "a growing body of evidence that the present State regulatory system is failing in its role" and suggested that prompt action be taken, particularly action that would "permit insurers the rating flexibility that they require" or else companies would have no choice but to "restrict further their automobile writings, withdraw automobile writings, withdraw entirely from the automobile market or seek relief in the Federal forum."[71]

Federal efforts first focused on the issue of insolvency among high-risk auto insurers. Between 1961 and 1966, seventy-two high-risk companies had been placed in liquidation or receivership, leaving an estimated three hundred thousand policyholders or accident victims with unsatisfied claims. At the time, only New York, New Jersey, and Maryland had guaranty funds for auto insurance. After a set of hearings in 1965, legislation was introduced in both the House and the Senate. In the Senate Chairman Dodd proposed a bill in 1966 that would have created the Federal Motor Vehicle Insurance Corporation, modeled on the FDIC, to guarantee the contractual performance of auto insurers engaged in interstate commerce. The Dodd Bill (S. 688) would have also imposed some other regulations on the auto insurance business. Companion legislation was introduced in the House.[72]

At the 1967 NAIC meeting, the threat of the Dodd Bill was palpable, and the mood was downbeat. In his president's address, Frank Barrett of Nebraska channeled the organization's malaise: "State regulation and the NAIC are being criticized. There are those who are possessed by the thought that any industry where abuses exist, the best way to correct those abuses is to destroy the industry. There are those who ascribe to State legislation all of the ills of the insurance industry." But even he could not offer a full-throated defense of state regulation, "a system which has performed well, although it has not always attained excellence. As a regulator of insurance, I am proud of my fellow States and their activities. My pride, of course, is tempered with the realization that we have weaknesses and problems which we must overcome and eliminate." To counter the perception that regulators were too close to industry, the president suggested that the NAIC employ "skilled experts in the technical fields of insurance regulation" so they did not have to rely "completely on the expertise of the industry which is being regulated." Developing this capacity will be "an important factor in determining whether the States will forfeit the regulation of insurance to the Federal Government."[73]

But the codependency of industry and state regulators was on full display as they gathered to issue a resolution opposing the Dodd Bill. Vestal Lemmon of the NAII tried to make the threat of federal takeover real for the commissioners: "The clear language of the Bill certainly tells anyone who has been around this insurance business or knows anything about regulation that federal examiners are coming into the insurance companies and the state insurance examiners might just as well stay home and play checkers, because they are not going to have anything to say about it." He implored the commissioners to join ranks with the companies: "I believe that if we can stick together, if the insurance commissioners will maintain the view which I hope they will have, and with the unified support of the industry, we can defeat the Dodd Bill." But even Lemmon struggled to unreservedly endorse the state system of regulation that he was purportedly so committed to defending: "Though we have had our ups and downs, all in all, there has been a pretty good job at the state level."[74]

When the NAIC president asked whether anyone else from industry would like to speak on the subject of the Dodd Bill, Commissioner Hunt of Oklahoma most colorfully represented the mind meld between regulators and insurers as he volunteered this response: "I not only represent the regulatory authority in Oklahoma, but I also represent the industry, and I represent the industry because I think the industry wants the same thing that we do—taking the damn fools and drunken drivers and those people who are causing these accidents off the highways. Then the states, with the help of industry, can strengthen their laws to require higher limits of capital and surplus, so these fly-by-night, moth-eaten companies can't get started." He inveighed against federal oversight and then offered a bit of western wisdom: "I think if each one of us will look at our hole card when we get back, we can do the things that will stop a lot of this foolishness."[75]

In 1969, Senate Commerce Committee chair Warren Magnuson (D-WA) broadened the federal effort and introduced a bill to create the Federal Insurance Guaranty Corporation to cover all property and casualty insurers. Though Chairman Magnuson claimed to only wish to supplement state regulation, the threat of federal oversight was real. The NAIC snapped into action, as states sensed that timely passage of state laws was the likeliest way to forestall federal legislation. A model guaranty fund law was created by December of 1969.[76] Around the country, state regulators rapidly attempted to establish guaranty funds, using the threat of potential federal intervention to make their case.[77] Thus, federal action on guaranty funds was averted, and the pattern of reactive state regulatory behavior persisted. By mid-1973, thirty-three states had established funds for property and casualty insurance; by 1981, fifty states had done so, and all fifty states had established funds for life and health insurance by 1991.[78]

Unlike the prospective approach of bank regulation, state insurance guaranty funds were triggered after an insolvency, which was thought to reduce complacency. Insurers were generally permitted to recoup payments through subsequent premium increases. In that sense "good companies" were not being asked to subsidize "bad companies," but consumers were protected and the cost of insolvencies was spread among all policyholders. States also encouraged a prohibition on mentioning the guaranty fund in advertising, to remove any attempt to claim a competitive advantage. The concept of insurance guaranty funds reflected the ascendence of consumer protection as an important social value. And while solvency regulation had always been a primary rationale for the regulation of insurance, there had not before been a consensus that the consumer was entitled to a fallback if that regulation did not prevent a company failure.[79]

A series of auto bills covering no-fault, group marketing, and damage reduction were introduced by Chairman Hart in 1970, after the conclusion of the Senate antitrust subcommittee hearings. While the auto damage and group marketing efforts did not advance, the no-fault legislation would become S. 495, the Uniform Motor Vehicle Insurance Act, with Senator Magnuson as a cosponsor. At around the same time, the highly critical results of the two-year study conducted by the Department of Transportation were released. As Jack Anderson cynically characterized the effort in his syndicated column, "Washington Merry Go Round": "The Department of Transportation just spent two years and $2 million to learn what any motorist could have told them for two cents—that the automobile insurance system in this country is an unmitigated mess."[80]

The Department of Transportation study made it clear that many of the problems of the auto insurance market, including high-risk insurers, assigned risk pools, cancellations, and high premiums, were difficult to solve unless losses could be reduced. In this sense it served to focus federal attention on reforming the tort liability system as the most likely path to reducing the cost of auto insurance. The basic protection plan was the first major proposal for systematic reform since the Columbia University study of 1932. A system of compulsory insurance was proposed that would replace third-party liability with first-party coverage to the insured regardless of fault. Tort action was permitted for severe injuries that exceeded $10,000 in damages. Keeton and O'Connell obtained an actuarial analysis that projected that the plan would reduce costs, due to both administrative savings and the elimination of pain and suffering from the first-party coverage.

Just as Massachusetts had been the first to enact compulsory insurance in 1927, it also became the first to try no-fault, with their bill going into effect January 1, 1971. Michael Dukakis was a former Keeton student and young Massachusetts legislator. He had also litigated accident cases and believed that the tort system needed to change.[81] Dukakis, who is credited with coining the term "no-fault," was instrumental in passing a version of the plan in his state, over the opposition of the trial lawyers and the insurance industry.[82] At around the same time, New York's governor Rockefeller appointed a committee to devise a system of compulsory first-party coverage. They would be the second state to pass a bill that went even further and established a true no-fault system.[83] As the consumer movement gained strength, many state legislatures around the country began to consider versions of no-fault.

Advocates lined up on both sides of this issue. The American Bar Association and the American Trial Lawyers Association (ATLA) emerged early as fierce opponents, since no-fault would greatly reduce the number of cases that went to trial. They emphasized that no-fault would eliminate a right of action, and some sought to make a constitutional claim that it violated due process. This is analogous to some of the early opposition to workers' compensation, which in New York State required an amendment of their constitution after a legal challenge. The issue split the consumer movement, with Ralph Nader and his organization siding with the trial bar, while other consumer groups and labor unions advocated for no-fault.[84]

The insurance industry was split as well. The AIA, the major trade association of the large bureau companies, had come out with a no-fault plan of their own in 1968, which went even further than Keeton and O'Connell in the direction of a compensation model and completely eliminated the tort liability system. Many companies, including State Farm, Travelers, and the INA, supported at least some form of no-fault, believing that the status quo had to change and that no-fault was more desirable than other potential policy remedies, such as rate regulation.[85] Some even supported federal legislation.

Yet others, including Allstate and most members of the NAII, persistently opposed any movement toward no-fault, especially at the federal level. Some resisted because their business model was based on rating the likelihood and cost of claims litigated through the current tort system, and a movement away from that system would potentially place them at a disadvantage.[86] Additionally, there was the fear of any opening that might lead to more federal regulation. The argument most often made by the NAII was that no-fault doesn't reduce costs but instead redistributes them in a way that eliminates accountability and "immunizes the wrong-doer." Vestal Lemmon claimed that federal no-fault amounted to a "declaration by Congress that the government no longer really cares how badly one maims his fellow citizen as long as he does it by car."[87]

President Nixon, who as a young lawyer had complained about the outsized role of juries in auto liability litigation, supported the concept of no-fault. But under pressure from insurance industry interests, his administration took the position that states first be given a chance to create their own laws.[88] The Hart-Magnuson Bill would have required states to enact laws that met a minimum federal standard, with federal law as the consequence for failure to act.[89] The Senate killed the bill in August of 1972 by referring it to the Judiciary Committee. Opponents argued that states needed more time and should be allowed to experiment with different forms of no-fault. Advocates expressed concern, which turned out to be well founded, that given the influence of the trial bar with state legislatures, these efforts would be heavily watered down, with low dollar thresholds that would preserve much of the traditional tort system.[90]

Meanwhile, due to pressure from consumer groups along with the threat of federal action, states began to pass various forms of no-fault laws. By 1974, seventeen states had enacted some form, but only one—Michigan—had come close to the federal standards of the 1972 bill. In some states, the adoption of no-fault was also an opportunity to advocate for compulsory insurance. Commissioner Samuel H. Weese employed this tactic in West Virginia.[91] In other states compulsory insurance was still not considered feasible, which limited the impact of no-fault. For example, New Mexico's moderate reform proposal of 1972 was thought to be as much as was possible for the state at the time, "due to the present clutter of records and confusion in the State Motor Vehicle Department."[92] In each state, the familiar array of interests lined up for and against any proposed legislation.

In 1974, the Senate Commerce Committee once again considered national no-fault insurance. By then, a new coalition of insurers, including some companies represented by the NAII as well as many of the AIA members, had come up with a plan of their own, the so-called Camelback Agreement, created at a meeting at the Camelback Inn in Scottsdale. This proposal created more flexible state guidelines and the use of dollar thresholds to set up no-fault. In his testimony, State Farm vice president Thomas C. Morrill complained about the public role forced upon insurers: "We know that when the professors, the bar, the consumer advocates and the legislators have finished with their handiwork, it is the automobile insurers of America that will be charged with implementing the theories of the law and that will bear the public burden of complaint for those features that prove to be unworkable or unfair."[93]

No-fault supporters had formed an umbrella advocacy organization—the National Committee for Effective No-Fault. The AIA and State Farm continued to support the bill, as did several other large insurers including Prudential and Nationwide. The NAIC opposed federal involvement in auto insurance regulation. The ATLA continued their opposition, and Ralph Nader and his organization aligned with the trial bar, while other consumer groups and labor unions supported the federal law.[94]

At the last minute, defection of key Republican support proved fatal. Senator Roman L. Hruska (R-NE), a strong advocate of state regulatory authority, offered a referral in 1972, essentially killing the bill. An account in the *Washington Post* suggested that the White House had quietly lobbied "pretty hard" with Republican members to defeat the bill.[95] In 1974, reintroduced legislation passed the Senate but not the House, which had become preoccupied with Nixon's impeachment. The Ford administration continued Nixon's opposition to federal action, preferring that the states be allowed to create their own laws. Advocates for this position pointed to ambiguous evidence from the twenty-four state no-fault laws currently in effect, which in some cases seemed to be raising costs.[96]

By 1976, approximately half of states passed some form of no-fault insurance, although this included some that did not include thresholds. There were important variations in state laws that had implications for costs. One distinction was between a verbal versus a monetary threshold for segmenting no-fault first-party cases from those that could access larger benefits in the tort system. A related distinction was whether health insurance or auto insurance would pay for medical expenses. Auto insurers advocated strongly for keeping auto insurance as the primary payer, but this, in combination with dollar limit thresholds, would ultimately increase costs in many state no-fault regimes, as rising medical costs increased the number of cases where damages crossed the threshold.[97] No-fault was resurrected once more in 1978, this time with the support of the Carter administration.[98] Yet the administration did not actively promote the bill's passage, and the energy behind the consumer movement was beginning to recede.[99] By this time, growing anti–federal government sentiment was increasing opposition from Republicans, who tended to get support from the insurance industry, while the influence of the ATLA diminished the enthusiasm of Democrats.

There were a variety of factors leading to the repeated failure of federal no-fault legislation during the 1970s. The Nixon administration had funded the Department of Transportation study but then was content to defer to states, as was the Ford administration. While Carter supported the federal approach, his administration did not prioritize the bill. The influence of the ATLA on the position of many Democrats was significant, and the alliance of Nader with the trial bar gave some Democrats cover for their opposition. Republicans received contributions from smaller mutual insurance companies, which tended to oppose federal involvement in insurance.[100]

As the threat of federal legislation started to recede, state incentives to reform their laws lessened, and fewer laws were passed. The case for the advantages of no-fault started to become less compelling, and a backlash emerged in some states. Over time, the low monetary thresholds in many state laws, which had often been inserted at the behest of the trial bar, became increasingly easy to cross, raising costs and muddying the waters about the impact of no-fault on premiums. Trial lawyers were able to argue that no-fault didn't really save money, and several states repealed their no-fault laws and returned to the tort system. In the absence of a clear effect on premiums, the issue of no-fault lacked salience to consumers. During the 1980s and 1990s, four states repealed their no-fault laws. An effort to establish no-fault was defeated in California, and Rhode Island rejected no-fault in 1993. In 2004 a no-fault bill was repealed in Colorado, and no-fault was nearly repealed in Florida in 2007.[101]

Support began to grow instead for "auto choice" legislation, an updated proposal that resolved some of the problems of no-fault. Auto choice was more palatable to Republicans, since motorists could choose to have either no-fault or tort coverage, and states could choose to adopt a federal law or keep their current laws. The pattern of partisan support for this version of federal legislation had shifted, with Republicans and moderate Democrats more supportive. President George W. Bush expressed support for auto choice in 1992, before losing his election. Senator Mitch McConnell (R-KY) supported it, as did Senators Joseph Lieberman (D-CT) and Daniel Patrick Moynihan (D-NY).

A coalition to lobby for auto choice, the Committee for Auto Insurance Reform (CAR), was formed in 1996 by former congressional staffer Peter Kinzler. Members included Michael Dukakis and Andrew Tobias, who had led the unsuccessful no-fault effort in California. Industry support was again divided. Large mutuals such as State Farm and United Services Automobile Association (USAA) signed on to the CAR effort, while Allstate and other stock companies opposed auto choice.[102] The continued importance of trial bar lobby support dissuaded some Democrats, and many prior supporters of no-fault were now nowhere to be found. Groups like the AARP that had fought for no-fault in the 1970s would not join the effort for auto choice. Both the Consumers Union and the Consumer Federation of America, which had been strong no-fault supporters in the 1970s, were similarly not on board.[103] The auto industry was divided as well, with Ford in favor and General Motors and Chrysler opposed, due to conflicting views about how the legislation would affect liability lawsuits. This division kept the chamber of commerce from supporting auto choice.

The Auto Choice Reform Act was introduced by Mitch McConnell in 1997, with cosponsorship from Senators Moynihan and Lieberman, but after several years of hearings and discussions and a significant amount of editorial endorsement, it failed to advance. Lack of enthusiasm from the Clinton administration followed by the disruption of the World Trade Center bombing were some of the many reasons. A final unsuccessful attempt at federal legislation came in 2004, when the Auto Choice Reform Act was introduced by Senator John Cornyn (R-TX), with support from Senators John McCain (R-AZ) and McConnell.[104]

No-fault was unique in that it was a consumer reform that sought to eliminate or greatly restrict a private right of action. This created strange and unstable political bedfellows that shifted over time. The influence of the trial bar may have been the single most important factor. Yet the resonance of the litigators' perspective with consumer advocates and many others reflected the innate desire on the part of Americans to have the right to sue, and perhaps a suspicion that insurance companies rather than consumers would benefit from any savings. This dynamic persuaded many of the most stalwart no-fault supporters in the insurance industry to ultimately drop their advocacy, since it was easy for opponents to generate suspicion about any policy supported by the insurers. One insurance spokesman noted that it was "easier to run a 'no' campaign."[105]

Columnist Jack Anderson made a less nuanced but generally accurate assessment in 1971 when he forecast the inevitable failure of federal efforts: "The injury industry—the insurance companies, agents, adjusters and lawyers—have been raking in billions of dollars with the auto insurance system just the way it is."[106] Auto insurance is no longer a major national issue, but the interest of the federal government continues. The Treasury Department's Federal Insurance Office announced plans to study the availability and affordability of auto insurance in 2021.[107]

In one sense, it would be easy to view the federal activity around auto insurance as a failure, since nothing was accomplished legislatively with respect to no-fault or anything else. But the threat of federal intervention and the publicity given to the issue accelerated state and industry action. The investigation of auto insurance also alerted members of Congress to the issue of state insurance regulation and strengthened among some a resolve to try to repeal the McCarran-Ferguson Act, which would reappear in other contexts.

Many of the problems in the auto insurance market reflected difficult tradeoffs between public and private objectives. A revealing set of comments by Russell Press, Travelers vice president for government affairs showed how the industry perceived this conflict. Advocating "cost-based pricing" as their preferred approach to rating, Press argued for a cleaner separation between public and private goals. Press grudgingly acknowledged the quasi-public responsibility of the insurance industry but warned that social expectations were rising to unsustainable levels: "Our business is being seen more and more as a necessity, as requiring a higher social standard than other businesses. There are differences of opinion on all of these issues, based on societal values. And, within bounds, we can live with these differences, because we recognize that the industry functions in the public interest." But there were limits: "The system should not be used for social engineering. Placing unworkable constraints on the rating system to achieve socially acceptable goals can cause the collapse of a viable insurance marketplace."[108]

The rise of consumer activism in the late 1960s and early 1970s was an important force behind the broad critique of auto insurance. Already deeply unpopular, insurers emerged with their reputations further damaged, coming across to consumers as opaque and bureaucratic. The public profile of state regulators was much lower, but their reputation also suffered. They were perceived as poorly qualified, unresponsive to consumers, and overly close to industry. It was true that insurance commissioners were sometimes appointed as a political payoff for large campaign contributions and often had little practical experience for the job. Many prioritized the concerns of the companies over the public interest.[109] An Illinois commissioner in the 1970s had to resign due to ties to organized crime. Ohio's commissioner was accused of facilitating the redlining of inner-city neighborhoods.[110] There was a clear revolving door between regulators and insurance companies in many states.

But in the 1970s, there was a short-lived second cohort of "new breed" re-formist commissioners. Like their Progressive Era counterparts, they were critical of the insurance industry and saw themselves as advocates for consumers. Yet these commissioners also had to forge a relationship with an ever more active federal government, whose interests were not limited to auto insurance. Members of this group included New York's Richard Stewart and Benjamin Schenk, John Ryan in Massachusetts, and Fred Maulk in Illinois. In the South there was Thomas O'Malley in Florida, and Samuel Weese in West Virginia.

Some of these commissioners took a harder line with industry and pushed back against rate increases. This was a characteristic of Weese, who was known as a "champion to the taxpayers."[111] Many focused more broadly on their responsibility to the public. New York's Stewart, for example, was keenly aware of the changing expectations of consumers and a rising level of accountability. He called upon state officials to break free from the "rituals of regulation," which he described as a "closed system." Regulators needed to embrace their primary responsibility—"helping the people get the most insurance for their money." Part of that job involved better communication with the public: "especially those who are most disaffected. This is not easy, and certainly it is not pleasant."[112] Many insurance departments focused more on the needs of consumers. Even the famously unregulated California department weighed the creation of a shopping resource for consumers so that competition could work better.[113] Another important thought leader in the area of state regulation was Spencer Kimball, an insurance professor who was behind much of Wisconsin's insurance regulation reform, and the originator of the broader practice of close collaboration between academia and state regulators—an approach that came to be known as the "Wisconsin idea."[114]

The most famous member of this new cohort was undoubtedly Herb Denenberg. Denenberg was the insurance commissioner in Pennsylvania for only a brief time (1971–1974) but during that period became famous and is quite likely the most well-known insurance commissioner ever, except perhaps Elizur Wright. The *Wall Street Journal* noted that Denenberg had become "a rarity among state officials, much less among state insurance commissioners, a household word."[115]

Denenberg had a law degree with a concentration in insurance and earned a doctorate at Wharton in 1962 before joining the faculty. He worked for the federal government as special counsel and research director on the National Advisory Panel on Insurance in Riot-Affected Areas and assisted Puerto Rico in creating the nation's first no-fault auto plan in 1969.[116]

Denenberg was a Ralph Nader protégé and came into office as a self-professed consumer advocate. Despite his professorial background, Denenberg was a brilliant and irreverent self-promoter who craved the limelight. His famous trademark slogan, reproduced on a desk sign and buttons that he handed out, was "Populus Iamdudum Defutatus Est"—translated loosely as "the public has been screwed long enough."

Insurance commissioners in the late nineteenth and early twentieth century faced consumer outrage over fire insurance rates. Some tried to battle companies using a variety of tactics, including antitrust measures and attempts at rate regulation. Little success came from these efforts, and improvements for consumers largely occurred later in the century when the incidence of fire began to decline and the threat posed by the *SEUA* decision made the industry somewhat more competitive. Commissioners in the later part of the twentieth century had more power than their predecessors but were also under more pressure, due to compulsory insurance laws and the ubiquitousness of driving. Even those like Denenberg who sought relief for consumers generally faced an unappealing choice between higher rates and reduced availability, as companies exercised their option to withdraw from markets or find other ways to write less insurance if they perceived rates to be inadequate. In both home and property markets, assigned risk pools became an important though imperfect strategy to bridge the gap between public demand and private supply.

12

Hard Markets

In 1944, a hurricane traveled up the Atlantic coast. The worst damage was in
New Jersey, where the storm washed away the fishing pier in Asbury Park, bat-
tered Atlantic City's Steel Pier, and damaged boardwalks up and down the Jersey
shore. Among those reporting losses was Governor Wally Edge:

> When I finally reached my home on the Boardwalk I was amazed at the damage.
> Huge planks were thrown across the walk and in many places the surging water
> had lifted the entire structure from the sand. Part of a lifeboat was floating
> around my garage. The foundations of the house were weakened and ten feet
> of water in the cellar had cut off my deep freeze unit. With Mrs. Edge worrying
> constantly about sufficient red ration points for meat, this was a tragedy in it-
> self. At the moment, however, I must admit that I was more concerned over my
> modest cellar. Precious bottles were floating around, clinking against the walls.
> Donning hip boots, my staff worked long into the night trying to minimize the
> damage.

Though clearly free from the concerns of the everyday man, Edge, like many
others, was surprised and dismayed to learn that his homeowners policy did not
cover "wave wash" or flood damage. Using the power of his office, he sought to
rectify the situation: "Almost immediately I became involved in a battle with insurance companies who insisted that the hurricane was not ordinarily compensable water damage. While my financial loss was small, many property owners
had lost everything."[1]

The inadequacy of insurance coverage for storm damage became an increasingly important issue in the latter half of the twentieth century. As this chapter
will show, this was just one of a number of affordability and availability problems
that emerged in residential and commercial property and liability insurance.
These issues highlighted tensions between insurer business models and the
public demand for coverage that could not be meaningfully resolved by the
state regulatory structure. After a number of failed attempts, the federal government became a provider of national flood insurance in the late 1960s, but the
program's impact was weakened by its fragmentary design and piecemeal implementation. A contemporaneous federal attempt to reduce insurer withdrawals
from urban areas faced similar challenges. The commercial liability crisis of the

Uncovered. Katherine Hempstead, Oxford University Press. © Oxford University Press 2024.
DOI: 10.1093/oso/9780190094157.003.0012

1980s led to a critique of state regulation and another round of unsuccessful calls for greater federal oversight. Hurricane Katrina, a super-catastrophe on par with the San Francisco earthquake and fire, revealed how little had changed in the relationship between insurers and government.

While auto insurers were trying to restrict coverage and be more selective as costs rose in the postwar period, a somewhat different trend was unfolding in home insurance. The long-hoped-for reduction in the incidence of fires began in the 1930s and continued as construction methods, materials, and building codes improved. While this had ostensibly been the lifelong desire of the National Board of Fire Underwriters declines in losses would soon lead to lower rates and premium volumes if nothing intervened. This long-term challenge to profitability led to a number of responses in the postwar period.

One was a movement to reduce costs by increasing the use of computer technology, which insurers had been incrementally adopting in the postwar period.[2] In response to threats posed by direct writers, there was a wave of new automation throughout the property and casualty industry as insurers computerized more of their business processes and began to bill policyholders directly. Some agents resisted, thinking that this would be the first step toward their elimination. Yet others realized it provided them with more opportunities for sales and servicing. In any case the change was inevitable. Increased hiring of women, even in "judgment-level" positions, was another tactic insurers used to cut costs.[3] Another strategy was diversification into more profitable noninsurance activities. In the 1960s and 1970s, many insurers reorganized themselves into holding companies, which allowed them to circumvent state laws that prohibited them from engaging in noninsurance activities.

Additionally, insurers focused on increasing lines of coverage and creating more comprehensive policies. Just as in auto insurance, a comprehensive multiperil homeowners policy was developed that covered property damage and liability. In addition to fire, these policies came bundled with "allied lines" that protected against many other perils, including windstorms, cyclones, hurricanes, and riots.[4] Increased comprehensiveness allowed agents to compete with direct writers and also increased customer satisfaction. An insurance textbook of the time described how the trend toward comprehensiveness was self-reinforcing: "A property owner who suffers losses not covered by his insurance program tends to feel some resentment, but every claim adjusted to the insured's satisfaction creates a more favorable attitude toward the institution of insurance. Hence the use of comprehensive policies helps to promote good will by facilitating the sale of complete protection."[5]

The bundling of home and auto was yet another practice that increased comprehensiveness. Integrating coverage helped to drive organizational simplifications that eliminated redundancies and administrative overhead, as one textbook noted, "beyond the fondest expectations of many insurance experts. Under the pressure of a variety of influences, the integrative process has proven stronger than the bonds of tradition."[6] Yet as coverage became more comprehensive, the expectations of consumers increased, and storm damage in particular became a growing source of friction.

In his high-level memoir, Edge recalls a fairly simple resolution: "Without going into details, I took up this fight until hundreds of claims were paid and in the end the basic shore coverage policy was clarified to meet such contingencies."[7] What really happened was that the insurance commissioner threatened that the state would mandate coverage for wave wash and flood damage unless insurers offered it voluntarily. The Insurance Company of North America (INA), aware of the "obvious public relations danger inherent in the failure to meet the public need" and looking for opportunities to exercise its independence from the bureau companies in the post–McCarran-Ferguson era, reluctantly stepped forward and offered the coverage. But as predicted, it soon proved to be a failure.[8]

By 1944, insurers were well aware that flood insurance was not a feasible line of business, and it hadn't been offered voluntarily in a long time. In the 1920s, at around the time that some insurers were unsuccessfully experimenting with all-peril crop insurance, some tried flood insurance as well. A devastating flood on the Mississippi River in 1927 caused major losses and basically put an end to the commercial market.[9] Flood risk was seen as a classic example of an uninsurable event. An account of the INA's misadventure in the 1940s made the point clearly: "INA proved that the only people who tended to buy this protection were persons whose houses were so close to the water that damage to their property was virtually inevitable."[10]

As a result, losses from floods and hurricanes were largely uncovered, and there was also little in the way of federal disaster policy in the early twentieth century. For example, at the time of the San Francisco earthquake and fire in 1906, the federal response was minimal by today's standards. The government appropriated a small amount of money, replaced their own damaged property, and sent in the army for a short period. President Roosevelt encouraged Americans to make donations to relief efforts. Voluntary donations to the American Red Cross were a major part of the nation's response, and in 1905 that organization was designated by Congress to be the agent of federal disaster assistance.

By the time of the Mississippi flood in 1927, the approach had not changed all that much. President Coolidge, who also served as president of the national American Red Cross, asked Americans to make donations. Just as life insurance was endorsed by government as a key element of a voluntary system of protection, and in fact Coolidge himself would later serve on the board of New York Life, the government also advocated a voluntary approach to disaster relief that was based on property insurance and charitable donations. In the case of floods, donations were more important, since fewer losses were covered by insurance.[11]

In the case of the Mississippi flood, which flooded 16.5 million acres and killed at least 250 people, the government donated boats and tents, while the Red Cross raised funds to provide additional relief. While this was the biggest federal response to a disaster in history, the share of losses covered by these efforts was approximately thirteen percent.[12] As the twentieth century progressed, losses from weather-related disasters mounted and began to strain the voluntary system, particularly when they involved water damage. The "big blow" was an extremely severe windstorm affecting eleven northeastern states for three days in November of 1950. At the time it was the most severe loss since the San Francisco earthquake and fire, causing more than $200 million in losses industry-wide and five hundred thousand claims.[13] The INA alone had claims of $10 million.[14]

Given the general absence of flood insurance, as the size of storms increased, along with the value of property, so did the amount of uncovered losses. Public expectations of the role of government were changing, leading to a call for a larger public response in the event of a disaster. The Federal Disaster Act of 1950 created a permanent relief fund and allowed the president to designate when a disaster was eligible for federal aid. The rising demand for disaster relief created a federal interest in the development of flood insurance. This development is comparable to the initial federal interest in crop insurance in the context of the agricultural depression.[15]

Following massive flooding in Kansas and Missouri that caused more than $870 million in damage, President Harry Truman called the lack of a national system of flood insurance "a major gap in the means by which a man can make his home, his farm, or his business secure against events beyond his control." Truman, who was at the same time also unsuccessfully advocating for national health insurance, proposed a $1.5 billion program administered by private companies with federal underwriting.[16] The policy failed to pass, as did a similar proposal in 1952.[17]

Hurricanes Carol, Edna, and Hazel landed in August, September, and October of 1954, causing 1.5 million claims and more than $200 million in covered losses, approximately $2.5 billion in 2019 dollars. Yet total losses were nearly three times higher.[18] The Eastern Underwriters Association released data to document the extent of the damage and to reinforce the point that flood insurance was not commercially feasible. A 1956 study for the American Insurance Association made the same point. On the strength of this evidence, President Eisenhower also advanced proposals for flood insurance during his administration. The Federal Flood Insurance Act of 1956 directed the Housing and Home Finance Agency to establish a program of federal insurance and reinsurance against the risks of losses resulting from floods and tidal disasters. Again, the program was designed to be sold and serviced by private companies, with the federal government providing reinsurance and subsidies. Congress authorized a $2.9 billion commitment but failed to pass the appropriation, and the program was abolished in 1957.[19]

In 1960 came Hurricane Donna, followed in 1961 by Hurricanes Carla and Esther. Carla and Donna were both Category 4 hurricanes that together killed approximately one hundred people and caused billions in damages, in today's dollars.[20] Even though companies weren't liable for flood damage, hurricanes also caused covered losses resulting from wind damage. In some states, insurers withdrew from areas where wind damage was likely. Tensions between state regulators and insurers in coastal states ran high. In fact, problems in New Jersey had not been resolved, and the state's insurance commissioner in 1965 threatened fire insurers with cancellation of their license if they ignored shore towns like Atlantic City and Asbury Park: "I would consider it sufficient grounds to cancel licenses if they only write the cream of the risks."[21]

President Johnson declared thirty-four natural disasters in 1964 and 1965. One of them was Hurricane Betsy, which landed in Louisiana in 1965 as a Category 3 storm. Lake Pontchartrain overflowed and caused widespread flooding, creating the first natural disaster to generate more than $1 billion in crop and property damages and killing approximately fifty people. Betsy was identified at the time as the costliest catastrophe since San Francisco, resulting in insured losses of $715 million, more than $4 billion in 2019 dollars.[22]

There was a growing consensus that federal flood insurance was in the public interest. The Southeast Hurricane Disaster Relief Act directed the Department of Housing and Urban Development (HUD) to assess the viability of federal flood insurance. By then, state regulators and the National Association of Insurance Commissioners (NAIC) had been working on the issue of flood insurance for more than twenty years. Commissioners had tried unsuccessfully to get companies to add the coverage to homeowners policies. Florida's insurance commissioner described the long struggle of state regulators to try to solve this problem on their own, reflecting their reluctance to seek a federal partnership: "Some 20 years ago, the National Association of Insurance Commissioners began to formulate a plan wherein our citizens could secure insurance protection against flood damage to their homes without the necessity of going to the Federal Government for relief. The Association envisioned the addition of this insurance to the fire and windstorm policies that people now carry on their dwelling."[23] But after decades of unsuccessful attempts to create flood protection at the state level, the NAIC ultimately supported federal action and, in 1965, created the All Industry Flood Insurance Committee, which recommended a federal plan based on the public-private model.[24]

The politics around federal involvement in flood insurance were very different than in the case of auto insurance. Federal involvement carried with it no critique of insurer or state regulator behavior. The absence of the private flood insurance market was well understood to be the result of a market failure, despite sporadic efforts by state regulators to force insurers to provide coverage. Subsidizing flood insurance was a way for the federal government to protect itself by reducing demand for disaster relief. It built on existing federal involvement in crop insurance.

Federal involvement in flood insurance also solved a problem for state regulators and created a new business opportunity for insurers, as it was designed to complement the existing system of homeowners insurance. George Romney, secretary of Housing and Urban Affairs, envisioned the program as a cooperative effort between industry and government. The new agency commissioned a two-year feasibility study in 1966, which brought together government, individual insurers, and trade associations, as well as the National Association of Insurance Agents.[25]

In 1968, Congress created the National Flood Insurance Program (NFIP). The goal was to provide subsidized insurance but to also foster activities that would reduce flood damage. National flood insurance included an element of prevention in its design, to minimize moral hazard and potentially reduce the trajectory of future losses by affecting where people lived and how communities managed water. It was designed to protect both homeowners and the federal government. The NFIP was conceived as a "unified floodplain management strategy to reduce property losses from flood peril and public spending to compensate disaster victims." Incentives within the program were designed to encourage better management of flood-prone areas. To be eligible for flood insurance under the program, communities located in designated flood hazard areas were required to adhere to certain land use controls and building requirements. The NFIP represented a new approach to floodplain management, and it was also an acknowledgment of a shift in the way in which people viewed disasters. A Congressional Research Service report observed, "Disasters, whether man-made or natural, were initially considered inevitable or 'acts of God' but came to be viewed as public problems that required government action to protect individuals, businesses, communities, and taxpayers."[26]

The same piece of legislation that established the NFIP also created another important partnership between the federal government and the insurance industry. The Urban Property Protection and Reinsurance Act (UPPRA) of 1968 provided for a series of federal activities designed to improve the availability of property insurance in urban areas. This was most immediately a response to recent demonstrations and protests in cities. There were several incidents in New York City in 1964, followed by a large-scale protest in the Watts section of Los Angeles. Over the next several years there were additional incidents in Chicago, Cleveland, Newark, Milwaukee, and a number of other cities. The assassination of Martin Luther King Jr. was followed by more incidents in the summer of 1968.[27]

These incidents resulted in significant property damage and led to losses for insurers. Earlier in the century, damages from civil disturbances were not covered by standard fire insurance policies. This was famously relevant during the Tulsa racial massacre of 1921, when insurers summarily denied claims from Black and White policyholders on the grounds that the fires that destroyed their property were not covered losses since they resulted from a civil disturbance. City officials played an important role in instigating the Tulsa massacre, yet attempts to hold them responsible in the courts failed due to the legal concept of "sovereign immunity." Despite the significant amount of property loss, victims recovered nothing, due to the terms of the policies and the prevailing racism that ruled out any kind of policyholder activism of the type that existed after the San Francisco earthquake and fire. Insurers were under no pressure to settle on more favorable terms. Lawsuits against insurance companies persist to this day.[28]

Racism was also behind the civil uprisings of the 1960s, which were triggered by recent events but also driven by decades of discrimination, poverty, and underinvestment in urban neighborhoods. An important factor contributing to urban poverty was "redlining," commonly understood to mean a discriminatory refusal to issue homeowners insurance or a mortgage for a property in a specific geographical area, regardless of the property in question and the qualifications of the applicant.[29]

A long history of discrimination by insurers and others had contributed to civil disturbances that caused significant property damage, and thanks to the comprehensive multiperil policies developed in the postwar period, these losses were generally covered. The "extended coverage endorsement," which was by now a standard part of homeowners and commercial property insurance, covered damages from windstorm, hail, explosion, riot, riot attending a strike, civil commotion, aircraft, vehicles, and smoke. Additionally, most policies carried an additional endorsement covering "vandalism and malicious mischief." Together, the extended coverage and the vandalism endorsement were known as "allied lines" and were generally sold along with the basic fire coverage as a "package policy."[30]

Covered losses were notable. For example, the Continental Insurance Company lost $1 million in the Watts uprising alone.[31] By 1967 the overall extent of damage was estimated at more than $1 billion.[32] Yet while significant, these events were by no means the largest losses of the time. Since 1953, there had been two hundred loss events of $1 million or more. Of these, all but eleven had been caused by storms. Hurricane Betsy in 1965 had caused $715 million in property damage, an amount greater than the total premiums for extended coverage that year. By comparison, riots and civil disturbances caused total losses of between $50 and $75 million in 1967, an estimated ten to fifteen percent of extended coverage premiums.[33]

Losses from these events soon led to policy cancellations, withdrawal from markets, and premium increases, exacerbating an already serious shortage of property insurance in urban areas. In 1967, President Johnson established the National Advisory Council on Insurance in Riot-Affected Areas. New Jersey governor Richard J. Hughes chaired the group, which came to be known as the "Hughes panel." Former Pennsylvania governor William Scranton served as vice chair. Three insurance company chief executive officers (CEOs) also served as members, and Herb Denenberg staffed the group as a special counsel and research director. The panel conducted surveys and held hearings, during which much evidence emerged to substantiate the concern that the availability of property insurance in urban areas was a longstanding and serious problem.

On January 1, 1968, the council released their findings in a report, *Meeting the Insurance Crises of Our Cities*, which contained the recommendations that formed the basis for UPPRA. The report highlighted the centrality of a functioning insurance market to the health of cities: "Without insurance, buildings are left to deteriorate; services, goods, and jobs diminish. Efforts to rebuild our nation's inner cities cannot move forward. Communities without insurance are communities without hope." It was also made clear that systemic disinvestment in urban areas had long preceded the recent disturbances. The council conducted surveys with business owners, homeowners, and agents and brokers in urban areas. They documented an unmet demand for insurance, finding that more than twenty percent of commercial respondents and six percent of homeowners they surveyed reported that they lacked basic fire insurance. They also demonstrated that insurers had made it a business practice to avoid business in certain urban areas.[34]

Avoidance of certain neighborhoods by insurers was by no means new. The term "redlining" originates from the practice of marking fire insurance maps to indicate areas where companies would not write policies. Redlining by insurers has occurred historically for many reasons, but in this context, it largely reflected racial discrimination against Blacks, although it was also used against other ethnic groups. The enduring historical impact of redlining on social and economic outcomes such as income, education, and health has been extensively documented and is an important element of structural racism. Insurance companies had also contributed to urban decline through their investment behaviors, which had in recent decades emphasized suburban development.[35]

Agents provided information about how this discrimination worked in practice. Many told the council that they had a difficult time placing business from certain areas and had learned to stop trying. One agent from New York City described how most companies mark off certain territories "to denote a lack of interest in business arising from those areas. In New York these are called K.O. areas, or knock-out areas; in Boston they are called redline districts. Same thing—don't write the business."[36] These underwriting practices by extension led to discrimination against Black agents, as evidenced in this account from a Cleveland agent:

AGENT: My difficulty is in trying to get a company that will license me to sell business, period. I think this is largely because they feel that anyone of my race would probably be selling in the ghetto areas, and they don't want that.

INTERVIEWER: Have you ever had in your experience any specific instances where that was stated to you by a particular company?

AGENT: Well, they don't state it to you in those words, but I have had them make an appointment to come and see me about an agency appointment, and they walk in and start talking about, "We are not placing any agents now, we are getting rid of agents." And I say, "Well, why did you come to see me in the first place if you weren't interested?"

INTERVIEWER: In other words, they take action upon your letter which does not reveal, of course, your race?

AGENT: That's right.[37]

Despite the presence of a number of insurance CEOs on the council, the report was deeply critical of the status quo, which was described as something that may be reasonable as a private business practice but did not well serve society. As one New York City agent observed, using a bit of period slang, "The property-casualty companies are in business to make a profit and not to make love."[38] The insurance companies and trade associations acknowledged that change was needed but also made it clear that they would not jeopardize the basic structure and profitability of their business. In property and casualty markets, where the threat of total government takeover was far lower, insurers did not feel pressured to try to prove that they could meet the public's needs, as they had in the case of health insurance. Insurers were comfortable withdrawing from markets that were not profitable but were also open to collaboration with government, if the terms were right.

The federal government assisted in this case by helping to finance Fair Access to Insurance Requirements (FAIR) plans, essentially guaranteeing through special risk pools the continued availability of property insurance. Insurers that participated in FAIR plans would be eligible for federal riot reinsurance. Congress appropriated money to states to be used in setting up the plans but left states considerable leeway in how to structure them. By 1971, twenty-seven states had FAIR plans, which had written more than five hundred thousand policies with $14 billion worth of coverage. In 1971 New York's FAIR plan had the largest share of the fire insurance market, twenty-five percent.

Insurance CEOs initially adopted a statesmanlike pose in describing their participation in FAIR plans. Victor Herd, CEO of Continental, referenced the quasi-public role of the insurance industry while expressing his support for FAIR plans. "FAIR plan pools were created to meet an extremely serious social problem and to distribute the responsibility for its solution fairly among not only insurance companies but the total community of the state."[39] Yet as operationalized, FAIR plans had the unintended effect of creating a "dumping ground" for properties that insurers didn't want to cover in the standard market. FAIR plans created a structure for the same discrimination that was already occurring, as risks were "written out" of the standard market and then "rated out" to an unaffordable level. Despite the intent of preventing rate discrimination, rates in FAIR plans soared in many states, sometimes reaching three times the standard rate, as insurers, citing losses, argued for rate increases. The federal government had limited oversight into how states ran their FAIR plans, and most states did little to counteract these trends. Few states adopted anti-redlining legislation.[40] Due to the fragmented implementation and lack of federal control, FAIR plans were in practice a weak tool.

Both the riot reinsurance program and the NFIP were designed to create voluntary partnerships between federal, state, and/or local government and the private insurance industry. The NFIP required local government to agree to certain flood plain management practices as a condition of participation. Flood insurance was provided through a cooperative agreement between the federal government and a pool of insurers. As a contingency, the NFIP contained provisions permitting the federal government to administer the program completely on its own if necessary. The riot reinsurance program would offer subsidized reinsurance to insurers on a voluntary basis, providing that they were members of their states' FAIR plans. States were responsible for creating FAIR plans and additionally creating assigned risk pools if necessary,

Neither of these arrangements was inconsistent with the McCarran-Ferguson Act, because the federal government was not literally supervising insurers or pre-empting state law. Yet in both instances, the possibility remained open for the federal government to take over these activities if the outcomes were not satisfactory. The NFIP was specifically designed to allow for that contingency. In the case of riot reinsurance, the potential clearly existed.

The Federal Insurance Office was created by HUD to administer these two initiatives. The first occupant of the office of the Federal Insurance Administration was George Bernstein, who was appointed by HUD secretary George Romney in 1967. Bernstein had most recently been deputy supervisor of insurance in New York, and before that had served as an assistant attorney general in that state. Bernstein was skeptical of the claims of New York's property insurers about their losses in the state's FAIR plan, accusing the New York Property Underwriters Association of using misleading financial data in an attempt to understate their profits, calling the practice "a disservice to the public and to the insurance business."[41]

Bernstein more generally soured on the insurance industry for their overall response to the problem of availability. In a remarkable and widely circulated statement, "The Federal Role in Meeting Consumer Insurance Needs," Bernstein accused insurers of abdicating their public responsibility: "It is rare to pick up a newspaper or trade journal without reading of a property insurance executive bemoaning the huge losses allegedly sustained by the FAIR Plans and the injustice of the companies having to write 'social insurance.'"[42]

Bernstein blamed insurers for necessitating federal involvement due to their passiveness and lack of initiative. There was something new in his critique. The industry was being criticized not only for putting profits over social responsibility but also for performing poorly by private sector standards and for lacking vision and imagination. He argued that the necessity of his office was a sign of the industry's inadequacy: "The very existence of a Federal Insurance Administration is evidence of the failure of the property insurance industry to meet the basic insurance needs of our citizens. Part of this failure can be attributed to a lack of will, part to an inability to operate effectively under internal and external strictures. All of it, to a greater or lesser degree, represents a stodginess, a lack of creative innovation, and a relatively low quotient of courage and responsibility."[43]

His critique calls to mind the intransigence of the insurance industry in the face of entreaties by federal officials to assist with all-peril crop insurance in the 1920s or the reluctance of "the companies" to break out of the bureau system of cartelized price setting. The FAIR plans had provided a new opportunity to revert to a comfortable mode of collective and conservative decision-making. Bernstein's overarching theme was that this private industry, which had long claimed an important public role in exchange for a good deal of consideration and special treatment, was now essentially walking off the job.

The growing trend among insurers during this time to form holding companies in order to engage in noninsurance business provided further support for this perspective: "What is occurring, however, is the accelerating withdrawal by the insurance industry from the insurance business. Whether these withdrawals occur from the city, the suburbs, rural areas, or along our coast lines—whether they represent reluctance to write fire, crime, auto, windstorm, or liability is less important than that collectively they represent a serious loss and the disintegration of our private insurance system."[44]

Bernstein did not spare federal and state regulators, and in fact castigated them as enablers that tiptoed around the established framework of the industry rather than risk challenging it. The unintentional consequence of the FAIR plans, which in a sense institutionalized discrimination, was a key example of the cost of this accommodation: "A first step is public awareness and acceptance of the incredible fact that many insurance companies do not want to write insurance. It is this phenomenon, of an industry in large measure abandoning its inherent role, that should have alerted us to the seriousness of the disease. Yet tragically, even when there was a recognition of the symptoms, the responses were inadequate or simply wrong. To a considerable extent, it was the palliatives adopted, with great fanfare, which led us to where we are today."[45] Bernstein's comments reflected the frustrating truth that the government was largely dependent on the voluntary participation of the private insurance industry and needed to offer incentives and hope for the best when that participation was not forthcoming.

Meanwhile, the NFIP had gotten off to a slow start. By 1970, only four communities had joined the program, and only sixteen policies had been sold.[46] One reason that participation was low was because communities had to provide assurances that they would adopt adequate flood plain management techniques. The fact that this could ultimately prohibit development in areas likely to flood was controversial. When Hurricane Camille struck in 1969, there were widespread critiques that the flood program was inadequate and there was too little participation. Congress responded by authorizing emergency flood insurance and postponing the requirement that rates be actuarially sound.[47]

Insurers were more enthusiastic. Within one year of the enabling legislation, eighty-one property and casualty carriers had elected to participate. In an article to agents, Travelers announced their participation in a program they described as "revolutionary" and "far-reaching" but also as an "experiment." The company spoke approvingly of the land use incentives built into the federal program, which, "while not reducing existing exposures, should tend to curb the increase in the number and value of properties exposed to flood damage." The power of the federal conditions as a quid pro quo for subsidized insurance had the potential to accomplish what state and local regulators and private industry could not. Travelers acknowledged that the program was untried and that many insurers had not yet chosen to participate. But they argued that the new effort deserved a chance, describing it as an opportunity to play a quasi-public role in a way that did not interfere with profitability. This opportunity was made possible by federal subsidies: "Flood insurance, long debated within the industry and in Congress, is now a reality. It is in the interest of the whole industry, companies, producers and claims men, to see that the program serves the public well within the framework of the profit system."[48]

By 1970, the NFIP was operating in thirteen states, and one hundred companies participated. Insurers had created an organization, the National Flood Insurers Association (NFIA), to interface with the federal government. Membership was open to all qualified companies licensed to write property insurance under the laws of any state. These companies would sell and service policies written as part of the NFIP. Samuel H. Weese left his position as insurance commissioner of West Virginia to become the leader of this group. To participate in the NFIP, local governments applied to the Federal Insurance Administration at HUD. Maps would then be shared with all local property insurance companies and agents, showing which areas were eligible. Anyone could sell flood insurance, but the NFIA designated one company as the "servicer" in each territory. Servicers would disseminate information to the public and insurance agents about the program, process the policies, and handle claims adjustment and payment for losses.[49]

Premiums were artificially low and were subsidized by the federal government. The question of appropriate rates was a critical one from the inception of the program. The National Flood Insurance Act of 1968 originally specified that actuarially sound rates would be charged, but it was quickly amended to create an emergency flood program that postponed that requirement for several years. Premium subsidies were considered necessary because residents of flood-prone areas arguably didn't understand flood risk when they originally built or bought their houses, and there were no public safeguards or methods to make people aware of the risk. During the early 1970s, the NFIP's subsidized rates were lowered several times to encourage participation in the program. The thought was that the premium subsidies would be phased out over several years, and actuarial values would be substituted.[50]

In June of 1972, a tropical storm shifted east and gained intensity, dumping a torrential amount of rain in the Middle Atlantic states, particularly Pennsylvania. Some of the worst impact occurred after the rain had ended, when the Susquehanna River flooded, essentially destroying the business district of Wilkes Barre and surrounding areas. Hurricane Agnes was at that time the largest natural disaster in history, in terms of financial loss, with a cost of $3 billion and 117 deaths.[51] And just as a storm in 1944 damaged the vacation home of New Jersey's governor, Agnes struck the official residence of Pennsylvania's governor, which was located on the banks of the Susquehanna.[52]

In the aftermath of Hurricane Agnes, the low penetration of flood insurance was recognized. At the time fewer than 1,200 communities participated in the NFIP. There were only 95,000 policies and $1.5 billion of coverage in force. National flood insurance, which was still voluntary, paid for less than one percent of damages from Agnes. Herb Denenberg, the Pennsylvania insurance commissioner, soon initiated an angry barrage of criticism of the federal government for having failed to sufficiently publicize the NFIP. In the short run, he required the state's property and casualty agents to advertise the availability of flood insurance, a responsibility he argued was actually the federal government's. Denenberg collaborated with Pennsylvania's attorney general to file a lawsuit against HUD, seeking $1 billion in damages, on the grounds that they failed to follow the intent of Congress and publicize the program. George Bernstein denounced the move as "political nonsense."[53]

In response, Congress passed the Flood Disaster Protection Act of 1973, which required mandatory flood insurance as a condition of mortgages. Federally regulated lenders were obligated to require flood insurance on any loan secured by improved real estate in designated flood areas in a participating community.[54] This effectively required communities in flood plains to participate.[55] The NFIA supported this effort toward mandatory insurance, believing that this would help to ultimately transition the program to the private sector. Samuel H. Weese, testifying before Congress in 1975, argued that this would "guarantee that we get a broad geographic spread of risk, and that, coupled with the larger numbers, makes insurance an attractive mechanism for the transfer of risk from the individual to the insurer."[56]

Not everyone agreed. Senator Tom Eagleton (D-MO), and cosponsors proposed an amendment that would allow communities to opt out of the requirements. Local lenders and officials from rural communities in Missouri, including the mayor of Cape Girardeau, testified that the requirements were heavy handed and essentially constituted a federal land use policy because they interfered with credit. The mayor testified that local communities should be able to determine their own flood risk. On the other hand, some argued for a more collective approach to flood insurance. Advocates for a broader risk pool supported national disaster insurance. An early version came from Congressman Daniel Flood (D-PA), who proposed a national catastrophe insurance that would be spread across all property owners.[57] This idea has repeatedly resurfaced.

In 1974, the NFIP reduced its subsidized rates for flood insurance by 37.5 percent to encourage acceptance of the new mandatory purchase requirement and to increase participation. By then, more than 2,850 communities (including 2,264 in the emergency program) were participating in the NFIP. Approximately 312,000 policyholders had about $5.5 billion of coverage.[58] Officials at HUD began to suspect that insurance companies were overcharging the government and underpaying homeowners. The Government Accountability Office (GAO) criticized the flood program and claimed that it was "impossible to tell whether the subsidies paid to private companies were proper and whether premium rates were reasonable."[59] As HUD officials sought to exert more control, insurers resisted the changes and resented what they perceived to be a fundamental change in the partnership.[60] After a bitter fight and a court challenge, the Federal

Insurance Administration prevailed and dissolved its partnership with the private insurers.[61] Under the new structure, the federal agency was responsible for the underwriting. They partnered with local agents, who sold and serviced the policies.

In 1978, the Federal Emergency Management Association (FEMA) was established as an independent agency within the executive branch and took responsibility for the NFIP and other federal disaster efforts. A 1983 GAO report found that the NFIP had not collected enough premiums to cover costs, with the result that FEMA had to borrow from the U.S. Treasury. Political fallout and pressure from the business-friendly Reagan administration led to re-engagement with the private sector, and later that year, the partnership between the federal government and the insurance industry was re-established. The participating companies administer most policies through a business arrangement with FEMA, although FEMA still writes some policies directly.[62] The rates are set by FEMA and the government carries the underwriting risk.

The dissolving of the partnership between HUD and insurers came in the context of a darkening view of the insurance industry by many in the federal government. In January of 1977, a Department of Justice report pondered the issue of the antitrust exemption and state regulation, finding recent events had made it "appropriate to inquire whether state regulation has provided the public with the benefits normally attributed to competition." Comparing the relatively unregulated market in California favorably to the prior approval regime in place in most states, the Department of Justice concluded that the property casualty industry was favorably structured for competition, and perhaps it was time to "surrender the cloak" of the McCarran-Ferguson exemption and "face the antitrust elements ungarbed."[63]

The Department of Justice proposed a system of dual regulation, where companies that wished to "adopt a more entrepreneurial approach" could opt for a federal charter and federal rating and underwriting requirements and be exempt from state rate regulation. A federal guaranty system, modeled on the Federal Deposit Insurance Corporation, would function to emphasize "early detection and swift removal" of failing companies, rather than the state approach of "keeping every insurer afloat."[64]

States would still be involved in certain aspects of regulation, such as policy cancellations, and companies that didn't wish to participate in this system could remain purely state regulated and retain the protections of the McCarran-Ferguson Act. Under a competitive system, affordability and availability issues would still be a problem. The Department of Justice proposed that these issues would be better handled through explicit subsidies that were legislatively established, versus rating laws that created internal subsidies from good risks to bad risks. The Federal Insurance Act introduced in 1977 by Senator Edward Brooke from Massachusetts would have established an independent insurance agency in the executive branch to carry out a program of federal charters and solvency regulation.[65]

By 1978, another round of hearings by the Senate Judiciary Committee focused on affordability and availability issues in the property insurance market, raising questions about the arbitrariness of underwriting that mirrored previous discussions about auto rating.[66] Metzenbaum was emerging as a key foe of the insurance industry. Along with Senator Donald Steward (D-AL), Metzenbaum chaired the new Senate Subcommittee on Insurance that was formed in 1979 and planned to hold hearings on the question of ending the exemption. That year the Commission on Antitrust Laws and Procedures, established by the Carter administration, recommended that the McCarran-Ferguson Act be repealed.[67] A report by the GAO suggested that federal regulation might be preferable.[68]

The climate was also changing in the courts, as after three quiet decades, the antitrust exemption granted by McCarran-Ferguson started to come under increased judicial scrutiny.[69] A series of decisions by the Supreme Court pointed to a narrowing interpretation of the antitrust exemption.[70] In 1978, the Supreme Court decided their first case involving an application of the McCarran-Ferguson Act, finding the exemption did not apply to medical malpractice insurers accused of boycotting a group of doctors.[71] The next year, in *Group Health and Life v. Royal Drug*, the Supreme Court affirmed a lower court ruling that narrowed the definition of what constituted the "business of insurance," in a case that involved the creation of a network of pharmacists to provide a prescription drug benefit.[72] In *Arizona v. Maricopa Medical Society*, the court in 1982 similarly found that the provider payment arrangements in question were not part of the business of insurance and were therefore not exempt from the antitrust laws.[73]

In the context of this increasingly critical climate, there arose in the mid-1980s another high-profile issue related to the unaffordability and unavailability of insurance. This time, the commercial liability market was most directly affected. The problems in this market developed relatively rapidly and briefly caused severe problems. Between 1983 and 1984, premiums for general commercial liability insurance rose by fourteen percent. In 1985, premiums increased by seventy-nine percent, and in 1986 by slightly over seventy percent. Medical malpractice premiums rose sharply as well.[74]

Stories of specific examples of outrageously large premium hikes made the news. For example, operators of passenger buses reported increases ranging from 300 to 1,200 percent. The day care industry was particularly hard hit, with increases ranging from 300 to 500 percent. Cities and local governments saw sharp increases. Even worse was the plight of those who couldn't get insurance at all. Some carriers dropped policies for school districts and local governments. Industries involved in any way with asbestos found insurance nearly impossible to get at any price. Other areas experiencing availability problems included day care centers, restaurants with liquor licenses, and any coverage for pollution exposures.[75]

Manufacturers that made products that lasted a long time had increased exposure due to the potential for a long time window for lawsuits. Chicago was forced to remove playground equipment from its parks after an accident causing an injury to a child led their liability carrier to first cancel, then renew a policy providing much less coverage at a far greater price. The cover of *Time* magazine in March of 1986 depicted a small town, the peaceful scene marred by a lightning bolt jaggedly descending to touch the top of a flagpole. The headline read: "Sorry America, your insurance has been cancelled."[76] By this point, the crisis for most industries had peaked, and by 1987, the worst was considered to be over, yet premiums remained high, and availability was still a challenge for some.[77]

A number of factors contributed to the liability crisis, although there is a lack of consensus about their relative importance. The insurance industry naturally emphasized the growth in losses, mainly driven by litigation and the expansion of tort law. This is similar to the explanation made by insurers about litigation as a factor in the rise in auto insurance premiums. Incurred losses had been rising far more quickly than gross domestic product in the decades preceding the crisis and increased very sharply in 1984 and 1985.[78]

These trends in part reflected changing legal doctrines, including, for example, those that shifted the burden of proof and changed the apportionment of damages.[79] In many states, strict liability standards replaced prior standards that required a plaintiff to demonstrate that a manufacturer was guilty of negligence. In *Beshada v. Johns-Manville* (1982), the asbestos manufacturer's defense that their product met the safety standards of the time was disallowed. This ruling facilitated many more product liability suits. Losses to self-insured entities and medical malpractice mutuals also reflected a growth in awards to victims.[80]

Aside from these general trends in liability claims, there were some particular segments of the market where losses grew even more sharply. One area was childcare centers, where a wave of highly publicized allegations of sexual abuse drove lawsuits. This issue was a major factor in the failure of the Mission Insurance Company. Enhanced enforcement of laws on driving under the influence increased liability for establishments with liquor licenses. The Superfund law increased exposure for liability for pollution. And for municipalities, there was an erosion of the long-established concept of sovereign immunity, which increased liability insurance costs for local governments substantially.

The other major factor behind the liability crisis had to do with the dynamics of the insurance underwriting cycle. Attracted to the investment opportunity provided by high interest rates, in the years before the crisis, insurers engaged in "cash-flow underwriting," purportedly accepting underpriced risks on the theory that investment income would provide adequate funds to pay claims. Despite clear evidence of mounting losses and an inflationary climate, liability premiums increased very little in the years before the crisis. For example, between 1978 and 1984, general liability premiums hardly increased, despite a seventy-two percent increase in losses and an eight percent increase in general prices.[81]

A 1985 report from the Insurance Services Organization acknowledged as much: "In an attempt to generate cash flow for investment, insurers competed aggressively for premium dollars, knocking prices more and more out of line with loss costs."[82] When interest rates started to decline, the companies were left with the risks but without the offsetting returns. The exposure was greater in commercial as compared with personal lines due to the "long tail" in commercial liability, meaning that claims can be made years after premiums are collected.[83] Contributing to the problem was a sudden contraction in the supply of reinsurance, exacerbated by the withdrawal of Lloyds of London from the U.S. market in 1985. This increased the share of risk falling on primary insurers.

The property and casualty underwriting cycle reflects the fact that the demand for insurance is less elastic than the supply. Imbalances in supply and demand correct themselves in ways that can be painful for market participants. As in the nineteenth-century price wars in the fire insurance market, too much supply leads to falling profits and the potential for insolvencies. The result can be a "hard market," where prices rise to reflect losses and availability becomes a problem.[84]

Insurance law expert Kenneth Abraham advised against simplistic interpretations of the crisis: "In fact, no single explanation fully accounts for the problems that have arisen, and no single reform is likely to prevent their recurrence."[85] While the basic facts contributing to the liability insurance crisis of the 1980s were widely accepted, there were significant differences in interpretation and proposed remedies. The insurance industry blamed excess litigation and claimed that only significant changes to tort law would return the market to a stable equilibrium.

Insurers argued that underwriting cycles were normal and that accruing investment income was used to offset underwriting losses. Yet to consumer advocates, there was nothing normal about it. As Robert Hunter, leader of the National Insurance Consumers Organization (NICO), explained it, "At the top of the cycle you write policies for everyone, no matter how bad, and at the bottom you cancel everybody, no matter how good. It's a manic-depressive cycle."[86]

Insurers found natural allies among the many policyholders facing canceled policies or sharply increasing costs. The Insurance Information Institute, an industry research and communications organization, began a widescale media campaign designed to impact public opinion about the damaging impact of excess litigation. Meanwhile, the property and casualty trade association, the Alliance of American Insurers, put forth an agenda to reform the tort system. Proposed changes included mandatory and binding arbitration, restrictions and limits on various kinds of damages, and the creation of a uniform federal product liability law. The proposals were basically similar to the American Medical Association proposals to reform medical malpractice law and were similarly designed to make it more difficult for plaintiffs to prevail in liability suits.[87]

On the other side, consumer groups and the trial bar, represented by the American Trial Lawyers Association, argued that the insurance industry itself was primarily responsible for the liability crisis. The advocacy of the Nader-affiliated NICO group fostered the participation of other consumer groups, which formed an umbrella coalition called the Coalition for Consumer Justice. This coalition argued that insurers had engaged in aggressive price wars in the 1970s to increase volume and invest premium income to take advantage of high interest rates. They labeled the episode a "manufactured crisis" and charged that the industry was now exaggerating the tort issue to promote legislative fixes that would benefit the insurance industry and take away consumers' right of action.[88]

The consumer organizations argued for reforms that would prevent cash flow underwriting; they advocated for strict prior approval laws and better state regulation. Additionally, they effectively attacked the industry's facts, contending that insurers overstated their losses by omitting capital gains, tax credits, and dividends. They also introduced data from comparative studies that showed that the prevalence of litigation and recent trends were not markedly different in the United States as compared with other countries.[89]

Around the country, state legislatures and insurance regulators were barraged with facts and arguments from both groups. Many states developed study commissions to consider the problem further. Some began to take action to prohibit midyear policy cancellations, and in 1985 the NAIC adopted a model resolution to ban the practice. New Jersey governor Tom Kean placed an emergency restriction on cancellations and nonrenewals that would be lifted only when companies participated in Market Assistance Plans (MAPs), a "voluntary" version of an involuntary assigned risk pool, which commissioners had the power to create. Insurance trade organizations acknowledged that targeted use of MAPs could be helpful as a short-term measure, provided that "regulators and others understand they were not a panacea." A number of states put together MAPs for particular industries, such as day care, liquor licenses, and municipalities.[90]

Under intense pressure from the insurance lobby, dozens of states adopted tort reform statutes recommended by the industry. Washington, for example, adopted nearly all of the proposed policies. Consumer advocates advocated against these changes, arguing that states that passed such laws have been "unpleasantly surprised" by continued increases in the price of insurance. Some states tried to exact a quid pro quo from insurers. Florida, for example, coupled some concessions on tort reform with a mandatory drop in rates on the theory that the reforms were designed to lower prices. This move led to a legal challenge from insurance companies and trade associations. Momentum for the industry's legislative agenda started to stall as larger states with more sophisticated insurance departments were better able to resist their pressure.[91]

At the federal level, the Reagan administration sympathized with the insurance industry's version of events, which was also the position of the chamber of commerce and other business groups, and supported the idea of tort reform as a necessary remedy. This positioning explains why the cause of no-fault auto insurance ultimately came to be embraced by Republicans and opposed by consumer advocates in the 1990s. The Tort Policy Working Group, jointly formed by the Departments of Justice and Commerce and the Small Business Administration, released a study in 1986 endorsing the industry's position and calling for preemptive federal legislation on product liability.

Product liability law had been an issue among federal lawmakers for some time. Prior congressional efforts in the 1970s had resulted in a proposed but not passed Model Uniform Product Liability Act that would limit damages. Among legal scholars, policymakers, and advocates, views about product liability were divided. Guido Calabresi, Yale law professor and supporter of no-fault, was credited with advancing the concept of strict liability for defective products that did not require proof of negligence.[92] The ascendence of this philosophy had shifted many states away from a negligence standard and toward a more expansive perspective on recovery. Yet the perception of a growing number of lawsuits, high jury awards, and an increase in punitive damages made the issue contentious. Selective anecdotes, like the case of the woman who sued after burning herself on hot coffee from a McDonald's drive-thru, powered a narrative that product liability law was out of control and antibusiness.[93]

The liability crisis provided further fuel for advocates of tort reform. In 1987, Republican Wisconsin senator Robert Kasten introduced an industry-friendly product liability bill that was supported by the Reagan administration. Senator Mitch McConnell (R-KY) proposed a measure that would cap pain and suffering awards. The National Association of Manufacturers descended upon Washington, DC in 1986 for "Operation Product Liability," a one-day lobbying effort for a proposed bill establishing a uniform federal standard that would require plaintiffs to establish fault.[94]

However, the industry faced significant opposition in Congress. The preexisting antipathy toward the insurance industry among some Democrats in Congress only intensified in light of the liability crisis. Close ties between Metzenbaum and Ralph Nader's consumer groups, along with more general support for Democrats from the trial bar, led most Democrats in Congress to oppose federal tort reform. The bullying tactics that insurance companies were exhibiting toward Florida and other states that had passed laws they considered unfriendly to their interests further aroused the industry's enemies.

Senator Paul Simon of Illinois introduced a bill at around the same time to modify the McCarran-Ferguson Act, an interest among some Democratic lawmakers that long predated the liability crisis. His bill was supported by Senators Metzenbaum, Kennedy (D-MA), and Biden (D-DE). Metzenbaum sponsored a similar bill in 1987.[95] Hearings revealed an area of agreement between administration officials and Democrats regarding the antitrust exemption. In the House, Pete Rodino (D-NJ) advocated for antitrust hearings and released data challenging the insurance industry's claims of financial losses.

A Congressional Research Service report in 1987 signaled that legislators' questions about the insurance industry were not resolved: "The United States is atypical among nations in not supervising its insurance industry at the national level. The U.S. system of insurance regulation may puzzle foreign observers who consider the free movement of trade and commercial services to be one of the prime responsibilities of a central government, and the existence of uniform legal rules for large scale business operations to be an essential condition for that free movement. Insurance is the only large-scale financial service sector not directly regulated at the Federal level."[96] By 1988, the liability crisis had largely subsided. In part, policyholders adjusted to higher prices. In some states MAPs were used to help service segments of the market that continued to have availability problems. The insurance industry was able to achieve only a share of its desired tort reforms. States with more sophisticated insurance regulators and elected officials were able to defuse the situation or extract concessions in exchange for some reforms.

The liability crisis showed the effectiveness of organized consumers, who were able to combat the insurance industry's presentation of the facts. Most particularly, they were able to effectively challenge the insurance industry's contention about the extent of their losses.[97] A joint statement by six state attorneys general revealed considerable skepticism about industry claims: "The facts do not bear out the allegations of an 'explosion' in litigation or in claim size, nor do they bear out the allegations of a financial disaster suffered by property/casualty insurers today. They finally do not support any correlation between the current crisis in availability and affordability of insurance and such a litigation 'explosion.' Instead, the available data indicate that the causes of, and therefore the solutions to, the current crisis lie with the insurance industry itself."[98]

In response to the crisis, some businesses became self-insured or banded together to form "captive" insurers, which were jointly owned by the insured. In 1981, responding to emerging issues in commercial liability insurance, Congress enabled this by passing the Product Liability Risk Retention Act, which permitted risk retention groups (RRGs), a group self-insurance mechanism or a self-insurer, to sell commercial liability insurance. In response to the liability crisis, Congress amended this act in 1986, renaming it the Liability Risk Retention Act (LRRA). The LRRA permitted RRGs to receive a charter in one state but operate in any other and exempted them from state regulation in all states other than the state of charter.[99]

Consumer advocates supported RRGs as a source of competition to the insurance industry, just as some consumer groups supported the concept of banks entering the insurance industry.[100] The LRRA was the only federal action taken in response to the insurance liability crisis aside from the Childhood Vaccine Injury Act of 1986, a highly specific instance of tort reform that required those claiming vaccine-related injuries to participate in a no-fault compensation program.

Between 1969 and 1986 there were approximately 140 insolvencies among property and casualty insurers, and more than forty percent of them occurred after 1983. While the earlier insolvencies had largely been confined to small auto companies serving the nonstandard market, the later wave was more diffuse and included larger companies. There was widespread concern that state financial supervision was not effective in preventing insolvencies and the system of state guaranty funds may not be able to satisfactorily respond to insolvencies on a larger scale. The NAIC had created a special joint committee and developed a new model act recommending more and better financial examinations, but take-up from the states was low.

In 1986, congressional hearings were held on the topic of insurer failures and state regulation, and the GAO prepared a report in response to requests from members, including James Florio (D-NJ), chairman of the House Subcommittee on Commerce, Consumer Protection, and Competitiveness, and Senators Henry Waxman (D-CA) and Paul Simon (D-IL). The study attributed the failures to a fairly inclusive list of problems, including underpricing, underreserving, reinsurance trouble, fraud or incompetence, and overexpansion.[101]

Democrat John Dingell of Michigan chaired the House Subcommittee on Oversight and Investigation. At Chairman Dingell's request, the GAO produced another report about insolvencies and state regulation. The report found that uncollectible reinsurance was a factor in the failures of both the Transit Casualty Company and Mission Insurance Company, the two largest companies to fail. Reinsurance, they concluded, was a particularly weak spot in state regulation since much of the industry was global and beyond the purview of state regulators.[102]

Shortly thereafter came the subcommittee's famous 1990 report, *Failed Promises*. The title alluded to the systemic problem caused by insolvencies: "When an insurer fails to honor its promise to pay, the whole concept of insurance also fails." The subcommittee members found "obvious and deeply disturbing" parallels to the contemporaneous savings and loan crisis, which also featured bad private sector behavior and lax regulation. Following the approach used in investigating the savings and loan crisis, the report included case studies of the largest insolvencies, Mission Insurance, Integrity Insurance, and Transit Casualty, which had an estimated total cost of approximately $5 billion.[103]

Failed Promises was designed to alarm, with detailed tales of "scandalous mismanagement and rascality by certain persons entrusted with operating insurance companies, along with an appalling lack of regulatory controls to detect, prevent, and punish such activities." Yet while the language was florid, the focus was narrowly trained on the bad apples, "the pirates and dolts who inevitably will plague an attractive industry such as insurance, where customers hand over large sums of cash in return for a promise of future benefits." Though it did not make specific recommendations, *Failed Promises* was a call to action, with a strong implication that federal action might be necessary if the status quo did not change.[104]

The subcommittee's report described state regulators as more underpowered than captured or corrupt, with an inadequate system that was particularly ill-equipped to assess the global nature of the reinsurance business. Despite laudable intentions, the NAIC's ability to actually get things to happen was in question, due in part to low uptake of model regulations.[105] Dingell characterized NAIC efforts as "very nice, but not adequate. The situation has changed where both the state and national economy are vanishing in favor of the international economy. Without greater cooperation between the state and federal government, we're going to see a continued impairment of the capability of state regulators to deal with broad national and international problems."[106] The Insurance Information Institute protested the comparison drawn to the savings and loan crisis. However, *Failed Promises* was not an indictment of the insurance industry as a whole, and the "good companies" were clearly whispering in the members' ears, letting them know that they were the ones stuck with the bills when it was time to pay into the guaranty funds.[107]

Dingell's aspirations for federal regulation of insurance were focused on oversight issues related to solvency. His version of a federal solvency regime was the latest in a long line of proposals from Congress, starting with Christopher Dodd's proposed legislation in 1966. The Federal Insurance Solvency Act of 1992, cosponsored with Senator Ron Wyden (D-OR), proposed a federal commission that would regulate the solvency of insurers and reinsurers. The act was introduced in April of 1992 and referred to the Subcommittee on Commerce, Consumer Protection, and Competitiveness, where it stayed.[108] Undaunted, Dingell followed up in 1994 with *Wishful Thinking*, another critique of the insurance industry and the system of state regulation, which was described as "dangerously inadequate for the supervision of $2.3 trillion dollar industry which depends substantially on offshore companies to pay its claims."[109]

Dingell's proposal was unpopular with state regulators; the NAIC issued a strong statement of disagreement, criticizing the "wishful-thinking vision of a perfect federal system that can never be." The split among insurers persisted, with some of the larger firms in the American Insurance Association favorably disposed to some type of federal solvency regulation. The smaller firms represented by the Alliance of American Insurers preferred the state system. David Farmer, vice president of the Alliance, found no need for the regulatory fix Dingell recommended: "There has been no rash of insolvencies. There is simply no reason for the federal government to become overly involved in insurance regulation."[110] Republicans in Congress, who would gain the majority of seats in the House in the midterms, advocated for a reduced role for federal government. The minority members of the subcommittee disagreed with the report's call for a stronger federal role, endorsing instead the process of accreditation that the NAIC had by then initiated.[111]

Chairman Dingell and his subcommittee had no legislative objectives around the McCarran-Ferguson Act. However, some Senate Democrats such as Howard Metzenbaum and Joe Biden had been proposing legislation to repeal the anti-trust exemption. This was also supported by a portion of industry, again larger firms, that thought the prospect of a federal charter might free them from "hyperregulation" from the states.

There was even an aspect of bipartisan concordance among policymakers, as conservatives who supported deregulation and free markets believed that competition would yield lower prices. Some conservatives had come to support the idea of repealing the McCarran-Ferguson Act but potentially preserving some safe harbors for activities like sharing loss information. Yet they opposed a federal role in solvency and supported a return to competitive rate setting at the state level.[112] In 1991, Representative Jack Brooks (D-TX) introduced the Insurance Competitive Pricing Act, which would replace McCarran-Ferguson with a set of narrower safe harbor exemptions. In 1994, after years of negotiations, the House Judiciary Committee passed a sharp cutback of the exemption in a bipartisan vote. Yet after the Republicans gained the majority in the 1994 midterms, the bill failed to advance.[113]

In August of 1992, Hurricane Andrew made landfall in South Florida as a Category 5 Hurricane. It was at the time the costliest and most destructive hurricane to have ever hit the United States, causing nearly $60 billion in damages (in today's dollars). Much of the damage was from wind rather than flooding, and therefore not covered by flood insurance. The property and casualty industry was not prepared for the extent of covered losses; eleven insurers became insolvent and nearly one million policyholders lost their coverage.[114] The state responded in part by creating a state insurer of last resort, Citizens Property Insurance. Other adjustments included a statewide building code and the establishment of a state hurricane catastrophe fund, financed through an assessment on premiums. The importance of wind damage from hurricanes led some states to create windstorm funds.

The extent of losses reignited questions about national catastrophe insurance and whether or not the private insurance industry would be able to withstand a "mega-catastrophe" that might be greater than Hurricane Andrew.[115] The World Trade Center attacks of 2001, which caused the largest losses ever from a man-made source, raised these questions again. As was the case with earthquake coverage after the San Francisco earthquake and fire, the events led to the immediate and widespread exclusion of terrorism coverage from insurance and reinsurance, leading to coverage gaps or very high premiums. As a result, real estate transactions and construction projects stalled, especially in New York City. With strong support from the insurance industry, the federal government responded with the Terrorism Risk Insurance Act of 2002, which created a risk-sharing mechanism to cap insurer losses due to terrorism. While some decried it as a "government bailout," federal terrorism insurance was broadly supported as a way to provide financial security and help restart development in the face of a risk that insurers could not price. The design, which included deductibles and coinsurance, was contrasted favorably with national flood insurance, which was described in one editorial as "encouraging people to build in flood-prone areas."[116]

While initially intended to be temporary, state regulators, insurers, the real estate industry, and many others lobbied successfully for its reauthorization, an acknowledgment that, as a former state regulator noted, "private insurance does not take care of catastrophes."[117] Concerns about the nation's ability to deal with a mega-catastrophe were again put to the test with Hurricane Katrina in 2005, the largest natural disaster since the San Francisco earthquake and fire. Katrina caused $84 billion in damages and more than 1,500 deaths.[118] Compared with Hurricane Andrew, much of the property damage and loss of life resulted from flooding. This created an unprecedented number of claims on the NFIP and forced the program to borrow $20 billion from the U.S. Treasury.[119]

Katrina revived conversations about the inadequacy of the nation's public and private system to guard against catastrophic risk. Despite the enormous volume of claims, uptake of flood insurance was thought to be too low, particularly among the roughly one-third of homes that did not have mortgages.[120] At the same time, it was argued that subsidized flood insurance rates did not sufficiently disincentivize development in flood-prone areas. Some called for the expansion of the NFIP to include wind risks or advocated for broader national disaster insurance.[121] By then a number of states had established state catastrophe funds, but efforts to create a national fund were unsuccessful, as members of Congress from interior states were relatively unsupportive. An unsuccessful effort to create a national fund that would backstop state catastrophe funds was supported by state regulators and the insurance industry but denounced by opponents as a "beach house bailout." The Homeowners' Defense Act of 2007 passed the House but failed to advance.[122]

While the poor disaster response of FEMA dominated national coverage of Katrina, there was also an important insurance angle. The insurance industry was able to survive Katrina from an underwriting perspective, but as was the case with the San Francisco earthquake and fire, the catastrophe instantly created a large group of policyholders with enormous losses, many literally depending on their insurance policy for economic survival. Widespread unhappiness ensued. Affected consumers and their representatives questioned insurance company practices. There were complaints about long waits, excessive attribution of damages to flooding, underpayment of claims, collusive decision-making, systematic lowballing of damages, manipulation of prediction models that forecast future rates, and withdrawal from markets.

These in turn led to broader questions about the insurance business, and the appropriateness of the McCarran-Ferguson Act was raised once again. A bipartisan group of senators seemed to rediscover the special status of the insurance industry anew, marveling at the antitrust exemption and describing it as a relic from another time. Chairman Patrick Leahy (D-VT), expressed puzzlement at the exemption: "I have never quite understood in today's day and age why they should have this special privilege that other companies do not have. It is time to pull back the curtain of immunity and let the light shine in." From the other side of the aisle, Trent Lott (R-MI), was feeling the same way:

> Somehow along the line there, I missed the point that McCarran-Ferguson actually gives an exemption from our antitrust laws to the insurance industry. And as I witnessed the behavior of the industry in their response to Katrina, which until this day continues, and denials that there was any kind of collusion or that there is any kind of price fixing, I got more and more curious about the history, the rationale, and the wisdom of such a broad exemption from Federal oversight.[123]

Senator Leahy sponsored the Insurance Industry Competition Act of 2007, which would have repealed the antitrust exemption of the McCarran-Ferguson Act.[124] Consumer groups testified in favor, while insurance industry associations were opposed.[125] An issue brief authored for the National Association of Mutual Insurance Companies made a comment that reverberated back to San Francisco: "Following nearly every significant loss-related event affecting insurance markets, proposed regulatory responses have involved changes in rating and underwriting practices, rather than addressing the underlying element that affects affordability and availability of insurance—losses."[126]

Despite the bipartisan energy created by the enormous catastrophe, the bill was referred to a subcommittee, where it remained. Five decades of congressional scrutiny of the property and casualty industry had resulted in neither federal solvency oversight nor a repeal of the McCarran-Ferguson exemption. While the courts had narrowed the exemptions, competition had disrupted the "private governments" to a certain extent, and the federal government had become a partner in some catastrophe markets, the insurance industry and its system of state regulation had come through the twentieth century with much of its structure intact.

Epilogue

This book has traced the origin of the insurance business in the United States and the development of its relationship with state and federal government. A major argument is that the fragmented nature of insurance regulation has impeded the development of effective national solutions to many insurance problems. To be fair, the *Paul* decision relegating the regulation of insurance to the states made some sense given the historical context. The enormous social impact of insurance and its closeness to the objectives of government led nineteenth-century insurers to claim that their business served a public purpose and therefore transcended commerce. By and large, the public sector at the time agreed. Yet over time, large gaps in coverage became increasingly apparent. While state regulators have been effective at solving those problems that can be addressed with regulation alone, they have struggled to address significant issues of unmet demand. A surplus of bad insurance products and a shortage of good ones has been the consequence.

As discussions took place about how to fill the enormous chasms in insurance protection in the early to mid-twentieth century, insurers argued against public solutions, and when they became inevitable, they did their best to consign them to the parts of the market they did not want to serve. In that effort they have largely succeeded. The fragmentation of the regulatory state and the power of industry have made private models more dominant and public programs comparatively smaller and more piecemeal. Despite mounting concern about the anticompetitive practices of the insurance industry, federal policymakers did not take the opportunity presented by the *United States v. South-Eastern Underwriters Association (SEUA)* decision of 1944 to undo the state-based system, and the McCarran-Ferguson Act was enacted to preserve the status quo. That era also saw the beginning of a pattern of episodic congressional hand-wringing about the state of the insurance industry, which continues to this day.

If the McCarran-Ferguson Act initially bound state regulators and insurers at the hip in alliance against the federal government, more recent events have created a codependency between the federal government and the insurance industry. Private insurers now directly provide a large share of publicly subsidized health insurance coverage. They depend on government as a major customer; government also depends on their continued participation. A somewhat different kind of symbiosis exists in property and casualty insurance, where insurers as well as leaders of high-exposure states want the federal government to provide a larger catastrophic backstop while government attempts to maximize private participation so as to minimize their own exposure.

From the vantage point of the twenty-first century, it is easy to identify much persistence in these patterns and also, perhaps, some opportunities for change. One may exist in health insurance, where the drawbacks of our piecemeal system are perhaps most clearly evident and receive sustained national attention. The Affordable Care Act (ACA) was a major policy achievement yet also quite incremental, demonstrating how resistant our privatized system of risk protection is to change. The ACA relies on private insurers to sell coverage in a standardized and heavily subsidized individual market. The ACA has extended coverage to more than twenty million additional people, banished much of the substandard medically underwritten individual market, and begun what will likely be a long but important process of delinking health insurance from employment. Yet it too is a patch, designed to fit around a system that was designed by insurers for the employer market.

Since the ACA, the share of the population enrolled in public coverage has grown due to a combination of population aging and increased eligibility for Medicaid. It is a trend that is not likely to be reversed. More than half of every dollar spent on health insurance is from state or federal government. Yet despite the opportunities that public funding has created for health insurers, private incentives intrude in ways that create constant friction, raise costs, and sow discontent. To provide three recent examples, it is widely believed that insurers providing Medicare Advantage inflate member risk scores to receive higher payments. The Federal Trade Commission has recently warned agents and brokers about misleading advertisements for Medicare Advantage plans that confuse consumers. Some of the same insurers that participate in the ACA market persist in selling short-term plans that serve their customers poorly and cannibalize the regulated and taxpayer-subsidized individual market, an opportunity that has been restricted by a 2024 federal rule. For reasons like these (and there are countless others), Americans pay more and get less for health care than any other country in the world.

While uninsurance is at an all-time low, there are still important coverage gaps, especially in those states that have not expanded Medicaid eligibility. Though racial differences in coverage and access to care have been lessened somewhat thanks to the ACA, they remain unacceptably large. Large markets still exist for low-value supplementary coverage. High out-of-pocket costs, the prevalence of medical debt, lack of providers, and arbitrary prior authorization rules by managed care companies have led many, even among those with insurance, to declare our system a failure. A growing share of the population wants the government to play a greater role in health care, including providing universal coverage and regulating the prices of health care services and prescription drugs.

In an important new book, economists Liran Einav and Amy Finkelstein call for a 'teardown', castigating the current system as "rotten to the core."[1]

The problems identified in the mid-twentieth century with discrimination and availability of auto insurance have persisted. Recent investigations have shown that Black drivers in particular are more likely to pay higher premiums and are more likely to have factors unrelated to driving ability used in rating.[2] In the absence of national standards, states have addressed the issue in a non-uniform way, with many taking no action. Insurers' increasing use of big data and complex algorithms complicates the effectiveness of reforms based on prohibiting the use of any particular data point. Dissatisfaction with claims adjustment practices after Superstorm Sandy recalled complaints made after Hurricane Katrina, which in turn recalled insurer responses to the San Francisco earthquake and fire. Members of Congress from affected states complained of lowball estimates and long claims adjustment practices on the part of insurers participating in the National Flood Insurance Program.[3] A contingent of these members have opposed a new National Flood Insurance Program (NFIP) rating structure that is designed to be more actuarially fair, calling instead for subsidies that will make flood insurance more affordable, with premiums pegged to income in a structure much like the premium tax credits in the ACA. Currently, the NFIP lacks permanent reauthorization and take-up is low. Protection from flood risk is greatly undersupplied.

In Florida, possibly the area with the world's highest hurricane exposure, the state-run insurer of last resort, Citizens, has the greatest market share, and its ability to withstand a major catastrophe is uncertain. Attempts to offload policyholders to other insurers have been complicated by market withdrawals and insolvencies. In California, insurers are responding to wildfire risk by withdrawing from markets, while condemning the insurance department's position on their use of catastrophe models. California has attempted to make use of its Fair Access to Insurance Requirements (FAIR) plan to compel more participation in fire-prone areas, but supply is currently inadequate.

The accumulating pace of disasters may ultimately be a force for change. Disasters affect the perception of risk in important ways, both for the insurance industry and for society writ large. Disasters cause insurers to withdraw from markets, exclude certain types of perils, and develop new models to forecast their likelihood. This was seen after the San Francisco earthquake and fire, after Hurricane Katrina, and after the Covid-19 pandemic. Disasters of sufficient magnitude and frequency could lead to a reconsideration of the structure of our risk protection system. As Hilary Clinton recently noted at a global climate summit, "We need to rethink the insurance industry. Insurance companies are pulling out of so many places. They're not insuring homes. They're not insuring businesses."[4]

For society at large, disasters can be unifying and can promote a sense of a shared fate, as seen, for example, after the events at the World Trade Center in 2001. Disasters can compel a new and more collective mode of risk sharing between public and private actors, which may or may not be permanent. For example, the attacks on the World Trade Center led to federal terrorism insurance. Though designed to be temporary, it has persisted. During the Covid pandemic access to health insurance was expanded by restricting eligibility determinations in the Medicaid program. This has not lasted and is in the process of being unwound, victim in part to the state-based politics of Medicaid.

What is less clear is how repeated and escalating cycles of disasters may affect our society's or perhaps even our planet's approach to sharing risk. With the accelerating frequency of deadly storms and fires, this question is more than theoretical. Such a pattern of events may push us toward a more collective national strategy for risk sharing, but it could instead subject us, or at least some of us, more fully to the shortcomings of the fragile state-based systems that are currently in place. It's not clear how our society will confront such a challenge, but as we experience the hottest summer in the earth's history, it seems likely that we will soon find out.

Finally, none of this should be taken to imply that state insurance regulation today is ineffective. While the historical fact of the state-based system has impeded national solutions to insurance problems, the quality of state insurance regulation today is generally high. Collectively, state regulators have responsibility for an estimated one-third of the world's insurance premiums, with more than $8 trillion in cash and invested assets at the end of 2021.[5] State insurance regulators have been critical to the effective implementation of the ACA, and in responding to significant climate issues that threaten state property markets. In light of the low penetration of the NFIP, some states are attempting to foster private flood insurance markets that are based on new data and risk-based pricing.[6] In some states, consumer-oriented regulators are trying to prevent insurers from using credit scores in auto ratings.[7]

The National Association of Insurance Commissioners (NAIC) has evolved to be a professional and deeply knowledgeable organization, interacting with the federal government and educating members on topics such as climate resilience, cyber risks, and the growing role of private equity in the industry. A relatively new federal addition to the insurance supervision infrastructure is the Federal Insurance Office (FIO), established by the Dodd-Frank Wall Street Reform and Consumer Protection Act of 2010, largely in response to the failure of insurance giant AIG. The office sits within the Department of Treasury and is charged with producing reports, advising federal agencies, and engaging in international discussions about insurance. The NAIC describes the FIO on its website by noting that it is not a regulator, and "its authorities do not displace the time-tested robust state insurance regulatory regime."[8]

In early 2024, the FIO abandoned its attempt to collect detailed climate risk data from property and casualty insurers after facing howls of protest from the insurance industry, state regulators, and conservative members of Congress. In an attempt to avoid a recurrence of this threat, Republican lawmakers introduced a bill to eliminate the FIO's subpoena powers, along with another one that went a bit further—The Federal Insurance Office (FIO) Elimination Act.[9] A property insurance agent's trade association, in a comment that echoes with history, wistfully observed that the bill's passage would "greatly reduce the threat of a wholesale takeover of the insurance industry by eliminating an unnecessary administrative office that relentlessly seeks to expand its own powers."[10]

Notes

Introduction

1. Sir H. Llewellyn Smith, "Economic Security and Unemployment Insurance," *Economic Journal,* December 1910, 513.
2. This organization is now known as the National Association of Insurance Commissioners.
3. See, for example, Mary Douglas, *Risk and Blame: Essays in Cultural Theory* (London: Routledge, 1992); Tom Baker and Jonathan Simon, eds., *Embracing Risk: The Changing Culture of Insurance and Responsibility* (Chicago: University of Chicago Press, 2002).
4. Francois Ewald, "Insurance and Risk," in *The Foucault Effect: Studies in Governmentality,* Graham Burchell, Colin Gordon, and Peter Miller (eds.), (Chicago: University of Chicago Press, 1991).
5. Smith, "Economic Security," 517.
6. See, for example, Jonathan Levy, *Freaks of Fortune: The Emerging World of Capitalism and Risk in America* (Cambridge, MA: Harvard University Press, 2012); David Beito, *From Mutual Aid to the Welfare State: Fraternal Societies and Social Services, 1890–1976* (Chapel Hill: University of North Carolina Press, 2000); Caley Horan, *Insurance Era: Risk, Governance, and the Privatization of Security in Postwar America* (Chicago: University of Chicago Press, 2021); Jennifer Klein, *For All These Rights: Business, Labor and the Shaping of America's Public-Private Welfare State* (Princeton, NJ: Princeton University Press, 2006).
7. Insurance Information Institute, *How Insurance Supports the Economy,* https://www.iii.org/publications/a-firm-foundation-how-insurance-supports-the-economy/introduction/to-the-reader.
8. OECD Data, *Insurance Spending,* 2022 https://data.oecd.org/insurance/insurance-spending.htm.
9. Grover Cleveland, speech given at Association of Life Insurance Presidents, 1907, R. Carlyle Buley, *The Equitable Life Assurance Society of the United States* (New York: Appleton-Century-Crofts, 1959), iii.
10. Gabriel Kolko, *The Triumph of Conservatism* (New York: Free Press, 1963).
11. Smith, "Economic Security," 517.

Chapter 1

1. Terry Mort, *Cheyenne Summer: The Battle of Beecher Island* (New York: Pegasus Books, 2021), 199.
2. Lee Zion, "History of the Regiment: Forsyth Scouts, Beecher Island 17–25, September 1868," http://abuffalosoldier.com/forsyth.htm.
3. Mort, *Cheyenne Summer,* 233; Dee Brown, *Action at Beecher Island* (New York: Curtis Books, 1967).
4. Agnes Howard, "The Beechers in Our Backyard," *Stillpoint,* Gordon College, 2011; Bowdoin College, "Short Sketch of the Life of Lieutenant Frederick Beecher," in *Fiftieth Anniversary of the Class of 1862* (Brunswick, ME: Bowdoin College, 1912).
5. War Department, 16th Maine Regiment, 353, "1863-11-10 Special Order 499 Granting Lieutenant Frederick Beecher a Leave of Absence Due to Wounds," Maine Archives; Bowdoin College, "Short Sketch"; War Department, 16th Maine Regiment, 353, "1864-09-30 Special Order 325 Honorably Discharging Lieutenant Frederick Henry Beecher from Service 1864," Maine Archives.
6. Bowdoin College, "Short Sketch"; Brown, *Action.*
7. Bowdoin College, "Short Sketch"; Obituary of Frederick H. Beecher, *New York Times,* October 4, 1868; Mort, *Cheyenne Summer,* 199.
8. Morton Keller, *The Life Insurance Enterprise, 1885–1910: A Study in the Limits of Corporate Power* (Cambridge, MA: Harvard University Press, 1963), 8.

9. Quoted in Vivian Zelizer, *Morals and Markets: The Development of Life Insurance in the United States* (New York: Columbia University Press, 1979), 34; also see Sharon Ann Murphy, *Investing in Life: Insurance in Antebellum America* (Baltimore: John Hopkins University Press, 2010).
10. Keller, *Life Insurance Enterprise*, 4.
11. Lawrence Abbott, *The Story of New York Life: A History of the Origin and Development of the New York Life Insurance company from 1845 to 1929* (New York: New York Life Insurance Company, 1930).
12. Quoted in Zelizer, *Morals and Markets*, 93.
13. Zelizer, *Morals and Markets*, 47.
14. Abbott, *The Story of New York Life*, 44. This law was sometimes referred to as the "Magna Carta" of life insurance.
15. Richard White, *The Republic for Which It Stands: The United States during Reconstruction and the Gilded Age, 1865–1896* (New York: Oxford University Press, 2017), 178.
16. Zelizer, *Morals and Markets*.
17. Abbott, *The Story of New York Life*, 81; also see Shepard B. Clough, *A Century of American Life Insurance: A History of the Mutual Life Insurance Company of New York, 1843–1953* (New York: Columbia University Press, 1946).
18. Drew Faust, *This Republic of Suffering: Death and the American Civil War* (New York: Vintage, 2008), 92; Zelizer, *Morals and Markets*, 47.
19. Zelizer, *Morals and Markets*, 122.
20. Faust, *Republic of Suffering*, 6; Abbott, *The Story of New York Life*, 36–46; see also Richard Hooker, *Aetna Life Insurance Company: Its First Hundred Years* (Hartford, CT: Aetna Life, 1956), 11. Hooker also describes a "similarly unwise insurance of Chinese coolies" in the early nineteenth century. More recently, a number of insurers, including New York Life, have disclosed records related to insurance on the lives of slaves: "Insurance Policies on Slaves: New York Life's Complicated Past," *New York Times*, December 18, 2016.
21. Clough, *A Century of American Life Insurance*; Keller, *Life Insurance Enterprise*, 7.
22. Keller, *Life Insurance Enterprise*, 6–9; Clough, *A Century of American Life Insurance*, 372; U.S. Bureau of the Census, *Census of 1870, Selected Statistics of Age and Sex by States and Territories Table XXIII* (Washington, DC: U.S. Bureau of the Census, 1870).
23. Marquis James, *Metropolitan Life: A Study in Business Growth* (New York: Penguin, 1947); William H. Carr, *From Three Cents a Week: The Story of the Prudential Insurance Company of America* (Englewood Cliffs, NJ: Prentice-Hall, 1975), 22; Keller, *Life Insurance Enterprise*. Until the mid-twentieth century, it was common to refer to insurance companies using the definite article—i.e., "the Equitable," "the Mutual," etc.
24. Abbott, *The Story of New York Life*, 56.
25. J. Owen Stalson, *Marketing Life Insurance* (Homewood, IL: Richard D. Irwin, 1969), 327.
26. Abbott, *The Story of New York Life*, 61.
27. Tom Nicholas, *Venture Capital: An American History* (Cambridge, MA: Harvard University Press, 2019).
28. Peter L. Bernstein, *Against the Gods: The Remarkable Story of Risk* (New York: Wiley, 1996), 88.
29. Ronald E. Seavoy, *The Origins of the American Business Corporation* (New York: Praeger, 1982); Zelizer, *Morals and Markets*, 122. Marquis James, *Biography of a Business, 1792–1942* (New York: Bobbs-Merrill, 1942).
30. Zelizer, *Morals and Markets*; Dalit Baranoff, "Fire Insurance in the United States," in *EH.net Encyclopedia*, 2008, http://eh.net/encyclopedia/fire-insurance-in-the-united-states; Mark Tebeau, *Eating Smoke: Fire in Urban America: 1800–1950* (Baltimore, MD: Johns Hopkins University Press, 2003).
31. William H. A. Carr, *Perils Named and Unnamed: The Story of the Insurance Company of North America* (New York: McGraw-Hill, 1967); James, *Biography of a Business*.
32. Baranoff, "Fire Insurance"; James, *Biography of a Business*; Tebeau, *Eating Smoke*.
33. National Insurance Convention, *Official Report* (New York, 1871), 65.
34. Tebeau, *Eating Smoke*; F. C. Oviatt, "Historical Study of Fire Insurance in the United States," *Annals of the American Academy of Political and Social Science* 26 (September 1905): 155–78.
35. A. L. Todd, *A Spark Lighted in Portland* (New York: McGraw Hill, 1966), 11.
36. Harry Chase Brearley, *Fifty Years of a Civilizing Force: A Historical and Critical Study of the Work of the National Board of Fire Underwriters* (New York: Stokes, 1916), 5–12
37. Brearley, *Civilizing Force*, 119; Todd, *Spark*.

38. Brearley, *Civilizing Force*, 20.
39. Brearley, *Civilizing Force*, 23.
40. *Insurance Times* 2 (July 1869): 491.
41. Brearley, *Civilizing Force*, 26.
42. Stalson, *Marketing Life Insurance*, 363.
43. Keller, *Life Insurance Enterprise*; Clough, *A Century of American Life Insurance*, 372.
44. Stalson, *Marketing Life Insurance*, 433.
45. Stalson, *Marketing Life Insurance*, 436, 439; Keller, *Life Insurance Enterprise*, 81–96.
46. Stalson, *Marketing Life Insurance*, 426–27; Keller, *Life Insurance Enterprise*, 16.
47. Bernstein, *Against the Gods*; Abbott, *The Story of New York Life*.
48. Stalson, *Marketing Life Insurance*, 329.
49. Jonathan Levy, *Freaks of Fortune: The Emerging World of Capitalism and Risk in America* (Cambridge, MA: Harvard University Press, 2012), 60; Lawrence B. Goodheart, *Abolitionist, Actuary, Atheist: Elizur Wright and the Reform Impulse* (Kent, OH: Kent State University Press, 1990).
50. David J. Cummins, *Development of Life Insurance Surrender Values in the United States* (Philadelphia: S. S. Heubner Foundation, 1973), 11.
51. Keller, *Life Insurance Enterprise*, 65.
52. Clough, *A Century of American Life Insurance*, 169.
53. P. Tertius Kempson, "Brief Memoir of Stephen English," *Insurance Times*, 1888, 30.
54. Scott M. Cutlip, *Public Relations History: From the Seventeenth to the Twentieth Century* (New York: Routledge, 2013), 191.
55. Kempson, "Brief Memoir," 17.
56. Zelizer, *Morals and Markets*, 119.
57. Walter C. Wright, "Life Insurance in the United States," *Publications of the American Statistical Association* 1, no. 4 (1888): 127–56, 143.
58. Stalson, *Marketing Life Insurance*, 454.
59. *Insurance Times* 2 (March 1869): 206
60. *Insurance Times* 2 (October 1869): 722.
61. *Insurance Times* 2 (February 1869): 91; *Insurance Times* 2 (June 1869): 424.
62. *Insurance Times* 2 (June 1869): 424.
63. *Insurance Times* 2 (February 1869): 142.
64. *Insurance Times* 2 (August 1869): 542.
65. *Insurance Times* 2 (November 1869): 801.
66. *Insurance Times* 2 (July 1869): 485.
67. *Insurance Times* 3 (October 1870): 715.
68. *Insurance Times* 3 (October 1870): 715.
69. *Insurance Times* 3 (November 1870): 781.
70. *Insurance Times* 3 (December 1870): 861
71. Letter from Charles Lathrop, vice president of New Jersey Mutual, to the editor of the *Brooklyn Eagle*, September 30, 1871, in *Insurance Gazette* 34 (November 1871): 15; *Insurance Times* 4 (September 1871): 655.
72. Letter from Charles Beecher to William M. Force, president of New Jersey Mutual Life, August 2, 1871, in *Insurance Gazette* 34 (November 1871): 16.
73. *Insurance Times* 4 (September 1871): 655. English also made a great show of insisting that the *Insurance Times* approached the Beecher case in a principled manner, in contrast to the "slavish conduct" of the rest of the insurance press, which "for the sake of a little advertising patronage," presumably from New Jersey Mutual, assailed the *Insurance Times* bitterly for their position.
74. *Insurance Times* 3 (November 1870): 781.
75. State of New Jersey, *Report by the Secretary of State as Commissioner of Insurance, Part II Life and Accident Insurance* (Trenton, NJ: Naar, Day and Naar, 1877), ix–x.
76. State of New Jersey, *Report by the Secretary of State*, ix–xlv.

Chapter 2

1. National Insurance Convention, *Official Report* (New York, 1871), 1.
2. *Insurance Times* 4 (February 1871): 97.
3. Paul v. Virginia, 75 U.S. 168 (1869).

4. Howard Dunham, "The Origins and Development of the National Convention of Insurance Commissioners and Insurance Supervision in the U.S.," in *Proceedings of the National Convention of Insurance Commissioners* (Toronto, 1929), 37–64.
5. Temporary National Economic Committee, *Investigation of Concentration of Economic Power; Monograph 28-A; Statement on Life Insurance* (Washington, DC: USGPO, 1941), 64.
6. Howard Bodenhorn, *A History of Banking in Antebellum America: Financial Markets and Economic Development in an Era of Nation-Building* (New York: Cambridge University Press, 2000); Alan Olmstead, *New York Savings Banks in the Antebellum Years, 1819–1861* (Chapel Hill: University of North Carolina Press, 1976); George Alter, Claudia Goldin, and Elyce Rotella, "The Savings of Ordinary Americans: The Philadelphia Saving Fund Society in the Mid-Nineteenth Century," *Journal of Economic History* 54, no. 4 (December 1994): 735–67; Dunham, "Origins and Development," 39.
7. National Insurance Convention, *Official Report*, 76.
8. Temporary National Economic Committee, *Statement on Life Insurance*.
9. *Insurance Times* 3 (June 1870): 440.
10. Lawrence Goodwyn, *The Populist Moment: A Short History of the Agrarian Revolt in America* (New York: Oxford University Press, 1978).
11. Charles Postel, *Equality: An American Dilemma 1866–1916* (New York: Macmillan, 2019).
12. Spencer Kimball, *Insurance and Public Policy: A Study in the Legal Implementation of Social and Economic Public Policy, Based on Wisconsin Records 1835–1959* (Madison: University of Wisconsin Press, 1960), 240.
13. J. Owen Stalson, *Marketing Life Insurance* (Homewood, IL: Richard D. Irwin, 1969); *Insurance Times* 2 (March 1869): 206.
14. David J. Cummins, *Development of Life Insurance Surrender Values in the United States* (Philadelphia: Huebner Foundation, 1973), 12.
15. Shepard B. Clough, *A Century of American Life Insurance: A History of the Mutual Life Insurance Company of New York, 1843–1953* (New York: Columbia University Press, 1946), 157.
16. Cummins, *Surrender Values*, 18
17. Cummins, *Surrender Values*, 23. Several other states passed nonforfeiture laws patterned after the Massachusetts bill, including Michigan (1869), California (1869), Maine (1877), and Missouri (1879).
18. Cummins, *Surrender Values*.
19. Richard White, *The Republic for Which It Stands: The United States during Reconstruction and the Gilded Age, 1865–1896* (New York: Oxford University Press, 2017); Stalson, *Marketing Life Insurance*, 347–50.
20. *Insurance Times* 2 (February 1869): 140.
21. *Insurance Times* 3 (February 1870): 118.
22. *Insurance Times* 2 (November 1869): 802.
23. Gabriel Kolko, *Railroads and Regulation, 1877–1916* (Princeton, NJ: Princeton University Press, 1965).
24. "Life Insurance Companies," *The Nation*, April 16, 1868, 304–9.
25. Paul v. Virginia, 75 U.S. 168 (1869); Scott Harrington, "The History of Federal Involvement in Insurance Regulation," in *Optional Federal Chartering and Regulation of Insurance Companies*, ed. Peter J. Wallison (Washington, DC: AEI Press, 2000), 21–47; A. L. Todd, *A Spark Lighted in Portland* (New York: McGraw Hill, 1966), 19: 18–21; Eric Nordman, "The Early History of the National Association of Insurance Commissioners," *Journal of Insurance Regulation* (2000): 164–78.
26. Harry Chase Brearley, *Fifty Years of a Civilizing Force: A Historical and Critical Study of the Work of the National Board of Fire Underwriters* (New York: Stokes, 1916), 23.
27. *Insurance Times* 2 (March 1869): 189.
28. *Insurance Times* 2 (March 1869): 189.
29. National Insurance Convention, *Official Report*. The states that sent representatives were California, Connecticut, Illinois, Indiana, Kansas, Kentucky, Maine, Maryland, Michigan, Minnesota, Missouri, New Hampshire, Nebraska, New Jersey, New York, Pennsylvania, Rhode Island, Tennessee, and Wisconsin. Clarke may have initially stayed away due to disagreements with New York over how to approach nonforfeiture values. He was present at the second part of the meeting.
30. National Insurance Convention, *Official Report*.
31. National Insurance Convention, *Official Report*, 5.

32. Jason H. Godman, *Fourth Annual Report of the Insurance Department, State of Ohio, Auditor of State's Office, Part 1, Fire and Marine Insurance* (Columbus: Nevins and Myers State Printers, 1871), 6.
33. National Insurance Convention, *Official Report*, 12.
34. National Insurance Convention, *Official Report*, v.
35. National Insurance Convention, *Official Report*, 3.
36. National Insurance Convention, *Official Report*, 137.
37. National Insurance Convention, *Official Report*, 7.
38. National Insurance Convention, *Official Report*, 77.
39. National Insurance Convention, *Official Report*, 13.
40. National Insurance Convention, *Official Report*, 130.
41. National Insurance Convention, *Official Report*, 30.
42. National Insurance Convention, *Official Report*, 19–30.
43. National Insurance Convention, *Official Report*, 22–30.
44. National Insurance Convention, *Official Report*, 29.
45. National Insurance Convention, *Official Report*, 79.
46. National Insurance Convention, *Official Report*, 16–17.
47. National Insurance Convention, *Official Report*, 25.
48. National Insurance Convention, *Official Report*, 66.
49. National Insurance Convention, *Official Report*, 22.
50. National Insurance Convention, *Official Report*, 22.
51. National Insurance Convention, *Official Report*, 68.
52. National Insurance Convention, *Official Report*, 130.
53. National Insurance Convention, *Official Report*, 103.
54. National Insurance Convention, *Official Report*, 125.
55. *New York Daily Herald*, June 1, 1871.
56. National Insurance Convention, *Official Report*, 62.
57. National Insurance Convention, *Official Report*, 63.
58. National Insurance Convention, *Official Report*, 102.
59. Temporary National Economic Committee, *Statement on Life Insurance*, 66.
60. Postel, *Equality*; White, *The Republic for Which It Stands*; Robert Wiebe, *The Search for Order, 1877–1920* (New York: MacMillan, 1967); Gabriel Kolko, *Railroads and Regulation, 1877–1916* (Princeton, NJ: Princeton University Press, 1965); Nordman, "The Early History of the National Association of Insurance Commissioners," 164–78.
61. "What the National Insurance Convention in New York Did," *Nashville Union*, November 4, 1871.
62. *Waterloo Courier*, November 25, 1871.
63. *Weekly Commonwealth* (Topeka, Kansas), August 1871.
64. *New York Times*, November 22, 1871.
65. *New York Times*, November 25, 1871.
66. *New York Times*, December 21, 1871.
67. *Insurance Times* 4 (July 1871): 477.
68. For example, English in 1871 referenced the original mention: "When we first proposed and advocated the Convention in the *Insurance Times*, September 1870, 639...," *Insurance Times* 4 (August 1871): 558.
69. *Insurance Gazette* 34, preface, iii–vi.
70. *Insurance Gazette* 34, preface, April 30, 1872, viii.
71. *Insurance Times* 4 (September 1871): 631.
72. R. Carlyle Buley, *The Equitable Life Assurance Society of the United States, 1859–1964* (New York: Appleton Century, 1967), 140.
73. Clough, *Century of American Life Insurance*, 212.
74. Buley, *The Equitable Life Assurance Society*, 99.
75. Buley, *The Equitable Life Assurance Society*, 149; *The condition of the life insurance companies of the State of New York: Investigation of the Assembly Committee* (Albany: W. S. Manning, 1877); *Documents of the Assembly of the State of New York, Ninety-Sixth Session*, vol. 7, no. 155 (Albany: Argus Company, 1873); Clough, *Century of American Life Insurance*, 212.
76. Stalson, *Marketing Life Insurance*, 543.
77. Clough, *Century of American Life Insurance*, 212; Buley, *The Equitable Life Assurance Society*, 98.

Chapter 3

1. *Black and White: A Monthly Magazine of Facts for Insurance Policy Investors* 10 (1895): 331.
2. "Wolf Silverman Acquitted," *New York Times*, May 21, 1896.
3. *St. Joseph Herald*, June 24, 1896.
4. *The Insurance Press*, May 12, 1897.
5. J. Owen Stalson, *Marketing Life Insurance: Its History in America* (Cambridge, MA: Harvard University Press, 1942)), appendix 25:814; *The Spectator Insurance Year Book for 1901: Life and Miscellaneous* (New York: Spectator Company, 1901), 185–86; *Statistical Abstract of the United States* (Washington, DC: USGPO, 1895), table 27; Amount of Resources and Liabilities of Savings Banks from 1884 to 1895, p. 55. The adult male population in 1890 was roughly sixteen million, implying a population prevalence of approximately fifteen percent: Department of the Interior, *Eleventh Census of the United States: 1890*, part 2, table 1.
6. Jonathan Levy, *Freaks of Fortune* (Cambridge, MA: Harvard University Press, 2012), 167; *Seventh Biennial Report of the Bureau of Labor, Census and Industrial Statistics, State of Wisconsin, 1895–1896; Life Insurance History, 1843–1910: Yearly Business of All Active Life Insurance Companies from Organization* (New York: Spectator Company, 1911).
7. Kent McKeever, "A Short History of Tontines," *Fordham Journal of Corporate and Financial Law* 15 (2010): 491.
8. Shepard B. Clough, *A Century of American Life Insurance: A History of the Mutual Life Insurance Company of New York 1843–1943* (New York: Columbia University Press, 1946), 139.
9. Morton Keller, *The Life Insurance Enterprise, 1885–1910: A Study in the Limits of Corporate Power* (Cambridge, MA: Harvard University Press, 1963), 29. Clough, *Century of American Life Insurance.*
10. Roger L. Ransom and Richard Sutch, "Tontine Insurance and the Armstrong Investigation: A Case of Stifled Innovation, 1868–1905," *Journal of Economic History* 47, no. 2 (1987): 379–90.
11. Clough, *Century of American Life Insurance*, 140.
12. Advertisement, Connecticut Mutual Insurance Company, *Weekly Underwriter* 54: 26 (1896), 427.
13. Clough, *Century of American Life Insurance*, 141.
14. *Conditions of the Life Insurance Companies in the State of New York*, Investigation by the Assembly Committee (Albany, 1877).
15. Ransom and Sutch, "Tontine Insurance." Some analyses have suggested that the deferred dividend plans were not bad investments and have been judged too harshly by critics.
16. Daniel T. Rodgers, *Atlantic Crossings: Social Politics in a Progressive Age* (Cambridge, MA: Harvard University Press, 1998), 219.
17. R. Carlyle Buley, *The American Life Convention 1906–1952—A Study in the History of Insurance* (New York: Appleton, 1953), 118. The basic idea behind assessment plans is still in use today by Christian sharing ministries, which are alternatives to health insurance that don't use actuarial methods but rather assess members to cover costs.
18. Walter C. Wright, "Life Insurance in the United States," *Publications of the American Statistical Association* 1, no. 4 (1888): 127–56, 144.
19. Wright, "Life Insurance," 142.
20. Stalson, *Marketing Life Insurance*; Levy, *Freaks of Fortune*, 194.
21. Wright, "Life Insurance," 147.
22. "In the Courts," *Weekly Underwriter* 54, no. 24 (1896): 395.
23. Buley, *The American Life Convention*, 119.
24. *Weekly Underwriter* 54, no. 21 (1896).
25. *Twenty-Seventh Annual Report of the Report of Superintendent of Insurance for the state of Kansas, For the year ending 1897*, Topeka, Kansas, 1898.
26. *Baltimore Underwriter*, September 20, 1895, 129.
27. *The Indicator*, November 5, 1908, 336.
28. Keller, *Life Insurance Enterprise.*
29. *The Metropolitan Life Insurance Company: Its History, Its Present Position in the Insurance World. Its Home Office and the Work Carried on Therein* (New York: Metropolitan Life, 1914), 12.
30. Marquis James, *The Metropolitan Life: A Study in Business Growth* (New York: Viking Press, 1947).
31. Buley, *The American Life Convention*, 108.
32. Stalson, *Marketing Life Insurance*, 350.

33. Roger Grant, *Insurance Reform: Consumer Action in the Progressive Era* (Ames: Iowa State Press, 1979), 8.
34. Grant, *Insurance Reform; Texas Insurance*, March 21, 1904.
35. Clough, *Century of American Life Insurance*, 91.
36. Stalson, *Marketing Life Insurance*, 350, 524.
37. Stalson, *Marketing Life Insurance*, 350.
38. "Connecticut Insurance Report of 1896," *Weekly Underwriter* 54, no. 20 (1896): 340.
39. Grant, *Insurance Reform*, 16; Wisconsin Life Insurance Company, "Collected Speeches and Statements on the Nature of the Life Insurance Business," pamphlet.
40. Clough, *Century of American Life Insurance*, 240; Keller, *Life Insurance Enterprise*, 9.
41. Grant, *Insurance Reform*, 16.
42. *Weekly Underwriter* 54, no. 17 (April 23, 1896): 273.
43. Grant, *Insurance Reform*, 12; Spencer L. Kimball, *Insurance and Public Policy: A Study in the Legal Implementation of Social and Economic Public Policy, Based on Wisconsin Records, 1835–1959* (Madison: University of Wisconsin, 1960).
44. Grant, *Insurance Reform*, 15; *Proceedings of the National Convention of Insurance Commissioners* (St. Louis, 1891), 54–55.
45. Gabriel Kolko, *Railroads and Regulation, 1877–1916* (Princeton, NJ: Princeton University Press, 1965).
46. *Weekly Underwriter* 54, no. 10 (March 7, 1896): 156.
47. "Missouri Report—Life Insurance," *Weekly Underwriter* 54, no. 19 (May 9, 1896): 322.
48. Grant, *Insurance Reform*, 13.
49. Keller, *Life Insurance Enterprise*, 27–29.
50. Buley, *The American Life Convention*, 100.
51. Grant, *Insurance Reform*, 135.
52. Grant, *Insurance Reform*, 18.
53. *Weekly Underwriter* 54, no. 15 (April 11, 1896): 234.
54. McNall v. Metropolitan Life Insurance Company, 65 Kan. 694 (1902).
55. *Kansas Agitator*, December 16, 1898, 8.
56. "The End of McNall," *Travelers Record*, April 4, 1899, 4.
57. Keller, *Life Insurance Enterprise*, 223.
58. New York Life advertisement, *Weekly Underwriter* 54, no. 1 (1896): 16.
59. Clough, *Century of American Life Insurance*, 190.
60. Levy, *Freaks of Fortune*, 266.
61. Grant, *Insurance Reform*, 16.
62. R. Carlyle Buley, *The Equitable Life Assurance Society of the United States, 859–1954* (New York: Appleton-Century-Crofts, 1967), 493.
63. Quoted in Grant, *Insurance Reform*, 26.
64. Grant, *Insurance Reform*, 27; *Spectator*, September 8, 1904.
65. Keller, *Life Insurance Enterprise*, 187.
66. Keller, *Life Insurance Enterprise*, 238.
67. Keller, *Life Insurance Enterprise*, 238.
68. Clough, *Century of American Life Insurance*, 163; Keller, *Life Insurance Enterprise*, 237.
69. Grant, *Insurance Reform*, 28–54.
70. Keller, *Life Insurance Enterprise*, 240.
71. Upton Sinclair, *The Jungle* (New York: Octavo Publishing, 1906); Ray Stannard Baker, "The Railroads on Trial," *McClure's, XXVI* (November, 1905–March, 1906): 47–59, 179–94, 318–31, 398–411, 535–49; XXVII (June, 1906): 131–45; Ida Tarbell, *The History of the Standard Oil Company* (New York: McClure Phillips and Company, 1904).
72. Clough, *Century of American Life Insurance*, 218.
73. Grant, *Insurance Reform*, 28; *American Underwriter* (New York), October 1904.
74. John Ryckman, "Despotism of Combined Millions," *The Era* 14, no. 5 (November 1904): 401–16.
75. Grant, *Insurance Reform*, 28–32.
76. *New York World*, February 12, 1905.
77. Keller, *Life Insurance Enterprise*, 251; Clough, *Century of American Life Insurance*, 218.
78. Keller, *Life Insurance Enterprise*, 252.
79. *Testimony Taken Before the Joint Committee of the Senate and Assembly of the State of New York to Investigate and Examine into the Business and Affairs of Life Insurance Companies Doing Business in the State of New York*, 1905.

80. Keller, *Life Insurance Enterprise*, 254.
81. *New York Tribune*, January 1, 1906.
82. *Passaic Daily News*, June 2, 1906.
83. Keller, *Life Insurance Enterprise*, 254.
84. Buley, *The Equitable Life Assurance Society*, 1:699.
85. Clough, *Century of American Life Insurance*, 231.
86. Keller, *Life Insurance Enterprise*, 269.
87. Levy, *Freaks of Fortune*.
88. "McCall Resigns," *Buffalo Evening News*, January 2, 1906.
89. Keller, *Life Insurance Enterprise*, 267.
90. *New York State Library Bulletin Review of Legislation* 326 (1906): 217–27.
91. Keller, *Life Insurance Enterprise*, 255.
92. "Does Connecticut Need These Laws?," *Hartford Courant*, November 21, 1906.
93. Keller, *Life Insurance Enterprise*, 255.
94. Grant, *Insurance Reform*, 55.

Chapter 4

1. *Proceedings of the Ninth Annual Meeting of the New Jersey State Conference on Charities and Corrections* (Camden: MacCrellish and Quigley, 1910), 185.
2. Roger H. Grant, *Insurance Reform: Consumer Action in the Progressive Era* (Ames: Iowa State University Press, 1979), 161.
3. Morton Keller, *The Life Insurance Enterprise, 1885–1910: A Study in the Limits of Corporate Power* (Cambridge, MA: Harvard University Press, 1963), 242.
4. *Passaic Daily News*, June 2, 1906.
5. *Hackensack Record*, November 28, 1906.
6. Keller, *Life Insurance Enterprise*, 261.
7. R. Carlyle Buley, *The American Life Convention 1906–1952—A Study in the History of Insurance* (New York: Appleton Century Crofts, 1953), 264.
8. Buley, *American Life Convention*, 264.
9. Buley, *American Life Convention*, 267.
10. Keller, *Life Insurance Enterprise*, 241.
11. Daniel T. Rogers, *Atlantic Crossings: Social Politics in a Progressive Age* (Cambridge, MA: Harvard University Press, 1998).
12. R. Carlyle Buley, *The Equitable Life Assurance Society of the United States, 1859–1964* (New York: Appleton Century Crofts, 1967), 301.
13. *El Paso Herald*, February 24, 1906.
14. *Houston Post*, September 30, 1906.
15. "Metropolitan Life Decides to Quite Lone Star State," *Eastern Underwriter* 9, no. 2 (January 2, 1908): 7.
16. Grant, *Insurance Reform*, 65; "Compulsory Investment Law," *Salt Lake Tribune*, June 3, 1912.
17. Buley, *American Life Convention*, 326.
18. Keller, *Life Insurance Enterprise*, 275; Buley, *American Life Convention*, 247.
19. *The Indicator*, July 20, 1909.
20. *The Indicator*, June 20, 1908.
21. "Mutual Interests," *The Indicator*, August 5, 1909.
22. Buley, *American Life Convention*.
23. Lawrence B. Goodheart, *Abolitionist, Actuary, Atheist: Elizur Wright and the Reform Impulse* (Kent, OH: Kent State University Press, 1990), 166.
24. Allan Gal, *Brandeis of Boston* (Cambridge, MA: Harvard University Press, 1980), 96–97.
25. *Proceedings of the Ninth Annual Meeting of the New Jersey State Conference on Charities and Corrections.*
26. *Proceedings of the Ninth Annual Meeting of the New Jersey State Conference on Charities and Corrections.*
27. *Proceedings of the Ninth Annual Meeting of the New Jersey State Conference on Charities and Corrections.*
28. *Proceedings of the Ninth Annual Meeting of the New Jersey State Conference on Charities and Corrections.*

29. Daniel R. Wadhwani, "The Institutional Foundations of Personal Finance: Innovations in U.S. Savings Banks, 1880–1920," *Business History Review* 85, no. 3 (2011): 499–528.
30. "Savings Bank Insurance," *The Indicator*, July 20, 1908.
31. "Rush in Where Angels Are Afraid to Tread," *Insurance Field*, April, 4, 1907.
32. Grant, *Insurance Reform*, 49.
33. "For State Insurance," *Oshkosh Northwestern*, April 24, 1907.
34. New Zealand Government Life Insurance Department, "A Brief Survey of New Zealand's State Life Insurance Specially Prepared for Distribution at the New Zealand International Exhibition, Christchurch, 1906–7," in The Pamphlet Collection of Sir Robert Stout, vol. 78, 1905.
35. "War on Wisconsin Laws," *The Insurance Field*, January 16, 1908.
36. Mark A. Smith, "The State Life Fund of Wisconsin," *Journal of Political Economy* 25, no. 5 (1917): 442–63.
37. "Life Insurance by the State Explained by the Wisconsin Commissioner of Insurance," *Plumas National Bulletin*, January 9, 1913.
38. "Socialism Denied," *Calgary Herald*, August 6, 1912.
39. "Life Insurance by the State Explained by the Wisconsin Commissioner of Insurance."
40. William Duffus, *Report on Agricultural Settlement and Farm Ownership, Part 1: State Loans to Farmers* (Wisconsin State Board of Public Affairs, 1912), 23.
41. Gal, *Brandeis of Boston*, 1980.
42. "State Insurance Is a Burden on the People," *Kansas Workman*, April 1, 1916.
43. "State Insurance Is a Burden on the People"; see also *Kansas Workman*, March 1, 1916.
44. *Proceedings of the Annual Session, National Convention* (Mutual Life Underwriters, 1913), 26.
45. Grant, *Insurance Reform*, 64.
46. Grant, *Insurance Reform*; Rogers, *Atlantic Crossings*.
47. *Wisconsin Medical Journal* 14 (January 1916): 314.
48. "La Folette in No Serious Danger," *Chippewa Herald-Telegram*, September 30, 1910.
49. "Knife Ordeal Over, Prospects Are Good," *Osh Kosh Northwestern*, October 4, 1910.
50. "Janicke Appointed to Fair Oaks Board," *Wisconsin State Journal*, April 18, 1913.
51. "In Sympathy," *Wisconsin State Journal*, March 5, 1915.
52. "Wisconsin Experiment Hurt," *Chicago Tribune*, April 15, 1915.
53. "State Life Fund Is Valid," *Journal Times*, April 8, 1915.
54. "State Insurance Failure," *Wichita Beacon*, May 14, 1916.
55. "State Life Fund Fiasco," *Hartford Courant*, September 2, 1916.
56. "State Insurance Favored," *Osh Kosh Northwestern*, March 13, 1916; *Fifty-First Annual Report of the Commissioner of Insurance, Life and Fraternal Insurance, State of Wisconsin* (Madison, 1920), 4. "How Individual Insurance Commissioners May Work Harm," *Hartford Courant*, July 22, 1917.
57. Grant, *Insurance Reform*, 63.
58. *Hartford Courant*, January 2, 1916.
59. "Old Age Pensions," *Insurance Press*, January 6, 1909.
60. "State Insurance Unsound Because There Is no Guarantee of Payment," *Kansas Workman*, September 1, 1916.
61. Mutual Life of New York Advertisement, *Eastern Underwriter* 9, no. 1 (January 2, 1908): 16.
62. New York Life Advertisement, *Eastern Underwriter* 9, no. 4 (January 23, 1908): 16.
63. "Can You Sell Life Insurance?," *Eastern Underwriter* 9, no. 40 (October 1, 1908): 3.
64. J. Owen Stalson, *Marketing Life Insurance: It's History in America* (Cambridge, MA: Harvard University Press, 1942), 578.
65. "Metropolitan Men Honored," *Eastern Underwriter* 9, no. 4 (January 23, 1908): 7.
66. *The Indicator*, August 5, 1908.
67. *The Indicator*, June 20, 1908.
68. *The Indicator*, July 5, 1909.
69. *The Indicator*, August 5, 1909.
70. Keller, *Life Insurance Enterprise*.
71. Keller, *Life Insurance Enterprise*, 263.
72. Rogers, *Atlantic Crossings*, 262–65.
73. *The Indicator*, August 5, 1909.
74. Keller, *Life Insurance Enterprise*, 290; Jonathan Levy, *Freaks of Fortune* (Cambridge, MA: Harvard University Press, 2012).

75. "Fighting Tuberculosis," *Insurance Press*, January 6, 1909. This is not completely without precedent. The Mutual distributed an emergency health guide to members in 1875. *Plain Directions for Accidents, Emergencies and Poisons* (New York: Mutual Life Insurance Company of America, 1875).

76. *The Metropolitan Life Insurance Company: Its History, Its Present Place in the Insurance World, Its Home Office Building and the Work Carried on Within* (New York: Metropolitan Life, 1914), 23.

77. Keller, *Life Insurance Enterprise*, 291.

78. *The Metropolitan Life Insurance Company*, 93.

79. Rogers, *Atlantic Crossings*, 262.

80. *The Metropolitan Life Insurance Company*.

81. *The Metropolitan Life Insurance Company*.

82. Louis Dublin, *Mortality Statistics of Insured Wage-earners and their Families: Experience of the Metropolitan Life Insurance Company Industrial Department, 1911–1916, in the United States and Canada* (New York: Metropolitan Life Insurance Company), 1919.

83. Met Life Report, iv.

84. Levy, *Freaks of Fortune*.

85. *Proceedings of the Annual Session, National Convention*.

86. *Proceedings of the Annual Session, National Convention*.

87. *Proceedings of the Annual Session, National Convention*.

88. *Spectator Yearbook of Insurance* (New York: Spectator Company, 1920), 834.

89. Lewell C. Butler, *Unveiling Tributes* (Nashville: Press of Brandon Printing Company, 1909), 8.

90. Walter S. Nichols, "Fraternal Insurance in the United States: Its Origin, Development, Character and Status," *Annals of the American Academy of Political and Social Science* 70 (1917): 109–22.

91. Stalson, *Marketing Life Insurance*.

92. *Proceedings of the National Conference of Insurance Commissioners* (Del Monte, CA, 1915), 23.

93. "The Fraternal Situation," in *Proceedings of the National Conference of Insurance Commissioners* (Denver, 1918), 176.

94. *Spectator Yearbook of Insurance* (New York: Spectator Company, 1920).

95. *Proceedings of the National Fraternal Conference of America* (Chicago, 1920), 102.

96. W. E. B. Dubois, *The Philadelphia Negro* (Philadelphia: University of Pennsylvania, 1899).

97. Walter B. Weare, *Black Business in the New South* (Durham, NC: Duke University Press, 1993).

98. Weare, *Black Business*, 16.

99. *Spectator Yearbook of Insurance* (New York: Spectator Company, 1920), 48.

100. *Green Bay Gazette*, April 16, 1917.

101. Douglas B. Craig, *Progressives at War: William F. McAdoo and Newton D. Baker, 1863–1941* (Baltimore: Johns Hopkins University Press, 2013), 107. War risk insurance was established in the Department of the Treasury on the insistence of William McAdoo, although Newton Baker tried to make a case that it belonged in the War Department. Bureau of War Insurance, *Annual Report of the Director of War Insurance* (Washington, DC: USGPO, 1920).

102. Theda Skocpol, *Protecting Soldiers and Mothers: The Political Origins of Social Policy in the United States* (Cambridge, MA: Harvard University Press, 1992).

103. Honorable Julian W. Mack, "Scope and Meaning of Act of October 02 2017 Providing for Family Allowances, Allotments, Compensation and Insurance, for the Military and Naval Forces of the United States," Bulletin No. 3, Bureau of War Risk Insurance, Department of the Treasury (Washington, DC: USGPO, 1917).

104. Samuel McCune Lindsay, "Purpose and Scope of War Risk Insurance," *Annals of the American Academy of Political and Social Science* 79, no. 1 (September 1918): 52–68.

105. Mack, "Scope and Meaning."

106. Mack, "Scope and Meaning."

107. Mack, "Scope and Meaning." In fact, there was considerable pressure on the government from insurers to not disparage the private industry or any particular company.

108. Mack, "Scope and Meaning."

109. Lindsay, "War Risk Insurance."

110. Bureau of War Insurance, *Annual Report of the Director of War Insurance* (Washington, DC: USGPO, 1920).

111. Bureau of War Insurance, *Annual Report of the Director of War Insurance*.

112. "War Halting Improvement," *Nebraska State Journal*, December 7, 1917.
113. *Proceedings of the National Convention of Insurance Commissioners* (Denver, 1918), 57.
114. "Insurance Men Keep Their Eyes on Washington," *Chicago Daily Tribune*, March 11, 1918.
115. "Aspersions upon Life Insurance Companies," Letter of William de Lancey, Director of the War Risk Insurance Bureau, December 24, 1917, Department of the Treasury, Compilation of War Risk Insurance Letters, Treasury Decisions and War Department Circulars, Relating to War Risk Insurance from December 21, 1917, to April 1, 1919, 5.
116. *Proceedings of the National Convention of Insurance Commissioners*, 186.
117. *War Risk Insurance Bills: Hearings Before the House Committee on Interstate and Foreign Commerce*, 66th Cong. 102 (1920) (statement by H. H. Raege, representative of the American Legion).
118. *War Risk Insurance Bills:* (letter from Private Sidney DeGraw, February 9, 1920).
119. *Establishment of a Veteran's Bureau: Hearings on H.R. 6611, Before the Senate Comm. on Finance*, 67th Cong. (1921), July 5 and 7, 1921.
120. "An Entering Wedge," *Los Angeles Times*, July 15, 1924.
121. *LaCross Tribune*, January 26, 1923.
122. "An Entering Wedge."
123. Modern Woodmen, "2021 Annual Report to Members," www.modernwoodmen.org/about-us/what-we-are/.
124. *Spectator Yearbook of Insurance.* Author's calculations.
125. Wisconsin State Life Fund, https://oci.wi.gov/.
126. Savings Bank Life Insurance, https://www.sbli.com/.

Chapter 5

1. Personal Recollection of Mr. Charles Stetson Wheeler Jr., San Francisco Fire and Earthquake Digital Collection, http://oac.cdlib.org.
2. Personal Recollection of Mr. Charles Stetson Wheeler Jr., San Francisco Fire and Earthquake Digital Collection, http://oac.cdlib.org.
3. Dennis Smith, *San Francisco Is Burning: The Untold Story of the 1906 Earthquake and Fire* (New York: Viking, 2005).
4. San Francisco Chamber of Commerce, *Report of the Special Committee of the Board of Trustees of the Chamber of Commerce of San Francisco on Insurance Settlements Incident to the San Francisco Fire* (1906), 7.
5. Personal Recollection of Mr. Charles Stetson Wheeler Jr., San Francisco Fire and Earthquake Digital Collection, http://oac.cdlib.org.
6. Jack London, "Story of an Eyewitness," *Colliers*, May 5, 1906.
7. Personal Recollection of Mr. Charles Stetson Wheeler Jr., San Francisco Fire and Earthquake Digital Collection, http://oac.cdlib.org.
8. Personal Recollection of Mr. Charles Stetson Wheeler Jr., San Francisco Fire and Earthquake Digital Collection, http://oac.cdlib.org.
9. London, "Story of an Eyewitness."
10. San Francisco Chamber of Commerce, *Report of the Special Committee.*
11. Personal Recollection of Mr. Charles Stetson Wheeler Jr., San Francisco Fire and Earthquake Digital Collection, http://oac.cdlib.org.
12. William H. A. Carr, *Perils Named and Unnamed: The Dramatic Story of the Insurance Company of North America* (New York: McGraw Hill, 1967), 75.
13. Lawrence Kennedy, *"Progress of the Fire in San Francisco as shown by an analysis of original documents,"* Collection of Documents of the Earthquake History Committee, Museum of the City of San Francisco, 1906.
14. "All America Quick at Relief Response," *Los Angeles Times*, April 20, 1906.
15. Smith, *San Francisco Is Burning*, 3.
16. John Eugene Pierce, *Development of Comprehensive Insurance for the Household* (Homewood, IL: Richard Irwin, 1958), 205.
17. Carr, *Perils Named and Unnamed*, 74.
18. *The Argonaut*, October 6, 1906, 118.
19. *Weekly Underwriter* 75, no. 3 (July 21, 1906): 48.
20. *The Argonaut*, October 6, 1906, 118, 1906; *Weekly Underwriter* 75, no. 2 (July 14, 1906): 22–23.
21. *Weekly Underwriter* 75, no. 2 (July 14, 1906): 22–23.

22. Carr, *Perils Named and Unnamed*, 75.
23. Ted Steinberg, *Acts of God: The Unnatural History of Natural Disaster in America* (New York: Oxford University Press, 2000).
24. St. Paul Fire and Marine Insurance Company to Governor George C. Pardee, June 16, 1906, Earthquake Settlements, George C. Pardee Papers, Bancroft Library, University of California Berkeley.
25. "Powerful Body Is to Demand Fair Treatment," *San Francisco Call*, June 26, 1906.
26. "Fire Insurance Roll of Honor Is Posted in the Ferry Building," *San Francisco Call*, July 11, 1906.
27. "The San Francisco Disaster: Honest and Dishonest Insurance," Speech of Julius Kahn, of California, in the House of Representatives, June 28, 1906.
28. "Unfair Tactics Here Costing Them Dearly. Policyholders Seek Terms That Are Just," *San Francisco Call*, July 2, 1906.
29. Atlas Insurance Company, "San Francisco Situation," April 30, 1906, The 1906 San Francisco Earthquake and Digital Collection, Bancroft Library, University of California Berkley.
30. Patricia Grossi and Robert Muir-Wood, *The 1906 San Francisco Earthquake and Fire: Perspectives on a Modern Super Cat* (Newark, CA: Risk Management Solutions, 2006).
31. A. M. Best, *Best's Special Report upon the San Francisco Losses and Settlements of the Two Hundred and Forty-three Institutions Involved in the Conflagration of April 18–21, 1906* (New York: A. M. Best, 1907).
32. A. M. Best, *A History of AM Best: The Company* (Oldwick, NJ: A. M. Best, 2020).
33. "President's Address," in *Proceedings of the National Convention of Insurance Commissioners* (Richmond, 1907), 19.
34. "Progressive Lessons in Insurance," *San Francisco Call*, June 30, 1906.
35. San Francisco Chamber of Commerce, *Report of the Special Committee*, 42.
36. Frank J. Devlin, "Some Lessons from the Conflagration and a Prophesy," Annual Meeting Fire Underwriters' Association of the Pacific, January 17, 1907.
37. Atlas Insurance Company, "San Francisco Situation," August 3, 1906, The 1906 San Francisco Earthquake and Digital Collection, Bancroft Library, (University of California Berkley).
38. Roger Lowenstein, *America's Bank: The Epic Struggle to Create the Federal Reserve* (New York: Penguin Press, 2015).
39. Harold James, Peter Borscheid, David Gugerli, and Tobias Straumann, *The Value of Risk: Swiss Re and the History of Reinsurance* (London: Oxford, 2013), 173.
40. See David A. Moss, *When All Else Fails: Government as the Ultimate Risk Manager* (Cambridge, MA: Harvard University Press, 2002); see Steinberg, *Acts of God*, for some perspective on the history of federal disaster relief.
41. Dalit Baronoff, "Fire Insurance in the United States," in *EH.net Encyclopedia*, ed. Robert Whaples, March 16, 2008, https://eh.net/encyclopedia/fire-insurance-in-the-united-states/.
42. Baronoff, "Fire Insurance in the United States."
43. Spencer L. Kimball and Ronald N. Boyce, "The Adequacy of State Insurance Rate Regulation: The McCarran Ferguson Act in Historical Perspective," *Michigan Law Review* 65, no. 4 (1958): 545–78.
44. Marquis James, *Biography of a Business* (New York: Bobbs-Merrill, 1942), 98.
45. Mark Tebeau, *Eating Smoke: Fire in Urban America, 1800–1950* (Baltimore: Johns Hopkins University Press, 2003), 61.
46. Kenneth J. Meier, *The Political Economy of Regulation: The Case of Insurance* (Albany: State University of New York, 1988), 51.
47. Meier, *Political Economy of Regulation*, 51.
48. Meier, *Political Economy of Regulation*, 52.
49. Harry Chase Brearley, *Fifty Years of a Civilizing Force: An Historical and Critical Study of the Work of the National Board of Fire Underwriters* (New York: Frederick A. Stokes, 1916).
50. Brearley, *Fifty Years*, 48.
51. Meier, *Political Economy of Regulation*, 52.
52. Brearley, *Fifty Years*, 227.
53. Tebeau, *Eating Smoke*, 177.
54. Spencer L. Kimball, *Insurance and Public Policy: A Study in the Legal Implementation of Social and Economic Policy, Based on Wisconsin Records, 1835–1959* (Madison: University of Wisconsin Press, 1960).
55. Meier, *Political Economy of Regulation*, 52
56. *Weekly Underwriter* 54, no. 4 (January 25, 1896): 52.

57. *Baltimore Underwriter*, August 20, 1895.
58. *Baltimore Underwriter*, October 21, 1895, 187.
59. H. Roger Grant, *Insurance Reform: Consumer Action in the Progressive Era* (Ames: Iowa State University Press, 1979), 73.
60. Brearley, *Fifty Years*, 75.
61. "Valued Policy Law in Georgia," *Baltimore Underwriter*, December 20, 1895, 278.
62. Grant, *Insurance Reform*, 74.
63. *Baltimore Underwriter*, October 21, 1895, 187.
64. *Baltimore Underwriter*, November 5, 1895, 1.
65. "In Sing-Sing for Life," *Democrat and Chronicle* (Rochester, New York), November 10, 1895.
66. *Weekly Underwriter* 54, no. 24 (June 13, 1896): 397.
67. *Weekly Underwriter* 54, no. 18 (May 2, 1896): 297.
68. Grant, *Insurance Reform*, 77.
69. Grant, *Insurance Reform*, 19.
70. *Twenty-Eighth Annual Report of the Superintendent of Insurance of the State of Kansas, For the Year ending December 31, 1897* (Topeka) June 1898, xxxi.
71. Grant, *Insurance Reform*, 19.
72. Ohio was followed by Michigan (1887); Arkansas, Nebraska, Texas, and Kansas (1889); and Missouri, Maine, New Hampshire, and Georgia (1891). Nearly twenty states had passed anticompact laws by 1906, and twenty-three had done so by 1913.
73. *The Chronicle, A Weekly Insurance Journal*, July 25, 1895.
74. Baronoff, "Fire Insurance in the United States." https://eh.net/encyclopedia/fire-insurance-in-the-united-states/.
75. *Weekly Underwriter* 54, no. 21 (May 23, 1896): 348.
76. *Kansas City Times*, July 25, 1897; Grant, *Insurance Reform*, 80–81.
77. Grant, *Insurance Reform*, 80–81.
78. Grant, *Insurance Reform*, 80–81.
79. Grant, *Insurance Reform*, 88.
80. "Twenty-Eighth Annual Report of the Superintendent of Insurance for the State of Kansas," 1898, xxxiv.
81. Grant, *Insurance Reform*, 88; Kimball, *Insurance and Public Policy*.
82. Tebeau, *Eating Smoke*, 194.
83. Tebeau, *Eating Smoke*.
84. Best, *A History of AM Best*.
85. Tebeau, *Eating Smoke*, 263.
86. Tebeau, *Eating Smoke*, 199.
87. Alfred A. Dean, "Fire Insurance Rates," in *Annual Proceedings of the National Convention of Insurance Commissioners* (Milwaukee, 1898), 583.
88. Alfred A. Dean, "Fire Insurance Rates," in *Annual Proceedings of the National Convention of Insurance Commissioners* (Milwaukee, 1898), 567.

Chapter 6

1. "Terrific Explosion in New York Harbor—Fire Companies Involved for Heavy Losses," *Weekly Underwriter*, August 5, 1916, 123.
2. "Affairs at Black Tom," *Weekly Underwriter*, September 23, 1916, 339. The National Board of Fire Underwriters unsuccessfully petitioned the Interstate Commerce Commission to investigate the railroads.
3. "Black Tom Explosion Loss—Committee Recommends Compromise," *Weekly Underwriter*, October 14, 1916, 455.
4. "Fire Insurance Is on Trial," *Fresno Morning Republican*, June 25, 1906.
5. Franklin Hichorn, "The Uncertain Basis of Fire Insurance," *San Francisco Call*, June 17, 1906, 18.
6. Hichorn, "The Uncertain Basis of Fire Insurance."
7. *The Indicator*, November 5, 1909, 339.
8. *The Indicator*, November 5, 1908, 333.
9. Gabriel Kolko, *Railroads and Regulation, 1877–1916* (Princeton, NJ: Princeton University Press, 1965).

10. H. Roger Grant, *Insurance Reform: Consumer Action in the Progressive Era* (Ames: Iowa State University Press, 1979), 102.
11. *Fortieth Annual Report of the Superintendent of Insurance for the State of Kansas* (Topeka: State Printing Company, 1910).
12. German Alliance Ins. Co v. Lewis, 233 U.S. 389 (1914).
13. *Agency History, Texas Department of Insurance*, Texas State Library and Archives Commission.
14. Grant, *Insurance Reform*.
15. Michael J. Lansing, *Insurgent Democracy: The Non-Partisan League in North American Politics* (Chicago: University of Chicago Press, 2015); Jack Lufkin, "Property Insurance for Iowa Farmers: The Rise of Mutuals," *Annals of Iowa* 54, no. 1 (Winter 1995): 25–45.
16. Lufkin, "Property Insurance."
17. Lufkin, "Property Insurance," 43.
18. Iowa, Illinois, and Wisconsin had far more mutuals than Nebraska, Kansas, Missouri, Ohio, and the Dakotas. Virginia Wadsley, *Bear Ye One Another's Burdens: The First 100 Years of Farmers Mutual Hail Insurance Company of Iowa* (Des Moines: Farmers Mutual Hail Insurance Company, 1993), 92.
19. Biographical sketch of Special Agent W. C. Bredenhagen, Hail Insurance Papers, St. Paul Fire and Marine Insurance Company archives. Bredenhagen, who was born in Germany, obtained the German government policies through an inheritance and brought them to the St. Paul.
20. Ann Kelchburg, *A History of the Continental Insurance Company* (New York: Continental Corporation, 1979).
21. "Protection for the Bread Basket of the Nation," *St. Paul Letter*, 1953, Hail Insurance Papers, St. Paul Fire and Marine Insurance Company archives.
22. Preference for cash is seen in letters to agents from St. Paul archives 1899 and 1909, Hail Insurance Papers, St. Paul Fire and Marine Insurance Company archives.
23. "Crop Hail Insurance and the St. Paul," April 1968, Hail Insurance Papers, St. Paul Fire and Marine Insurance Company archives.
24. Wadsley, *Bear Ye One Another's Burdens*, 70.
25. Wadsley, *Bear Ye One Another's Burdens*, 366.
26. Lufkin, "Property Insurance."
27. Advertisement, St. Paul Mutual Hail and Cyclone Company 1914, Hail Insurance Papers, St. Paul Fire and Marine Insurance Company archives. "Not ours" written on the top of the page.
28. Wadsley, *Bear Ye One Another's Burdens*, 20.
29. W. C. Taylor, "*Biennial Report for 1916*," in *Public Documents for 1916* (Bismark: North Dakota, 1916), 1309.
30. Lansing, *Insurgent Democracy*, 156.
31. "North Dakota Hail Affairs," *Weekly Underwriter*, December 2, 1916, 627; "North Dakota Hail Writings," *Weekly Underwriter*, April 26, 1919, 618.
32. Gilbert W. Cooke, "North Dakota State Hail Insurance, 1911–1936," *Journal of the Business of the University of Chicago* 11, no. 3 (July 1938): 277–307.
33. "Enormous Hail Business," *Weekly Underwriter*, May 7, 1919, 740.
34. "Hail Problems Continue," *Weekly Underwriter*, November 11, 1922, 970.
35. Spencer L. Kimball, *Insurance and Public Policy: A Study in the Legal Implementation of Social and Economic Policy, Based on Wisconsin Records, 1835–1959* (Madison: University of Wisconsin Press, 1960), 55.
36. "Ohio Farmers' Field Outing," *Weekly Underwriter*, June 24, 1916.
37. *Wisconsin State Journal*, March 24, 1916.
38. In 1915, the state treasurer unsuccessfully tried to get the attorney general to bring a "friendly suit" to see whether the state could truly be liable for these obligations, but the attorney general found that the insurance laws were constitutional and declined "to become a party to any arrangement" for the purpose of "attacking the law in the courts." "State Treasurer Johnson Seeks Friendly Suits Over 3 Funds," *Watertown News*, April 9, 1915, 1915.
39. "Wisconsin State Fund Hit," *Chicago Tribune*, March 27, 1916.
40. *Wassau Daily Herald*, April 11, 1916.
41. *Chicago Tribune*, March 27, 1916.
42. As recently as the 1950s, the fund charged half of bureau rates. Kimball, *Insurance and Public Policy*, 55.
43. "The Attitude of Investigating Committees Regarding Ratemaking Bureaus," in *Annual Proceedings of the National Convention of Insurance Commissioners* (Asheville, NC, 1914), 119.

44. "Saving Mississippi," *Weekly Underwriter*, June 3, 1922, 118.
45. "Constant Drain on Tennessee," *Nashville American*, April 11, 1907, letter to the editor signed "Home Lover."
46. *Insurance Field*, April 27, 1907.
47. "Negro Fire Insurance Company Needed," *Nashville Globe*, February 4, 1910.
48. "First Negro Fire Insurance Company Now Organized," *Buffalo American*, August 12, 1920.
49. "Negro Fire Insurance Company Gets Charter," *Arkansas Democrat*, June 10, 1921.
50. William Hotchkiss, "What Hughes Did for Insurance," *Nebraska State Journal*, September 24, 1916.
51. Kenneth J. Meier, *The Political Economy of Regulation: The Case of Insurance* (Albany: State University of New York, 1988), 59.
52. Meier, *Political Economy of Regulation*.
53. Hotchkiss, "What Hughes Did."
54. Kimball, *Insurance and Public Policy*.
55. Kimball, *Insurance and Public Policy*.
56. Alfred Dean, "Fire Hazard, Is It Measurable?," in *Modern Insurance Theory and Education*, Vol 1: *The Formative Era: Progress and Developments to 1949*, ed. Kailin Tuan (Orange, NJ: Varsity Press, 1971), 61.
57. "Expense and Rates of Fire Insurance Companies," in *Annual Proceedings of the National Convention of Insurance Commissioners* (Spokane, WA, 1912), 159.
58. President's Address, in *Annual Proceedings of the National Convention of Insurance Commissioners* (Spokane, WA, 1912), 28.
59. *Annual Proceedings of the National Convention of Insurance Commissioners* (Del Monte, CA, 1915).
60. Meier, *Political Economy of Regulation*, 60.
61. Frederick Crane, "Insurance Rate Regulation: The Reasons Why," *Journal of Risk and Insurance* (1972): 511–34.
62. "Report of the Committee on Rates and Rate-making," in *Annual Proceedings of the National Convention of Insurance Commissioners* (Del Monte, CA, 1915), Adjourned Meeting, 11.
63. "President's Address," *Annual Proceedings of the National Convention of Insurance Commissioners* (Del Monte, CA, 1915), 19.
64. "The Value of Schedule Rating in Securing Equitable Fire Insurance Rates," in *Annual Proceedings of the National Convention of Insurance Commissioners* (Richmond, VA, 1916), 299.
65. *Weekly Underwriter* 54, no. 15 (1896): 367.
66. "Repeal of Valued Policy Asked by Texas Commission," *Weekly Underwriter*, February 5, 1916.
67. "Gave Agents a Lesson," *Weekly Underwriter*, February 5, 1916.
68. "President' Address," *Annual Proceedings of the National Convention of Insurance Commissioners* (Del Monte, CA, 1915), 20.
69. *Annual Proceedings of the National Convention of Insurance Commissioners* (Del Monte, CA, 1915), 207.
70. "President's Address," *Annual Proceedings of the National Convention of Insurance Commissioners* (Del Monte, CA, 1915), 20.
71. "Reserves of Fire Insurance Companies," in *Annual Proceedings of the National Convention of Insurance Commissioners* (Richmond, VA, 1916), 207.
72. "Reciprocal or Inter-Insurance," in *Annual Proceedings of the National Convention of Insurance Commissioners* (Del Monte, CA, 1915), 220.
73. "Anti-Discrimination Laws in Fire Insurance," in *Annual Proceedings of the National Convention of Insurance Commissioners* (Richmond, VA, 1916), 240. One example of the reported "hue and cry" over insurance matters was a furious and unsuccessful effort to repeal the Ramsay Act in 1917, instigated by famous political boss Frank Hague, then commissioner of public safety in Jersey City, who argued that his constituents had their rates unfairly raised. "Jersey's Rate Agitation," *Pittsburgh Post*, February 3, 1916.
74. *Weekly Underwriter*, May 27, 1916.
75. Frank Block, "Fire Insurance Year," *Weekly Underwriter*, January 8, 1917.
76. "War Cover Rates," *Weekly Underwriter*, April 28, 1917, 556. Variation in rates reflected the level of police and fire protection as well as proximity to the coast.
77. John Eugene Pierce, *Development of Comprehensive Insurance for the Household* (Homewood, IL: S.S. Heubner Foundation for Insurance Education, 1958), 223.
78. "Volume of Side Lines," *Weekly Underwriter*, March 30, 1917, 430.

79. Spectator Company, *The Insurance Yearbook* (New York: Spectator Company, 1917).
80. A. J. Wilson, "Business Builder Possibilities for Fire Insurance Agents in the Writing of Casualty Lines," *Weekly Underwriter*, June, 1916.
81. "Insurance is Preparedness," *Weekly Underwriter*, April 15, 1916, 430.
82. "Agents as Preventionists," *Weekly Underwriter*, September 21, 1918, 410.
83. "Agents as Preventionists," *Weekly Underwriter*, September 21, 1918, 410.
84. "Americanization Plan Is Launched by Fire Underwriters," *St. Louis Globe-Democrat*, January 18, 1920.
85. Lansing, *Insurgent Democracy*.
86. The War Risk Insurance Act created access to government life insurance policies for men and women serving in the military. The federal government also carried some of the workers' compensation and employers' liability hazard on some of the construction work on the Emergency Fleet Corporation.
87. Douglas B. Craig, *Progressives at War: William G. McAdoo and Newton D. Baker, 1863–1941* (Baltimore: Johns Hopkins University Press, 2013), 207.
88. "Great Income Lost on Railroad Insurance," *Weekly Underwriter*, July 20, 1918.
89. "Government Encroachment in the Field of Insurance," *Weekly Underwriter*, September 21, 1918.
90. Robert D. Cuff, *The War Industries Board: Business-Government Relations during World War I* (Baltimore: Johns Hopkins University Press, 1973).
91. Cuff, *The War Industries Board*, 180.
92. A thank you letter from Chairman Baruch at the WIB's cessation thanked Evans for the "harmonious spirit of cooperation" from the fire prevention committee. "Epistolary Compliments," *Weekly Underwriter* December 7, 1918, 818.
93. "Government Encroachment in the Field of Insurance," *Weekly Underwriter*, September 21, 1918.
94. Lansing, *Insurgent Democracy*.
95. Representative Julius Kahn, "Honest and Dishonest Insurance," U.S. House of Representatives, June 28, 1906.
96. "Encroachment of Government Insurance," *Weekly Underwriter*, August 3, 1918.

Chapter 7

1. Kansas Historical Society, Smoky Hill Trail and Butterfield Overland Despatch, https://www.kshs.org/kansapedia/smoky-hill-trail-and-butterfield-overland-despatch/17320.
2. Anne F. Hyde, *Born of Lakes and Plains* (New York: Norton, 2022), 275.
3. "Our Indian Troubles," *New York Times*, December 4, 1865.
4. "Our Indian Troubles."
5. "The Beginnings," in *The Travelers 100 Years*, Travelers Archives, 1.
6. "The Beginnings," 13.
7. "The Beginnings"; "Growing Pains," in *The Travelers 100 Years*, Travelers Archives, 13; Richard Hooker, *Aetna Life Insurance Company: Its First Hundred Years* (Hartford, CT: Aetna Life Insurance Company, 1956).
8. "The Beginnings," 17.
9. Obituary, James G. Batterson, *New York Tribune*, September 19, 1901.
10. "The Beginnings," 16.
11. "The Beginnings," 15.
12. "The Beginnings," 13.
13. "The Beginnings," 11.
14. *Travelers Record* 1, no. 11 (January 1866).
15. "Killed by Indians," *Hartford Courant*, December 9, 1865.
16. *Berkshire County Eagle*, December 21, 1865.
17. "Growing Pains," 19.
18. Mark Aldrich, *Safety First: Technology, Labor and Business and the Building of American Workplace Safety, 1870–1939* (Baltimore: Johns Hopkins University, 1997).
19. *Travelers Record* 34, no. 12 (March 1899): 4.
20. "The Beginnings," 11.
21. Accident Policy Application and Agent's Guide, 1865, Travelers Archives.

22. *Yearbook of Insurance* (New York: Spectator Publishing Company, 1899).
23. State of Connecticut, *Thirty-Second Annual Report of the Insurance Commissioner, Part II Life and Accident Companies* (Hartford, CT: Fowler and Miller Company, 1896).
24. Hooker, *Aetna Life Insurance Company.*
25. *Annual Proceedings of the National Convention of Insurance Commissioners* (Springfield, IL, 1898), 918.
26. *Baltimore Underwriter*, September 5, 1895.
27. *Travelers Record*, (34:11) February, 1899, 8.
28. *The Insurance Yearbook 1901–1902 Life and Miscellaneous* (New York: Spectator Publishing Company, 1902), 122.
29. Randolph E. Bergstrom, *Courting Danger: Injury and Law in New York City, 1870–1910* (Ithaca, NY: Cornell University, 1992), 168.
30. Liability Application, Mather Electric Company, Travelers Archives.
31. *The Story of the Travelers*, Travelers Archives, 1968.
32. Edwin W. DeLeon, "Hints to Agents," in *The Insurance Yearbook 1901–1902 Life and Miscellaneous* (New York: Spectator Publishing Company, 1902).
33. *Annual Proceedings of the National Convention of Insurance Commissioners* (Springfield, IL, 1898).
34. *Annual Proceedings of the National Convention of Insurance Commissioners* (Springfield, IL, 1898).
35. Farwell v. Boston & Worcester Railroad Corporation, 4 Met. 49 (Mass. 1842).
36. Jonathan Levy, *Freaks of Fortune: The Emerging World of Capitalism and Risk in America* (Cambridge, MA: Harvard University Press, 2012).
37. *The Insurance Yearbook 1901–1902 Life and Miscellaneous.*
38. Aldrich, *Safety First.*
39. Price V. Fishback and Shawn Everett Kantor, *A Prelude to the Welfare State: The Origins of Workman's Compensation* (Chicago: University of Chicago Press, 2000).
40. Upton Sinclair, *The Jungle* (New York: Octavo Publishing, 1906).
41. William Hard, "Making Steel and Killing Men," *Everybody's Magazine*, November 1907.
42. Aldrich, *Safety First*, 92.
43. U.S. Commissioner of Labor, *Fourth Special Report: Compulsory Insurance in Germany* (Washington, DC: USGPO, 1893).
44. *The Insurance Yearbook 1901–1902 Life and Miscellaneous*, 340.
45. Aldrich, *Safety First.*
46. Fishback and Kantor, *A Prelude to the Welfare State*, 97.
47. *Yearbook for the Forty-Eighth Year of the Travelers Insurance Company*, Travelers Archives, 1912, 15.
48. James Weinstein, *The Corporate Ideal in the Liberal State, 1900–1918* (Boston: Beacon Press, 1968), 44.
49. Fishback and Kantor, *A Prelude to the Welfare State.*
50. Daniel T. Rodgers, *Atlantic Crossings: Social Politics in a Progressive Age* (Cambridge, MA: Harvard University Press, 1998).
51. Fishback and Kantor, *A Prelude to the Welfare State*, 129.
52. Weinstein, *Corporate Ideal*, 60.
53. Alan Brinkley, *Voices of Protest: Huey Long, Father Coughlin and the Great Depression* (New York: Vintage Books, 1983), 110.
54. Carl Hookstadt, "Comparison of Workman's Compensation Laws of the United States and Canada up to September 1920," in *United States Bureau of Labor Statistics*, no. 275 (Washington, DC: USGPO, 1920), 125
55. "Edge Bill Provides for Mutuals in New Jersey," *Eastern Underwriter*, March 21, 1912.
56. Hookstadt, "Comparison of Workman's Compensation Laws."
57. Hookstadt, "Comparison of Workman's Compensation Laws."
58. Hookstadt, "Comparison of Workman's Compensation Laws."
59. Fishback and Kantor, *A Prelude to the Welfare State.*
60. "Liability Men Organize to Oppose State Insurance Program," *Minnesota Labor World*, May 27, 1916.
61. Honorable T. J. Duffy, "Ohio's Experience with State Insurance," *Dayton Daily News*, April 30, 1916.

62. Spencer Baldwin and Thomas Duffy, *The State Fund Versus Casualty Companies* (New York State Federation of Labor, 1918).
63. *Yearbook for the Forty-Seventh Year of the Travelers Insurance Company, 1911*, Travelers Archives, 1911.
64. "Indorse Compensation Laws," *Eastern Underwriter*, March 21, 1912.
65. *Yearbook for the Forty-Eighth year of the Travelers Insurance Company, 1912*, Travelers Archives, 1912, 15.
66. Aldrich, *Safety First*, 96.
67. Morrison H. Beach, *A Century of Security: The Story of the Travelers Insurance Companies* (New York: Newcomen Society of North America, 1973), 11.
68. *Yearbook for the Forty-Seventh Year of the Travelers Insurance Company, 1911*, Travelers Archives, 1911, 17.
69. Aldrich, *Safety First*, 96.
70. Samuel P. Hays, *Conservation and the Gospel of Efficiency* (Pittsburgh, PA: University of Pittsburgh Press, 1957).
71. Aldrich, *Safety First*, 111.
72. *The Travelers Standard* 1 (October 1912): 2.
73. C. A. Kulp, *Casualty Insurance: An Analysis of Hazards, Policies, Companies and Rates* (New York: Ronald Press, 1942), 72.
74. "Safety Engineering," *The Traveler's Standard* 1, no. 8 (May 1913): 149.
75. "Safety Engineering," 149.
76. Franz Kafka, "Measures for Preventing Accidents from Woodplaning Machines (1910)," In *Franz Kafka: The Office Writings*, ed. Stanley Corngold, Jack Greenburg, and Benno Wagner (Princeton, NJ: Princeton University Press, 2009), 109–15.
77. "Indorse Compensation Laws," *Eastern Underwriter*, March 21, 1912.
78. "Whither Are We Drifting?," *The Indicator*, 1911.
79. "Stock Companies Superior to State Plan," *Weekly Underwriter*, February 5, 1916.
80. Fishback and Kantor, *Prelude to the Welfare State*, 151.
81. *Yearbook for the Fiftieth Year of the Travelers Insurance Company, 1911*, Travelers Archives, 1914, 18.
82. Baldwin and Duffy, *State Fund Versus Casualty Companies*.
83. A. M. Best, *Best's Insurance Report—Casualty and Miscellaneous* (New York: Alfred M. Best Company, 1921), 458.
84. Duffy, "Ohio's Experience."
85. Hookstadt, "Comparison of Workman's Compensation Laws," 73.
86. Hookstadt, "Comparison of Workman's Compensation Laws."
87. Duffy, "Ohio's Experience."
88. Faribault Woolen Mills Co. vs. District Court, Rice County, 1917, Supreme Court of Minnesota, 164 N.W. Rep. 810.
89. State ex rel. Rau v District Court, Ramsey County, 1917, Supreme Court of Minnesota 165 N.W. Rep. 916.
90. Kulp, *Casualty Insurance*, 83.
91. Hookstadt, "Comparison of Workman's Compensation Laws," 73–74.
92. Hookstadt, "Comparison of Workman's Compensation Laws," 98
93. Hookstadt, "Comparison of Workman's Compensation Laws," 95–105.
94. Hookstadt, "Comparison of Workman's Compensation Laws," 106
95. Rodgers, *Atlantic Crossings*, 285.
96. Rodgers, *Atlantic Crossings*, 290.
97. Fishback and Kantor, *Prelude to the Welfare State*, 198.
98. Fishback and Kantor, *Prelude to the Welfare State*.
99. Baldwin and Duffy, *The State Fund Versus Casualty Companies*, 6.
100. "Disquieting Conditions," *Weekly Underwriter*, November 16, 1918.
101. Robert D. Cuff, *The War Industries Board: Business-Government Relations during World War I* (Baltimore: Johns Hopkins University Press, 1973).
102. "Setbacks for Monopoly," *Weekly Underwriter*, April 19, 1919, 570.
103. "Strongly Condemns Monopolistic Idea," *Weekly Underwriter*, March 6, 1920, 440.
104. "The Fitzgerald Bill," *Weekly Underwriter*, May 21, 1921, 922.
105. Rodgers, *Atlantic Crossings*.

106. Walter King, *Proceedings of the Casualty Actuarial and Statistical Society* 4, no. 9, pt. 1 (1917): 192.
107. *Twenty-Fourth Annual Report of the U.S. Department of Commerce and Labor* (Washington, DC: USGPO, 1917), 226.
108. Weinstein, *Corporate Ideal*, 11.
109. Edward B. Morris, "Group Life Insurance and Its Possible Developments," *Proceedings of the Casualty Actuarial and Statistical Society* 3 (1917): 149.
110. "Employees Insured Free," *Central New Jerseys Home News* (New Brunswick), October 23, 1918.
111. "Schenectady Insures Employees," *Weekly Underwriter*, March 6, 1920, 435.
112. William F. Chamberlain, "Group Insurance," in *The Travelers: A Series of Lectures* (Hartford, CT: Travelers Insurance Company, 1921), Travelers Archives.
113. "Group Paid Premiums by Years—1913–1940," Travelers Archives.
114. Chamberlain, "Group Insurance."
115. *The Travelers Yearbook for 1923* (Hartford, CT: Travelers Insurance Company, 1923), Travelers Archives, 17.
116. *The Travelers Yearbook for 1924* (Hartford, CT: Travelers Insurance Company, 1924), Travelers Archives, 19.
117. *Proceedings*, no. 9, pt.1 (1917): 199.
118. "Those Health Rates," *Weekly Underwriter*, March 6, 1920.
119. *Annual Proceedings of the National Convention of Insurance Commissioners* (New York, 1920), 70.
120. *Annual Report of Insurance Commissioner State of Tennessee for the Year Ending December 31, 1921, Fire Life, Casualty and Fraternal* (Nashville: Brandon Printing Company, 1922), 15. This comment is often made of short-term health insurance policies today, which are largely mounted on the chassis of these casualty policies from one hundred years ago.

Chapter 8

1. William Larsen, *Pendergast!* (St. Louis: University of Missouri, 1997), 150.
2. Larsen, *Pendergast!*, 130.
3. "Judge Says O'Malley Betrayed Missouri for 30000 Pieces of Silver," *St. Louis Post Dispatch*, May 29, 1939.
4. A. L. Todd, *A Spark Lighted in Portland: The Record of the National Board of Fire Underwriters* (New York: McGraw Hill, 1966).
5. *Hearings Before a Select Subcommittee on Investigation of Crop Insurance*, 67th Cong. (1923), 35.
6. James L. Novak, James W. Pease, and Larry D. Sanders, *Agricultural Policy in the United States: Evolution and Economics* (New York: Routledge, 2015).
7. "May Hire Untermyer to Fight Insurance Rates," *Boston Globe*, April 7, 1922.
8. "Fire Insurance Firms Accused of Speculation," *Democrat and Chronicle* (Rochester, NY), June 2, 1921.
9. "Best Throws Wrench," *Weekly Underwriter*, May 28, 1921, 950.
10. "On with the New," *Weekly Underwriter*, January 3, 1920.
11. Morrison Beach, *A Century of Security: The Story of the Travelers Insurance Companies* (New York: Newcomen Society of North America, 1973), 20.
12. "Rain Cover Proving Worth," *Weekly Underwriter*, July 8, 1922.
13. "Minnesota and the Surcharge," *Weekly Underwriter*, August 23, 1919.
14. Letter to the editor, "The Fire Insurance," *Cleveland Star* (Shelby, NC), February 6, 1920.
15. "Supreme Court Affirms Decision in Insurance Case," *Vardaman's Weekly*, November 23, 1922.
16. "Kansas Opinion Charges Monopoly," *Weekly Underwriter*, December 31, 1922.
17. Hallie L. Jameson, *The Flame Fiend* (New York: J. J. Little and Ives Co., 1921), 50.
18. Kenneth J. Meier, *The Political Economy of Regulation: The Case of Insurance* (Albany: State University of New York Press, 1988), 60.
19. "Rating Reform Defended by Morton," *Weekly Underwriter*, October 21, 1922.
20. *Annual Proceedings of the National Convention of Insurance Commissioners*, Seattle, WA, 1924, 6–8.
21. Albert Henry Mowbray and Ralph Harrub Blanchard, *Insurance* (New York: McGraw Hill, 1961).

348   NOTES

22. William H.A. Carr, *Perils Named and Unnamed: The Insurance Company of North America* (New York: McGraw Hill, 1967), 109.
23. Meier, *Political Economy of Regulation*, 65.
24. Carr, *Perils*, 113.
25. Carr, *Perils*, 157.
26. Carr, *Perils*, 113.
27. Carr, *Perils*, 116.
28. "State's Cut in Fire Insurance Rates is Upheld," *Dexter Statesman*, January 6, 1928.
29. "Stalling Off Repayment," *Dexter Statesman*, July 19, 1929.
30. "Companies Must Show Cause for Excess Fire Rates," *St. Louis Star and Times*, February 8, 1933.
31. "Time to Make an Example of Them," *Ralls County Record*, August 25, 1933.
32. Larsen, *Pendergast!*, xi.
33. Larsen, *Pendergast!*, xi.
34. "O'Malley Ousted; Successor Is Man He Discharged," *St. Louis Post-Dispatch*, October 20, 1937.
35. "O'Malley Asked Pay," *Kansas City Star*, May 27, 1939.
36. "Milligan Tells Case," *Weekly Kansas City Star*, May 24, 1939.
37. Walter Licht, *American Capitalisms*, forthcoming.
38. Ellis Hawley, *The New Deal and the Problem of Monopoly* (Princeton, NJ: Princeton University Press, 1966), 472–90.
39. Meier, *Political Economy of Regulation*, 65.
40. Carr, *Perils*, 137.
41. Carr, *Perils*, 138.
42. Carr, *Perils*, 139.
43. Carr, *Perils*, 141.
44. Carr, *Perils*, 141. Black was joined in the majority opinion by William O. Douglas, Frank Murphy, and Wiley B. Rutledge. Chief Justice Harlan Stone dissented, as did Felix Frankfurter and Robert H. Jackson. (Justices Owen Roberts and Stanley Reed did not participate in the decision.)
45. United States v. South-Eastern Underwriters Association, 322 U.S. 533 (1944), at 586, Jackson J. dissenting in part.
46. "Joe's Blow," *Time*, December 13, 1943.
47. Carr, *Perils*, 142.
48. Charles D. Weller, "The McCarran-Ferguson Act's Antitrust Exemption for Insurance: Language, History, and Policy," *Duke Law Journal* 27, no. 2 (1978): 587–643.
49. Carr, *Perils*, 143.
50. *Annual Proceedings of the National Association of Insurance Commissioners* (Atlantic City, NJ, 1947), 69–74.
51. Eric Nordman, "The Early History of the National Association of Insurance Commissioners," *Journal of Insurance Regulation* 19, no. 2 (2000): 164–78.
52. Scott E. Harrington, "Insurance Rate Regulation in the 20th Century," *Journal of Insurance Regulation* 19, no. 2 (2000): 214–18.
53. Meier, *Political Economy of Regulation.*
54. Meier, *Political Economy of Regulation*, 7.
55. "What Price Competition?," *Time*, March 23, 1942.
56. Carr, *Perils*, 158.
57. *The Insurance Industry: Second Session Pursuant to S. Res. 231, Part I. Aviation Insurance, Hearings Before the Subcommittee on Antitrust and Monopoly of the Committee on the Judiciary,* 85th Cong. 1159 (1958).
58. Carr, *Perils*, 173.
59. Carr, *Perils*, 176.
60. Carr, *Perils*, 176.
61. Carr, *Perils*, 265.
62. National Archives, *Guide to Senate Records: Chapter 13: Judiciary, 1947–1968* (Washington, DC: USGPO).
63. *The Insurance Industry: Second Session Pursuant to S. Res. 231, Part I. Aviation Insurance, Hearings Before the Subcommittee on Antitrust and Monopoly of the Committee on the Judiciary,* 85th Cong. 2 (1958).

64. *The Insurance Industry: First Session Pursuant to S. Res 57, Part 2. Ocean Marine, Rating and State Regulation, Hearings Before the Subcommittee on Antitrust and Monopoly of the Committee on the Judiciary,* 86th Cong. 1275 (1960).
65. *The Insurance Industry: First Session Pursuant to S. Res 57, Part 2. Ocean Marine, Rating and State Regulation, Hearings Before the Subcommittee on Antitrust and Monopoly of the Committee on the Judiciary,* 86th Cong. 1049 (1960).
66. Richard A. Wiley, "Pups, Plants, and Package Policies—Or the Insurance Antitrust Exemption Re-Examined," *Villanava Law Review* 31 (December 1960): 281.
67. *The Insurance Industry: First Session Pursuant to S. Res 57, Part 2. Ocean Marine, Rating and State Regulation, May 28th, Hearings Before the Subcommittee on Antitrust and Monopoly of the Committee on the Judiciary,* 86th Cong. 1159 (1960).
68. Meier, *Political Economy of Regulation,* 73.
69. Spencer Kimball and W. Eugene Hansen, "The Utah Insurance Commissioner: A Study of Administrative Regulation in Action, Part I," *Utah Law Review* 5, no. 4 (Fall 1957): 429–55.
70. Spencer L. Kimball, *Insurance and Public Policy: A Study in the Legal Implementation of Social and Economic Public Policy, Based on Wisconsin Records, 1835–1959* (Madison: University of Wisconsin Press, 1960).
71. Bruce McCandless III and Patricia Fuller McCandless, "The Texas Department of Insurance: Where It Came From, Where It's Headed," State Bar of Texas, Ninth Annual Advanced Insurance Law Course, Dallas, 2012.
72. Committee of the Judiciary, The Insurance Industry: Rates, Rating Organizations, and State Rate Regulations, Together with Individual Views Made by the Subcommittee on Antitrust and Monopoly, Pursuant to S.R. 52, 87–831, at 6 (1961).
73. S. Rep. 87–831, at 45 (1961).
74. S. Rep. 87–831, at 44 (1961).
75. S. Rep. 87–831, at 114 (1961).
76. S. Rep. 87–831, at 114 (1961).
77. S. Rep. 87–831, at 112, fn. 106 and 107 (1961).
78. S. Rep. 87–831, at 116 (1961).
79. S. Rep. 87–831, at 126 (1961).
80. U.S. Congressional Serial Set, Insurance Industry, Aviation, Ocean Marine, and State Regulation (1960), pp. 1–338, 249.
81. *The Insurance Industry: First Session Pursuant to S. Res 57, Part 2. Ocean Marine, Rating and State Regulation, May 28th, Hearings Before the Subcommittee on Antitrust and Monopoly of the Committee on the Judiciary,* 86th Cong. 4127 (1960).
82. S. Rep. 87–831, at 165 (1961).
83. "Dirksen Seeks to Curb Kevauver Probes," *Capital Times,* January 26, 1960.
84. David Houston, "The Insurance Industry: Hearings, Parts 1-10 and Reports of the SubCommittee on Antitrust and Monopoly," *Journal of Insurance* 29, no. 1 (March 1962): 126–29.
85. Wiley, "Pups, Plants, and Package Policies," 345.
86. "The Underwriters," *Fortune,* July 1950, 77–108.
87. Houston, "The Insurance Industry."
88. *The Insurance Industry: First Session Pursuant to S. Res 57, Part 2. Ocean Marine, Rating and State Regulation, May 28th, Hearings Before the Subcommittee on Antitrust and Monopoly of the Committee on the Judiciary,* 86th Cong. 4127 (1960).
89. Peter Drucker, "The Theory of the Business," *Harvard Business Review* (September–October 1994).
90. Meier, *Political Economy of Regulation,* 77.
91. Harrington, "Insurance Rate Regulation."
92. Todd, *Spark Lighted,* 222.
93. Todd, *Spark Lighted,* 218.
94. "Crop Hail Insurance and the St. Paul," Hail Insurance Papers, The St. Paul Fire and Marine Insurance Archives, April 1968.

Chapter 9

1. Mary L. Heen, "Ending Jim Crow Life Insurance Rates," *Northwestern Journal of Law and Social Policy* 4, no. 2 (2009): 360–99; *Wisconsin State Journal,* December 30, 1949.

2. These are Connecticut, 1887; Ohio, 1889; New York, 1891; Michigan, 1893; Minnesota, 1895; and New Jersey, 1902.
3. Frederick Hoffman, "Race Traits and Tendencies of the American Negro," *Publications of the American Economic Association* 11, no. 103 (1896): 1–329.
4. Megan Wolf, "The Myth of the Actuary: Life Insurance and Frederick L. Hoffman's Race Traits and Tendencies of the American Negro," *Public Health Reports* 121, no. 1 (2006): 84–91.
5. Heen, "Ending Jim Crow Life Insurance Rates," 362.
6. Marquis James, *The Metropolitan Life: A Study in Business Growth* (New York: Viking Press, 1947), 339.
7. Louis Dublin, Edwin William Kopf, and George H. Van Buren, *Mortality Statistics of Insured Wage-Earners and Their Families: Experience of the Metropolitan Life Insurance Company, Industrial Department, 1911 to 1916, in the United States and Canada* (New York: Metropolitan Life Insurance Company, 1919), 22.
8. James, *The Metropolitan Life*, 339.
9. Heen, "Ending Jim Crow Insurance Rates," 379.
10. James, *The Metropolitan Life*, 339.
11. Editorial, *Capital Times*, September 19, 1949.
12. "Negro Mortality Rate Said Lower," *Wisconsin State Journal*, December 30, 1949.
13. Lange v. Rancher, 56 N.W. 2d at 543–44 (Wis. 1953).
14. "An Important Civil Rights Decision," *Capital Times*, January 7, 1953.
15. "Rule Wisconsin Can't Bar Negro from Insurance," *Chicago Tribune*, January 7, 1953.
16. Heen, "Ending Jim Crow Life Insurance Rates."
17. *Annual Proceedings of the National Association of Insurance Commissioners* (Philadelphia, 1961), 521–43; also Heen, "Ending Jim Crow Life Insurance," 380.
18. Louis Dublin, *A Family of Thirty Million: The Story of the Metropolitan Life Insurance Company* (New York: Metropolitan Life Insurance Company, 1943), 88.
19. James, *The Metropolitan Life*, 261.
20. Lawrence F. Abbott, *The Story of NYLIC: A History of the Origin and Development of the New York Life Insurance Company from 1845 to 1929* (New York: New York Life Insurance Company, 1930).
21. James, *The Metropolitan Life*, 260.
22. Thomas C. Cochran, *The American Business System* (Cambridge, MA: Harvard University Press, 1957), 75.
23. Abbott, *The Story of NYLIC*, 125.
24. Abbott, *The Story of NYLIC*, 245.
25. Abbott, *The Story of NYLIC*, 166–99.
26. James, *The Metropolitan Life*, 214.
27. Dublin, *Family of Thirty Million*, 80.
28. James, *The Metropolitan Life*, 259.
29. "Americanism in Milwaukee," *Weekly Underwriter*, March 6, 1920, 435.
30. *Investigation of Concentration of Economic Power: Final Report and Recommendations of the Temporary National Economic Committee*, S. Doc. 77-35 (1941).
31. Morton Keller, *The Life Insurance Enterprise, 1885–1910: A Study in the Limits of Corporate Power* (Cambridge, MA: Harvard University Press, 1963).
32. Abbott, *The Story of NYLIC*, 271.
33. James, *The Metropolitan Life*, 262.
34. Dublin, *Family of Thirty Million*, 87.
35. Abbott, *The Story of NYLIC*, 271.
36. Abbott, *The Story of NYLIC*, 287.
37. James, *The Metropolitan Life*, 268.
38. Dublin, *Family of Thirty Million*, 266.
39. James, *The Metropolitan Life*, 268.
40. Dublin, *Family of Thirty Million*, 88.
41. Abbott, *The Story of NYLIC*, 166.
42. Abbott, *The Story of NYLIC*, 161.
43. Walter B. Weare, *Black Business in the New South* (Durham, NC: Duke University Press, 1993).
44. Weare, *Black Business*, 135.
45. Weare, *Black Business*, 141.
46. Weare, *Black Business*, 98.

47. Weare, *Black Business*, 99.
48. Bureau of the Census, *Negroes in the United States, 1920–1932* (Washington, DC: USGPO, 1932), 443.
49. R. Carlyle Buley, *The American Life Convention, 1906–1952: A Study in the History of Life Insurance*, vol. 1 (New York: Appleton-Century-Crofts, 1953), xii.
50. Buley, *The American Life Convention*, 520.
51. James, *The Metropolitan Life*, 272.
52. James, *The Metropolitan Life*, 227.
53. James, *The Metropolitan Life*, 227.
54. Dublin, *A Family of Thirty Million*, 93; James, *The Metropolitan Life*, 230.
55. James, *The Metropolitan Life*, 273.
56. Dublin, *A Family of Thirty Million*, 96.
57. Abbott, *The Story of NYLIC*, 329.
58. Buley, *The American Life Convention*.
59. Owen J. Stalson, *Marketing Life Insurance: It's History in America* (Cambridge, MA: Harvard University Press, 1942), appendix 19.
60. E. B. White, "Notes and Comment," *New Yorker*, January 8, 1930.
61. Daniel T. Rodgers, *Atlantic Crossings: Social Politics in a Progressive Age* (Cambridge, MA: Harvard University Press, 1998), 252; Julia E. Johnson, *The Handbook Series: Social Insurance* (New York: H. W. Wilson, 1922).
62. Theodore Gaty, "Insurance against Unemployment," *Journal of Commerce* 88, no. 4 (August 1915).
63. Quoted in Roy Lubove, *The Struggle for Social Security 1900–1935* (Cambridge, MA: Harvard University Press, 1968).
64. John Andrews, "Unemployment Prevention and Insurance," *American Labor Legislation Review* 10 (December 1920): 233–39; Johnson, *The Handbook Series*, 322.
65. Spencer L. Kimball, *Insurance and Public Policy: A Study in the Legal Implementation of Social and Economic Policy, Based on Wisconsin Records, 1835–1959* (Madison: University of Wisconsin Press, 1960), 22.
66. David Moss, *When All Else Fails: Government as the Ultimate Risk Manager* (Cambridge, MA: Harvard University Press, 2002), 183.
67. Moss, *When All Else Fails*, 193–94.
68. Ira Katznelson, *Fear Itself: The New Deal and the Origins of Our Time* (New York: Liveright, 2013), 386.
69. Moss, *When All Else Fails*, 193–98.
70. Moss, *When All Else Fails*, 198; Committee on Economic Security, *Report to the President* (Washington, DC: USGPO, 1935), 22–23.
71. Abraham Epstein, *The Challenge of the Aged* (New York: Macy-Masius Vanguard Press, 1928); Moss, *When All Else Fails*.
72. Lubove, *The Struggle for Social Security*, 37.
73. As covered in Chapter 4.
74. Abraham Epstein, "Present Status of Old Age Legislation in the United States," *Monthly Labor Review* 19, no. 4 (1924): 26–33.
75. Lubove, *The Struggle for Social Security*, 118.
76. Lubove, *The Struggle for Social Security*, 116–17.
77. Rodgers, *Atlantic Crossings*, 378; Moss, *When All Else Fails*, 198.
78. National Industrial Conference Board, *Industrial Pensions in the United States* (New York, 1925), 2.
79. National Industrial Conference Board, *Industrial Pensions*, 2.
80. National Industrial Conference Board, *Industrial Pensions*, 23.
81. National Industrial Conference Board, *Elements of Industrial Pension Plans* (New York, 1931), 3.
82. National Industrial Conference Board, *Elements of Industrial Pension Plans*, 12.
83. Epstein, *The Challenge of the Aged*.
84. National Industrial Conference Board, *Industrial Pensions*.
85. Lubove, *Struggle for Social Security*, 176.
86. Rodgers, *Atlantic Crossings*; Huey Long's Share Our Wealth movement and Father Townsend were two prominent examples. See Alan Brinkley, *Voices of Protest: Huey Long, Father Coughlin and the Great Depression* (New York: Vintage Books, 1983).

87. Rodgers, *Atlantic Crossings*, 439.
88. Moss, *When All Else Fails*, 204.
89. Lubove, *Struggle for Social Security*, 177.
90. James, *The Metropolitan Life*, 336–37.
91. James, *The Metropolitan Life*, 338.
92. James, *The Metropolitan Life*, 269–90.
93. "Welfare Board Aims to Collect for Families," *Boston Globe*, December 10, 1934.
94. "Speaker Opposes Experiments on Welfare Clients," *Waterloo Courier*, September 24, 1937.
95. "ERB Office Explains Its Life Insurance Adjustment Service," *Kingston Daily Freeman*, April 11, 1935.
96. Charles J. Harnett, "This Policy Should Be Reversed," *Brooklyn Daily Eagle*, March 6, 1935.
97. Kimball, *Insurance and Public Policy*, 32.
98. Morris Siegel, letter to the editor, "Defends Policyholders' Advisors Council," *The Tablet*, August 13, 1938.
99. James, *The Metropolitan Life*, 272.
100. *Verbatim Report of the Proceedings of the Temporary National Economic Committee V*, no. 5, August 29, Bureau of National Affairs (Washington, DC: USGPO, 1939), 135, Exhibit 980.
101. Dublin, *A Family of Thirty Million*, 106.
102. *Verbatim Report of the Proceedings of the Temporary National Economic Committee V*, 1.
103. James, *The Metropolitan Life*, 349–55.
104. Gerhard Gessell, *My "Jealous Mistress": 1932–1984*, Unpublished memoir, August, 1984, 26.
105. *Verbatim Report of the Proceedings of the Temporary National Economic Committee*, 1.
106. "Squirrel cage" was a reference to exercise wheels or cylinders created for small rodents to run in endless circles.
107. *Verbatim Report of the Proceedings of the Temporary National Economic Committee*, 117, 127.
108. James, *The Metropolitan Life*, 356.
109. *Verbatim Report of the Proceedings of the Temporary National Economic Committee*, 147.
110. *Verbatim Report of the Proceedings of the Temporary National Economic Committee*, 147.
111. *Verbatim Report of the Proceedings of the Temporary National Economic Committee*, 127.
112. Gessell, *My "Jealous Mistress,"* 22.
113. *Verbatim Report of the Proceedings of the Temporary National Economic Committee*, 275.
114. *Verbatim Report of the Proceedings of the Temporary National Economic Committee*, 275.
115. "Report of the Executive Committee," in *Annual Proceedings of the National Association of Insurance Commissioners* (Quebec, 1938), 23–27.
116. *Annual Proceedings of the National Association of Insurance Commissioners* (Quebec, 1938), 147.
117. *Temporary National Economic Committee, Statement on Life Insurance, Monograph No. 28-A*, Sen. Doc. 76th Cong. (1941), Section I; James, *The Metropolitan Life*, 360. Four companies did not sign on to the statement—Prudential, New York Life, Mutual, and Northwest Mutual.
118. James, *The Metropolitan Life*, 358; Dublin, *Family of Thirty Million*.
119. Stalson, *Marketing Life Insurance*, 561.
120. *Temporary National Economic Committee, Statement on Life Insurance, Monograph No. 28-A*, Sen. Doc. 76th Cong. (1941), Section II; James, *The Metropolitan Life*, 360.
121. *Investigation of Concentration of Economic Power: Final Report and Recommendations of the Temporary National Economic Committee*, S. Doc. 77-35 (1941), 559–602.
122. Gessell, *My "Jealous Mistress,"* 26.
123. Weltha Van Eenam, "Life Insurance and Annuities on United States Lives, 1935–1943," *Social Security Administration Bulletin 7*, no. 12 (December 1944): 14–15.
124. Stalson, *Marketing Life Insurance*, 561.
125. Dublin, *A Family of Thirty Million*, 198.
126. Stalson, *Marketing Life Insurance*, appendix 24, 815.
127. *Verbatim Report of the Proceedings of the Temporary National Economic Committee*, 197.
128. Malvin E. Davis, "Modern Industrial Life Insurance," in *Life Insurance Trends at Mid-Century*, ed. David McCahon (Philadelphia: University of Pennsylvania Press, 1950), 115–32.
129. Dublin, *A Family of Thirty Million*, 105.
130. Weare, *Black Business in the New South*, 157.
131. Weare, *Black Business in the New South*, 166.
132. Weare, *Black Business in the New South*, 205.

133. "Life Insurance Companies Owned and Operated by Negroes Reveal Increased Income Over Last Year," *New York Age*, September 2, 1939.
134. Weare, *Black Business in the New South*, 270.
135. Weare, *Black Business in the New South*, 280.
136. Interview with Michael Lawrence, *Black History Month Extra*, February 28, 2017.
137. Zachary Eanes, "N.C. Mutual Rebrands as It Attempts to Secure Its Longevity," *Herald Sun*, March 22, 2017.
138. "Ex-Investment Manager Accused of Defrauding North Carolina Mutual," *Coastland Times*, December 4, 2020.
139. Zachary Eanes, "North Carolina Mutual Was Once a Titan of Durham's Black Wall Street. Its Future Is Up in the Air," *News Observer*, June 6, 2019.
140. Lauren Ohnesosrge, "New York CEO Charged with Defrauding North Carolina Mutual, Setting in a Path to Insolvency," *Triangle Business Journal*, December 4, 2020.
141. Heen, *Ending Jim Crow Life Insurance Rates*, 383.

Chapter 10

1. Albert H. Mowbray, *Insurance: Its Theory and Practice in the United States* (New York: McGraw Hill, 1930), 163.
2. Mowbray, *Insurance*; C. A. Kulp, *Casualty Insurance: An Analysis of Hazards, Policies, Companies, and Rates* (New York: Ronald Press Company, 1942). There were several earlier companies that did not achieve commercial success. The early development of accident insurance is described in more detail in Chapter 7.
3. Travelers Insurance Company, *Agent's Manual, 1865*, Travelers Archives, 20–21.
4. Kulp, *Casualty Insurance*, 372.
5. Edwin Faulkner, "The Replacement of Income—Personal Contracts," in *Accident and Sickness Insurance*, ed. David McCahon (Homewood, IL: Richard Irwin, 1954), 16–34.
6. Kulp, *Casualty Insurance*, 373.
7. James M. Cain, "Double Indemnity," in *Three of a Kind* (New York: Alfred A. Knopf, 1936).
8. Travelers Insurance Company, *Travelers Record*, 1892, Travelers Archives.
9. Mowbray, *Insurance*, 161.
10. Faulkner, "Replacement of Income," 33.
11. Billy Wilder, "Double Indemnity," *Paramount Pictures*, 1944.
12. Faulkner, "Replacement of Income," 19.
13. Kulp, *Casualty Insurance*, 374.
14. John H. Miller, *Accident and Sickness Insurance Provided through Individual Policies* (Chicago: Society of Actuaries, 1956), 6.
15. Louis Dublin, *A Family of Thirty Million: The Story of the Metropolitan Life Insurance Company* (New York: Metropolitan Life Insurance Company, 1943).
16. Miller, *Accident and Sickness*, 2
17. Mowbray, *Insurance*, 160.
18. Travelers Insurance Company, *Travelers Record*, April 1899, Travelers Archives.
19. Travelers Insurance Company, *Travelers Record*, April 1899, Travelers Archives.
20. Faulkner, "Replacement of Income," 19.
21. Miller, *Accident and Sickness*, 1.
22. Marquis James, *Biography of a Business* (New York: Bobbs-Merrill, 1942).
23. Kulp, *Casualty Insurance*, 369.
24. Travelers Insurance, "Report in Recognition of Seventy-Fifth Anniversary of Employee Benefits Department," Internal document, 1988, Travelers Archives.
25. Kulp, *Casualty Insurance*, 365.
26. Mowbray, *Insurance*, 172.
27. Mowbray, *Insurance*, 173.
28. Mowbray, *Insurance*, 179.
29. Joseph B. Maclean, "Development of Disability Benefits in Life Insurance Contracts," in *Life Insurance Trends at Mid-Century*, ed. David McCahan (Philadelphia: University of Pennsylvania Press, 1950), 100–113.
30. Kulp, *Casualty Insurance*, 376.

31. *1916 Proceedings of the National Conference of Insurance Commissioners* (Portland, OR, 1931), 119.
32. A. M. Best, *Best's Compilation of Disability and Double Indemnity Provisions of All Legal Reserve Life Insurance Companies Operating in the United States* (New York: A. M. Best Co., 1922).
33. *1931 Proceedings of the National Conference of Insurance Commissioners* (Portland, OR, 1931), 119.
34. *1931 Proceedings of the National Conference of Insurance Commissioners*, 121.
35. *1931 Proceedings of the National Conference of Insurance Commissioners*, 126.
36. *1931 Proceedings of the National Conference of Insurance Commissioners*, 128.
37. Kulp, *Casualty Insurance*, 367.
38. Committee on the Cost of Medical Care, *Medical Care for the American People*, no. 28 (Washington, DC, 1932).
39. Robert Cunningham III and Robert M. Cunningham Jr., *The Blues: A History of the Blue Cross and Blue Shield System* (DeKalb, IL: Northern Illinois University Press, 1997), 10.
40. Cunningham, *The Blues*, 19.
41. Christy Ford Chapin, *Ensuring America's Health: The Public Creation of the Corporate Health System* (New York: Cambridge University Press, 2015); Paul Starr, *The Social Transformation of American Medicine* (New York: Basic Books, 2017).
42. Cunningham, *The Blues*, 18.
43. Cunningham, *The Blues*, 23.
44. "Report on Group Hospitalizations," in *1938 Proceedings of the National Conference of Insurance Commissioners* (Quebec, Canada, 1938), 117.
45. Cunningham, *The Blues*, 31.
46. Henry S. Beers, "The Growing Field of Group Coverages," in *Life Insurance Trends at Mid-Century*, ed. David McCahan (Philadelphia: University of Pennsylvania, 1950), 133–55, 133.
47. Edison L. Bowers, "The Nature of Accident and Sickness Insurance," in *Accident and Sickness Insurance*, ed. David McCahan (Homewood, IL: Richard D. Irwin, 1954), 1–13, 9.
48. Starr, *Social Transformation*, 314.
49. C. Manton Eddy, "Replacement of Income—Group Contracts," in *Accident and Sickness Insurance*, ed. David McCahan (Homewood, IL: Richard Irwin, 1952), 35–49, 36.
50. Bowers, "The Nature of Accident and Sickness Insurance," 9.
51. Cunningham, *The Blues*.
52. Edward A. Green, "Underwriting, Reinsurance and Claim Adjustment—Group Contracts," in *Accident and Sickness Insurance*, ed. David McCahan (Homewood, IL: Richard Irwin, 1954), 164–83, 165.
53. Gabriel Winant, *The Next Shift: The Fall of Industry and the Rise of Health Care in Rust Belt America* (Cambridge, MA: Harvard University Press, 2021), 10; Jennifer Klein, *For All These Rights: Business, Labor and the Shaping of America's Public-Private Welfare State* (Princeton, NJ: Princeton University Press, 2003).
54. Starr, *Social Transformation*, 313.
55. Winant, *Next Shift*, 18.
56. Julian Zelizer, "The Contentious Origins of Medicare and Medicaid," in *Medicare and Medicaid at Fifty*, ed. David C. Colby, Keith A. Wailoo, and Alan Cohen (New York: Oxford University Press, 2015), 3–20, 6.
57. Ira Katznelson, *Fear Itself: The New Deal and the Origins of Our Time* (New York: Liveright, 2013).
58. Zelizer, "Contentious Origins," 7; Caley Horan, *Insurance Era: Risk, Governance, and the Privatization of Security in Postwar America* (Chicago: University of Chicago Press, 2021).
59. Bowers, "The Nature of Accident and Sickness Insurance," 14.
60. Chapin, *Ensuring America's Health*, 110.
61. Eddy, "Replacement of Income," 47.
62. Eddy, "Replacement of Income," 47.
63. Eddy, "Replacement of Income," 49.
64. Eddy, "Replacement of Income," 45.
65. Bowers, "The Nature of Accident and Sickness Insurance," 10.
66. Faulkner, "Replacement of Income," 31.
67. Gilbert W. Fitzhugh, "Meeting Hospital Costs," in *Accident and Sickness Insurance*, ed. David McCahan (Homewood, IL: Richard Irwin, 1954), 50–75, 59.
68. Fitzhugh, "Meeting Hospital Costs," 59.
69. Kenneth Babcock, "The Excessive Use of Blue Cross Benefits," *Hospitals*, 26 (July 1952): 49–51.

70. *Chicago Daily News*, November 28, 1950.
71. Starr, *Social Transformation*, 328.
72. Fitzhugh, "Meeting Hospital Costs," 74.
73. J. Henry Smith, "Meeting Surgical and Medical Expense," in *Accident and Sickness Insurance*, ed. David McCahan (Homewood, IL: Richard Irwin, 1952), 76–97, 77.
74. Smith, "Meeting Expenses."
75. William H. Carr, *From Three Cents a Week* (Newark, NJ: Prudential Insurance Company, 1975), 214.
76. Chapin, *Ensuring America's Health*, 117.
77. Winant, *Next Shift*, 145.
78. Cunningham, *The Blues*, 113.
79. Chapin, *Ensuring America's Health*, 117.
80. Maclean, "Disability Benefits."
81. Faulkner, "Replacement of Income," 34.
82. Grant M. Osborn, *Compulsory Temporary Disability in the United States* (Philadelphia: S.S. Heubner Foundation for Insurance Education, 1958), 31.
83. Joe Nocera, "A Tale of Two Companies," *Fortune*, April 5, 2004, 232–38.
84. Smith, "Meeting Expenses," 95.
85. Smith, "Meeting Expenses," 95; Laura McCarty, "John Amos," *New Georgia Encyclopedia*, https://www.georgiaencyclopedia.org/articles/business-economy/john-amos-1924-1990.
86. Smith, "Meeting Expenses," 96.
87. Faulkner, "Replacement of Income," 34.
88. Smith, "Meeting Expenses," 96.
89. Edward M. Neumann, "Rates and Reserves—Group Contracts," in *Accident and Sickness Insurance*, ed. David McCahan (Homewood, IL: Richard Irwin, 1954), 200–225.
90. Green, *Underwriting*, 167.
91. Bowers, "The Nature of Accident and Sickness Insurance," 3.
92. J. F. Folmann, "Regulation of Accident and Sickness Costs," in *Accident and Sickness Insurance*, ed. David McCahan (Homewood, IL: Richard Irwin, 1954), 257.
93. Green, *Underwriting*, 183
94. Smith, "Meeting Expenses."
95. Miller, *Accident and Sickness*, 187.
96. Armand Sommer, "Underwriting, Reinsurance and Claim Adjustment—Personal Commercial Contracts," in *Accident and Sickness Insurance*, ed. David McCahan (Homewood, IL: Richard Irwin, 1954), 129–45, 129.
97. Alfred W. Perkins, "Underwriting, Reinsurance and Claim Adjustment—Personal Noncancellable Contracts," in *Accident and Sickness Insurance*, ed. David McCahan (Homewood, IL: Richard Irwin, 1954), 146–63, 146.
98. Smith, "Meeting Expenses," 93.
99. Wendell Milliman, "Contract Provisions of Group Accident and Sickness Insurance," in *Accident and Sickness Insurance*, ed. David McCahan (Homewood, IL: Richard Irwin, 1954), 114–28, 115.
100. Milliman, "Contract Provisions," 114–28.
101. Perkins, "Underwriting."
102. Mortimer Spiegelman, *Ensuring Medical Care for the Aged* (Homewood, IL: Richard Irwin, 1960), 210.
103. Spiegelman, *Ensuring Medical Care*, 214, 247–48; Chapin, *Ensuring America's Health*, 107–18.
104. Quoted in Smith, "Meeting Expenses," 91.
105. Smith, "Meeting Expenses," 92.
106. Zelizer, "Contentious Origins," 3–14; Heather McGhee, *The Sum of Us: What Racism Costs Everyone and How We Can Prosper Together* (New York: One World, 2021), 50; Chapin, *Ensuring America's Health*, 41–45; Starr, *Social Transformation*, 280–86.
107. Starr, *Social Transformation*, 367–70.
108. Chapin, *Ensuring America's Health*, 198.
109. "Special Health Insurance Available During October 1963," *Del Rio News Standard*, October 6, 1963.
110. "Because of State Program, TMA Official Says Medicare a Needless Expense in Texas 1963," *Abilene Reporter-News*, April 6, 1963.

111. "George Bush—How He Stands" (advertisement), *Austin American Statesman*, October 15, 1964.
112. Chapin, *Ensuring America's Health*, 198.
113. David Barton Smith, "Civil Rights and Medicare," in *Medicare and Medicaid at 50*, ed. David C. Colby, Keith A. Wailoo, Julian E. Zelizer, and Alan B. Cohen (New York: Oxford University Press, 2015), 21–38.
114. Zelizer, "Contentious Origins," 16.
115. Chapin, *Ensuring America's Health*, 219.
116. "Two Medicare Amendments Shake Insurance Industry," *Hartford Courant*, April 12, 1965.
117. Starr, *Social Transformation*.
118. Continental Casualty Company, "Golden 65" (advertisement), *New York Daily News*, June 12, 1966.
119. Aflac, "Our History," https://www.aflac.com/about-aflac/our-company/default.aspx.
120. Louis S. Reed and Willine Carr, *The Benefit Structure of Private Health Insurance, Research Report 32*. U.S. Department of Health Education and Welfare, Office of Research and Statistics, Social Security Administration (Washington, DC: US GPO, 1970), 111.
121. National Health Expenditure Accounts, Centers for Medicare and Medicaid Studies, Office of the Actuary, National Health Statistics Group. https://www.cms.gov/data-research/statist ics-trends-and-reports/national-health-expenditure-data/historical.
122. Charles T. Hall, "The Future of Health Insurance and Medicine: A 20 Year Forecast," *Journal of Insurance Issues and Practices* 6, no. 2 (June 1983): 46.
123. Lynn Gruber, Maureen Shadle, and Cynthia L. Polich, "From Movement to Industry: The Growth of HMOs," *Health Affairs* 7, no. 3 (1988): 197–208.
124. Thomas B. Morehart, "HMOs: A Historical Perspective," *Journal of Insurance Issues and Practice* 1, no. 2 (1977): 28–38.
125. Starr, *Social Transformation*, 460.
126. Ellen M. Morrison and Harold S. Luft, "Health Maintenance Organization Environments in the 1980s and Beyond," *Health Care Finance Review* 12, no. 1 (1990): 81–90; Jessica Banthin and Amy Taylor, *Research Findings #15: HMO Enrollment in the United States: Estimates Based on Household Reports, 1996* (Rockville, MD: Agency for Healthcare Research and Quality, 2001).
127. Patricia Mortenson, "The Future of Health Insurance," *Best's Review—Life Health Insurance Edition* 85 (July 1984).
128. Jeffrey O'Connell, "Your Protection or Their Profit?," *Press-Telegram* (Long Beach, California), July 7, 1974.
129. Mortenson, "Future of Health Insurance."
130. Mortenson, "Future of Health Insurance."
131. Sidney W. Bishop and Angela Kachadour, "Potential to Mislead—Life and Health Insurance Advertising Regulation," *The Forum (ABA Section of Insurance, Negligence and Compensation Law)* 11, no. 4 (1976): 1040–53, 1042.
132. Federal Trade Commission, *Cancer Insurance: A Review of Publicly Available Documents.* (Washington, DC: USGPO, 1980), 9.
133. Equity Research Associates, June 30, 1978, quoted in Federal Trade Commission, *Cancer Insurance*, 59.
134. Steve Flowers, "The Story of Aflac," *The Blount Countian*, August 12, 2015.
135. Federal Trade Commission, *Cancer Insurance*, iii.
136. U.S. Senate Subcommittee on Monopoly Antitrust and Business Interests, *Cancer Insurance Industry Practices and Procedures* (Washington, DC: USGPO, 1980), 3.
137. Federal Trade Commission, *Cancer Insurance*, iii.
138. Federal Trade Commission, *Cancer Insurance*, appendix B, B-4-B-5.
139. *Hearings on Cancer Insurance Industry Practices and Procedures, Before the Subcommittee on Monopoly, Antitrust and Business Interests*, 96th Cong. 3 (1980); John T. Dauner, "Teasdale Wins Suit on Cancer Insurance," *Kansas City Times*, May 13, 1983; "American Family Life: Expanding Beyond Its Cancer Insurance Market," *Business Week*, January 5, 1979.
140. *Hearings on Cancer Insurance Industry Practices and Procedures.*
141. Federal Trade Commission, *Cancer Insurance*, 100.
142. Susan Marquis and Charles E. Phelps, *The Demand for Supplementary Health Insurance R-3285-HSS* (Los Angeles: RAND Corporation, 1985).

143. After his death, ten U.S. senators praised Amos in the *Congressional Record* on April 16, 1991. McCarty, "John Amos."
144. Chapin, *Ensuring America's Health*, 243.
145. A. M. Best, *Best's Aggregates and Averages—Life-Health* (Oldwick, NJ: A. M. Best, 1994), 74.
146. Chapin, *Ensuring America's Health*.
147. NAIC Accident and Health Policy Experience Exhibit, 2021, Mark Farrah Associates. Nearly six million lives were enrolled in individually named disease policies in 2021.

Chapter 11

1. *Annual Proceedings of the National Association of Insurance Commissioners* (Miami, FL, 1957), 34–37.
2. Lynn O. Borchert, *Competition under the California Rating Law and Its Effect on Private Passenger Automobile and Homeowners Insurance* (Sacramento: California Insurance Department, 1974).
3. Spencer L. Kimball and Ronald N. Boyce, "The Adequacy of State Insurance Rate Regulation: The McCarran-Ferguson Act in Historical Perspective," *Michigan Law Review* 56, no. 4 (1958): 545–78; 91 Congressional Record Part 2, 1992 (1945) Franklin D. Roosevelt, Statement on Signing S. 340, Online by Gerhard Peters and John T. Woolley, The American Presidency Project https://www.presidency./ucsb.edu/node/210053.
4. Kenneth Meier, *The Political Economy of Regulation: The Case of Insurance* (Albany: State University of New York Press, 1988); FTC v. National Casualty 357 U.S. 560 (1958).
5. United States v. South-Eastern Underwriters' Association, 322 U.S. 533 (1944).
6. *Annual Proceedings of the National Association of Insurance Commissioners* (Miami, FL, 1957), 34–37.
7. *Annual Proceedings of the National Association of Insurance Commissioners* (Miami, FL, 1960), 31–34.
8. FTC v. Traveler's Health Association, 362 U.S. 293 (1960).
9. Kimball and Boyce, "The Adequacy of State Insurance Rate Regulation."
10. Spencer Kimball, *Insurance and Public Policy: A Study in the Legal Implementation of Social and Economic Public Policy, based on Wisconsin Records 1835–1959* (Madison: University of Wisconsin Press, 1960); Meier, *Political Economy of Regulation*.
11. Kimball and Boyce, "The Adequacy of State Insurance Rate Regulation."
12. Meier, *Political Economy of Regulation*.
13. Scott Harrington, "Insurance Rate Regulation in the 20th Century," *Journal of Insurance Regulation* 19 (2000): 204–18.
14. Ambrose Ryder, *Automobile Insurance: A Description of the Various Forms of Coverage, Underwriting Methods and Selling Plans* (Chicago: Spectator Company, 1924), 3.
15. C. A. Kulp, *Casualty Insurance: An Analysis of Hazards, Policies, Companies and Rates* (New York: Ronald Press, 1942), 164.
16. Ryder, *Automobile Insurance*, 1.
17. Kulp, *Casualty Insurance*, 163.
18. Charles Newton Hulvey and Williman Hamlin Wandel, *Workman's Compensation and Automobile Liability Insurance in Virginia* (New York: Century Company, 1931).
19. Albert H. Mowbray, *Insurance: Its Theory and Practice in the United States* (New York: McGraw Hill, 1930).
20. James M. Anderson, Paul Heaton, and Stephen J. Carroll, *The U.S. Experience with No-Fault Auto Insurance: A Retrospective* (Santa Monica, CA: RAND Institute for Civil Justice, 2010).
21. Columbia University Council for Research in the Social Sciences, *Report by the Committee to Study Compensation for Automobile Accidents* (Philadelphia: International Printing Company, 1932), 18.
22. Hulvey and Wandel, *Workman's Compensation and Automobile Liability Insurance in Virginia*, 141.
23. Kulp, *Casualty Insurance*, 169–200.
24. Ryder, *Automobile Insurance*, 199.
25. Columbia University Council for Research in the Social Sciences, *Report*.
26. Ryder, *Automobile Insurance*, 233.
27. Kulp, *Casualty Insurance*, 57.

28. Ryder, *Automobile Insurance*, 209.
29. Association of Casualty and Surety Executives, *Comments on Report by the Committee to Study Compensation for Automobile Accidents to the Columbia University Council for Research in the Social Sciences* (New York, 1932), 33.
30. Mowbray, *Insurance*.
31. Association of Casualty and Surety Executives, *Comments*, 13.
32. Kulp, *Casualty Insurance*.
33. *Proceedings of the National Convention of Insurance Commissioners* (Cincinnati, 1927), 192–98.
34. Mowbray, *Insurance*.
35. *Proceedings of the National Convention of Insurance Commissioners* (Seattle, 1935), 82.
36. Kulp, *Casualty Insurance*, 209.
37. "Frontiers of Liability Insurance," *Best's Insurance News (Fire and Casualty Edition)*, 1939, 439.
38. Albert A. Ehrenzweig, *"Full Aid" Insurance for the Traffic Victim* (Berkeley: University of California Press, 1954).
39. William H. A. Carr, *Perils Named and Unnamed: The Story of the Insurance Company of North America* (New York: McGraw-Hill, 1967), 301.
40. Joseph Martin, Leonard Scandur, and Theo Wilson, "Law Means Well but Works Badly," *New York Daily News*, April 26, 1963.
41. Carr, *Perils Named and Unnamed*, 291–95.
42. "Insurance: Paying the Highway Toll," *Time*, November 19, 1956.
43. Ann Kelchberg, *A History of the Continental Insurance Company* (New York: Continental Corporation, 1979), 62.
44. Travelers Insurance Company, "Rx for the Automobile Problem," *Protection*, March 1966, Travelers Archives, 1966.
45. Carr, *Perils*, 299.
46. Mike Morgan, "Mike Morgan Says," *Miami Herald*, November 3, 1967.
47. "Older American Citizens Facing Cancellation of Auto Insurance Policies," *Johnson City Press* (Tennessee), April 5, 1967.
48. "No Bias Claim of Insurers Is Doubted," *Daily Record* (Long Branch), August 22, 1964.
49. "Middlesex Agents Berate Insurance Firms at Hearing," *Central New Jersey Home News*, July 14, 1965.
50. Progressive Insurance Company, 2022, https://www.progressive.com/about/history/.
51. Robert L. Jackson, "Insurance Hoodlums Probed," *Austin American Statesman*, November 16, 1967.
52. Douglas G. Olson, *Insolvencies among Auto Insurers: Advisory Report to the Division of Industry Analysis*, Department of Transportation Automobile Insurance and Compensation Study (Washington, DC: USGPO, 1970).
53. William T. Hold, *Motor Vehicle Assigned Risk Plans*, Department of Transportation, Automobile Insurance and Compensation Study (Washington, DC: USGPO, 1970); Olson, *Insolvencies among Auto Insurers*, 33.
54. Hold, *Assigned Risk Plans*, 22.
55. Hold, *Assigned Risk Plans*, 57.
56. Caley Horan, *Insurance Era: Risk, Governance, and the Privatization of Security in Postwar America* (Chicago: University of Chicago Press, 2021), 66.
57. Hold, *Assigned Risk Plans*; Travelers Insurance Company, "Toward Solving the Auto Problem— Full Speed Ahead!," *Protection*, April 1969, Travelers Archives, 1969.
58. Robert L. Jackson, "Congress May Hold Hearings on Auto Insurance Industry," *Courier Journal and Times* (Louisville), October 15, 1967.
59. Olson, *Insolvencies among Auto Insurers*; Ralph Nader, *Unsafe at Any Speed: The Designed-In Dangers of the American Automobile* (New York: Grossman Publishers, 1965); Robert E. Keeton and Jeffrey O'Connell, *Basic Protection for the Traffic Victim* (Boston: Little, Brown and Company, 1968).
60. Automobile Insurance Study, H.R. Rep. No. 90-815 (1967).
61. Automobile Insurance Study, H.R. Rep. No. 90-815 (1967).
62. Automobile Insurance Study, H.R. Rep. No. 90-815 (1967).
63. Automobile Insurance Study, H.R. Rep. No. 90-815 (1967).
64. Tom Talburt, "Some Who Never Had Wreck Considered Substandard Risk," *Evansville Press*, December 12, 1967.

65. Robert F. Buckhorn, "Soaring Auto Insurance Costs in Spotlight," *Fort Lauderdale News and Sun-Sentinel*, December 10, 1967.
66. Robert W. Lucas, "Congressional Investigation of Auto Insurance Seems Likely," *Courier News* (Bridgewater), July 13, 1967.
67. Automobile Insurance Study, H.R. Rep. No. 90-815 (1967), 35.
68. Lucas, "Congressional Investigation of Auto Insurance Seems Likely."
69. *Investigation of Auto Insurance: Hearings on S.J. Res. 129 Before the Consumer Subcommittee of the Committee on Commerce*, 90th Cong. 2-3 (1968).
70. *Automobile Liability Insurance: Hearings on S. Res. 40 Before the Subcommittee on Antitrust and Monopoly*, 91st Cong. 7391, 1969.
71. *Automobile Insurance Study*, H.R. Rep. No. 90-815, 128 (1967).
72. *Federal Motor Vehicle Insurance Guaranty Corporation: Hearings on S. Res. 3919*, 89th Cong. (1966); 89 Cong. Rec. S27311 (October 18, 1966).
73. *Proceedings of the National Association of Insurance Commissioners* (Dallas, 1967), 33–36.
74. *Proceedings of the National Association of Insurance Commissioners* (Dallas, 1967), 98.
75. *Proceedings of the National Association of Insurance Commissioners* (Dallas, 1967), 99.
76. David A. Moss, *When All Else Fails: Government as the Ultimate Risk Manager* (Cambridge, MA: Harvard University Press, 2002), 269.
77. Richard Grimes, "Legislature Could Offer Insurance Buyer Safety," *Charleston Daily Mail*, January 7, 1970.
78. Moss, *When All Else Fails*.
79. Moss, *When All Else Fails*.
80. Jack Anderson, "Auto Insurance 'Unmitigated Mess' Washington Merry Go Round," *Sheboygan Press*, September 23, 1971.
81. Anderson, Heaton, and Carroll, *U.S. Experience with No-Fault Auto Insurance*.
82. Peter Kinzler, *Highway Robbery: The Two Decade Battle to Reform America's Automobile Insurance System* (Lawrence: University of Kansas, 2021), 23.
83. U.S. Department of Transportation, *Constitutional Problems in Automobile Accident Compensation Reform* (Washington, DC: USGPO, 1970).
84. Kinzler, *Highway Robbery*.
85. Travelers Insurance Company, "No Fault Auto Insurance and the Travelers Official Position," *Protection*, July 1971, Travelers Archives.
86. Anderson, Heaton, and Carroll, *U.S. Experience with No-Fault Auto Insurance*.
87. "No Fault Bill to Up Insurance 18 Percent?," *Clarion-Ledger* (Jackson Mississippi), August 13, 1972.
88. Kinzler, *Highway Robbery*.
89. "No-Fault Auto Insurance: Senate Action Delayed," *Congressional Quarterly Almanac 1973*, 1974, 395–400.
90. Kinzler, *Highway Robbery*, 33.
91. "No Fault Insurance," *Weirton Daily Times*, October 11, 1971.
92. W. Wilson Cliff, "Bill Is Step Toward No-Fault Insurance," *Albuquerque Journal*, January 16, 1972.
93. "No-Fault Auto Insurance: Senate Action Delayed."
94. Kinzler, *Highway Robbery*.
95. "No-Fault Auto Insurance: Senate Action Delayed."
96. "No-Fault Auto Insurance," *Congressional Quarterly Almanac 1976*, 1977, 447–48.
97. Anderson, Heaton, and Carroll, *U.S. Experience with No-Fault Auto Insurance*.
98. "No-Fault Auto Bill Rejected," *Congressional Quarterly Almanac 1978*, 1979, 482–85.
99. Meier, *Political Economy of Regulation*.
100. Kinzler, *Highway Robbery*, 120.
101. Kinzler, *Highway Robbery*; Scott Harrington, "State Decisions to Limit Tort Liability: An Empirical Analysis of No-Fault Automobile Insurance Laws," *Journal of Risk and Insurance* 61, no. 2 (1994): 276–94; Anderson, Heaton, and Carroll, *U.S. Experience with No-Fault Auto Insurance*."
102. Kinzler, *Highway Robbery*, 163.
103. Andrew Tobias, *My Vast Fortune: The Money Adventures of a Quixotic Capitalist* (New York: Random House, 1997), 111.
104. Kinzler, *Highway Robbery*, 201.
105. Anderson, Heaton, and Carroll, *U.S. Experience with No-Fault Auto Insurance*, 58.

106. Anderson, "Auto Insurance 'Unmitigated Mess.'"
107. Federal Insurance Office, Department of the Treasury, *Monitoring Availability and Affordability of Auto Insurance: Assessing Potential Evolution of the Auto Insurance Market,* Federal Register (2021).
108. Travelers Insurance Company, "The Right to Rates: Travelers Takes Stand on Key Rate Regulation Issues," *Protection,* February 1990, Travelers Archives.
109. Herb Denenberg, "The Story of Insurance Regulation: Regulation of, by and for the Insurance Companies," Unpublished address.
110. Roger Grant, *Insurance Reform in the Progressive Era* (Des Moines: University of Iowa Press, 1979).
111. Richard Grimes, "High Pay Brings Quality?," *Berkley Post-Herald,* June 21, 1977.
112. Richard E. Steward, "Ritual and Reality in Insurance Regulation," in *Insurance, Government, and Social Policy: Studies in Insurance Regulation,* ed. Spencer L. Kimball and Herbert S. Denenberg (Homewood, IL: Richard Irwin, 1969), 22–32.
113. Borchert, *Competition under the California Rating Law,* 252.
114. Spencer L Kimball and Herbert S Denenberg, *Insurance, Government, and Social Policy: Studies in Insurance Regulation* (Homewood, IL: Richard Irwin, 1969), xiv.
115. Jeffrey O'Connell, "Your Protection or Their Profit?," *Press-Telegram* (Long Beach, California), July 7, 1974.
116. Kimball and Denenberg, *Insurance, Government, and Social Policy.*

Chapter 12

1. Walter Evans Edge, *A Jerseyman's Journal: Fifty Years of American Business and Politics* (Princeton, NJ: Princeton University Press, 1948), 280–300.
2. Joanne Yates, *Structuring the Information Age: Life Insurance and Technology in the Twentieth Century* (Baltimore: Johns Hopkins University Press, 2005), 113.
3. William H. A. Carr, *Perils Named and Unnamed: The Story of the Insurance Company of North America* (New York: McGraw-Hill, 1967).
4. Carr, *Perils Named and Unnamed,* 311.
5. John Eugene Pierce, *Development of Comprehensive Insurance for the Household* (Homewood, IL: Richard Irwin, 1958), 347.
6. Pierce, *Development of Comprehensive Insurance,* 401.
7. Edge, *A Jerseyman's Journal,* 280–300.
8. Carr, *Perils Named and Unnamed,* 323.
9. David A. Moss, *When All Else Fails: Government as the Ultimate Risk Manager* (Cambridge, MA: Harvard University Press, 2002), 262.
10. Carr, *Perils Named and Unnamed,* 323.
11. Moss, *When All Else Fails,* 255–58.
12. American Institutes for Research, *A Chronology of Major Events Affecting the National Flood Insurance Program, Evaluation of the National Flood Insurance Program* (Washington, DC: American Institutes for Research, 2005).
13. Ann Kelchberg, *A History of the Continental Insurance Company* (New York: Continental Corporation, 1979), 56.
14. Carr, *Perils Named and Unnamed.*
15. Moss, *When All Else Fails,* 255.
16. American Institutes for Research, *A Chronology of Major Events.*
17. Kenneth Meier, *The Political Economy of Regulation: The Case of Insurance* (Albany: State University of New York Press, 1988).
18. Hurricanes: Science and Society https://hurricanescience.org/index.html.
19. American Institutes for Research, *A Chronology of Major Events*; Meier, *Political Economy of Regulation.*
20. Eric S. Blake, Edward N. Rappaport, and Christopher W. Landsea, *The Deadliest, Costliest, and Most Intense United States Hurricanes of This Century (and Other Frequently Requested Hurricane Facts)* (Miami, FL: National Hurricane Center, 2011).
21. "Fire Insurance Companies Get Ultimatum from State," *Central New Jersey Home News,* May 26, 1965.

22. Blake, Rappaport, and Landsea, *The Deadliest, Costliest, and Most Intense United States Hurricanes of This Century*; Kelchberg, *A History of the Continental Insurance Company*; see also Ted Steinberg, *Acts of God: The Unnatural History of Natural Disaster in America* (New York: Oxford University Press, 2006) on the impact of Hurricane Betsy on federal disaster relief.
23. National Flood Insurance Act of 1967, 90th Congress, 1st Session, Senate Report No. 549, p. 3.
24. Meier, *Political Economy of Regulation*; American Institutes for Research, *A Chronology of Major Events*.
25. Meier, *Political Economy of Regulation*, 136.
26. Congressional Research Service, *The National Flood Insurance Program: Status and Remaining Issues for Congress* (Washington, DC: USGPO, 2013), 13.
27. Thomas Sugrue, *The Origins of the Urban Crisis: Race and Inequality in Postwar Detroit* (Princeton, NJ: Princeton University Press, 1996).
28. Pierce, *Development of Comprehensive Insurance*. On the estimated amount of losses, see Chris M. Messer, Thomas E. Shriver, and Alison E. Adams, "The Destruction of Black Wall Street: Tulsa's 1921 Riot and the Eradication of Accumulated Wealth," *American Journal of Economics and Sociology* 77, no. 3–4 (2018): 789–819. For an example of a lawsuit where the plaintiff unsuccessfully tried to apply case law from the San Francisco earthquake and fire, see Redfern v. American Central Ins. Co., 116 Okla. 137 (1926). For the persistence of litigation, see Jared Council, "Insurance Exclusions Left Black Tulsans Footing the Bill for the Massacre," *Wall Street Journal*, May 29, 2022.
29. John Hugh Gilmore, "Insurance Redlining and the Fair Housing Act: the Lost Opportunity of Mackey versus Nationwide Insurance Company," *Catholic University Law Review* 34, no. 2 (1985): 563–93.
30. *Meeting the Insurance Crisis of Our Cities: A Report by the President's National Advisory Panel on Insurance in Riot-Affected Areas* (Washington, DC, 1968); Pierce, *Development of Comprehensive Insurance*.
31. Kelchberg, *A History of the Continental Insurance Company*.
32. Carr, *Perils Named and Unnamed*, 397.
33. *Meeting the Insurance Crisis of Our Cities.*
34. *Meeting the Insurance Crisis of Our Cities.*
35. Caley Horan, *Insurance Era: Risk, Governance, and the Privatization of Security in Postwar America* (Chicago: University of Chicago Press, 2021).
36. *Meeting the Insurance Crisis of Our Cities*, 30.
37. *Meeting the Insurance Crisis of Our Cities*, 25.
38. *Meeting the Insurance Crisis of Our Cities*, 31.
39. Kelchberg, *History of Continental Insurance Company.*
40. Gilmore, "Insurance Redlining and the Fair Housing Act"; Horan, *Insurance Era.*
41. Robert J. Cole, "State Fire Insurance Pool Said to Try to Hide Profit," *New York Times*, January 4, 1972.
42. *The Insurance Industry: Hearings Before the Subcommittee on Antitrust and Monopoly Pursuant to S. Res. 40*, 91st Cong. 14313 (1971), statement of George K. Bernstein.
43. *The Insurance Industry: Hearings Before the Subcommittee on Antitrust and Monopoly Pursuant to S. Res. 40*, 91st Cong. 14313 (1971), statement of George K. Bernstein.
44. *The Insurance Industry: Hearings Before the Subcommittee on Antitrust and Monopoly Pursuant to S. Res. 40*, 91st Cong. 14313 (1971), statement of George K. Bernstein.
45. *The Insurance Industry: Hearings Before the Subcommittee on Antitrust and Monopoly Pursuant to S. Res. 40*, 91st Cong. 14313 (1971), statement of George K. Bernstein.
46. American Institutes for Research, *Chronology of Major Events.*
47. Meier, *Political Economy of Regulation.*
48. Travelers Insurance Company, "Flood Insurance—Once Only a Dream Now a Reality," *Protection*, October 1969, Travelers Archives, 1969.
49. American Academy of Actuaries, *The National Flood Insurance Program: Past, Present and . . . Future?* (Washington DC: American Academy of Actuaries Flood Insurance Subcommittee, 2011), 103.
50. Travelers Insurance Company, "Flood Insurance Program Efficiently Established in 13 States," *Protection*, November 1970, Travelers Archives.
51. Steinberg, *Acts of God*, 135.
52. Howard S. Shapiro, *How to Keep Them Honest* (Emmaus, Pennsylvania: Rodale Press, 1974), 80.

53. Shapiro, *How to Keep Them Honest*; Meier, *The Political Economy of Regulation*, 116.
54. Congressional Research Service, *The National Flood Insurance Program*, 12.
55. Meier, *The Political Economy of Regulation*.
56. *Federal Flood Insurance Program: Hearings Before the Subcommittee on Housing and Community Development*, 94th Cong. 578 (1975).
57. Robert Hunter (former federal insurance administrator), interview with the author, March 2022; *Federal Flood Insurance Program: Hearings Before the Subcommittee on Housing and Community Development*, 94th Cong. (1975); *National Catastrophic Disaster Insurance Act*, H.R. 9712, 93rd Cong. (1973).
58. American Institutes for Research, *A Chronology of Major Events Affecting the National Flood Insurance Program*; Meier, *Political Economy of Regulation*, 117.
59. "U.S. Flood Program Computer Errors Revealed," *Des Moines Register*, April 22, 1977.
60. American Institutes for Research, *A Chronology of Major Events Affecting the National Flood Insurance Program*.
61. Fred B. Power and E. Warren Shows, "A Status Report on the National Flood Insurance Program," *Journal of Risk and Insurance* 46, no. 2 (1979): 61–76.
62. American Institutes for Research, *A Chronology of Major Events Affecting the National Flood Insurance Program*, 27; Robert Hunter (former federal insurance administrator), discussion with the author, March 2022; see also Steinburg *Acts of God* on broader aspects of the deregulation of the NFIP.
63. *Pricing and Marketing of Insurance: A Report of the Department of Justice to the Task Force on Antitrust Immunities* (Washington, DC, 1977), xii.
64. Department of Justice, *Pricing and Marketing of Insurance*.
65. *Federal Insurance Act, S. Res. 1710*, 95th Cong. (1977).
66. *Rights and Remedies of Insurance Policyholders: Hearings Before the Subcommittee on Citizens and Shareholders Rights and Remedies*, Senate Judiciary Committee, 95th Cong., 2nd Sess., Part 1 (1978).
67. National Commission on Antitrust Laws and Procedures, *A Report to the President and the Attorney General for the Review of Antitrust Laws and Procedures*, 1979.
68. Comptroller General of the United States, *Report to Congress: Issues and Needed Improvements in State Regulation of the Insurance Business*, 1979, 213–16.
69. Alan Anderson, "Insurance and Anti-Trust Law: The McCarran-Ferguson Act and Beyond," *William and Mary Law Review* 25 (1983): 81.
70. Charles D. Weller, "The McCarran-Ferguson Act's Exemption for Insurance: Language, History, and Policy," *Duke Law Journal* (1978): 587–643.
71. St. Paul Fire and Marine Insurance Company v. Barry, 438 U.S. 531 (1978).
72. Group Life and Health Insurance Co. v. Royal Drug Co., 440 U.S. 205 (1979).
73. Arizona v. Maricopa Medical Society, 457 U.S. 332 (1982).
74. *Best's Averages and Aggregates, Property/Casualty* (Oldwick, NJ: A. M. Best Co., 1986).
75. Sean F. Mooney, "The Liability Crisis: A Perspective," *Villanova Law Review* 32, no. 6 (1987): 1235.
76. George J. Church, "Sorry, Your Policy Is Cancelled," *Time*, March 24, 1986, 16–25.
77. Meier, *Political Economy of Regulation*, 94.
78. *Best's Averages and Aggregates, Property/Casualty*.
79. Mooney, "The Liability Crisis."
80. Mooney, "The Liability Crisis"; Beshada v. Johns-Manville 447 A 2d 539 (1982); Meier, *Political Economy of Regulation*, 93.
81. Mooney, "The Liability Crisis."
82. Insurance Services Office, *A Critical Year*, (Jersey City, NJ, 1985), 4–6.
83. Meier, *The Political Economy of Regulation*, 91.
84. Mooney, "The Liability Crisis."
85. Kenneth S. Abraham, "The Causes of the Insurance Crisis," *Proceedings of the Academy of Political Science* 37, no. 1 (1988): 54–66.
86. Church, "Sorry, Your Policy Is Cancelled," 16–25.
87. Meier, *Political Economy of Regulation*.
88. Robert J. Hunter, "Taming the Latest Insurance 'Crisis,'" *New York Times*, April 13, 1985.
89. Meier, *Political Economy of Regulation*.
90. *Proceedings of the National Association of Insurance Commissioners* (Reno, 1986), 714–16.
91. Meier, *Political Economy of Regulation*.

92. John B. Attanasio, "Foreword: The Tension between Intervention and Resignation: Symposium on Product Liability," *Journal of Legislation* 14, no. 2 (1987): 128.
93. Moss, *When All Else Fails*, 216.
94. Matt O'Connor, "Manufacturers Seeking Help on Liability," *Chicago Tribune*, February 26, 1986.
95. *A Bill to Repeal the McCarran-Ferguson Act and for Other Purposes*, S. 80, 100th Cong. (1987).
96. Congressional Research Service, *The Liability Insurance Crisis*.
97. Meier, *Political Economy of Regulation*, 108.
98. National Association of Attorneys General Ad Hoc Committee on Insurance, *An Analysis of the Causes of the Current Crisis of Unavailability and Unaffordability of Liability Insurance*, 1986.
99. Lawrence S. Powell, *Should Congress Allow Risk Retention Groups to Offer Property Insurance? A Critical Examination of the Case for Expanding the Liability Risk Retention Act* (Washington, DC: National Association of Mutual Insurance Companies, 2014).
100. J. Robert Hunter, "Banks in Insurance: A Consumer Viewpoint," *Banks in Insurance Report* 1 (April 1985): 6–8.
101. General Accounting Office, *Insurer Failures: Property/Casualty Insurer Insolvencies and State Guaranty Funds* (Washington, DC, 1987), 87–100.
102. General Accounting Office, *Insurance Regulation State Reinsurance Oversight Increased, but Problems Remain* (Washington, DC, 1990), 90–82.
103. Committee on Energy and Commerce, *Failed Promises: Insurance Company Insolvencies, Report by the Subcommittee on Oversight and Investigations of the Committee on Energy and Commerce*, H.R. Rep. 101st Cong. (1990).
104. Committee on Energy and Commerce, *Failed Promises*, iii.
105. Committee on Energy and Commerce, *Failed Promises*.
106. Laurie Cohen, "A Quest for a National Policy to Cover Insurance Industry Risk," *Chicago Tribune*, March 24, 1991.
107. Robert Rosenblatt, "House Report Sees Peril in Insurance Industry: Regulators: Parallels to the S&L Crisis are Cited," *Los Angeles Times*, February 24, 1990.
108. Federal Insurance Solvency Act of 1992, H.R. 4900, 102nd Cong. (1992).
109. Committee on Energy and Commerce, *Wishful Thinking: A World View of Insurance Solvency Regulation*, 103rd Cong. (1994).
110. John A. McDonald, "State Controls on Insurers Termed Flawed," *Hartford Courant*, November 2, 1994.
111. Michael Quint, "New Report Is Critical of States on Regulation of Insurers," *New York Times*, October 20, 1994.
112. Jonathan R. Macey and Geoffrey P. Miller, "The McCarran-Ferguson Act of 1945: Reconceiving the Federal Role in Insurance Regulation," *NYU Law Review* 68, no. 13 (1993): 13–88.
113. *Insurance Competitive Pricing Act of 1994*, H.R. 9, 103rd Cong. (1994).
114. Gavin Bradshaw, "Viewpoint: Can the Florida Insurance Market Withstand Another Hurricane Andrew?," *Insurance Journal*, August 29, 2022.
115. Congressional Research Service, *Hurricanes and Disaster Risk Financing through Insurance: Challenges and Policy Options* (Washington, DC: USGPO, 2008)
116. Tom Baker and Peter Siegelman, "Congress Should OK Terrorism-Insurance," *Newsday*, September 17, 2002.
117. Thomas Lee, "Insurers at Risk as Bills Stall," *Journal News (Minneapolis)*, July 8, 2007.
118. Blake, Rappaport, and Landsea, *The Deadliest, Costliest, and Most Intense United States Hurricanes of This Century*.
119. James W. Macdonald, Lloyd Dixon, and Laura Zakaras, *Call for Reform in the Residential Insurance Market after Hurricane Katrina* (Santa Monica, CA: RAND Corporation, 2010).
120. Howard Kunreuther, "Has the Time Come for National Disaster Insurance?" in *Lessons from Hurricane Katrina*, Ronald J. Daniels, Donald F. Kettle, and Howard Kunreuther, (eds.) (Philadelphia: University of Pennsylvania Press, 2006), 175–202.
121. Macdonald, Dixon, and Zakaras, *Call for Reform in the Residential Insurance Market after Hurricane Katrina*.
122. H.R. 3355 Homeowners' Defense Act of 2007, 110th Congress.
123. *McCarran-Ferguson and Antitrust Immunity: Good for Consumers? Hearings Before the Senate Committee on the Judiciary*, 110th Cong. (2007).
124. *Insurance Industry Competition Act of 2007*, S.R. 618, 110th Cong. (2007).

125. Robert Hunter of the Nader-affiliated Consumer Federation of America testified in favor. The American Insurance Association opposed.

126. Lawrence Powell, *Issue Analysis: The Assault on the McCarran-Ferguson Act and the Politics of Insurance in the Post-Katrina Era* (Washington DC: National Association of Mutual Insurance Companies, 2007).

Epilogue

1. Liran Einav and Amy Finkelstein, *We've Got You Covered: Rebooting American Health Care* (New York: Penguin Random House, 2023).

2. Lyle Adriano, "State Farm Hit by Class Action Lawsuit Claiming Racial Discrimination," *Insurance News*, December 16, 2022.

3. *Hearings Before the Senate Subcommittee on Housing, Transportation and Community Development*, July 30, 2014.

4. Elizabeth Piper and Valerie Volcovici, "Hillary Clinton Calls for Reform of Insurance Sector at COP28 Climate Talks," *Insurance Journal*, December 4, 2023.

5. Testimony of Kathleen A. Birrane, on behalf of the National Association of Insurance Commissioners, Senate Committee on Banking, Housing and Urban Affairs, "Current Issues in Insurance," September 8, 2022.

6. Rebecca Williams, Lorilee Medders, David Marlett, Catherine Lattimore, and David Evans, "Flood Insurance Redesigned: Regulatory Conditions for a Viable and Sustainable Private Market," *Journal of Insurance Regulation*, April 12, 2023.

7. "Washington AG Investigating 'Possible Discrimination' for Insurers Using Credit Scores, *Insurance Journal*, November 9, 2022.

8. National Association of Insurance Commissioners, Center for Insurance Policy and Research, "Federal Insurance Office (FIO)," Updated February 16, 2024, https://content.naic.org/cipr-topics/federal-insurance-office-fio.

9. H.R. 4866–Federal Insurance Elimination Act, 117th Congress 2021–22.

10. "In PIA Victory, FIO Cancels Climate Data Collection," March 8, 2024, https://piaadvocacy.com/2024/03/08/in-pia-victory-fio-cancels-climate-data-collection-plan-allowing-naic-to-lead-data-call/.

Index

For the benefit of digital users, indexed terms that span two pages (e.g., 52–53) may, on occasion, appear on only one of those pages.

Tables and figures are indicated by *t* and *f* following the page number